Delicious IN DUNGEON

RYOKO KUI

1

Delicious IN DUNGEON

1

Contents

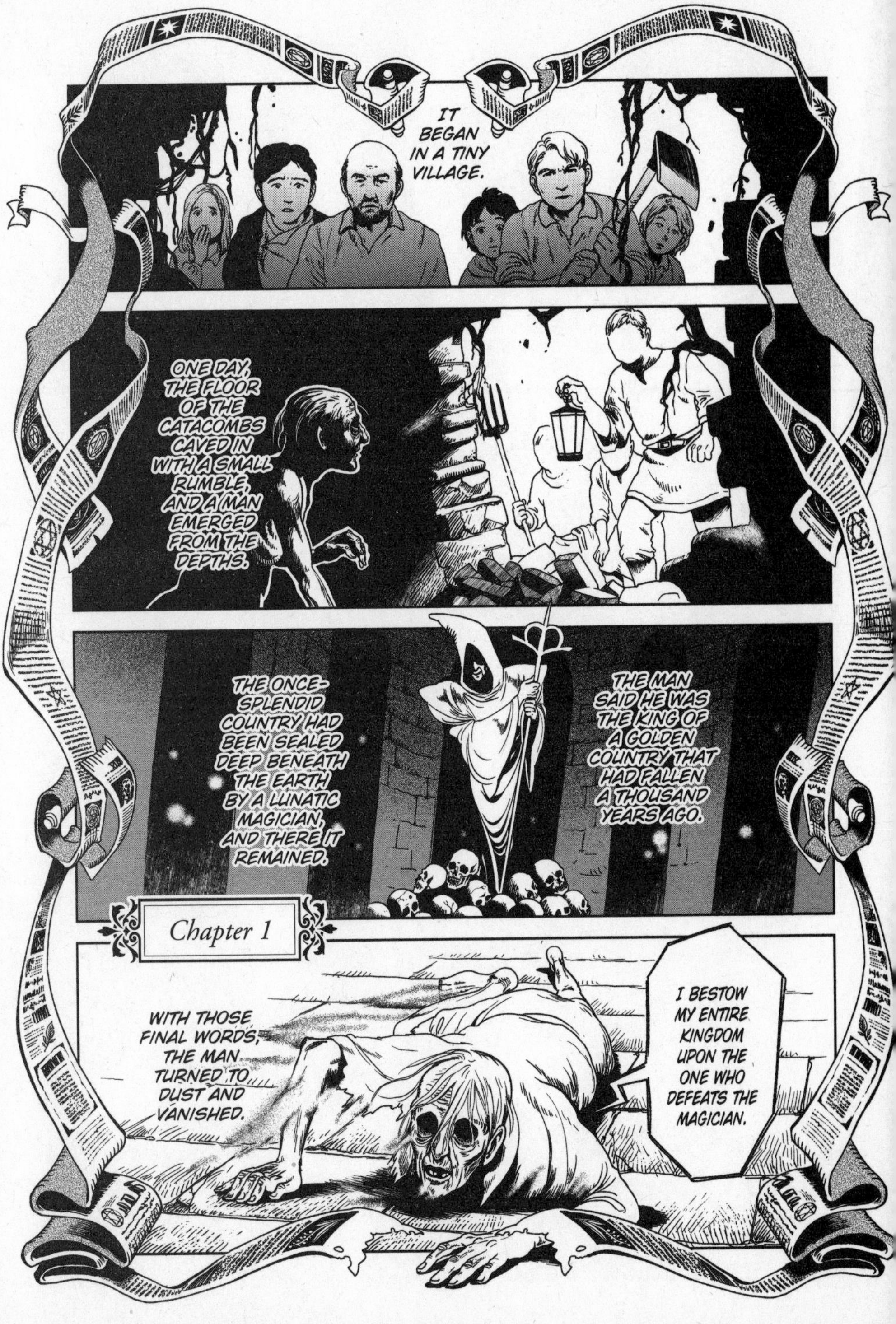
IT BEGAN IN A TINY VILLAGE.
ONE DAY, THE FLOOR OF THE CATACOMBS CAVED IN WITH A SMALL RUMBLE, AND A MAN EMERGED FROM THE DEPTHS.
THE MAN SAID HE WAS THE KING OF A GOLDEN COUNTRY THAT HAD FALLEN A THOUSAND YEARS AGO.
THE ONCE-SPLENDID COUNTRY HAD BEEN SEALED DEEP BENEATH THE EARTH BY A LUNATIC MAGICIAN, AND THERE IT REMAINED.
Chapter 1
I BESTOW MY ENTIRE KINGDOM UPON THE ONE WHO DEFEATS THE MAGICIAN.
WITH THOSE FINAL WORDS, THE MAN TURNED TO DUST AND VANISHED.

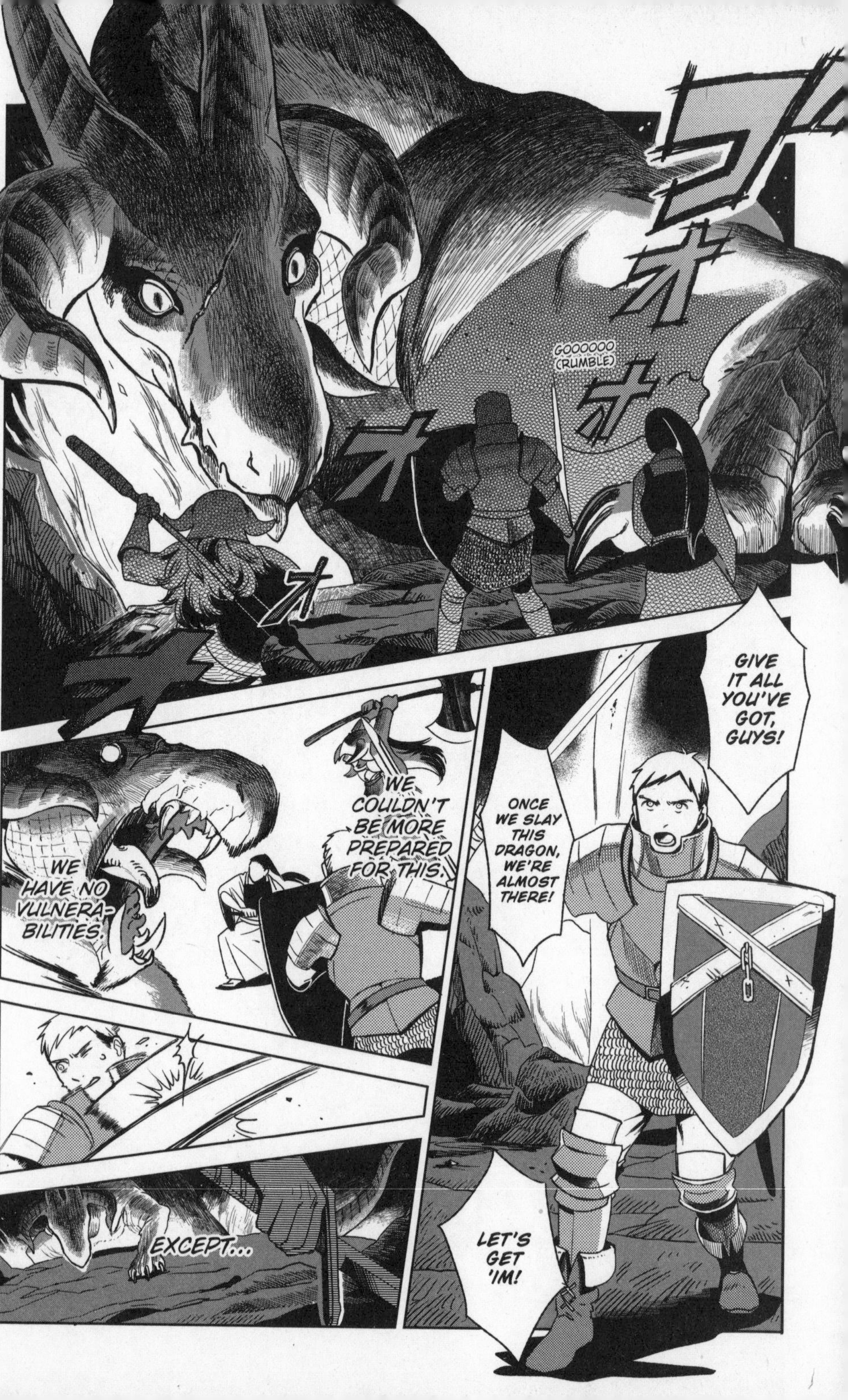
GOOOOOO
(RUMBLE)
GIVE IT ALL YOU'VE GOT, GUYS!
ONCE WE SLAY THIS DRAGON, WE'RE ALMOST THERE!
LET'S GET 'IM!
WE COULDN'T BE MORE PREPARED FOR THIS.
WE HAVE NO VULNERA-BILITIES.
EXCEPT...

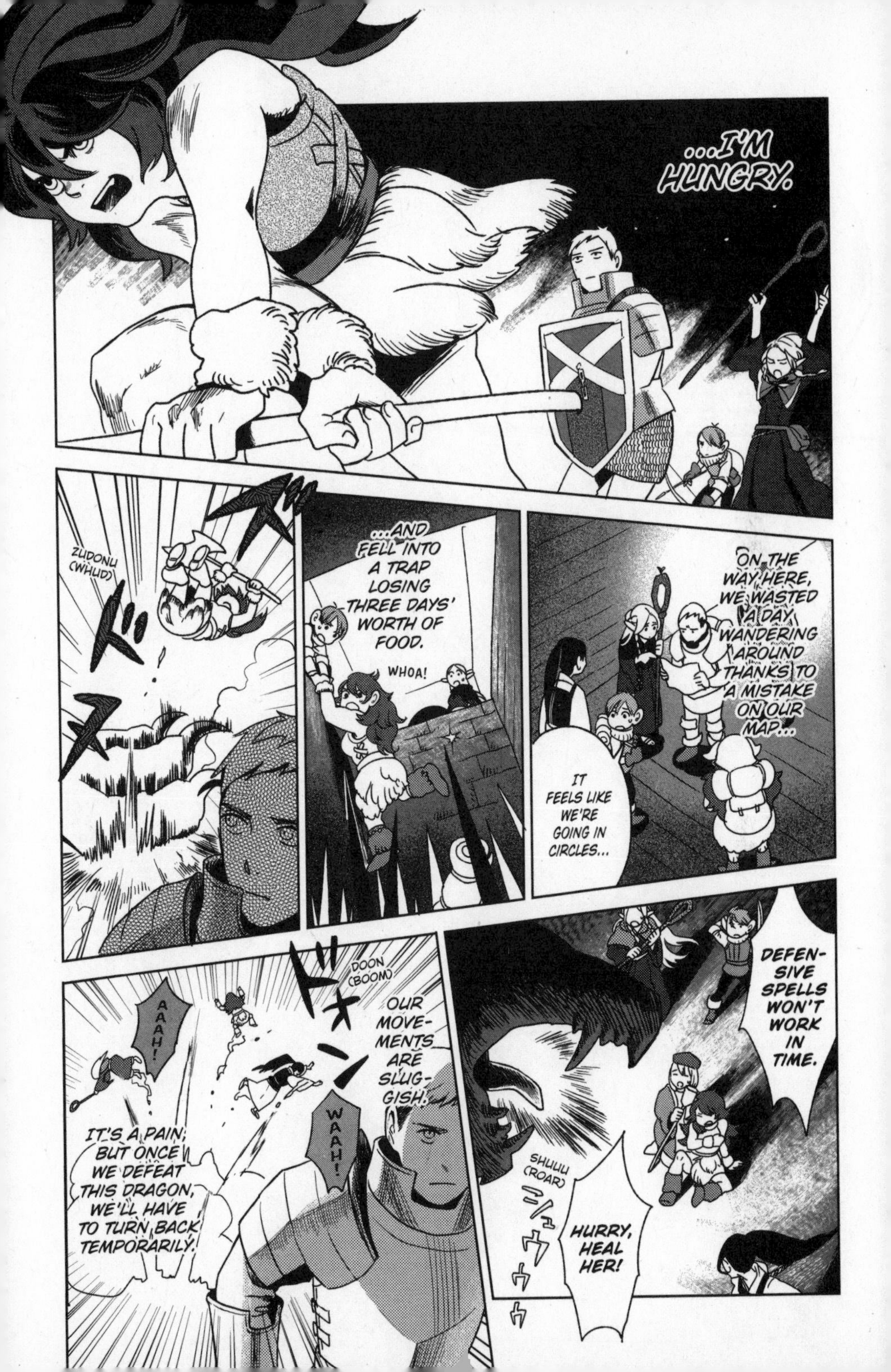
...I'M HUNGRY.
ON THE WAY HERE, WE WASTED A DAY WANDERING AROUND THANKS TO A MISTAKE ON OUR MAP...
IT FEELS LIKE WE'RE GOING IN CIRCLES...
...AND FELL INTO A TRAP LOSING THREE DAYS' WORTH OF FOOD.
WHOA!
ZUDONU (WHUD)
DEFENSIVE SPELLS WON'T WORK IN TIME.
SHUUU (ROAR)
HURRY, HEAL HER!
DOON (BOOM)
OUR MOVEMENTS ARE SLUGGISH.
WAAH!
AAAH!
IT'S A PAIN, BUT ONCE WE DEFEAT THIS DRAGON, WE'LL HAVE TO TURN BACK TEMPORARILY.

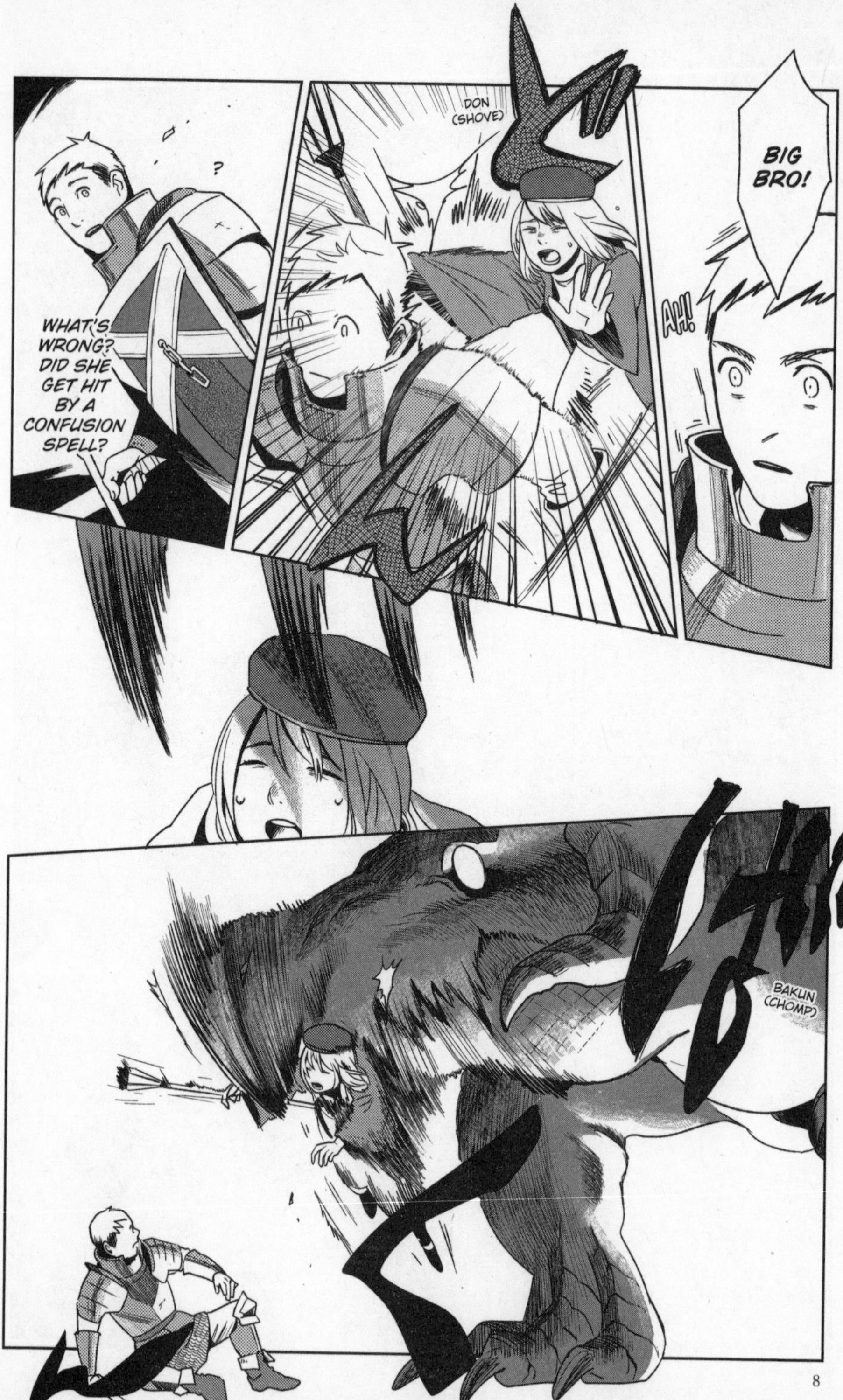
BIG BRO!
AH!
DON (SHOVE)
?
WHAT'S WRONG? DID SHE GET HIT BY A CONFUSION SPELL?
BAKUN (CHOMP)

HUH??

BOKI
(SNAP)

NO WAY...

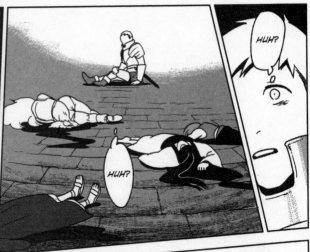

HUH?

HUH?

WHEN WE'VE COME THIS FAR...

ZO
(SHUDDER)

WIPED OUT.

KA
(FLASH)

MISHI
(CREAK)

R...

MISHI

RUN...

MISHI

9

1. Hot Pot

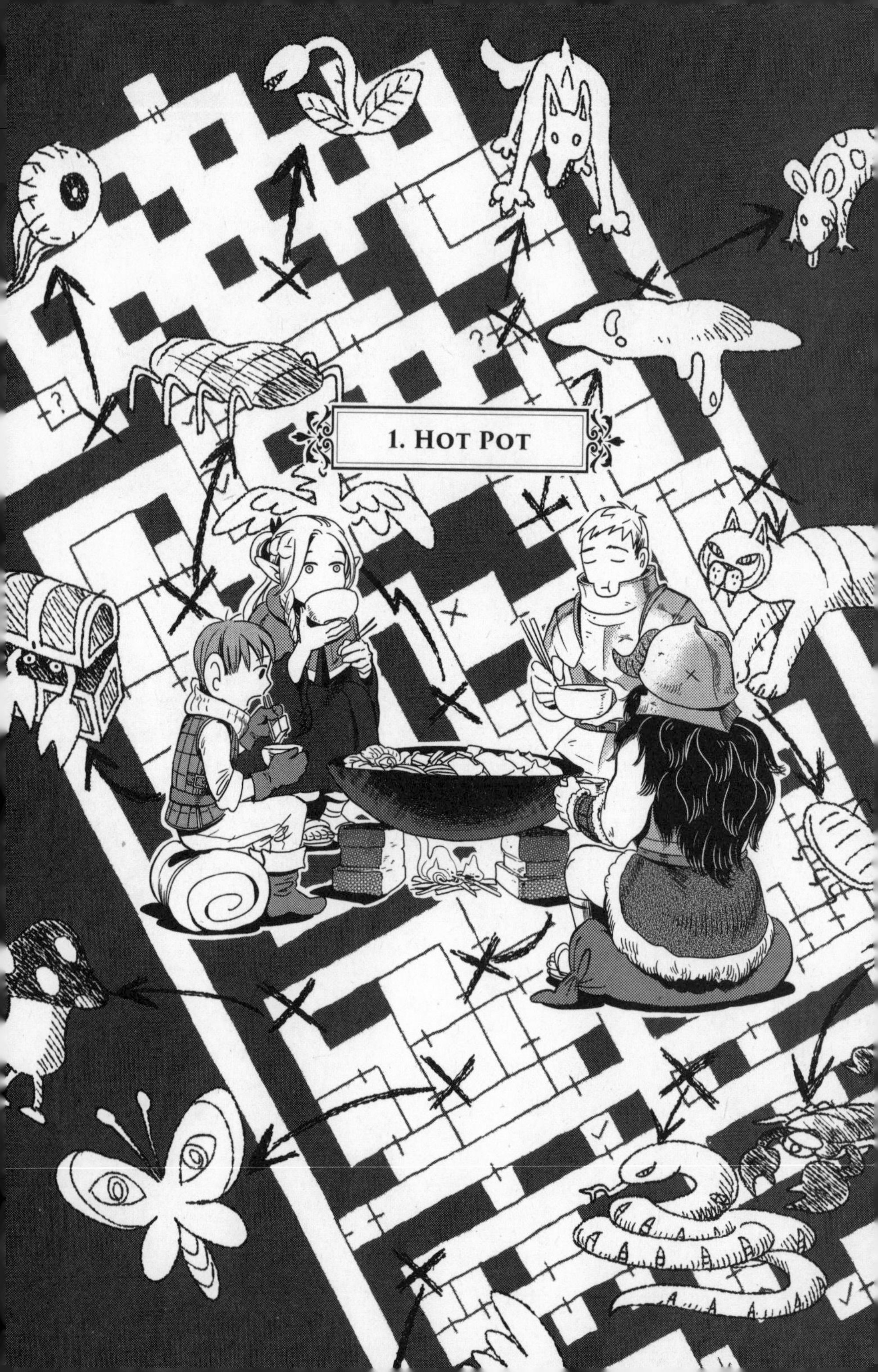

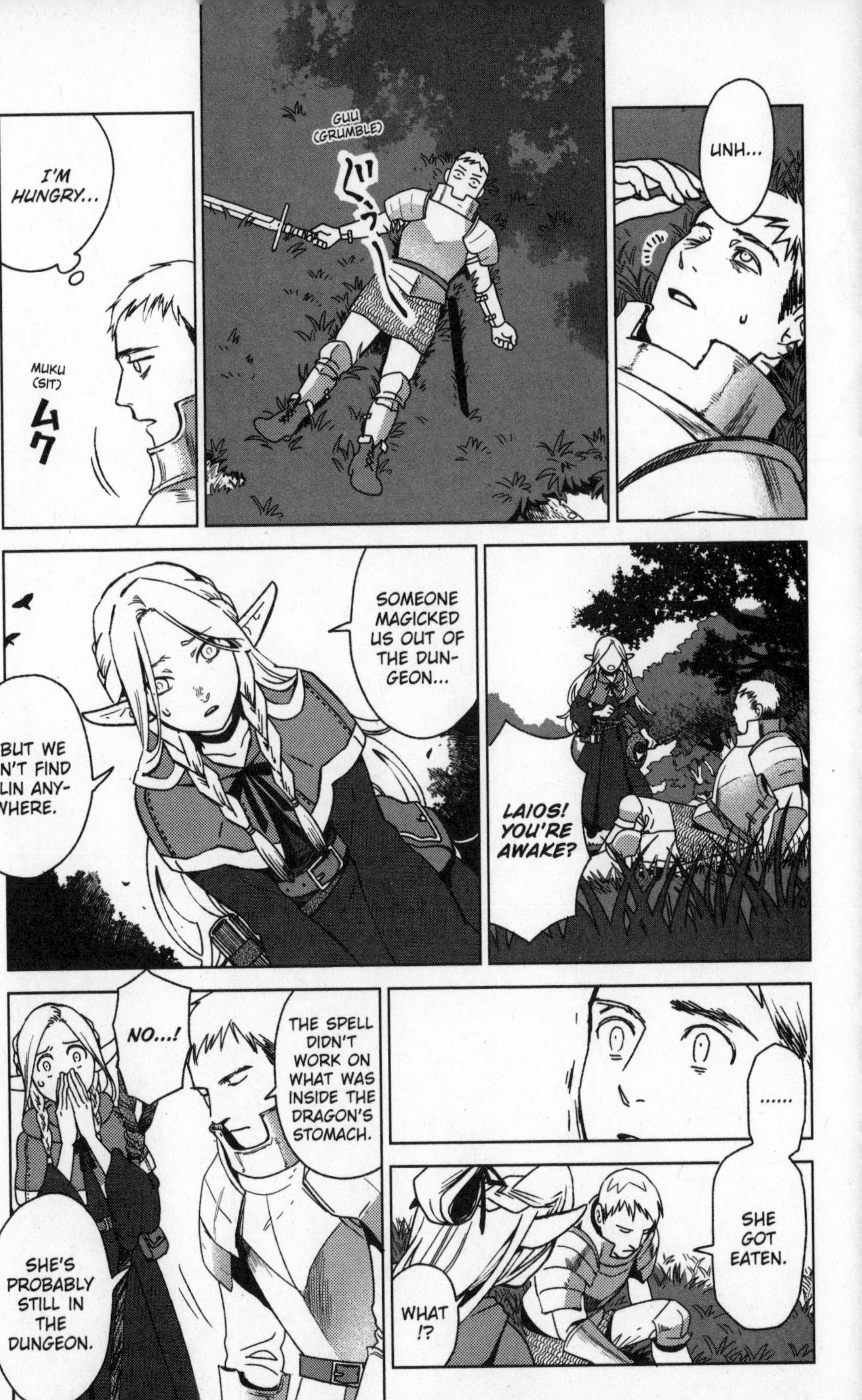
UNH...
GUU (GRUMBLE)
I'M HUNGRY...
MUKU (SIT)
ムク
LAIOS! YOU'RE AWAKE?
SOMEONE MAGICKED US OUT OF THE DUN-GEON...
...BUT WE CAN'T FIND FALIN ANY-WHERE.
......
SHE GOT EATEN.
WHAT!?
THE SPELL DIDN'T WORK ON WHAT WAS INSIDE THE DRAGON'S STOMACH.
NO...!
SHE'S PROBABLY STILL IN THE DUNGEON.

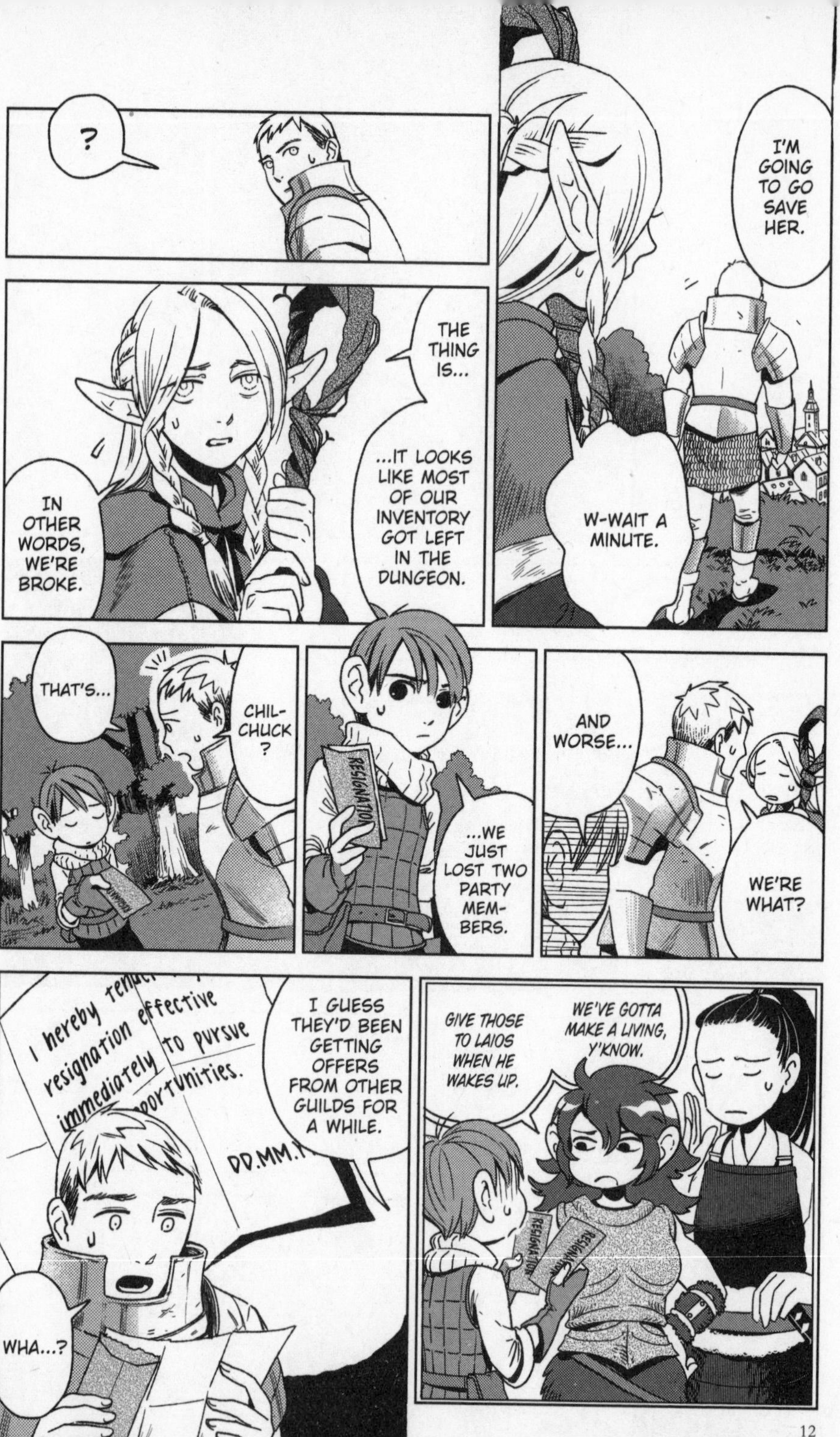

I'M GOING TO GO SAVE HER.
W-WAIT A MINUTE.
?
THE THING IS...
...IT LOOKS LIKE MOST OF OUR INVENTORY GOT LEFT IN THE DUNGEON.
IN OTHER WORDS, WE'RE BROKE.
AND WORSE...
WE'RE WHAT?
RESIGNATION
...WE JUST LOST TWO PARTY MEMBERS.
CHIL-CHUCK?
THAT'S...
WE'VE GOTTA MAKE A LIVING, Y'KNOW.
GIVE THOSE TO LAIOS WHEN HE WAKES UP.
RESIGNATION
RESIGNATION
I GUESS THEY'D BEEN GETTING OFFERS FROM OTHER GUILDS FOR A WHILE.
I hereby tend
resignation effective
immediately to pursue
pportunities.
DD.MM.Y
WHA...?

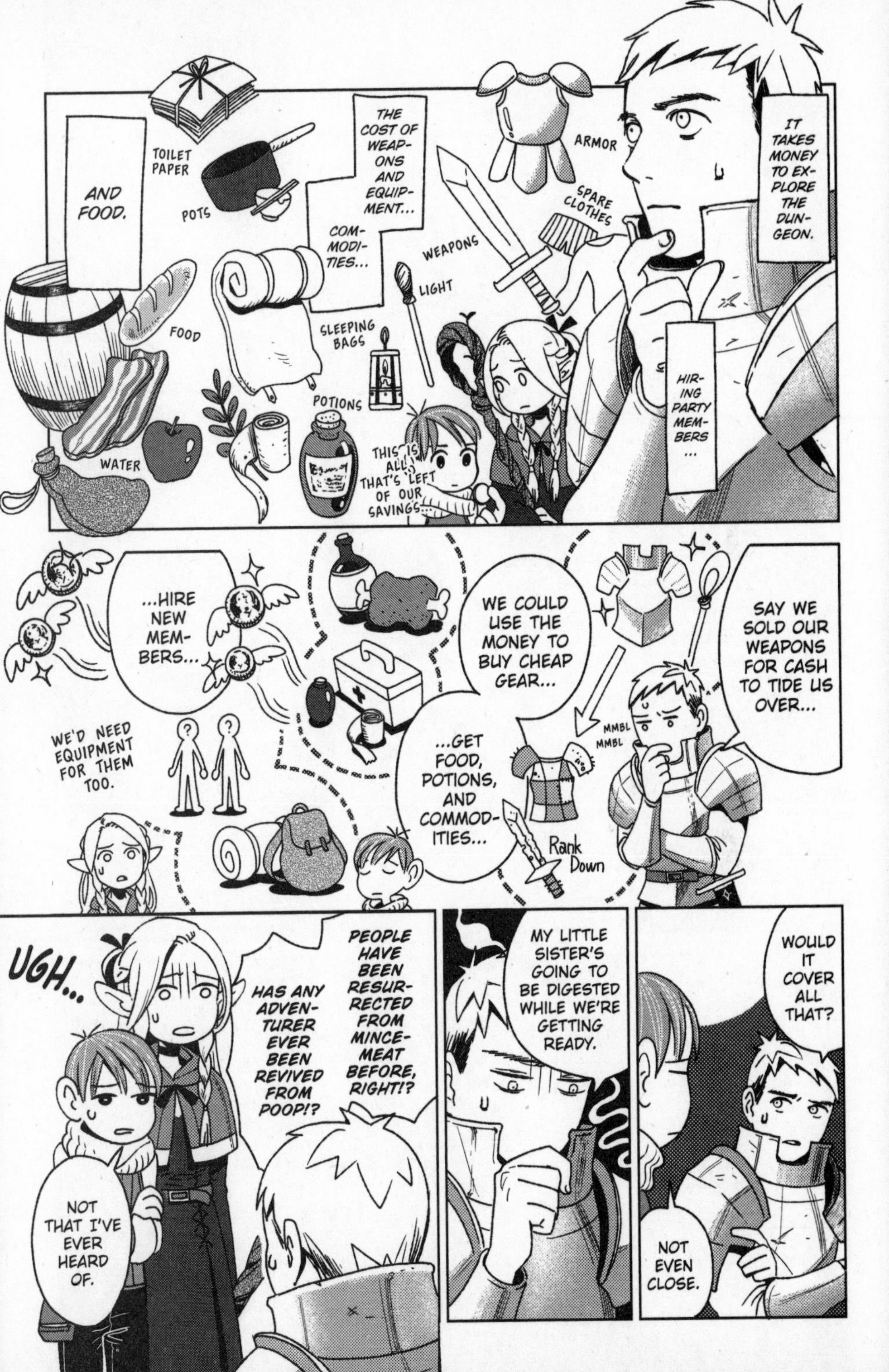

IT TAKES MONEY TO EXPLORE THE DUNGEON.
HIRING PARTY MEMBERS...
ARMOR
SPARE CLOTHES
THE COST OF WEAPONS AND EQUIPMENT...
WEAPONS
COMMODITIES...
LIGHT
SLEEPING BAGS
THIS IS ALL THAT'S LEFT OF OUR SAVINGS...
POTIONS
TOILET PAPER
POTS
AND FOOD.
FOOD
WATER
SAY WE SOLD OUR WEAPONS FOR CASH TO TIDE US OVER...
MMBL MMBL
WE COULD USE THE MONEY TO BUY CHEAP GEAR...
Rank Down
...GET FOOD, POTIONS, AND COMMODITIES...
...HIRE NEW MEMBERS...
WE'D NEED EQUIPMENT FOR THEM TOO.
WOULD IT COVER ALL THAT?
NOT EVEN CLOSE.
MY LITTLE SISTER'S GOING TO BE DIGESTED WHILE WE'RE GETTING READY.
PEOPLE HAVE BEEN RESURRECTED FROM MINCEMEAT BEFORE, RIGHT!?
HAS ANY ADVENTURER EVER BEEN REVIVED FROM POOP!?
UGH...
NOT THAT I'VE EVER HEARD OF.

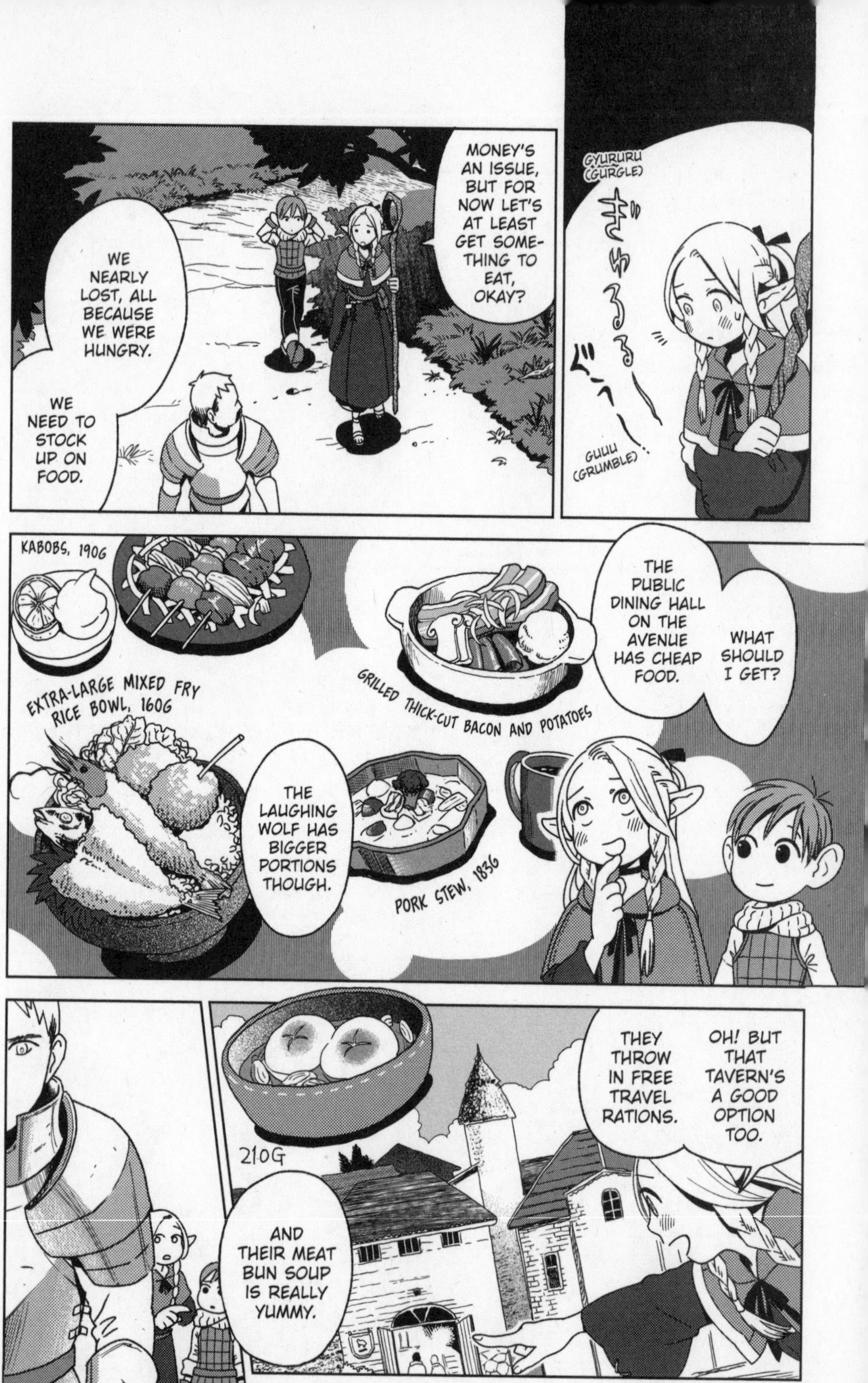
GYURURU (GURGLE)
GUUU (GRUMBLE)
MONEY'S AN ISSUE, BUT FOR NOW LET'S AT LEAST GET SOME-THING TO EAT, OKAY?
WE NEARLY LOST, ALL BECAUSE WE WERE HUNGRY.
WE NEED TO STOCK UP ON FOOD.
WHAT SHOULD I GET?
THE PUBLIC DINING HALL ON THE AVENUE HAS CHEAP FOOD.
GRILLED THICK-CUT BACON AND POTATOES
KABOBS, 190G
EXTRA-LARGE MIXED FRY RICE BOWL, 160G
THE LAUGHING WOLF HAS BIGGER PORTIONS THOUGH.
PORK STEW, 183G
OH! BUT THAT TAVERN'S A GOOD OPTION TOO.
THEY THROW IN FREE TRAVEL RATIONS.
210G
AND THEIR MEAT BUN SOUP IS REALLY YUMMY.

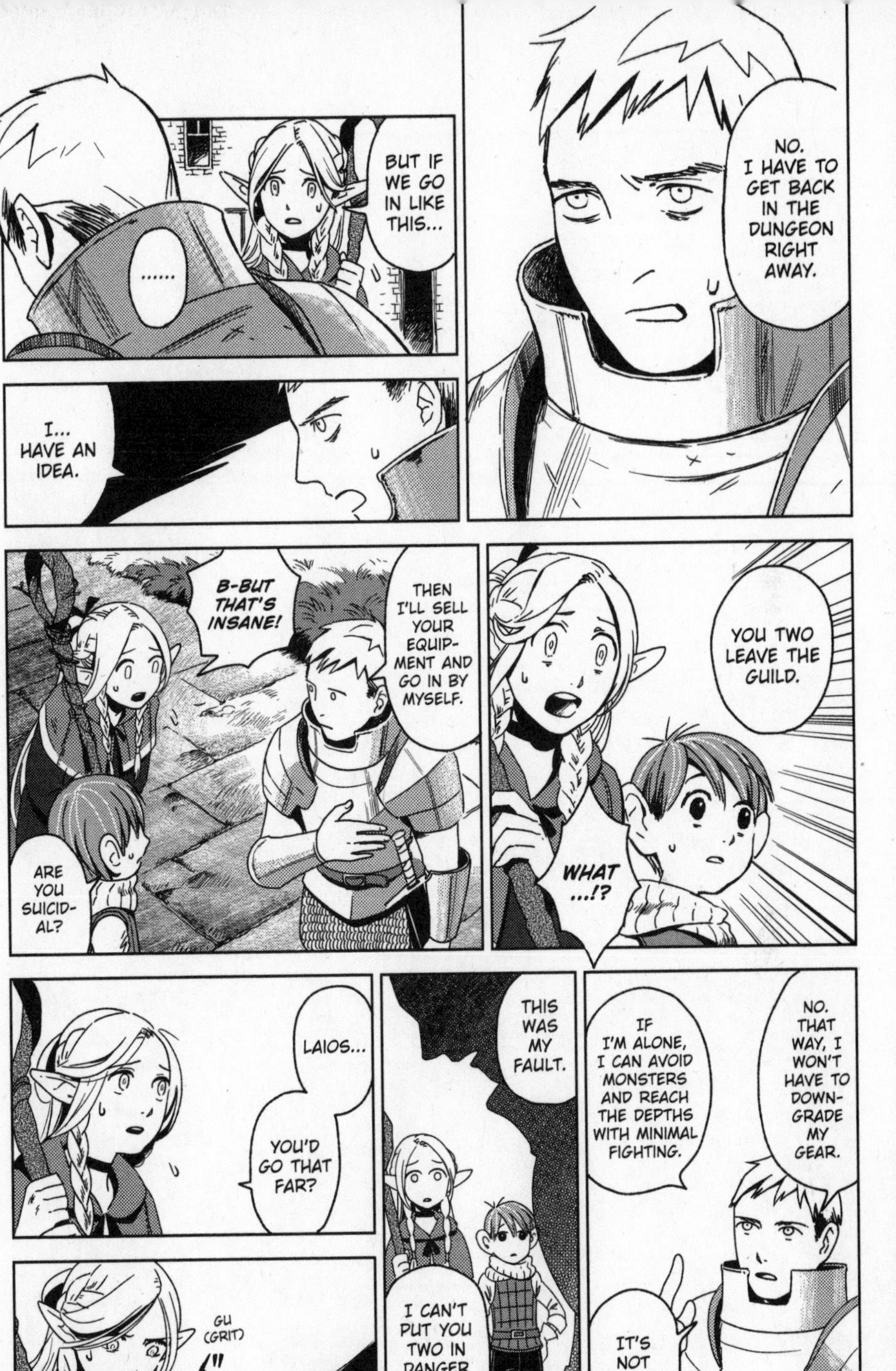
NO. I HAVE TO GET BACK IN THE DUNGEON RIGHT AWAY.
BUT IF WE GO IN LIKE THIS...
......
I... HAVE AN IDEA.
YOU TWO LEAVE THE GUILD.
WHAT ...!?
THEN I'LL SELL YOUR EQUIPMENT AND GO IN BY MYSELF.
B-BUT THAT'S INSANE!
ARE YOU SUICIDAL?
NO. THAT WAY, I WON'T HAVE TO DOWNGRADE MY GEAR.
IF I'M ALONE, I CAN AVOID MONSTERS AND REACH THE DEPTHS WITH MINIMAL FIGHTING.
IT'S NOT IMPOSSIBLE.
THIS WAS MY FAULT.
I CAN'T PUT YOU TWO IN DANGER AS WELL.
LAIOS...
YOU'D GO THAT FAR?
GU (GRIT)

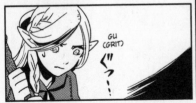

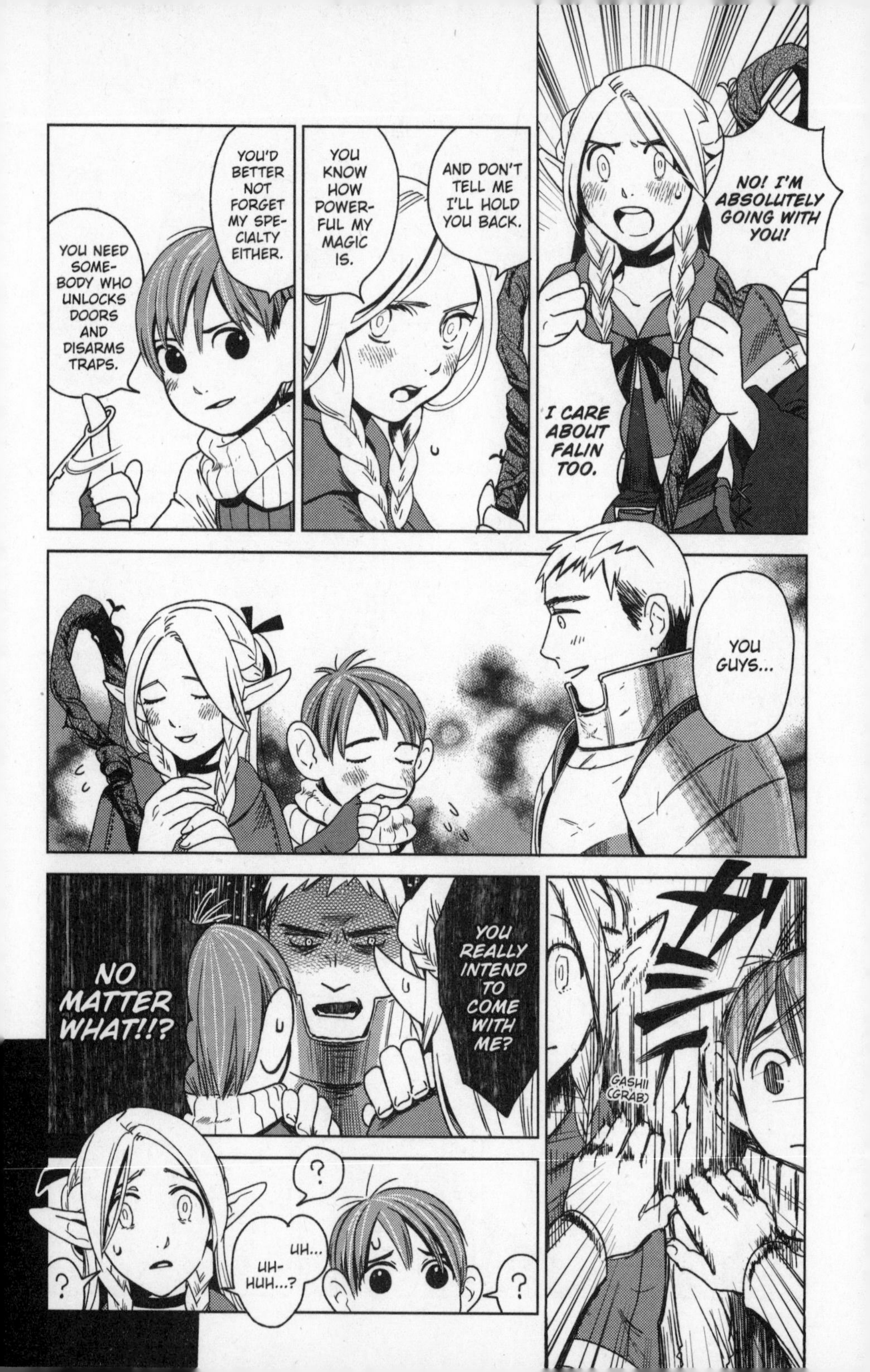
NO! I'M ABSOLUTELY GOING WITH YOU!
I CARE ABOUT FALIN TOO.
AND DON'T TELL ME I'LL HOLD YOU BACK.
YOU KNOW HOW POWERFUL MY MAGIC IS.
YOU'D BETTER NOT FORGET MY SPECIALTY EITHER.
YOU NEED SOMEBODY WHO UNLOCKS DOORS AND DISARMS TRAPS.
YOU GUYS...
GASHII (GRAB)
YOU REALLY INTEND TO COME WITH ME?
NO MATTER WHAT!!?
?
UH... UH-HUH...?
?
?

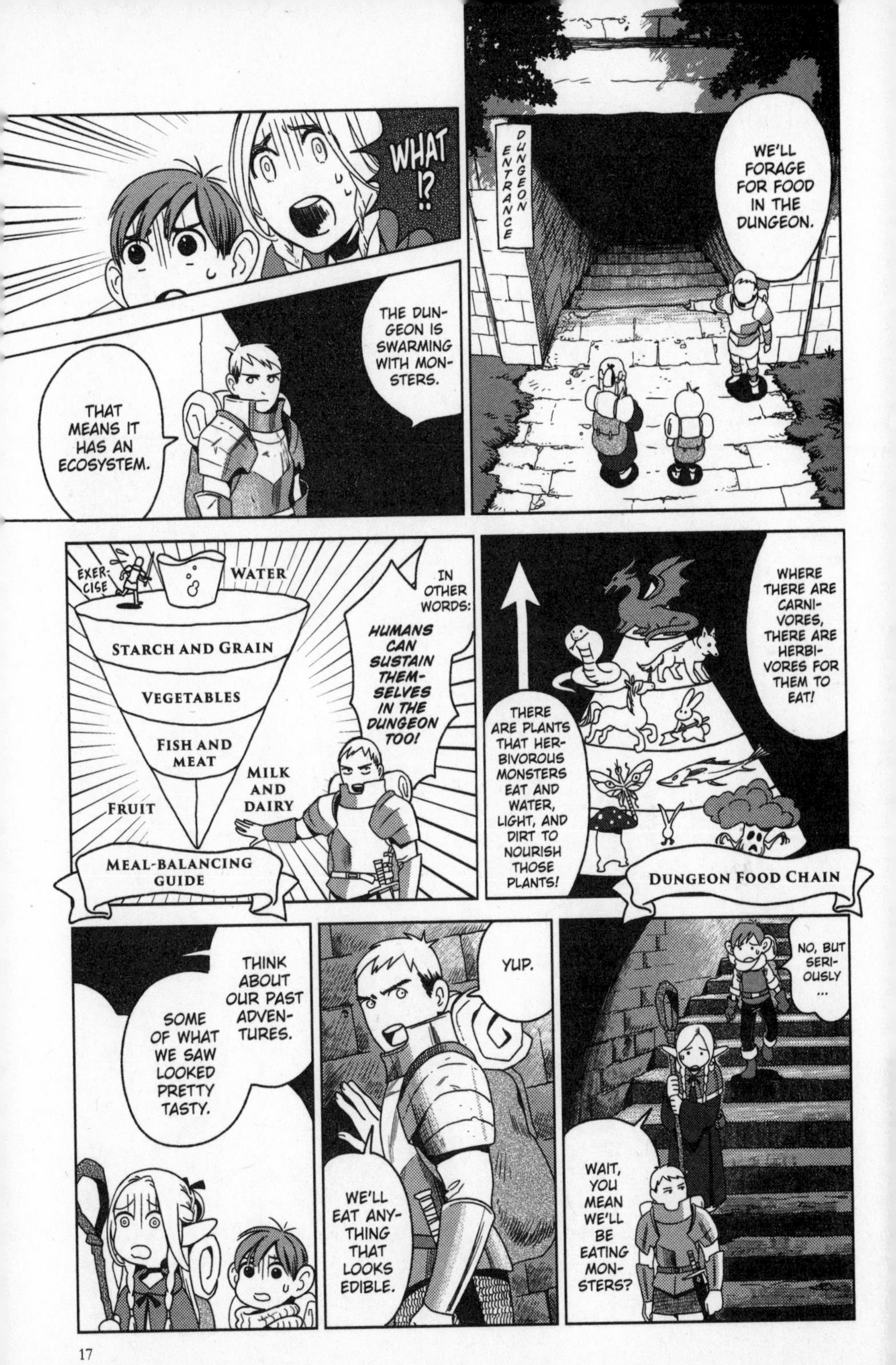
DUNGEON ENTRANCE
WE'LL FORAGE FOR FOOD IN THE DUNGEON.
WHAT!?
THE DUNGEON IS SWARMING WITH MONSTERS.
THAT MEANS IT HAS AN ECOSYSTEM.
WHERE THERE ARE CARNIVORES, THERE ARE HERBIVORES FOR THEM TO EAT!
THERE ARE PLANTS THAT HERBIVOROUS MONSTERS EAT AND WATER, LIGHT, AND DIRT TO NOURISH THOSE PLANTS!
DUNGEON FOOD CHAIN
IN OTHER WORDS:
HUMANS CAN SUSTAIN THEMSELVES IN THE DUNGEON TOO!
EXERCISE
WATER
STARCH AND GRAIN
VEGETABLES
FISH AND MEAT
MILK AND DAIRY
FRUIT
MEAL-BALANCING GUIDE
NO, BUT SERIOUSLY ...
WAIT, YOU MEAN WE'LL BE EATING MONSTERS?
YUP.
WE'LL EAT ANYTHING THAT LOOKS EDIBLE.
THINK ABOUT OUR PAST ADVENTURES.
SOME OF WHAT WE SAW LOOKED PRETTY TASTY.

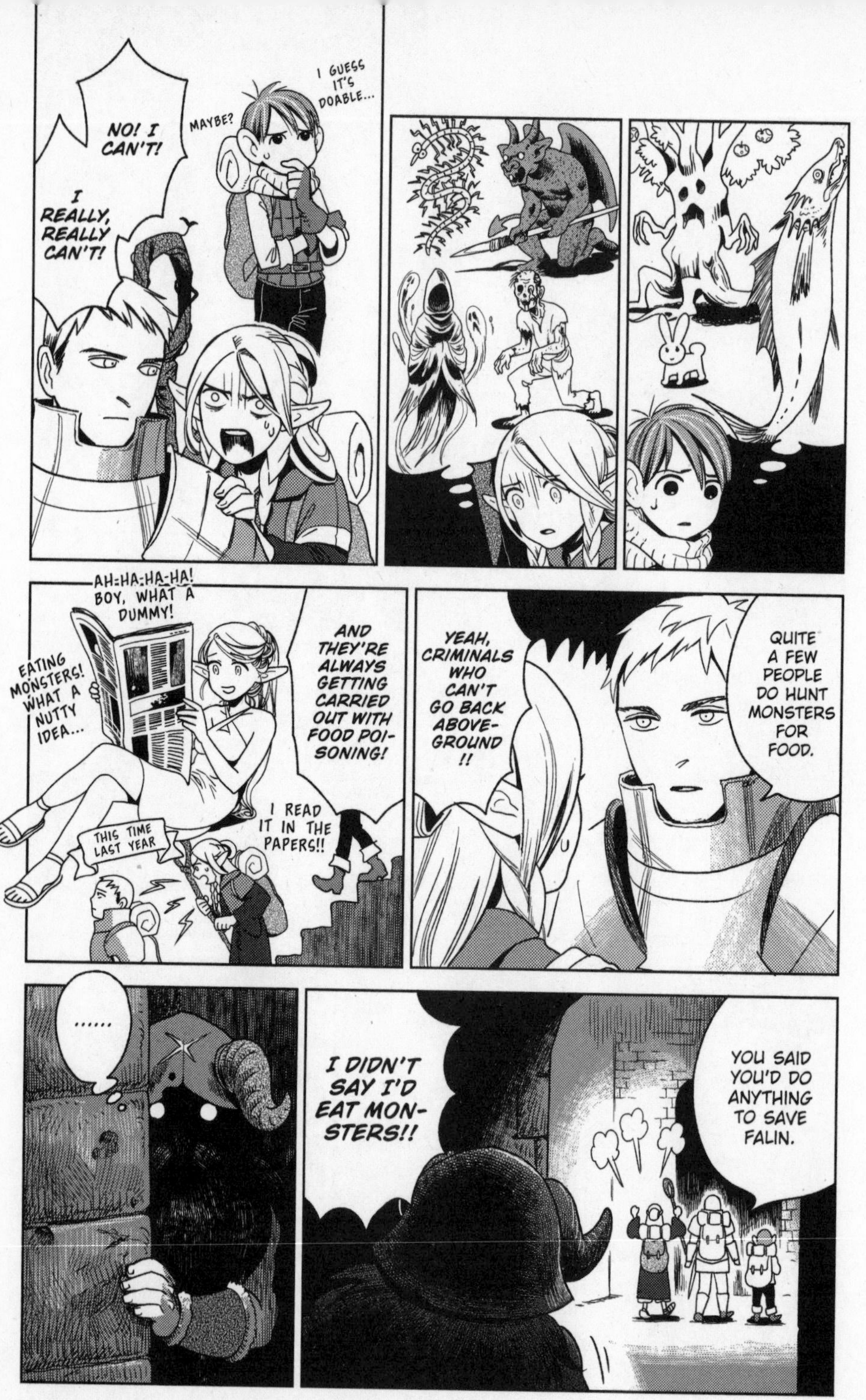
I GUESS IT'S DOABLE...
MAYBE?
NO! I CAN'T!
I REALLY, REALLY CAN'T!
QUITE A FEW PEOPLE DO HUNT MONSTERS FOR FOOD.
YEAH, CRIMINALS WHO CAN'T GO BACK ABOVE-GROUND!!
AND THEY'RE ALWAYS GETTING CARRIED OUT WITH FOOD POI-SONING!
AH-HA-HA-HA! BOY, WHAT A DUMMY!
EATING MONSTERS! WHAT A NUTTY IDEA...
I READ IT IN THE PAPERS!!
THIS TIME LAST YEAR
YOU SAID YOU'D DO ANYTHING TO SAVE FALIN.
I DIDN'T SAY I'D EAT MON-STERS!!
......

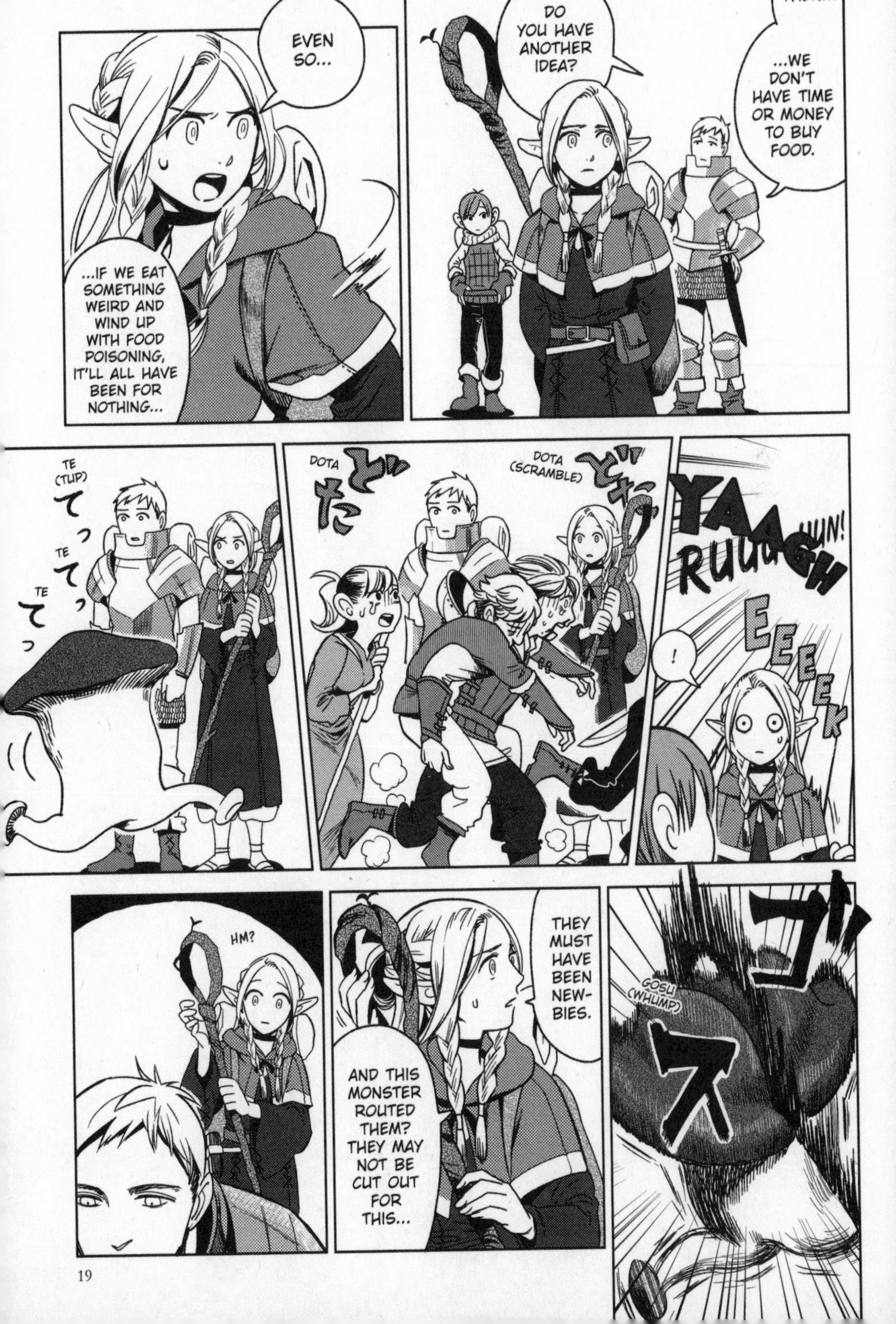

THEN...
...WE DON'T HAVE TIME OR MONEY TO BUY FOOD.
DO YOU HAVE ANOTHER IDEA?
EVEN SO...
...IF WE EAT SOMETHING WEIRD AND WIND UP WITH FOOD POISONING, IT'LL ALL HAVE BEEN FOR NOTHING...
YAAAGH
RUUUUN!
EEEEEK
!
DOTA (SCRAMBLE)
どた
DOTA
どた
TE (TUP)
て
TE
て
TE
て
ゴッ
GOSU (WHUMP)
ス
THEY MUST HAVE BEEN NEW-BIES.
AND THIS MONSTER ROUTED THEM? THEY MAY NOT BE CUT OUT FOR THIS...
HM?

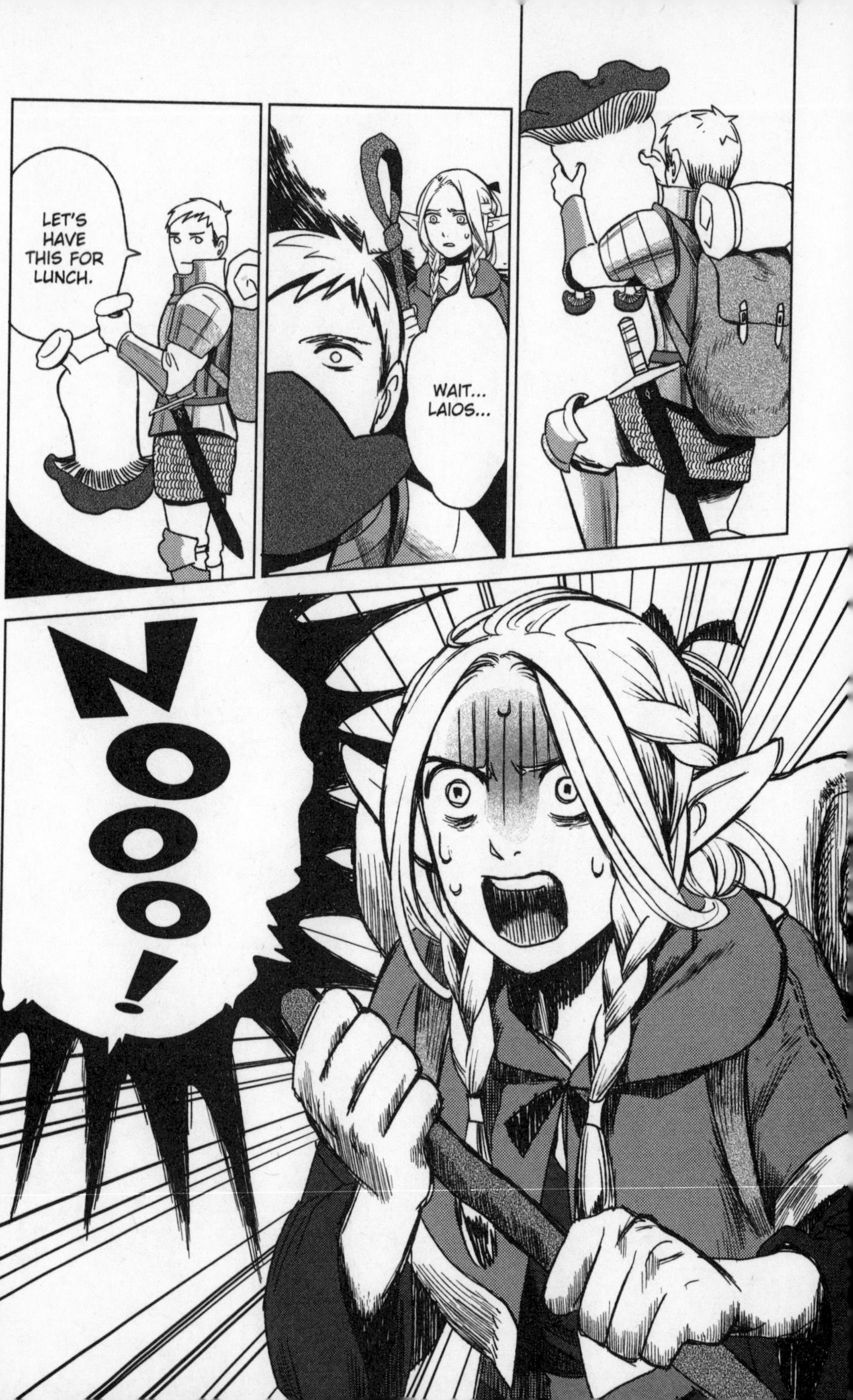
WAIT... LAIOS...
LET'S HAVE THIS FOR LUNCH.
NOOO!

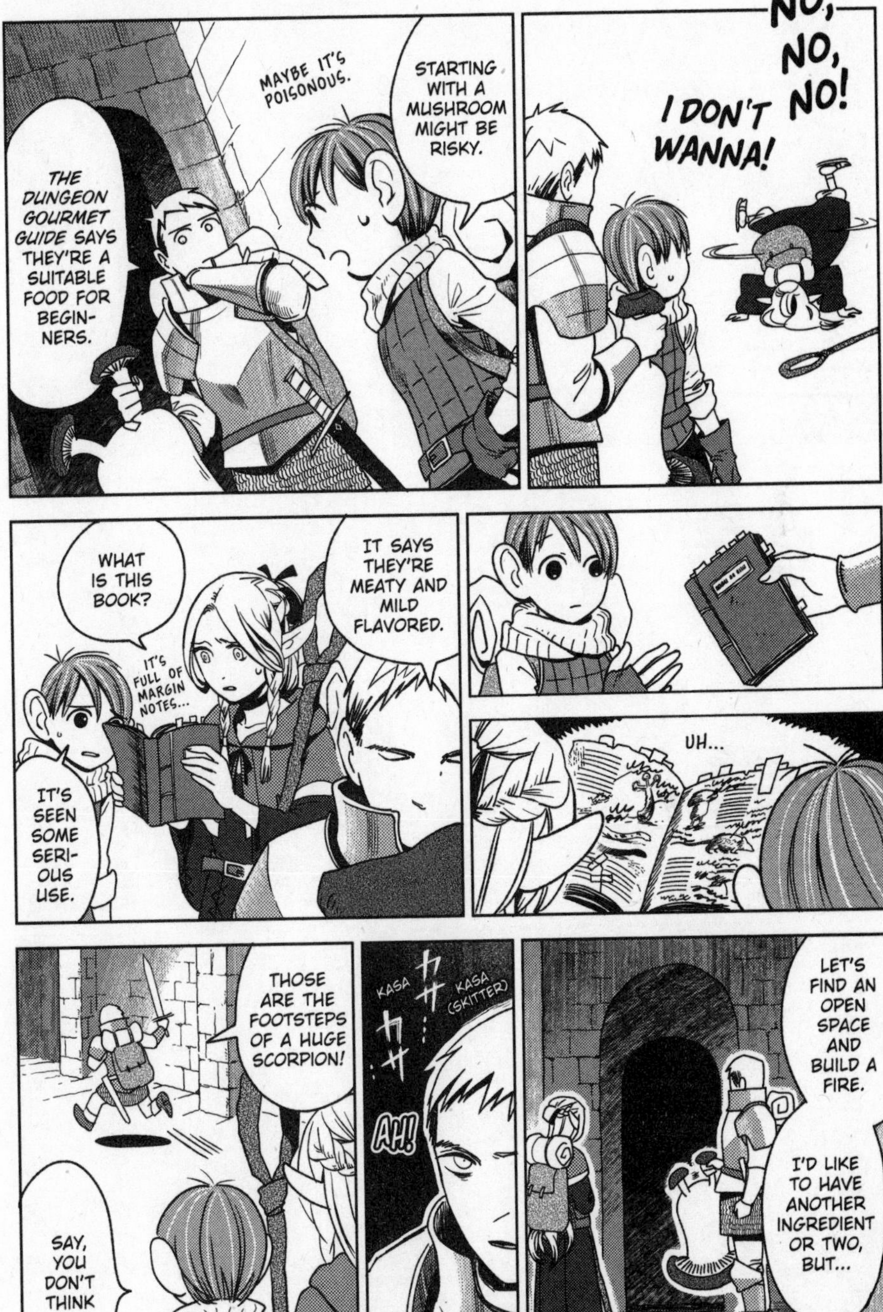

NO, NO, NO!
I DON'T WANNA!
STARTING WITH A MUSHROOM MIGHT BE RISKY.
MAYBE IT'S POISONOUS.
THE DUNGEON GOURMET GUIDE SAYS THEY'RE A SUITABLE FOOD FOR BEGIN-NERS.
UH...
IT SAYS THEY'RE MEATY AND MILD FLAVORED.
WHAT IS THIS BOOK?
IT'S FULL OF MARGIN NOTES...
IT'S SEEN SOME SERI-OUS USE.
LET'S FIND AN OPEN SPACE AND BUILD A FIRE.
I'D LIKE TO HAVE ANOTHER INGREDIENT OR TWO, BUT...
KASA
KASA (SKITTER)
AH!
THOSE ARE THE FOOTSTEPS OF A HUGE SCORPION!
SAY, YOU DON'T THINK HE'S...

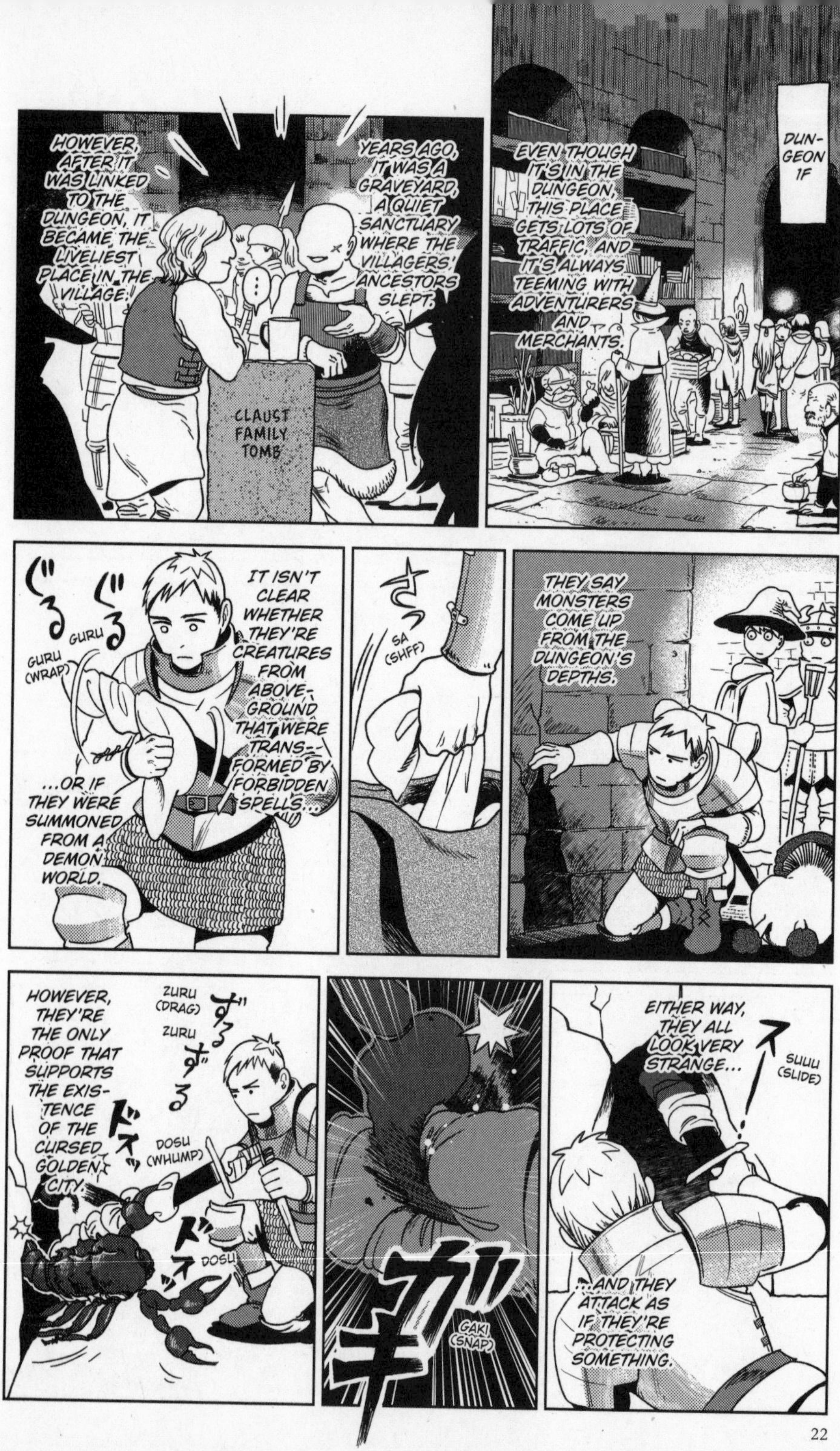
DUNGEON 1F
EVEN THOUGH IT'S IN THE DUNGEON, THIS PLACE GETS LOTS OF TRAFFIC, AND IT'S ALWAYS TEEMING WITH ADVENTURERS AND MERCHANTS.
YEARS AGO, IT WAS A GRAVEYARD, A QUIET SANCTUARY WHERE THE VILLAGERS' ANCESTORS SLEPT.
HOWEVER, AFTER IT WAS LINKED TO THE DUNGEON, IT BECAME THE LIVELIEST PLACE IN THE VILLAGE!
…
CLAUST FAMILY TOMB
THEY SAY MONSTERS COME UP FROM THE DUNGEON'S DEPTHS.
さっ
SA (SHFF)
IT ISN'T CLEAR WHETHER THEY'RE CREATURES FROM ABOVE-GROUND THAT WERE TRANS-FORMED BY FORBIDDEN SPELLS...
ぐる ぐる
GURU
GURU (WRAP)
...OR IF THEY WERE SUMMONED FROM A DEMON WORLD.
EITHER WAY, THEY ALL LOOK VERY STRANGE...
ス
SUUU (SLIDE)
...AND THEY ATTACK AS IF THEY'RE PROTECTING SOMETHING.
ガキ
GAKI (SNAP)
HOWEVER, THEY'RE THE ONLY PROOF THAT SUPPORTS THE EXISTENCE OF THE CURSED GOLDEN CITY.
ずる ずる
ZURU (DRAG)
ZURU
ドスッ
DOSU (WHUMP)
ドスッ
DOSU

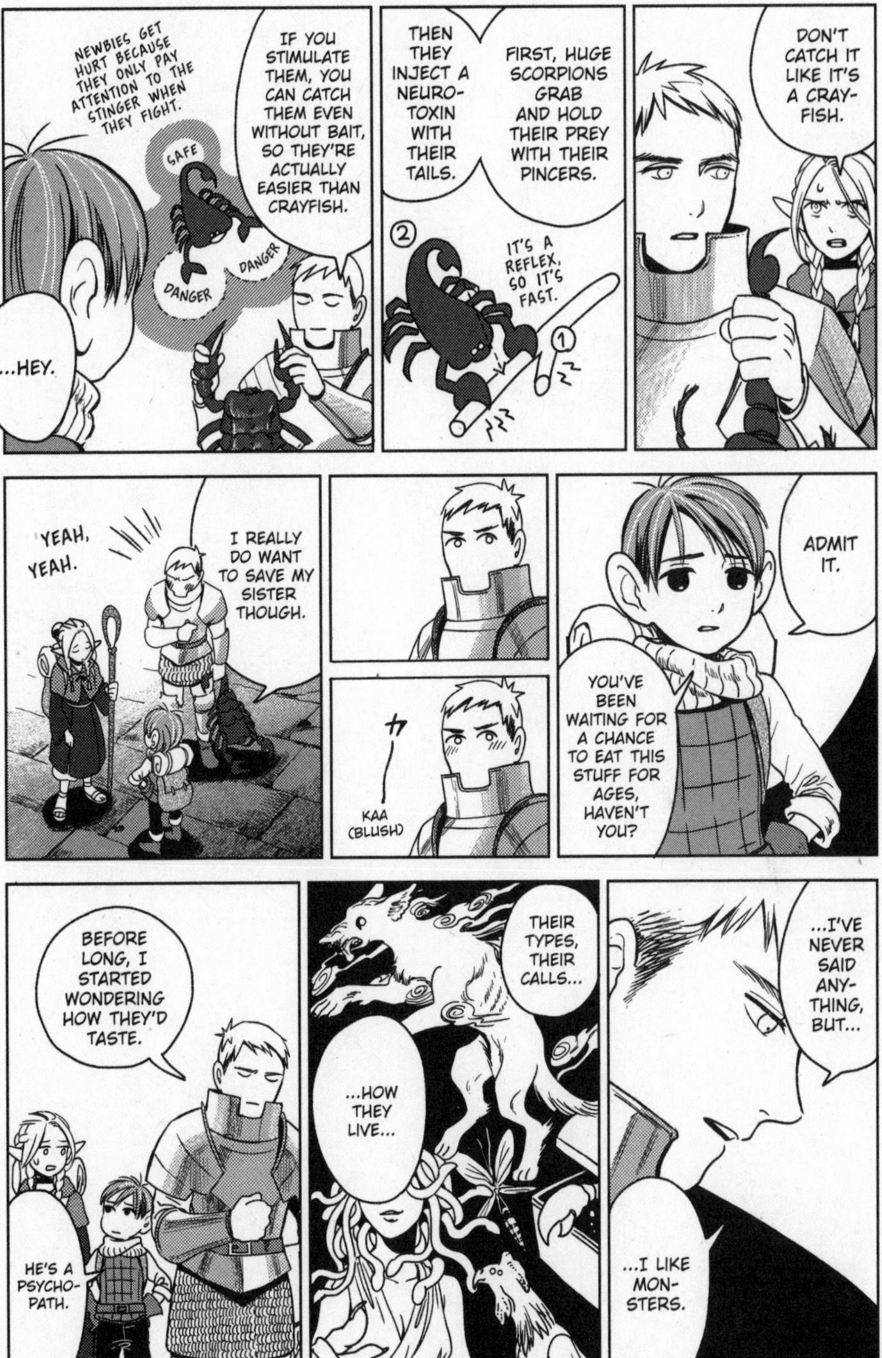
DON'T CATCH IT LIKE IT'S A CRAY-FISH.
FIRST, HUGE SCORPIONS GRAB AND HOLD THEIR PREY WITH THEIR PINCERS.
THEN THEY INJECT A NEURO-TOXIN WITH THEIR TAILS.
②
IT'S A REFLEX, SO IT'S FAST.
①
IF YOU STIMULATE THEM, YOU CAN CATCH THEM EVEN WITHOUT BAIT, SO THEY'RE ACTUALLY EASIER THAN CRAYFISH.
NEWBIES GET HURT BECAUSE THEY ONLY PAY ATTENTION TO THE STINGER WHEN THEY FIGHT.
SAFE
DANGER
DANGER
...HEY.
ADMIT IT.
YOU'VE BEEN WAITING FOR A CHANCE TO EAT THIS STUFF FOR AGES, HAVEN'T YOU?
カ
KAA (BLUSH)
I REALLY DO WANT TO SAVE MY SISTER THOUGH.
YEAH, YEAH.
...I'VE NEVER SAID ANY-THING, BUT...
...I LIKE MON-STERS.
THEIR TYPES, THEIR CALLS...
...HOW THEY LIVE...
BEFORE LONG, I STARTED WONDERING HOW THEY'D TASTE.
HE'S A PSYCHO-PATH.

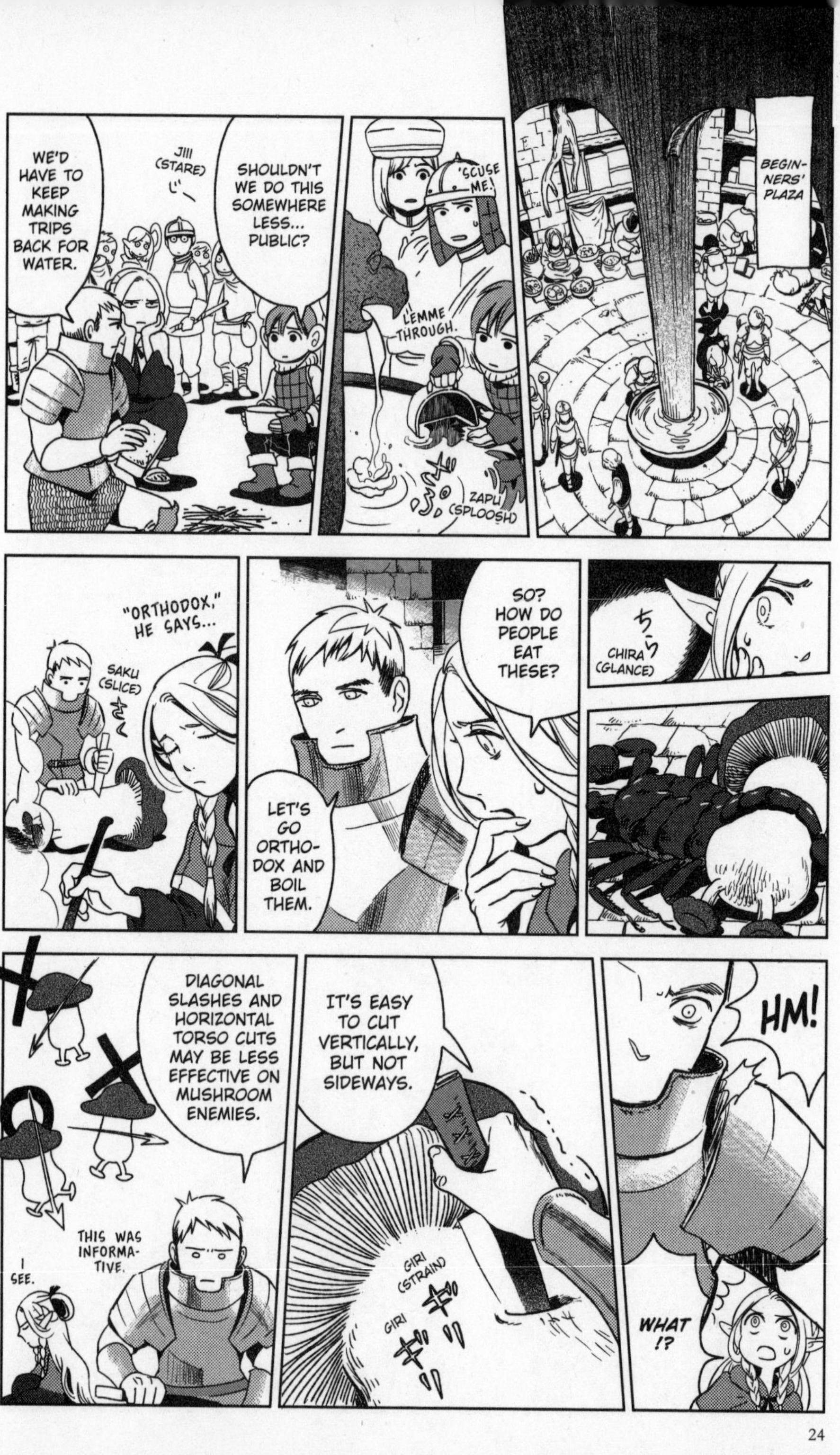
BEGINNERS' PLAZA
'SCUSE ME!
LEMME THROUGH.
ZAPU (SPLOOSH)
SHOULDN'T WE DO THIS SOMEWHERE LESS... PUBLIC?
JIII (STARE)
WE'D HAVE TO KEEP MAKING TRIPS BACK FOR WATER.
CHIRA (GLANCE)
SO? HOW DO PEOPLE EAT THESE?
LET'S GO ORTHODOX AND BOIL THEM.
"ORTHODOX," HE SAYS...
SAKU (SLICE)
HM!
WHAT!?
IT'S EASY TO CUT VERTICALLY, BUT NOT SIDEWAYS.
GIRI (STRAIN)
GIRI
DIAGONAL SLASHES AND HORIZONTAL TORSO CUTS MAY BE LESS EFFECTIVE ON MUSHROOM ENEMIES.
THIS WAS INFORMATIVE.
I SEE.

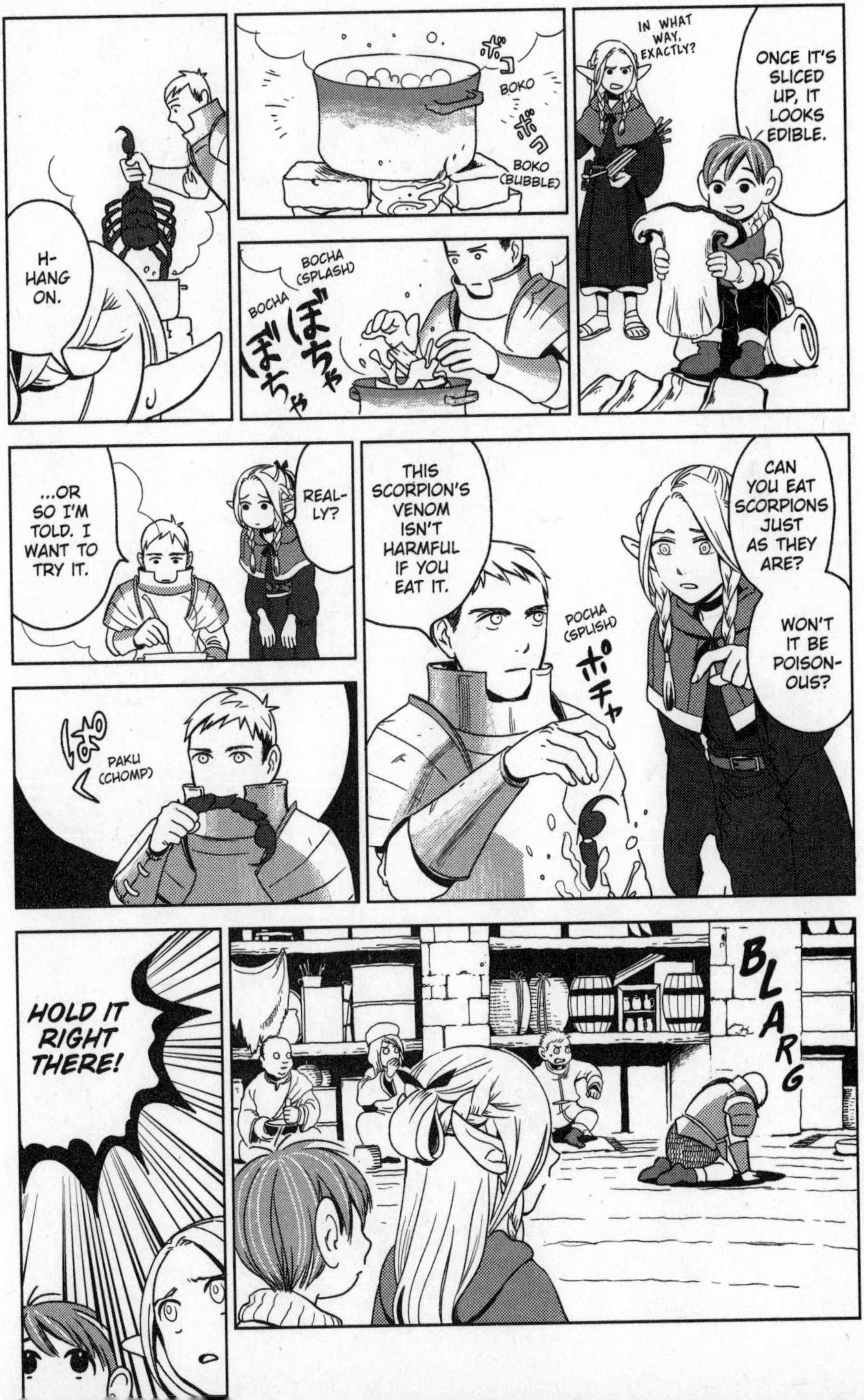
ONCE IT'S SLICED UP, IT LOOKS EDIBLE.
IN WHAT WAY, EXACTLY?
ボコ
BOKO
ボコ
BOKO (BUBBLE)
ぼちゃ
BOCHA (SPLASH)
ぼちゃ
BOCHA
H-HANG ON.
CAN YOU EAT SCORPIONS JUST AS THEY ARE?
WON'T IT BE POISONOUS?
THIS SCORPION'S VENOM ISN'T HARMFUL IF YOU EAT IT.
ポチャ
POCHA (SPLASH)
REAL-LY?
...OR SO I'M TOLD. I WANT TO TRY IT.
ぱく
PAKU (CHOMP)
BLARG
HOLD IT RIGHT THERE!

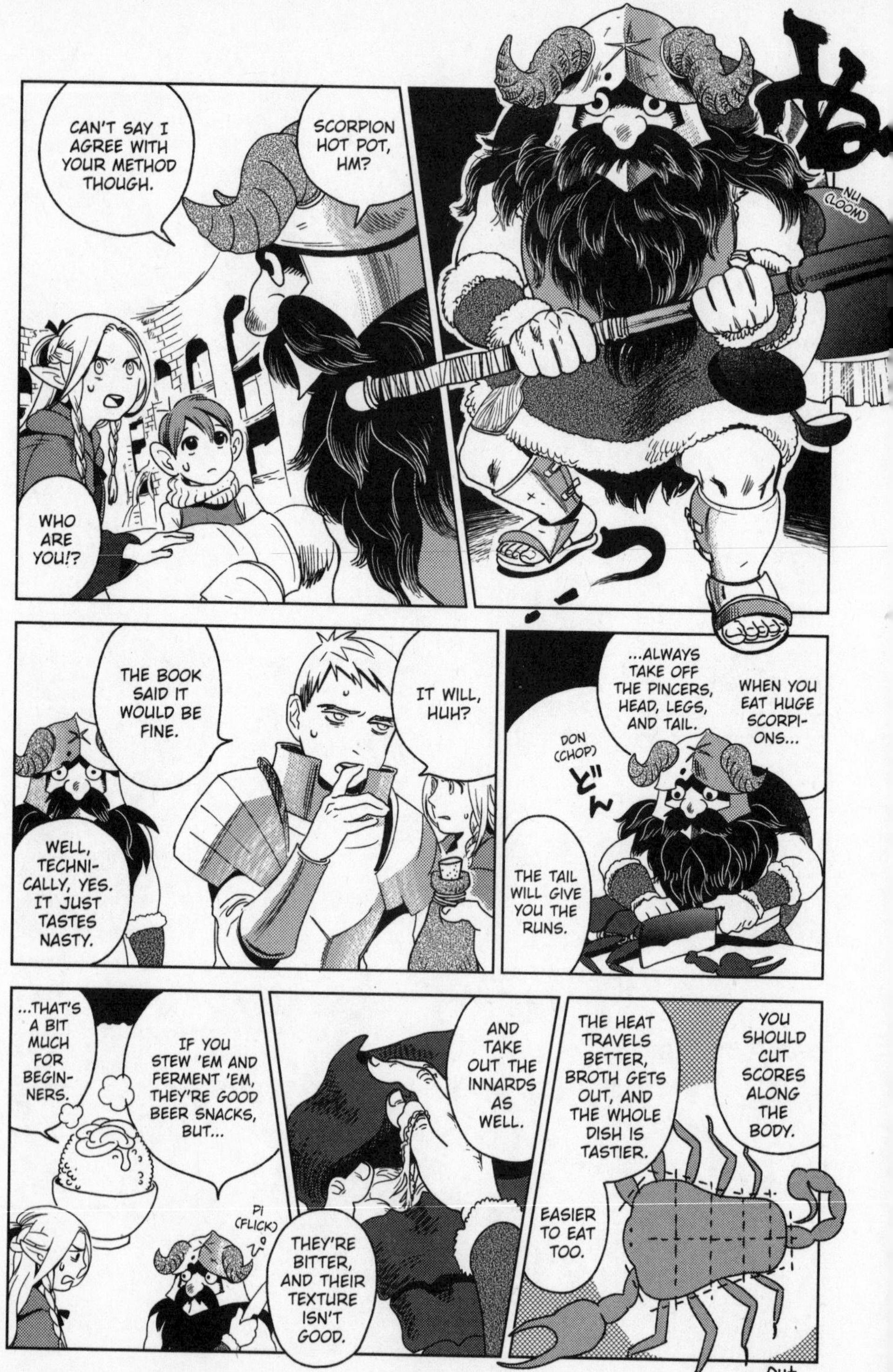
NU (LOOM)
SCORPION HOT POT, HM?
CAN'T SAY I AGREE WITH YOUR METHOD THOUGH.
WHO ARE YOU!?
WHEN YOU EAT HUGE SCORPIONS...
...ALWAYS TAKE OFF THE PINCERS, HEAD, LEGS, AND TAIL.
DON (CHOP)
THE TAIL WILL GIVE YOU THE RUNS.
IT WILL, HUH?
THE BOOK SAID IT WOULD BE FINE.
WELL, TECHNICALLY, YES. IT JUST TASTES NASTY.
YOU SHOULD CUT SCORES ALONG THE BODY.
THE HEAT TRAVELS BETTER, BROTH GETS OUT, AND THE WHOLE DISH IS TASTIER.
EASIER TO EAT TOO.
---Cut
AND TAKE OUT THE INNARDS AS WELL.
PI (FLICK)
THEY'RE BITTER, AND THEIR TEXTURE ISN'T GOOD.
IF YOU STEW 'EM AND FERMENT 'EM, THEY'RE GOOD BEER SNACKS, BUT...
...THAT'S A BIT MUCH FOR BEGINNERS.

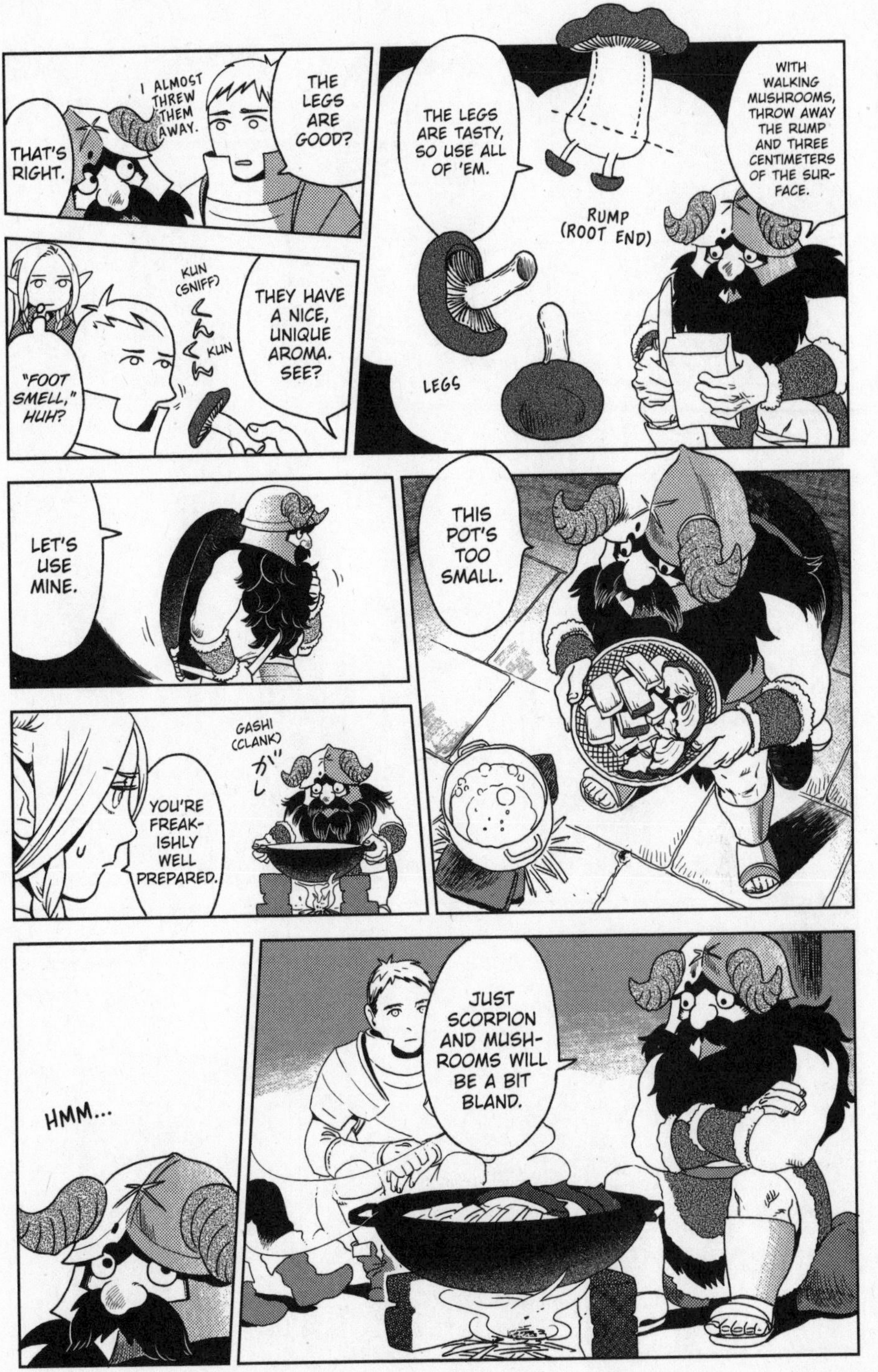
WITH WALKING MUSHROOMS, THROW AWAY THE RUMP AND THREE CENTIMETERS OF THE SURFACE.
THE LEGS ARE TASTY, SO USE ALL OF 'EM.
RUMP (ROOT END)
LEGS
THE LEGS ARE GOOD?
I ALMOST THREW THEM AWAY.
THAT'S RIGHT.
THEY HAVE A NICE, UNIQUE AROMA. SEE?
KUN (SNIFF)
くんくん
KUN
"FOOT SMELL," HUH?
THIS POT'S TOO SMALL.
LET'S USE MINE.
GASHI (CLANK)
がし
YOU'RE FREAKISHLY WELL PREPARED.
JUST SCORPION AND MUSHROOMS WILL BE A BIT BLAND.
HMM...

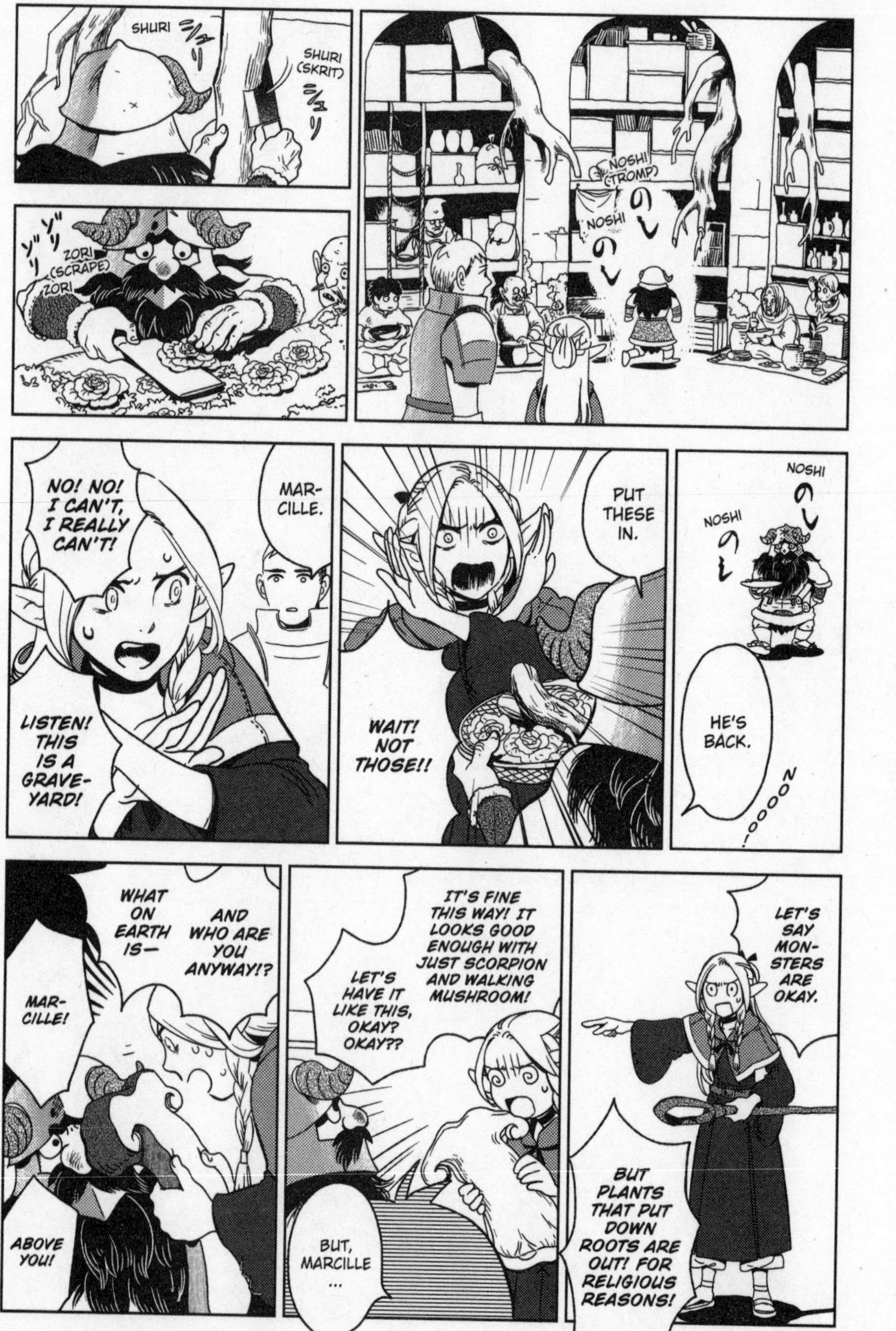
NOSHI (TROMP)
のし
NOSHI
のし
SHURI
シュリ
SHURI (SKRIT)
シュリ
ゾリ
ゾリ
ZORI (SCRAPE) ZORI
NOSHI
のし
NOSHI
のし
HE'S BACK.
NOOOOO!
PUT THESE IN.
WAIT! NOT THOSE!!
MARCILLE.
NO! NO! I CAN'T, I REALLY CAN'T!
LISTEN! THIS IS A GRAVEYARD!
LET'S SAY MONSTERS ARE OKAY.
BUT PLANTS THAT PUT DOWN ROOTS ARE OUT! FOR RELIGIOUS REASONS!
IT'S FINE THIS WAY! IT LOOKS GOOD ENOUGH WITH JUST SCORPION AND WALKING MUSHROOM!
LET'S HAVE IT LIKE THIS, OKAY? OKAY??
BUT, MARCILLE...
AND WHO ARE YOU ANYWAY!?
WHAT ON EARTH IS—
MARCILLE!
ABOVE YOU!

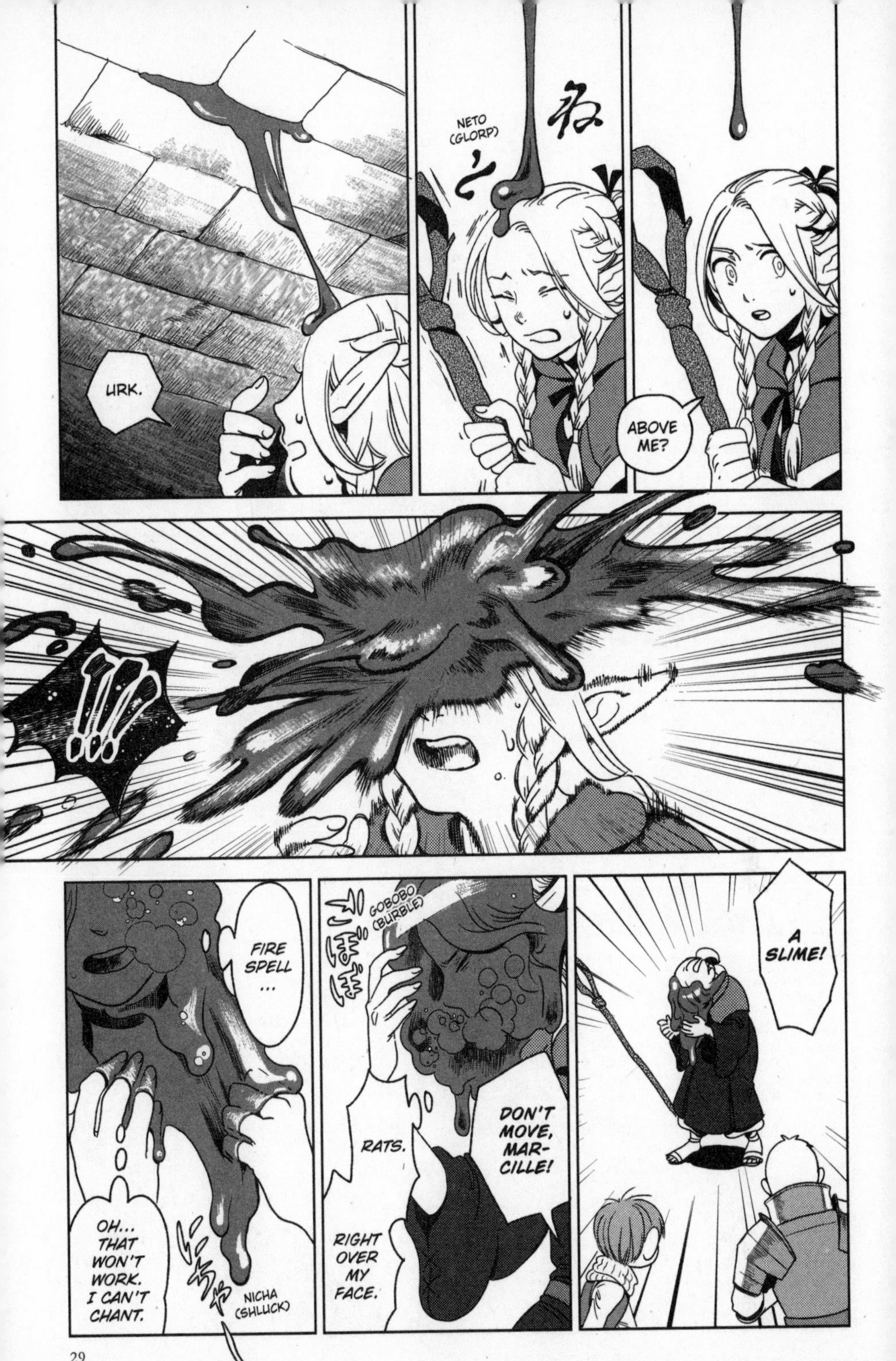
ABOVE ME?
NETO (GLORP)
URK.
!!!
A SLIME!
GOBOBO (BURBLE)
DON'T MOVE, MARCILLE!
RATS.
RIGHT OVER MY FACE.
FIRE SPELL...
OH... THAT WON'T WORK. I CAN'T CHANT.
NICHA (SHLUCK)

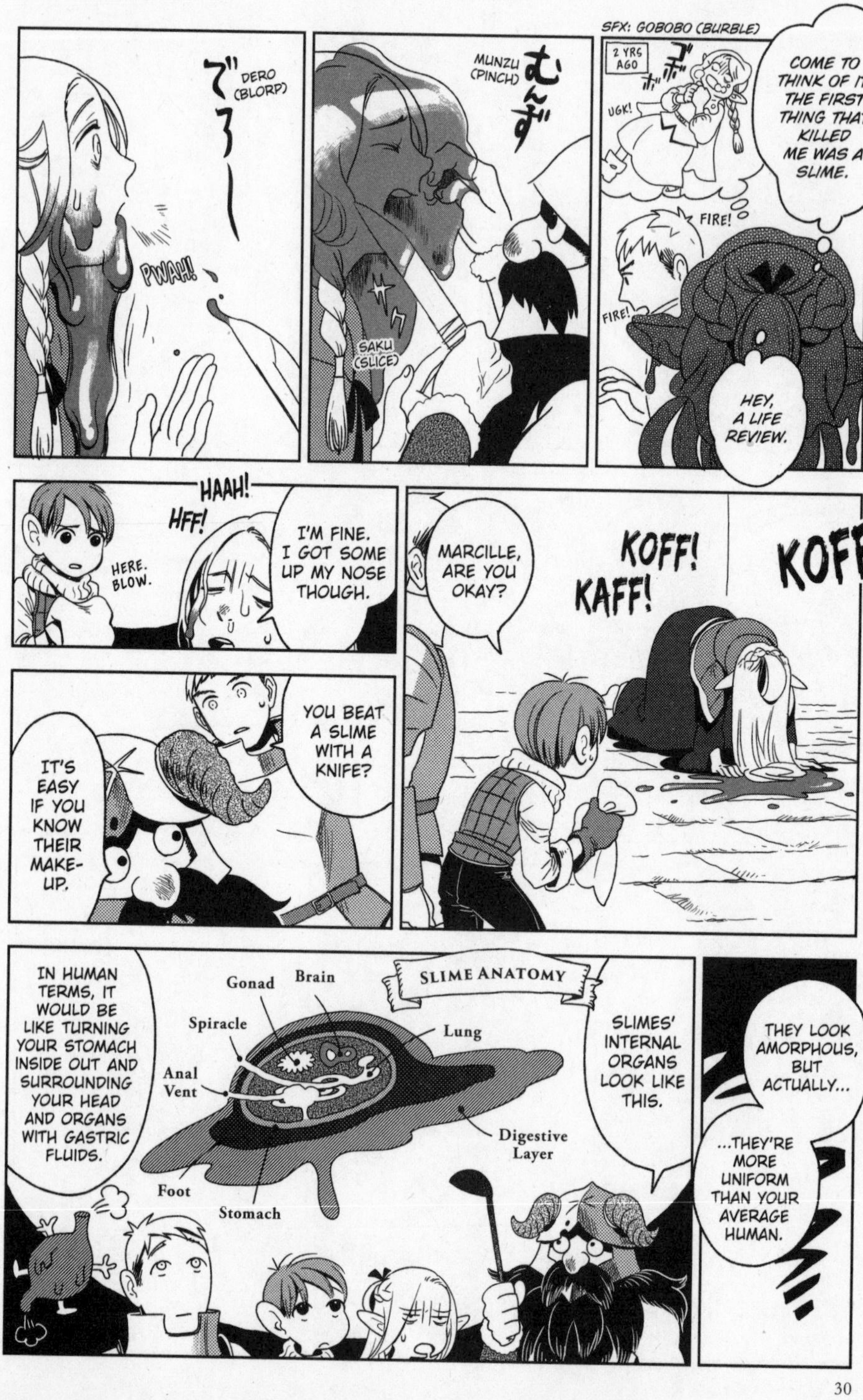
SFX: GOBOBO (BURBLE)
2 YRS AGO
COME TO THINK OF IT, THE FIRST THING THAT KILLED ME WAS A SLIME.
UGK!
FIRE!
FIRE!
HEY, A LIFE REVIEW.
むんず
MUNZU (PINCH)
SAKU (SLICE)
でろー
DERO (BLORP)
PWAH!
MARCILLE, ARE YOU OKAY?
KOFF!
KOFF!
KAFF!
HAAH!
HFF!
I'M FINE. I GOT SOME UP MY NOSE THOUGH.
HERE. BLOW.
YOU BEAT A SLIME WITH A KNIFE?
IT'S EASY IF YOU KNOW THEIR MAKE-UP.
THEY LOOK AMORPHOUS, BUT ACTUALLY...
...THEY'RE MORE UNIFORM THAN YOUR AVERAGE HUMAN.
SLIMES' INTERNAL ORGANS LOOK LIKE THIS.
SLIME ANATOMY
Gonad
Brain
Spiracle
Lung
Anal Vent
Digestive Layer
Foot
Stomach
IN HUMAN TERMS, IT WOULD BE LIKE TURNING YOUR STOMACH INSIDE OUT AND SURROUNDING YOUR HEAD AND ORGANS WITH GASTRIC FLUIDS.

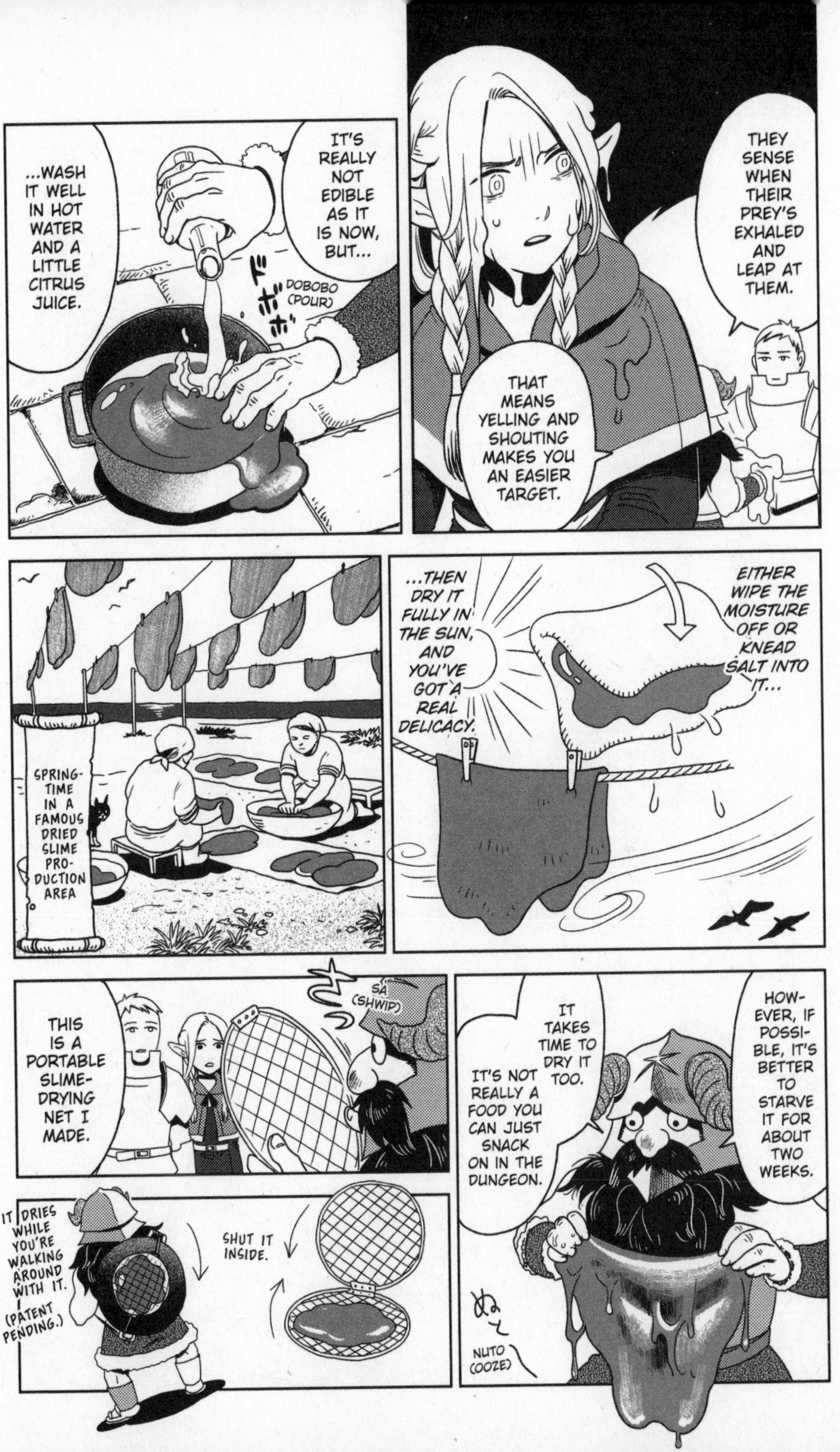
THEY SENSE WHEN THEIR PREY'S EXHALED AND LEAP AT THEM.
THAT MEANS YELLING AND SHOUTING MAKES YOU AN EASIER TARGET.
IT'S REALLY NOT EDIBLE AS IT IS NOW, BUT...
...WASH IT WELL IN HOT WATER AND A LITTLE CITRUS JUICE.
ドボボ
DOBOBO (POUR)
EITHER WIPE THE MOISTURE OFF OR KNEAD SALT INTO IT...
...THEN DRY IT FULLY IN THE SUN, AND YOU'VE GOT A REAL DELICACY.
SPRING-TIME IN A FAMOUS DRIED SLIME PRO-DUCTION AREA
HOW-EVER, IF POSSI-BLE, IT'S BETTER TO STARVE IT FOR ABOUT TWO WEEKS.
IT TAKES TIME TO DRY IT TOO.
IT'S NOT REALLY A FOOD YOU CAN JUST SNACK ON IN THE DUNGEON.
ぬと
NUTO (OOZE)
さ
SA (SHWIP)
THIS IS A PORTABLE SLIME-DRYING NET I MADE.
SHUT IT INSIDE.
IT DRIES WHILE YOU'RE WALKING AROUND WITH IT. (PATENT PENDING.)

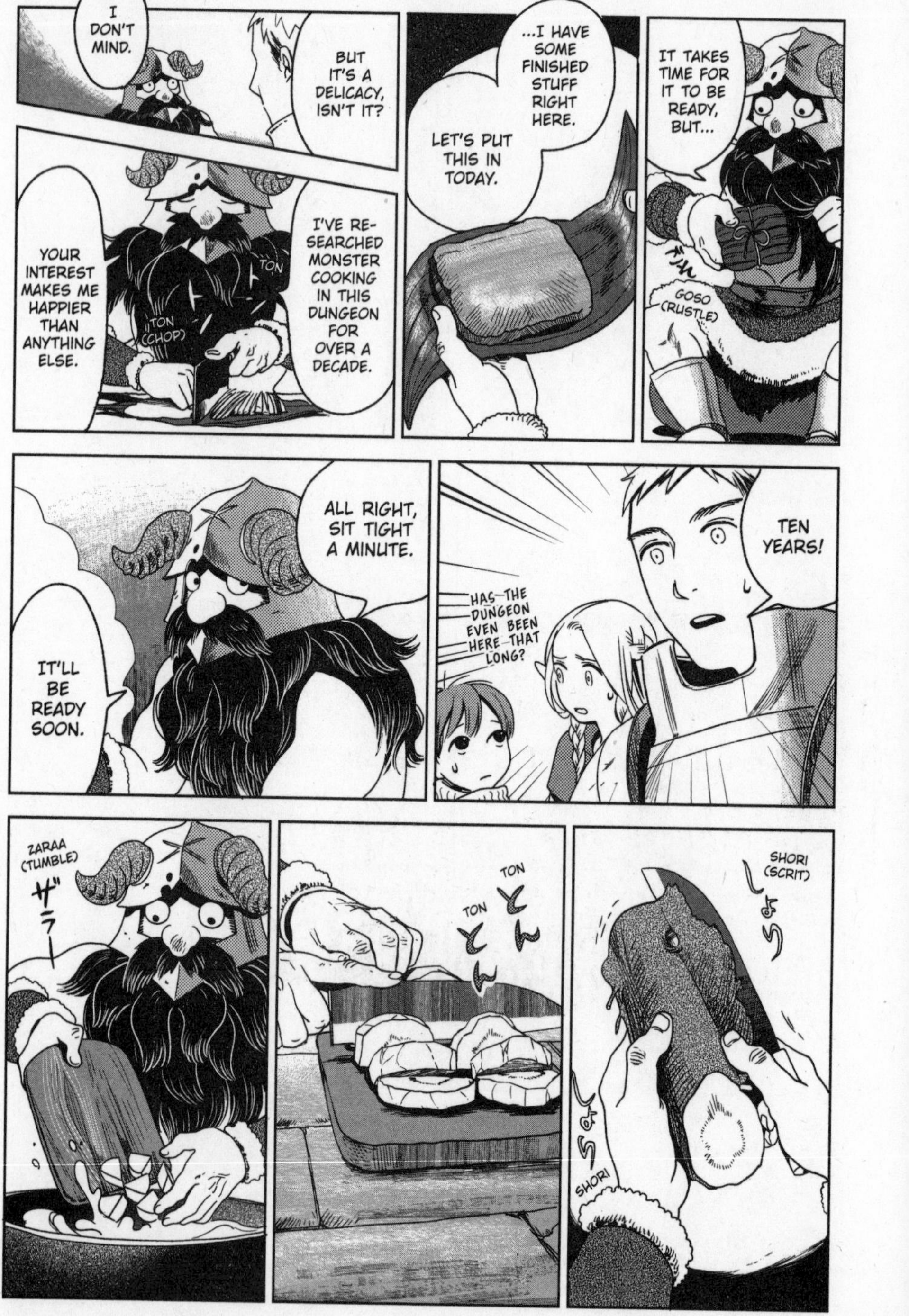
IT TAKES TIME FOR IT TO BE READY, BUT...
GOSO (RUSTLE)
...I HAVE SOME FINISHED STUFF RIGHT HERE.
LET'S PUT THIS IN TODAY.
BUT IT'S A DELICACY, ISN'T IT?
I DON'T MIND.
I'VE RE-SEARCHED MONSTER COOKING IN THIS DUNGEON FOR OVER A DECADE.
TON
TON (CHOP)
YOUR INTEREST MAKES ME HAPPIER THAN ANYTHING ELSE.
TEN YEARS!
HAS THE DUNGEON EVEN BEEN HERE THAT LONG?
ALL RIGHT, SIT TIGHT A MINUTE.
IT'LL BE READY SOON.
SHORI (SCRIT)
SHORI
TON
TON
ZARAA (TUMBLE)

HUGE SCORPION AND WALKING MUSHROOM HOT POT

Ingredients (Serves 3~4)

Huge scorpion	1
Walking mushroom	1
Mushroom feet	2
Seaweed (arctic moss, star jelly)	To taste
Invertatoes	About 5 medium
Dried slime	As much as you like
Water	To taste

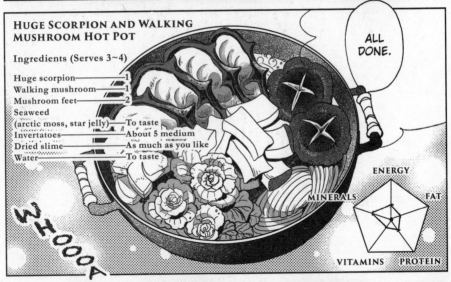

WHOOOA

ALL DONE.

ENERGY
FAT
PROTEIN
VITAMINS
MINERALS

I WONDER IF IT'S REALLY A SCORPION...

SO HUGE SCORPION TURNS RED WHEN YOU BOIL IT?

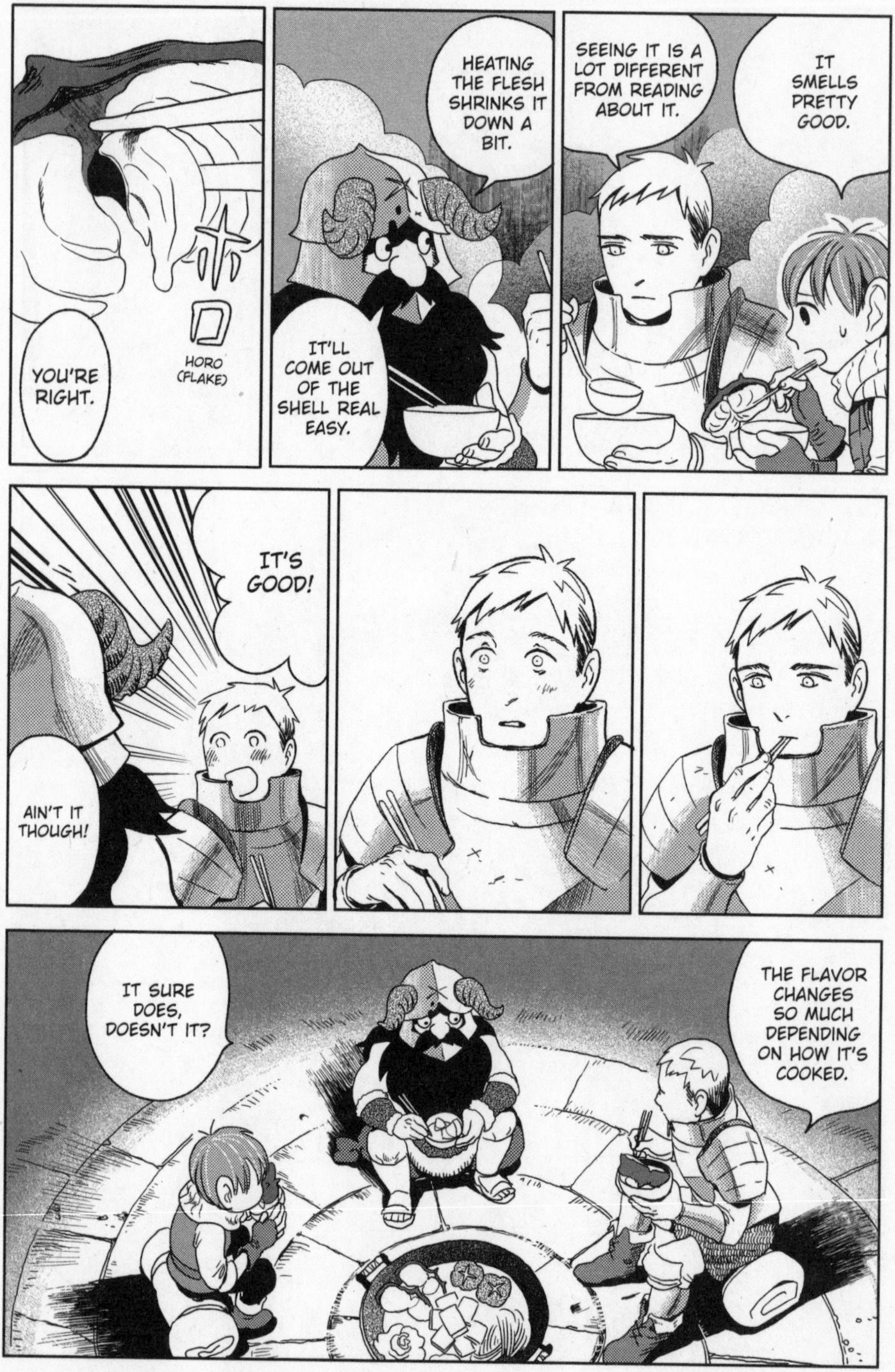
IT SMELLS PRETTY GOOD.
SEEING IT IS A LOT DIFFERENT FROM READING ABOUT IT.
HEATING THE FLESH SHRINKS IT DOWN A BIT.
IT'LL COME OUT OF THE SHELL REAL EASY.
ホロ
HORO (FLAKE)
YOU'RE RIGHT.
IT'S GOOD!
AIN'T IT THOUGH!
THE FLAVOR CHANGES SO MUCH DEPENDING ON HOW IT'S COOKED.
IT SURE DOES, DOESN'T IT?

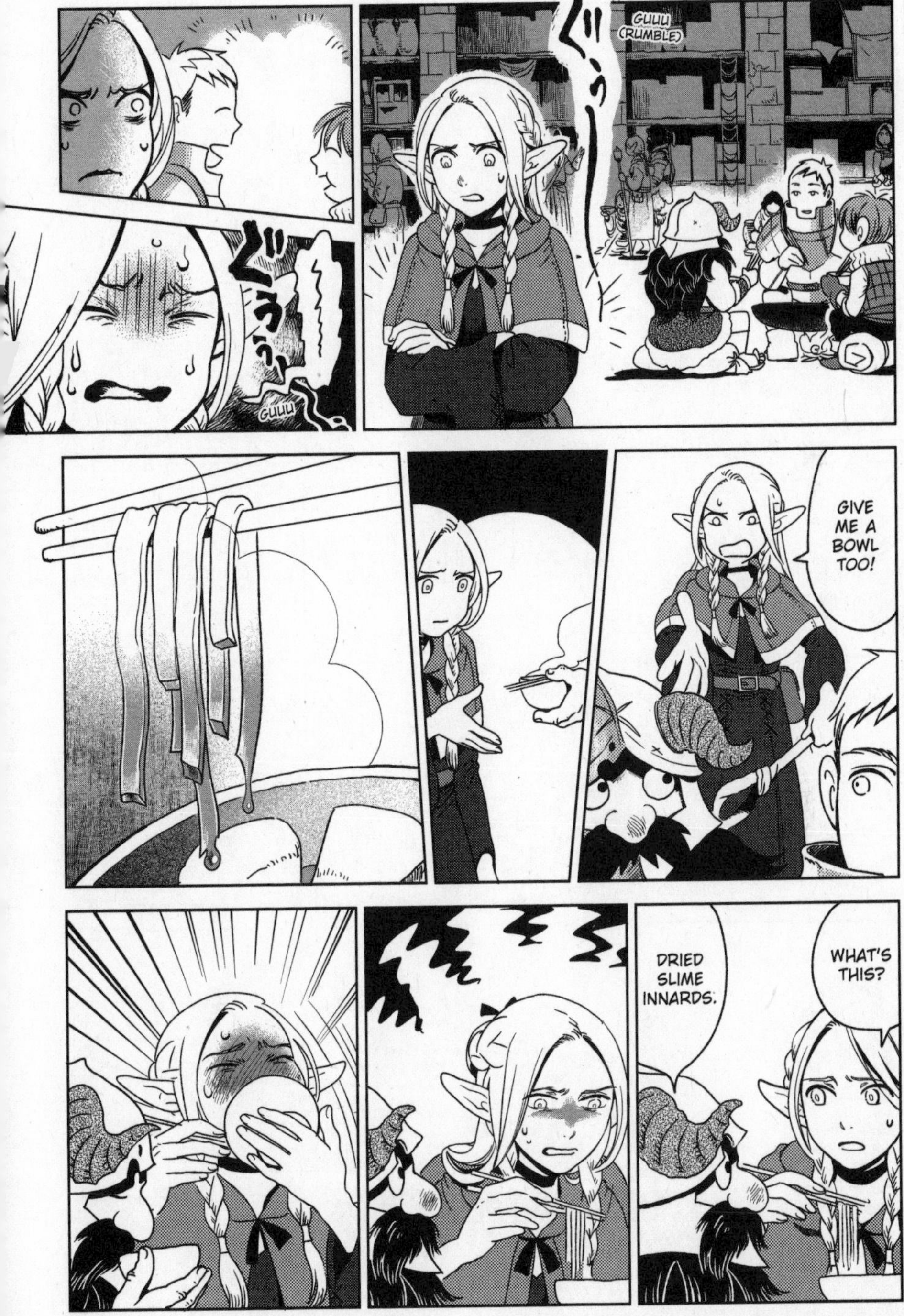
GUUU
(RUMBLE)
GUUU
GIVE ME A BOWL TOO!
WHAT'S THIS?
DRIED SLIME INNARDS.

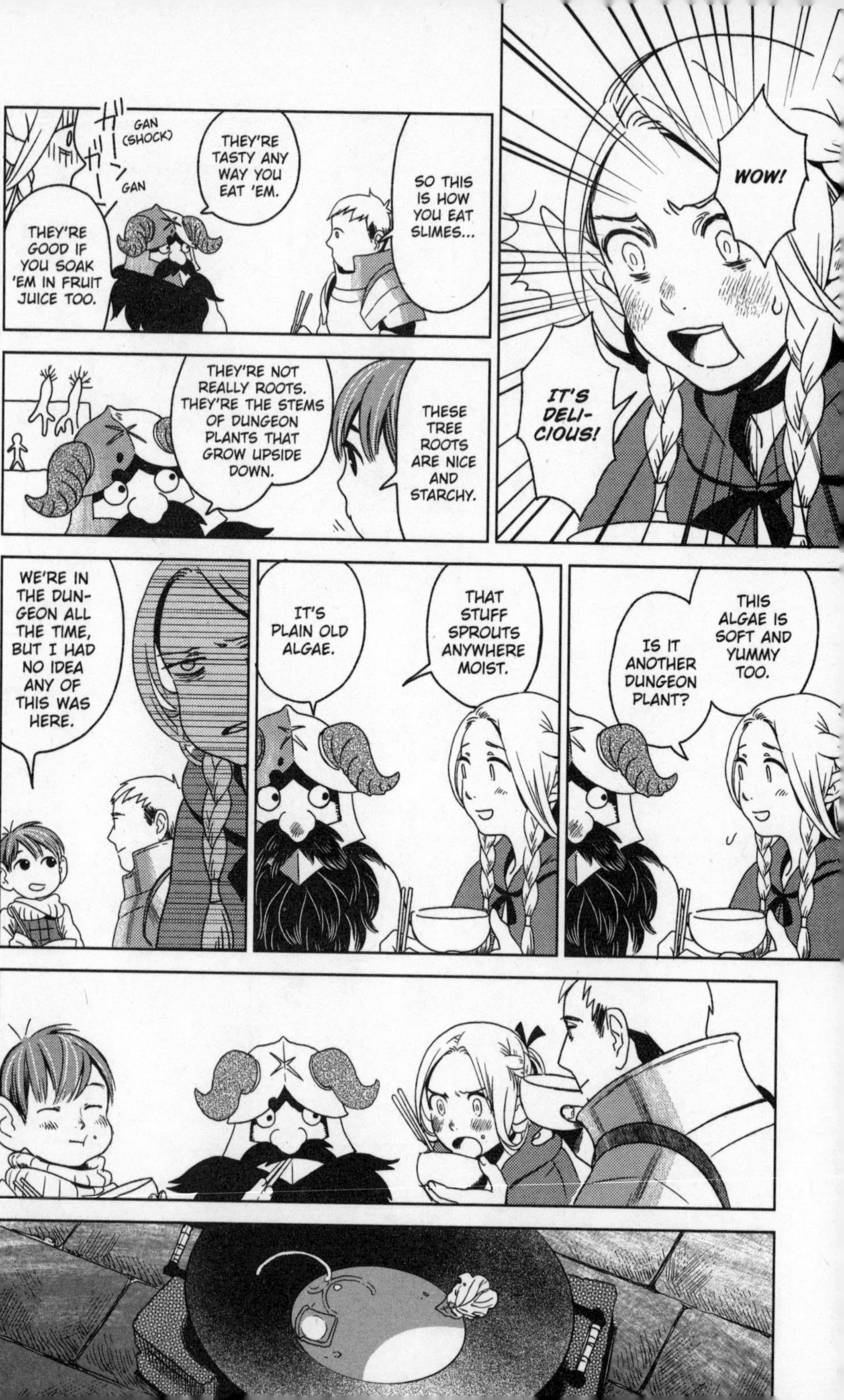
WOW!
IT'S DELICIOUS!
SO THIS IS HOW YOU EAT SLIMES...
THEY'RE TASTY ANY WAY YOU EAT 'EM.
GAN (SHOCK)
GAN
THEY'RE GOOD IF YOU SOAK 'EM IN FRUIT JUICE TOO.
THESE TREE ROOTS ARE NICE AND STARCHY.
THEY'RE NOT REALLY ROOTS. THEY'RE THE STEMS OF DUNGEON PLANTS THAT GROW UPSIDE DOWN.
THIS ALGAE IS SOFT AND YUMMY TOO.
IS IT ANOTHER DUNGEON PLANT?
THAT STUFF SPROUTS ANYWHERE MOIST.
IT'S PLAIN OLD ALGAE.
WE'RE IN THE DUNGEON ALL THE TIME, BUT I HAD NO IDEA ANY OF THIS WAS HERE.

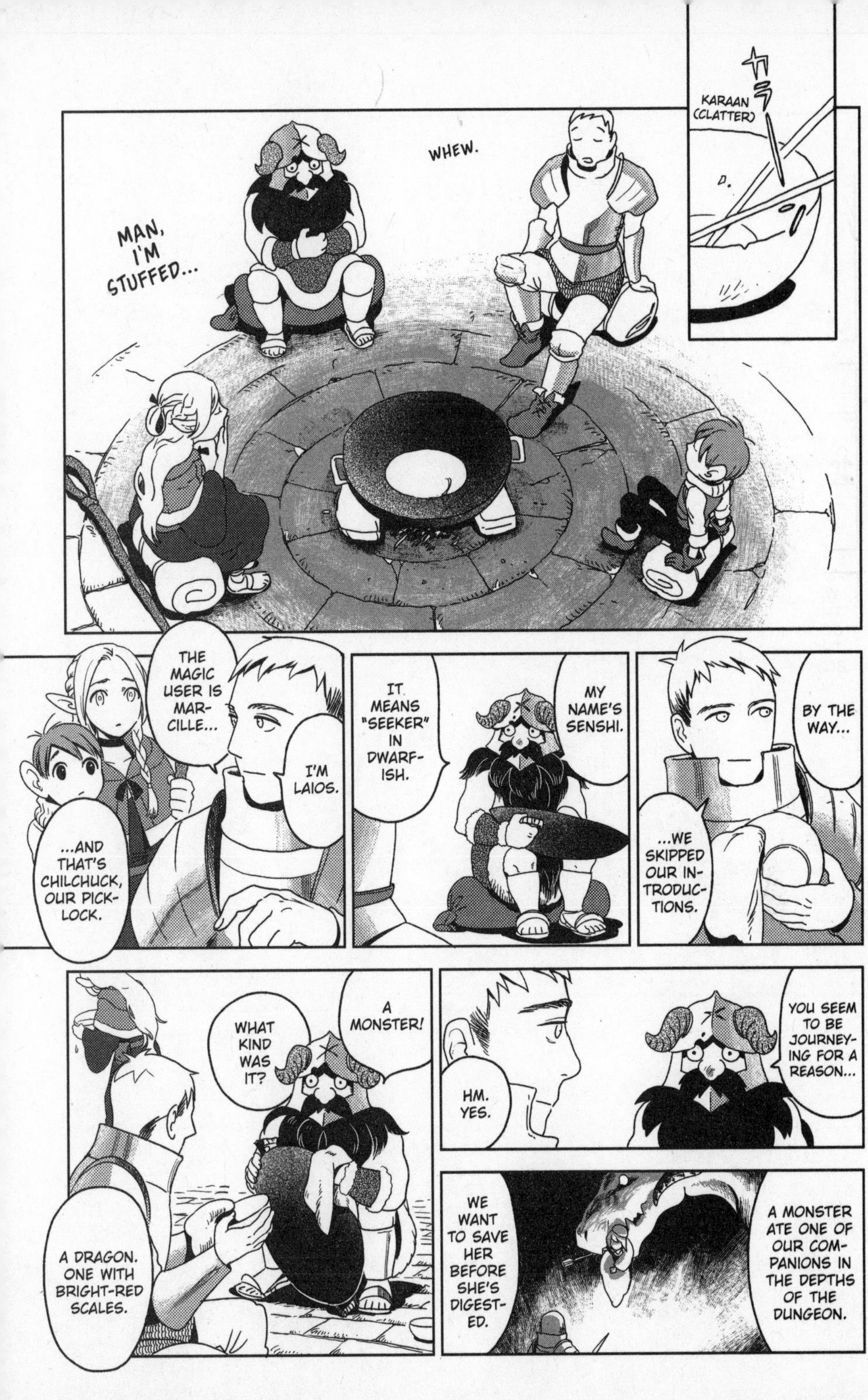
カラ
KARAAN (CLATTER)
WHEW.
MAN, I'M STUFFED...
BY THE WAY...
...WE SKIPPED OUR INTRODUCTIONS.
MY NAME'S SENSHI.
IT MEANS "SEEKER" IN DWARFISH.
I'M LAIOS.
THE MAGIC USER IS MARCILLE...
...AND THAT'S CHILCHUCK, OUR PICKLOCK.
YOU SEEM TO BE JOURNEYING FOR A REASON...
HM. YES.
A MONSTER ATE ONE OF OUR COMPANIONS IN THE DEPTHS OF THE DUNGEON.
WE WANT TO SAVE HER BEFORE SHE'S DIGESTED.
A MONSTER!
WHAT KIND WAS IT?
A DRAGON. ONE WITH BRIGHT-RED SCALES.

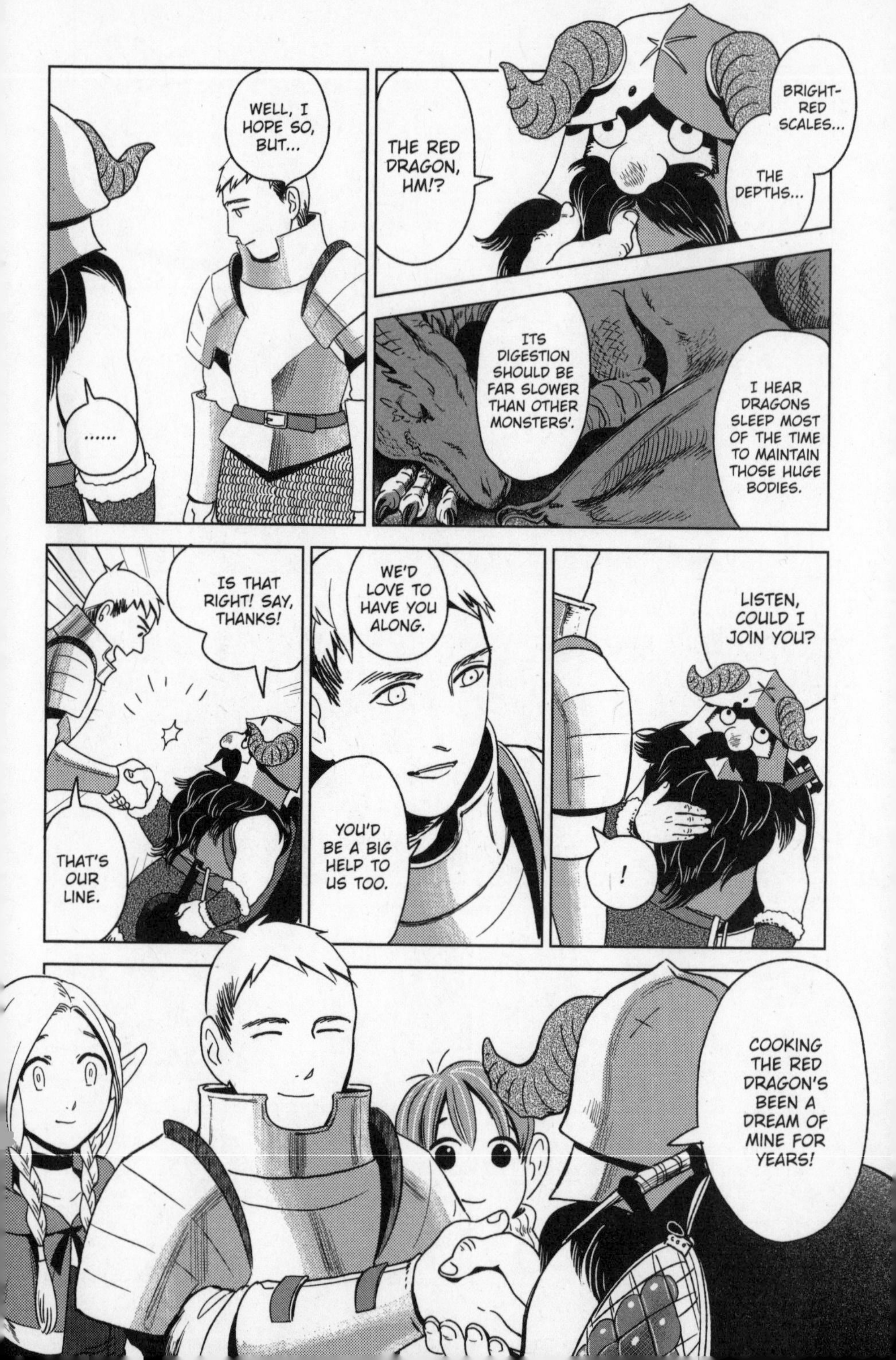
BRIGHT-RED SCALES...
THE DEPTHS...
THE RED DRAGON, HM!?
I HEAR DRAGONS SLEEP MOST OF THE TIME TO MAINTAIN THOSE HUGE BODIES.
ITS DIGESTION SHOULD BE FAR SLOWER THAN OTHER MONSTERS'.
WELL, I HOPE SO, BUT...
....
LISTEN, COULD I JOIN YOU?
!
WE'D LOVE TO HAVE YOU ALONG.
YOU'D BE A BIG HELP TO US TOO.
IS THAT RIGHT! SAY, THANKS!
THAT'S OUR LINE.
COOKING THE RED DRAGON'S BEEN A DREAM OF MINE FOR YEARS!

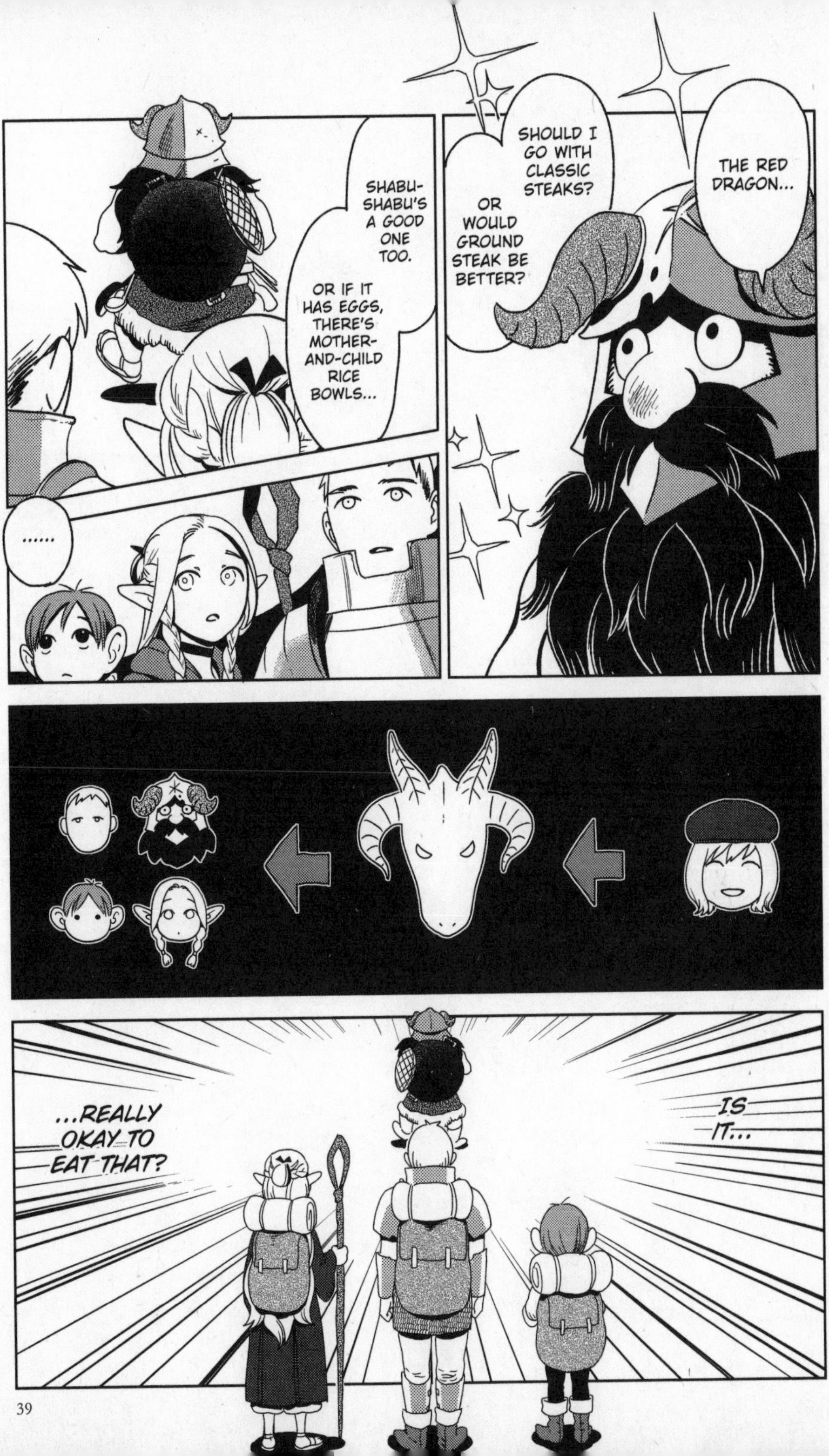
THE RED DRAGON...
SHOULD I GO WITH CLASSIC STEAKS?
OR WOULD GROUND STEAK BE BETTER?
SHABU-SHABU'S A GOOD ONE TOO.
OR IF IT HAS EGGS, THERE'S MOTHER-AND-CHILD RICE BOWLS...
......
IS IT...
...REALLY OKAY TO EAT THAT?

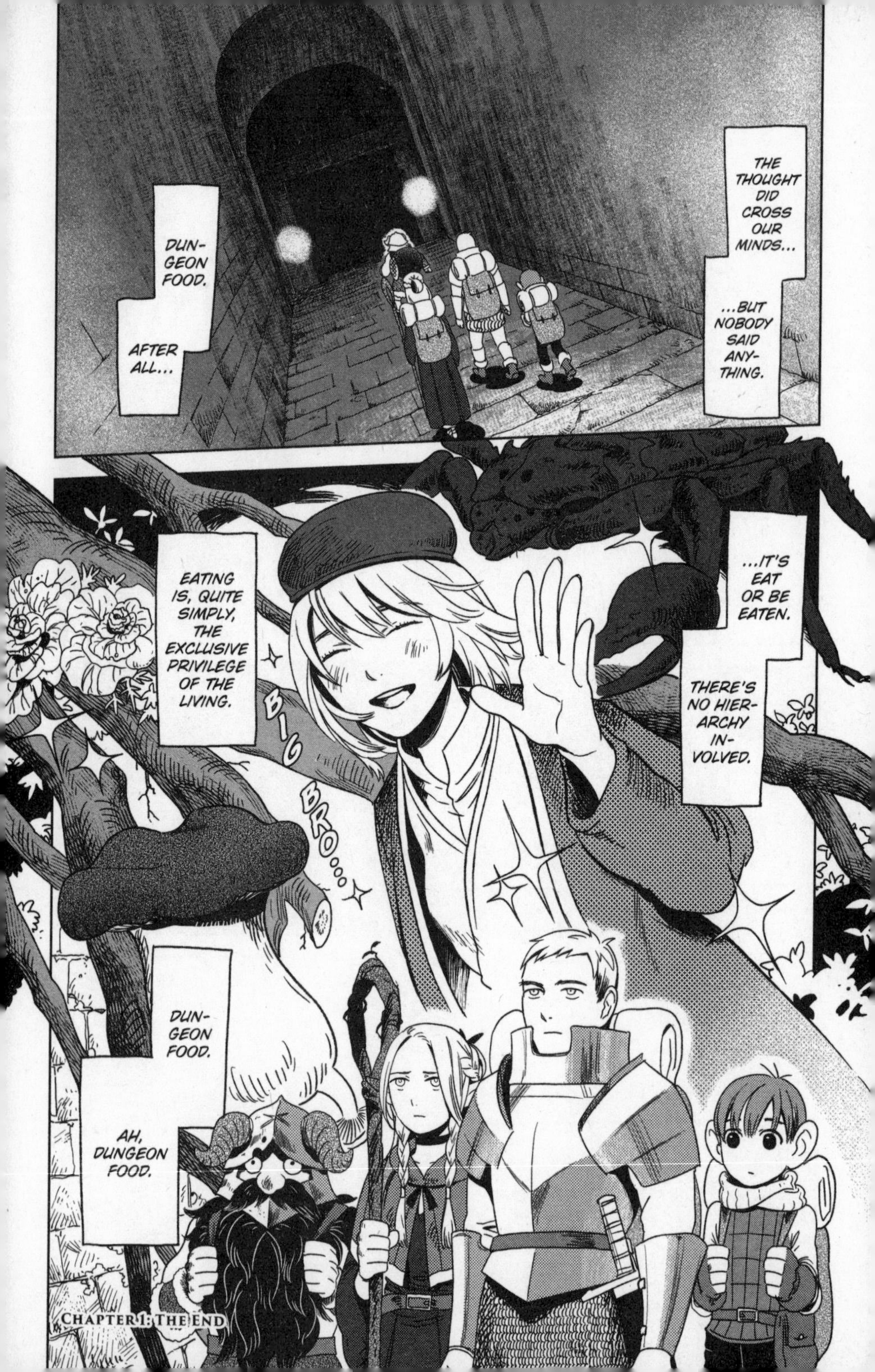
THE THOUGHT DID CROSS OUR MINDS...
...BUT NOBODY SAID ANYTHING.
DUNGEON FOOD.
AFTER ALL...
...IT'S EAT OR BE EATEN.
THERE'S NO HIERARCHY INVOLVED.
EATING IS, QUITE SIMPLY, THE EXCLUSIVE PRIVILEGE OF THE LIVING.
BIG BRO...
DUNGEON FOOD.
AH, DUNGEON FOOD.
CHAPTER 1: THE END

2. Tart

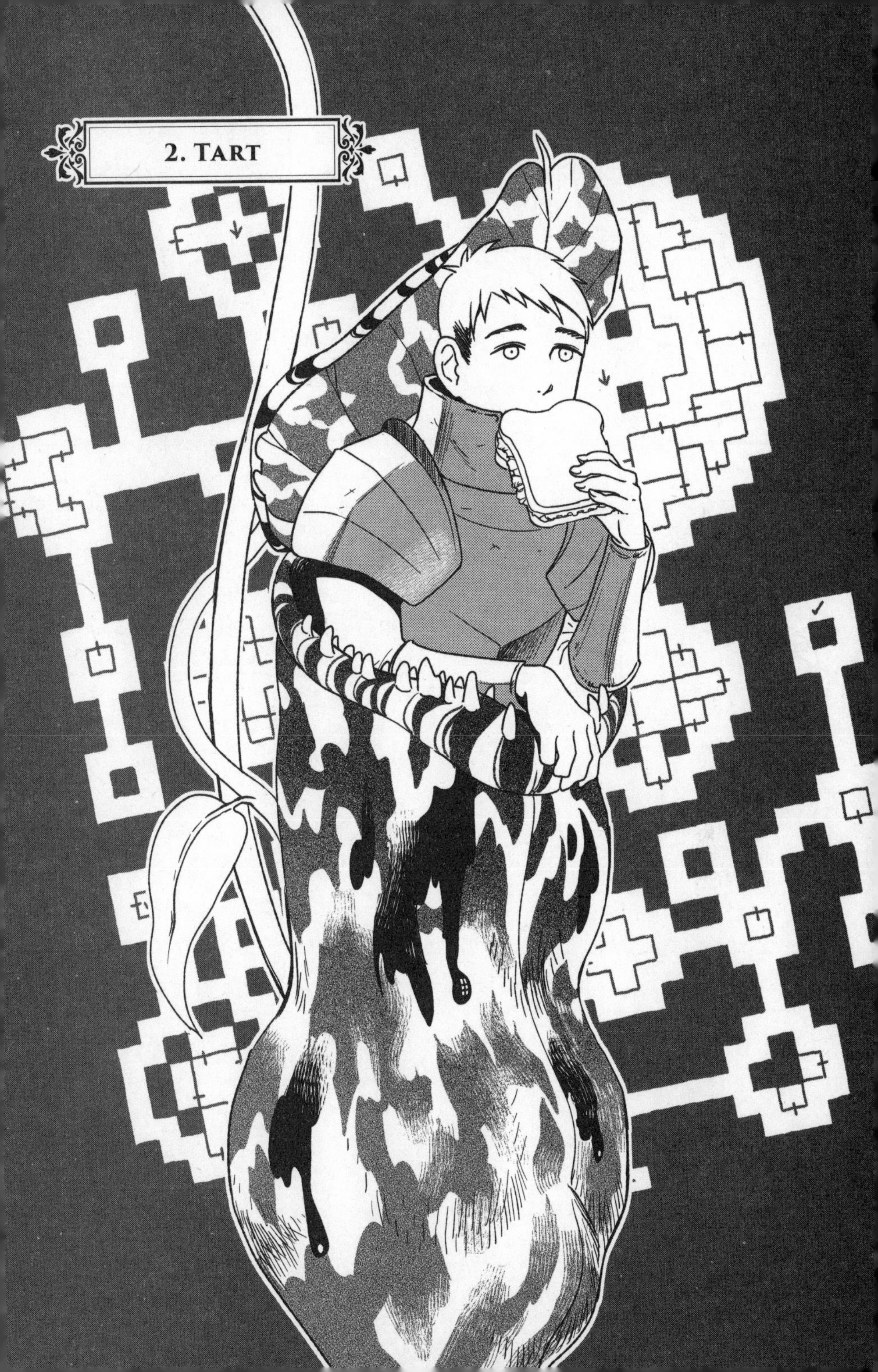

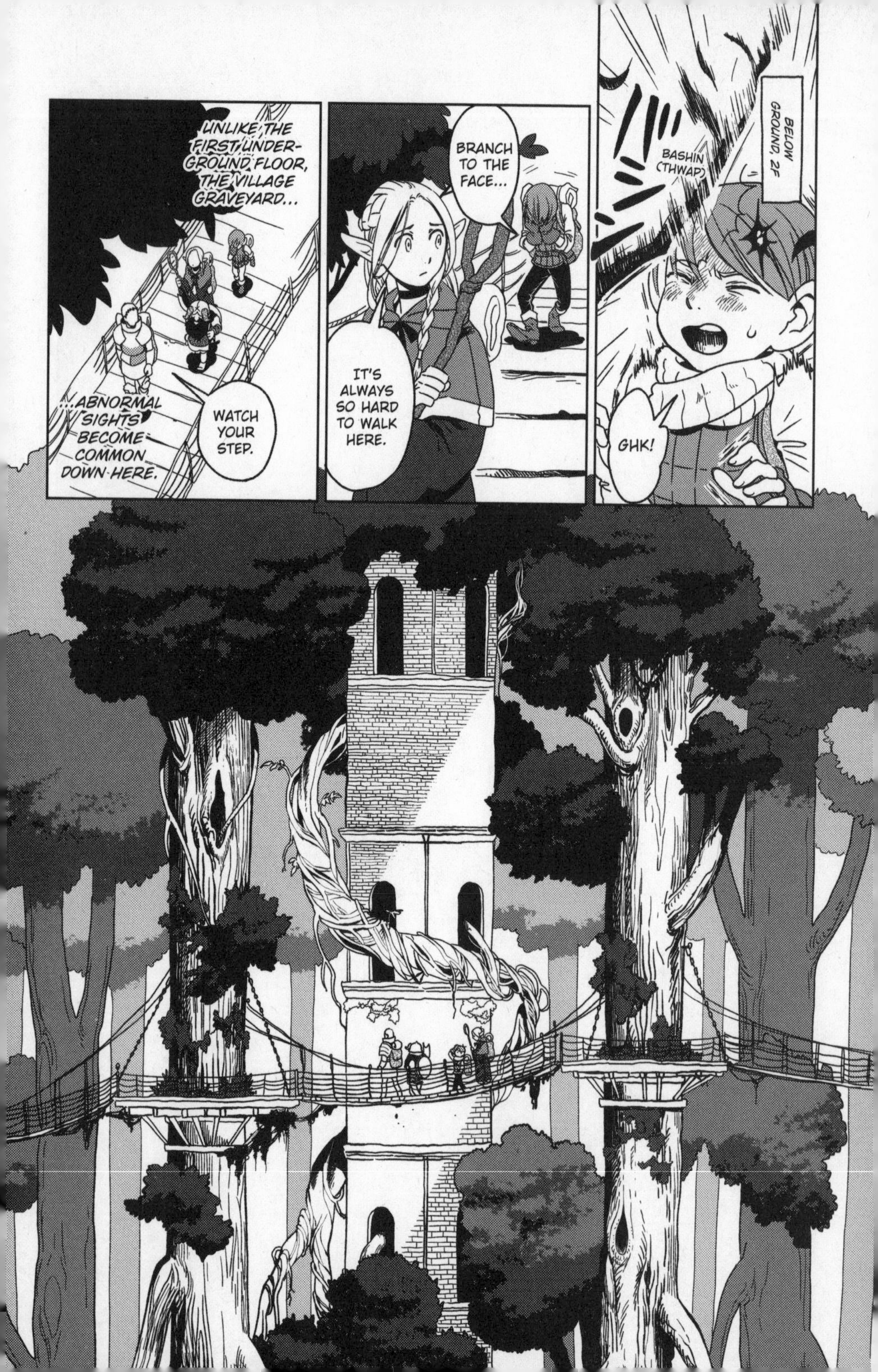
BELOW GROUND, 2F
BASHIN (THWAP)
GHK!
BRANCH TO THE FACE...
IT'S ALWAYS SO HARD TO WALK HERE.
UNLIKE THE FIRST UNDER-GROUND FLOOR, THE VILLAGE GRAVEYARD...
WATCH YOUR STEP.
...ABNORMAL SIGHTS BECOME COMMON DOWN HERE.

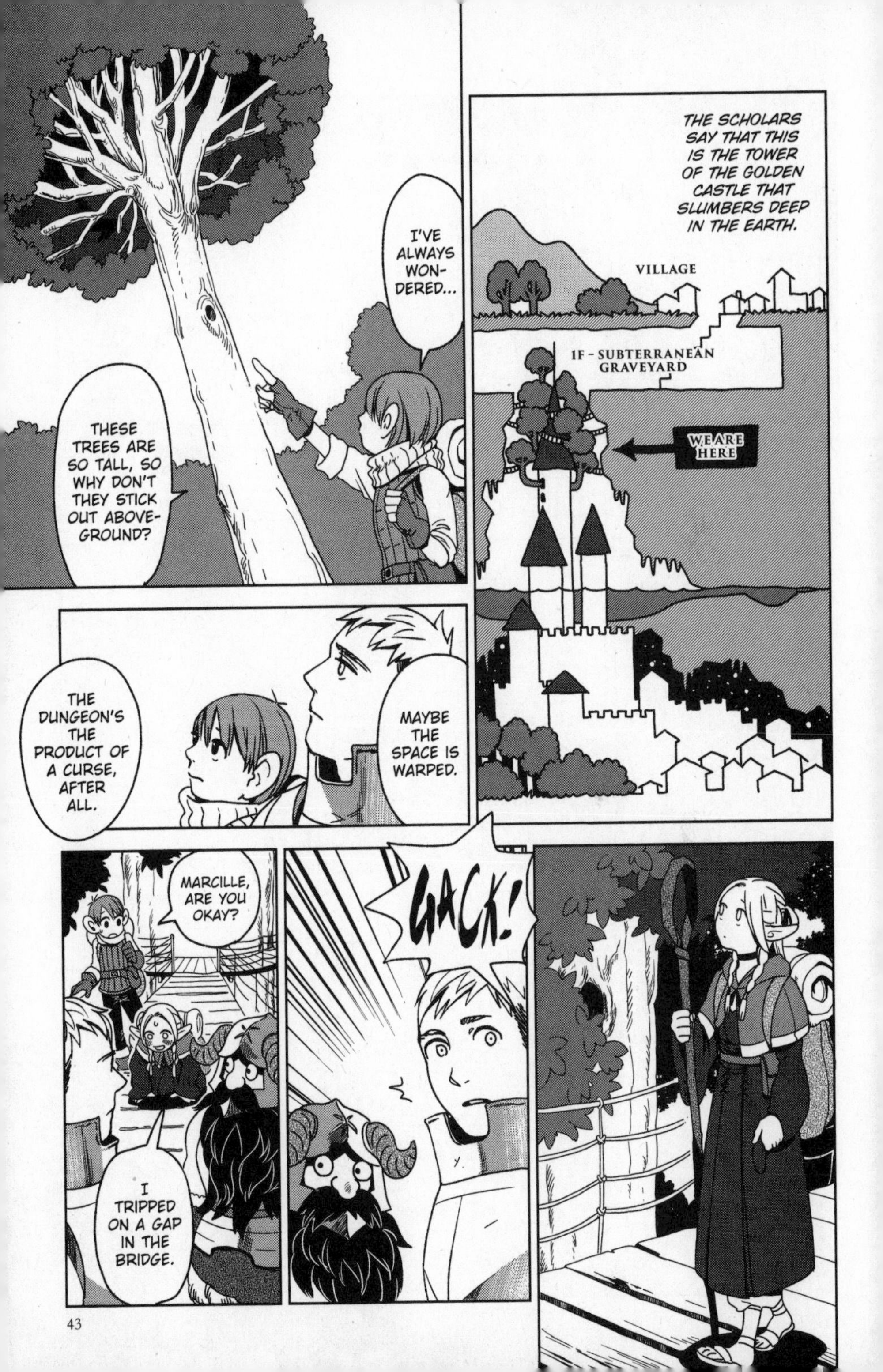
THE SCHOLARS SAY THAT THIS IS THE TOWER OF THE GOLDEN CASTLE THAT SLUMBERS DEEP IN THE EARTH.
VILLAGE
1F - SUBTERRANEAN GRAVEYARD
WE ARE HERE
I'VE ALWAYS WONDERED...
THESE TREES ARE SO TALL, SO WHY DON'T THEY STICK OUT ABOVEGROUND?
MAYBE THE SPACE IS WARPED.
THE DUNGEON'S THE PRODUCT OF A CURSE, AFTER ALL.
GACK!
MARCILLE, ARE YOU OKAY?
I TRIPPED ON A GAP IN THE BRIDGE.

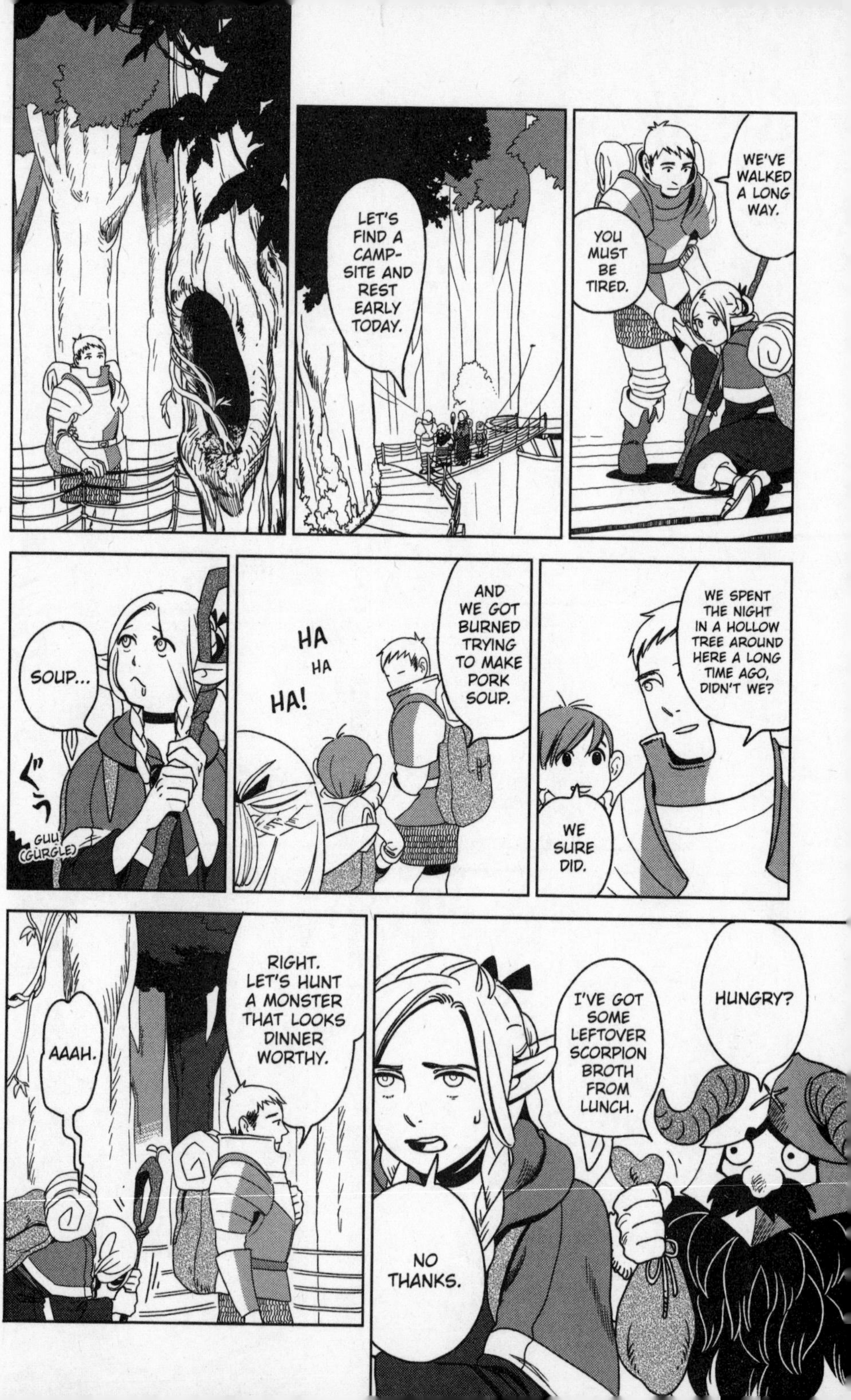
WE'VE WALKED A LONG WAY.
YOU MUST BE TIRED.
LET'S FIND A CAMP-SITE AND REST EARLY TODAY.
WE SPENT THE NIGHT IN A HOLLOW TREE AROUND HERE A LONG TIME AGO, DIDN'T WE?
WE SURE DID.
AND WE GOT BURNED TRYING TO MAKE PORK SOUP.
HA HA HA!
SOUP...
GUU (GURGLE)
HUNGRY?
I'VE GOT SOME LEFTOVER SCORPION BROTH FROM LUNCH.
NO THANKS.
RIGHT. LET'S HUNT A MONSTER THAT LOOKS DINNER WORTHY.
AAAH.

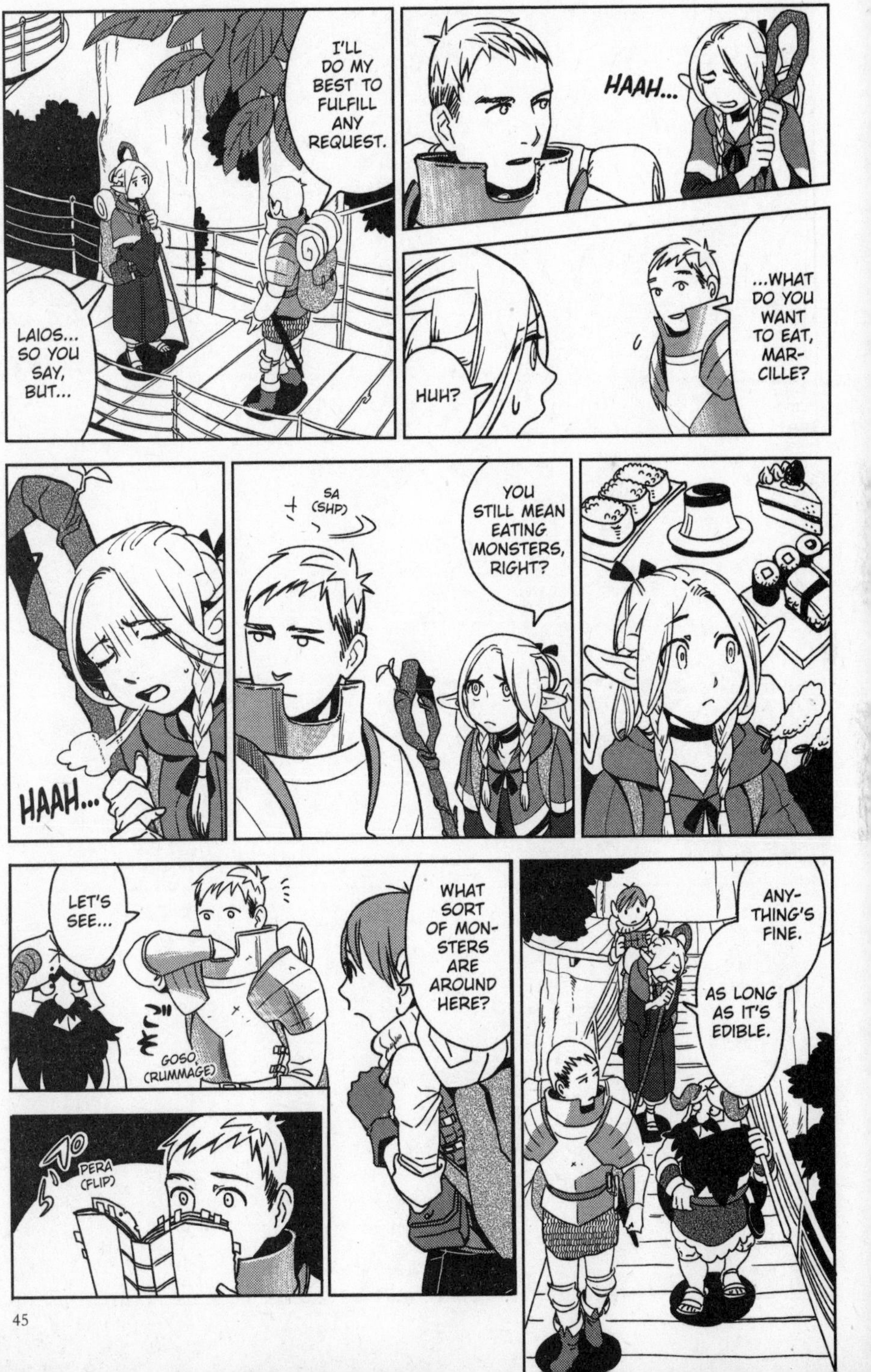
HAAH...
...WHAT DO YOU WANT TO EAT, MARCILLE?
HUH?
I'LL DO MY BEST TO FULFILL ANY REQUEST.
LAIOS... SO YOU SAY, BUT...
YOU STILL MEAN EATING MONSTERS, RIGHT?
SA (SHP)
HAAH...
ANY-THING'S FINE.
AS LONG AS IT'S EDIBLE.
WHAT SORT OF MON-STERS ARE AROUND HERE?
LET'S SEE...
GOSO (RUMMAGE)
PERA (FLIP)

NOT IF WE WANT TO KEEP GOING!

Big Bat

Enormous vampire

ts prey with its c

dropping it, blood

Giant Rat

nout like a pig's

n be violent and

ressive when an

NO! NOTHING UNSANITARY!

BIG BATS.

GIANT RATS.

DEMI-HUMANS ARE OUT!!

Earth spirits

t live

rk behind tr

hrough the gaps bet

leaves and branches

Especially good with bows

swiftly, from the shadow

FOREST GOBLINS.

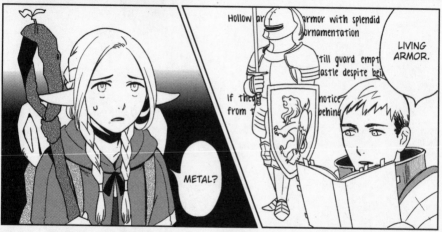

Hollow ar

armor with splendid ornamentation

till guard empt

astle despite bei

If the

notice

from

behin

METAL?

LIVING ARMOR.

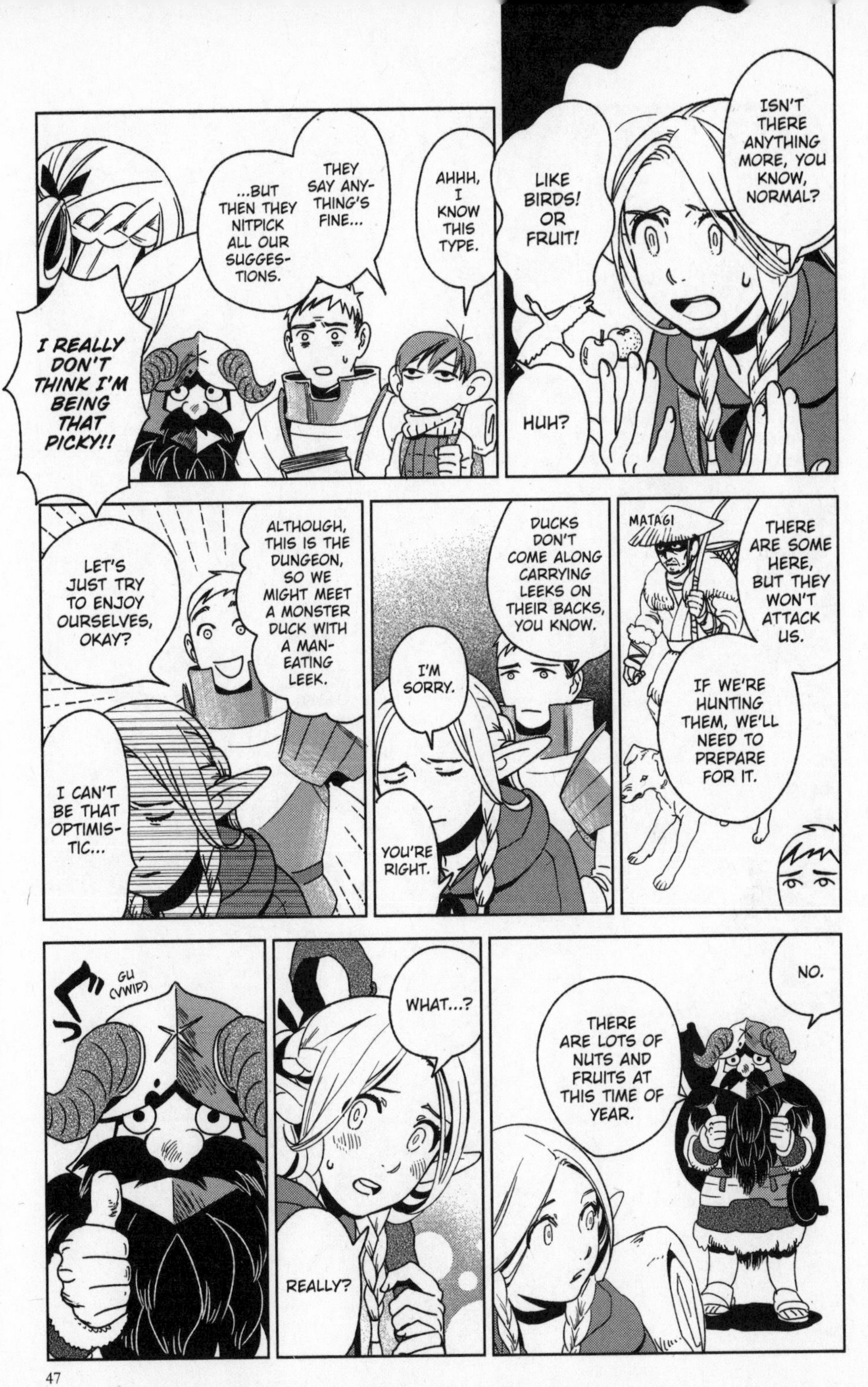
ISN'T THERE ANYTHING MORE, YOU KNOW, NORMAL?
LIKE BIRDS! OR FRUIT!
HUH?
AHHH, I KNOW THIS TYPE.
THEY SAY ANYTHING'S FINE...
...BUT THEN THEY NITPICK ALL OUR SUGGESTIONS.
I REALLY DON'T THINK I'M BEING THAT PICKY!!
MATAGI
THERE ARE SOME HERE, BUT THEY WON'T ATTACK US.
IF WE'RE HUNTING THEM, WE'LL NEED TO PREPARE FOR IT.
DUCKS DON'T COME ALONG CARRYING LEEKS ON THEIR BACKS, YOU KNOW.
I'M SORRY.
YOU'RE RIGHT.
ALTHOUGH, THIS IS THE DUNGEON, SO WE MIGHT MEET A MONSTER DUCK WITH A MAN-EATING LEEK.
LET'S JUST TRY TO ENJOY OURSELVES, OKAY?
I CAN'T BE THAT OPTIMISTIC...
NO.
THERE ARE LOTS OF NUTS AND FRUITS AT THIS TIME OF YEAR.
WHAT...?
REALLY?
GU (VWIP)

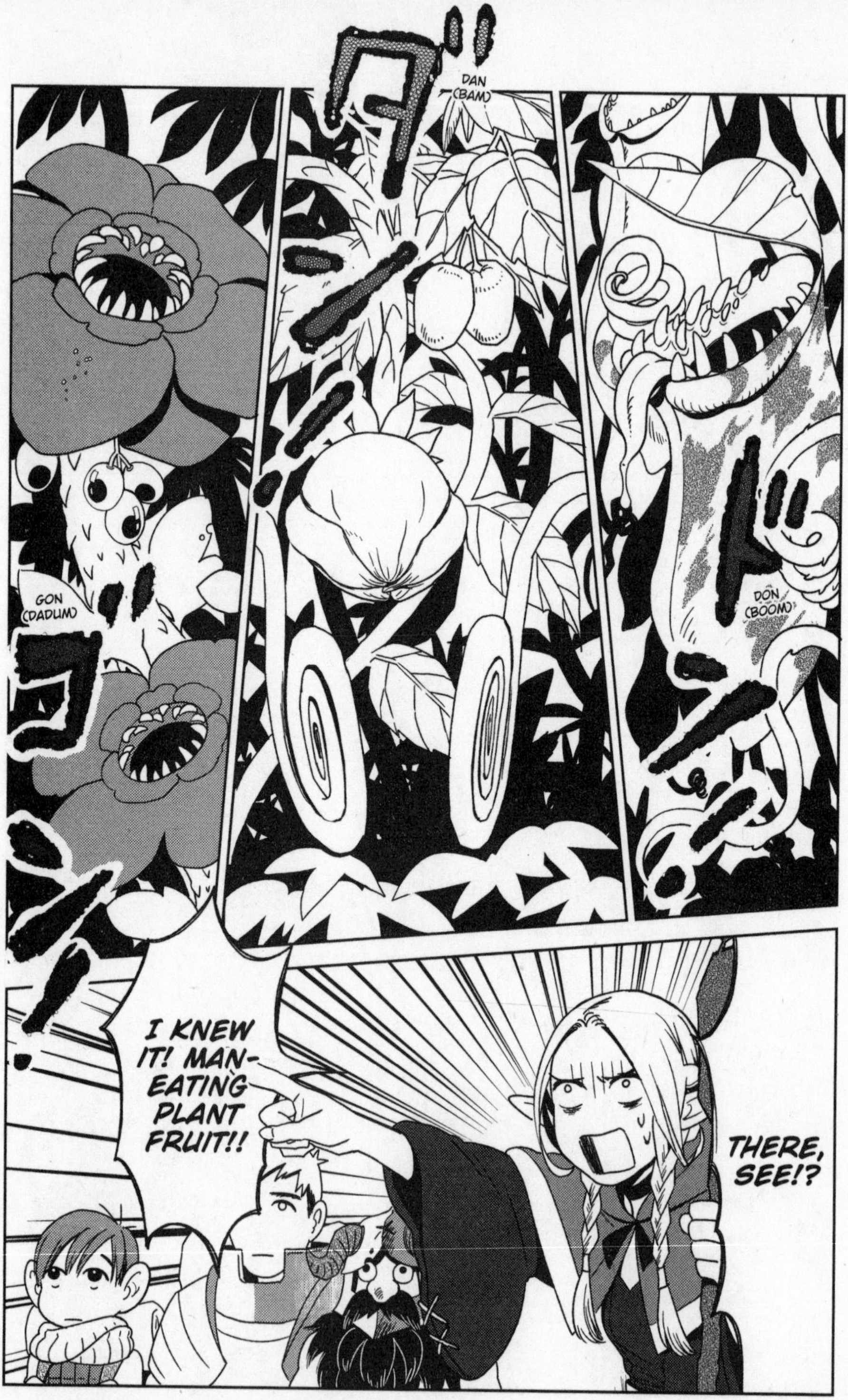
DON (BOOM)
DAN (BAM)
GON (DADUM)
THERE, SEE!?
I KNEW IT! MAN-EATING PLANT FRUIT!!

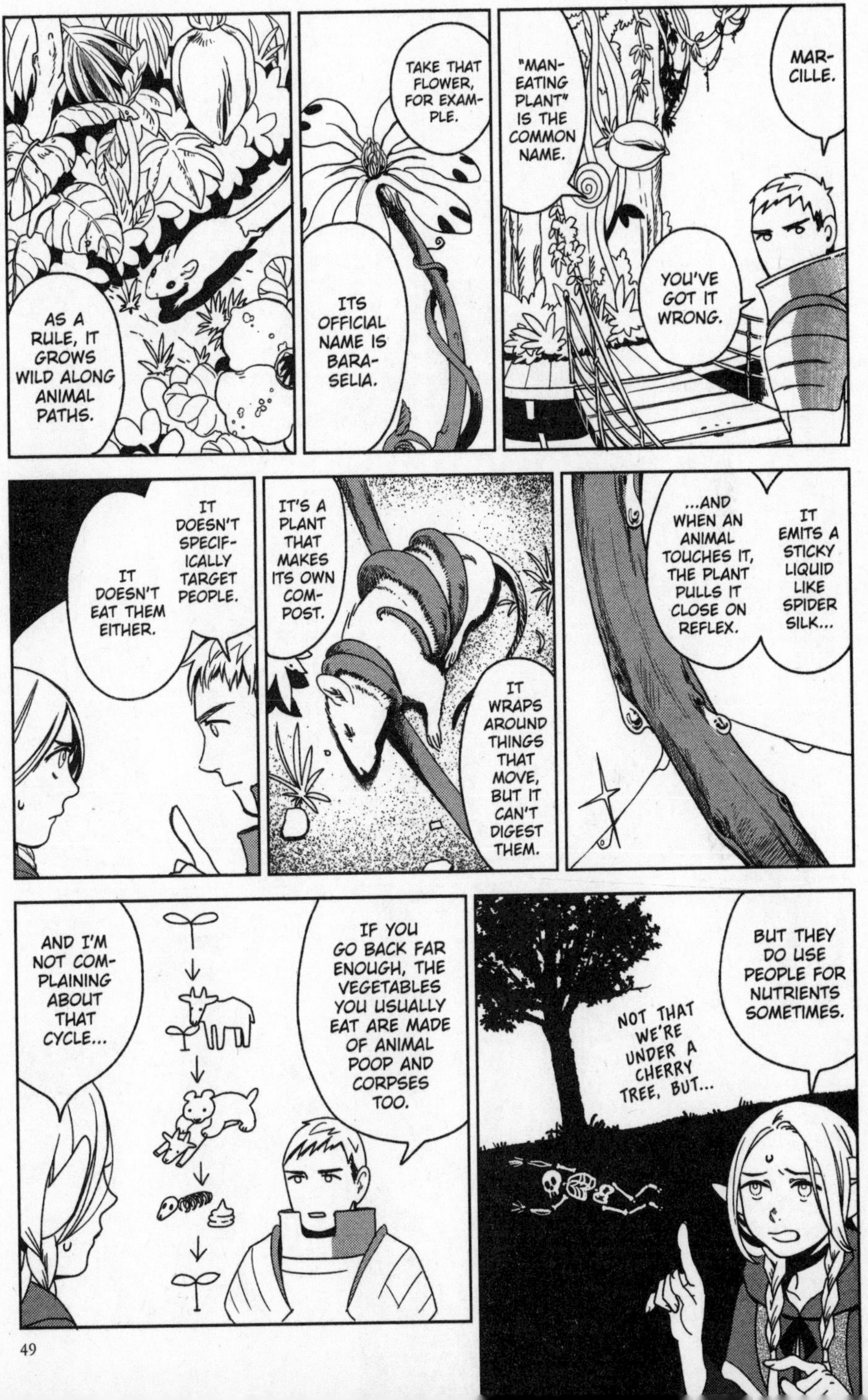
MARCILLE.
"MAN-EATING PLANT" IS THE COMMON NAME.
YOU'VE GOT IT WRONG.
TAKE THAT FLOWER, FOR EXAMPLE.
ITS OFFICIAL NAME IS BARASELIA.
AS A RULE, IT GROWS WILD ALONG ANIMAL PATHS.
IT EMITS A STICKY LIQUID LIKE SPIDER SILK...
...AND WHEN AN ANIMAL TOUCHES IT, THE PLANT PULLS IT CLOSE ON REFLEX.
IT'S A PLANT THAT MAKES ITS OWN COMPOST.
IT WRAPS AROUND THINGS THAT MOVE, BUT IT CAN'T DIGEST THEM.
IT DOESN'T SPECIFICALLY TARGET PEOPLE.
IT DOESN'T EAT THEM EITHER.
BUT THEY DO USE PEOPLE FOR NUTRIENTS SOMETIMES.
NOT THAT WE'RE UNDER A CHERRY TREE, BUT...
IF YOU GO BACK FAR ENOUGH, THE VEGETABLES YOU USUALLY EAT ARE MADE OF ANIMAL POOP AND CORPSES TOO.
AND I'M NOT COMPLAINING ABOUT THAT CYCLE...

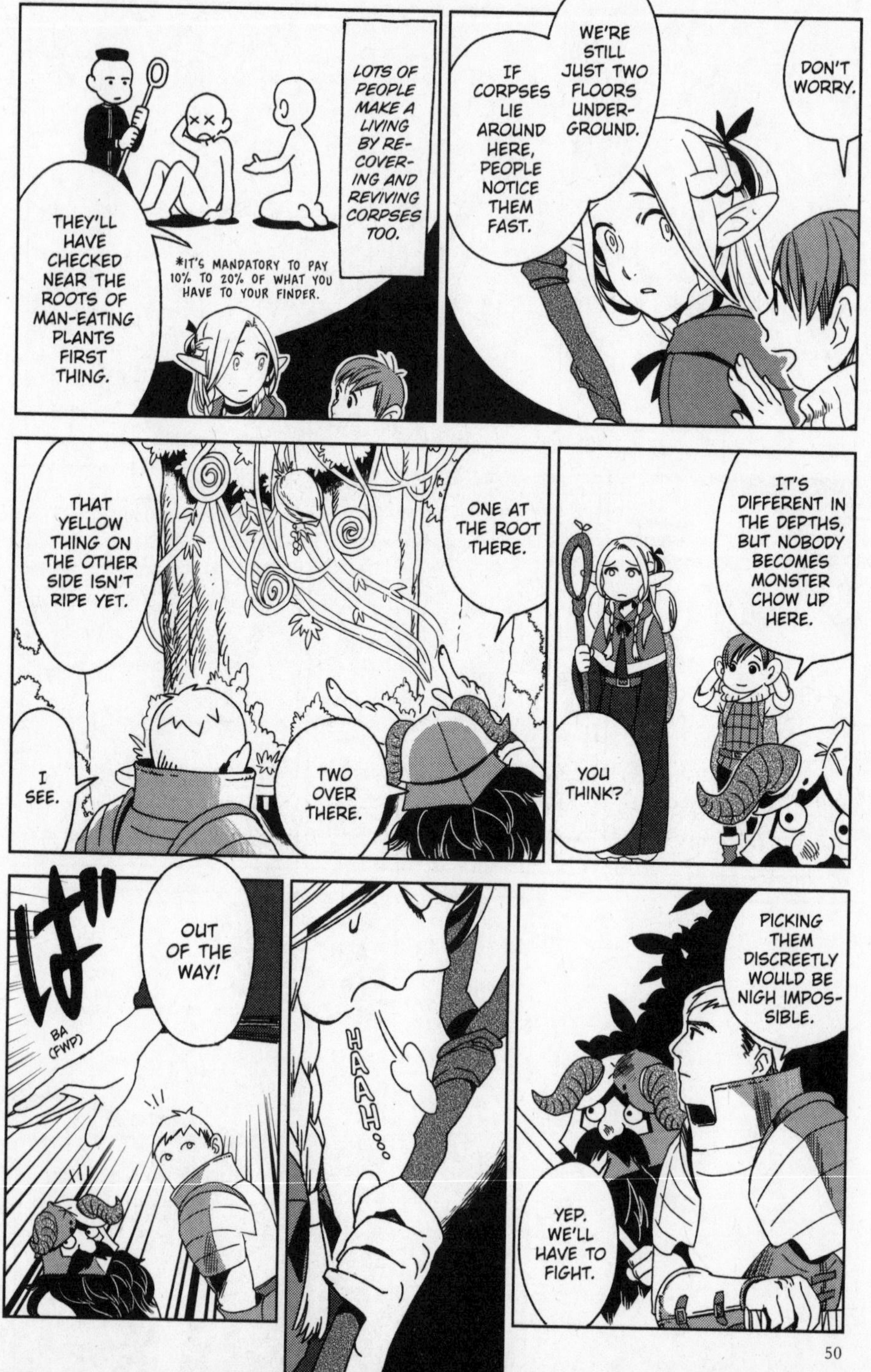
DON'T WORRY.
WE'RE STILL JUST TWO FLOORS UNDER-GROUND.
IF CORPSES LIE AROUND HERE, PEOPLE NOTICE THEM FAST.
LOTS OF PEOPLE MAKE A LIVING BY RE-COVER-ING AND REVIVING CORPSES TOO.
THEY'LL HAVE CHECKED NEAR THE ROOTS OF MAN-EATING PLANTS FIRST THING.
*IT'S MANDATORY TO PAY 10% TO 20% OF WHAT YOU HAVE TO YOUR FINDER.
IT'S DIFFERENT IN THE DEPTHS, BUT NOBODY BECOMES MONSTER CHOW UP HERE.
YOU THINK?
ONE AT THE ROOT THERE.
THAT YELLOW THING ON THE OTHER SIDE ISN'T RIPE YET.
TWO OVER THERE.
I SEE.
PICKING THEM DISCREETLY WOULD BE NIGH IMPOS-SIBLE.
YEP. WE'LL HAVE TO FIGHT.
HAAAH...
OUT OF THE WAY!
ばっ
BA (FWP)

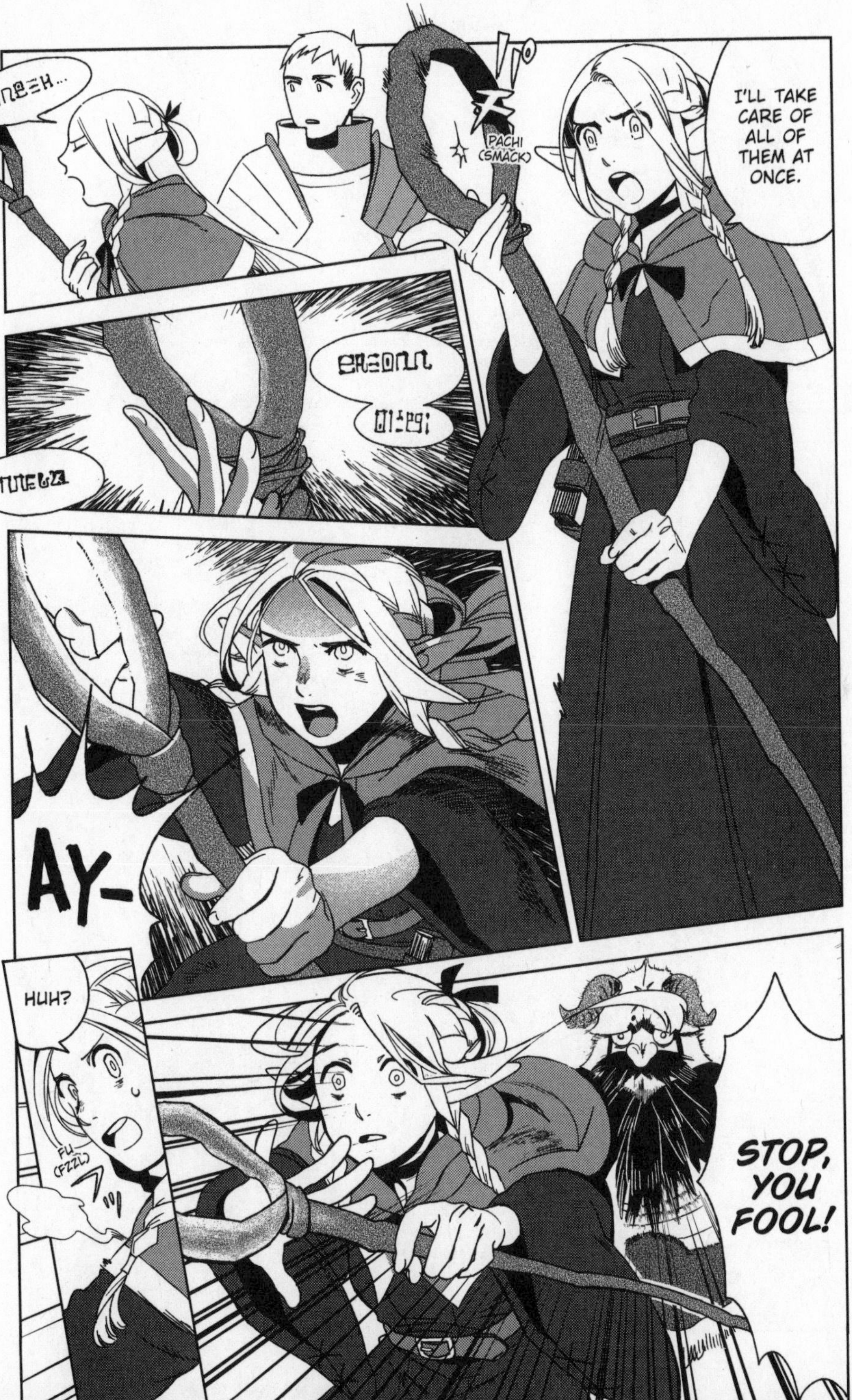
PACHI (SMACK)
I'LL TAKE CARE OF ALL OF THEM AT ONCE.
AY-
STOP, YOU FOOL!
HUH?
FU (FZZL)

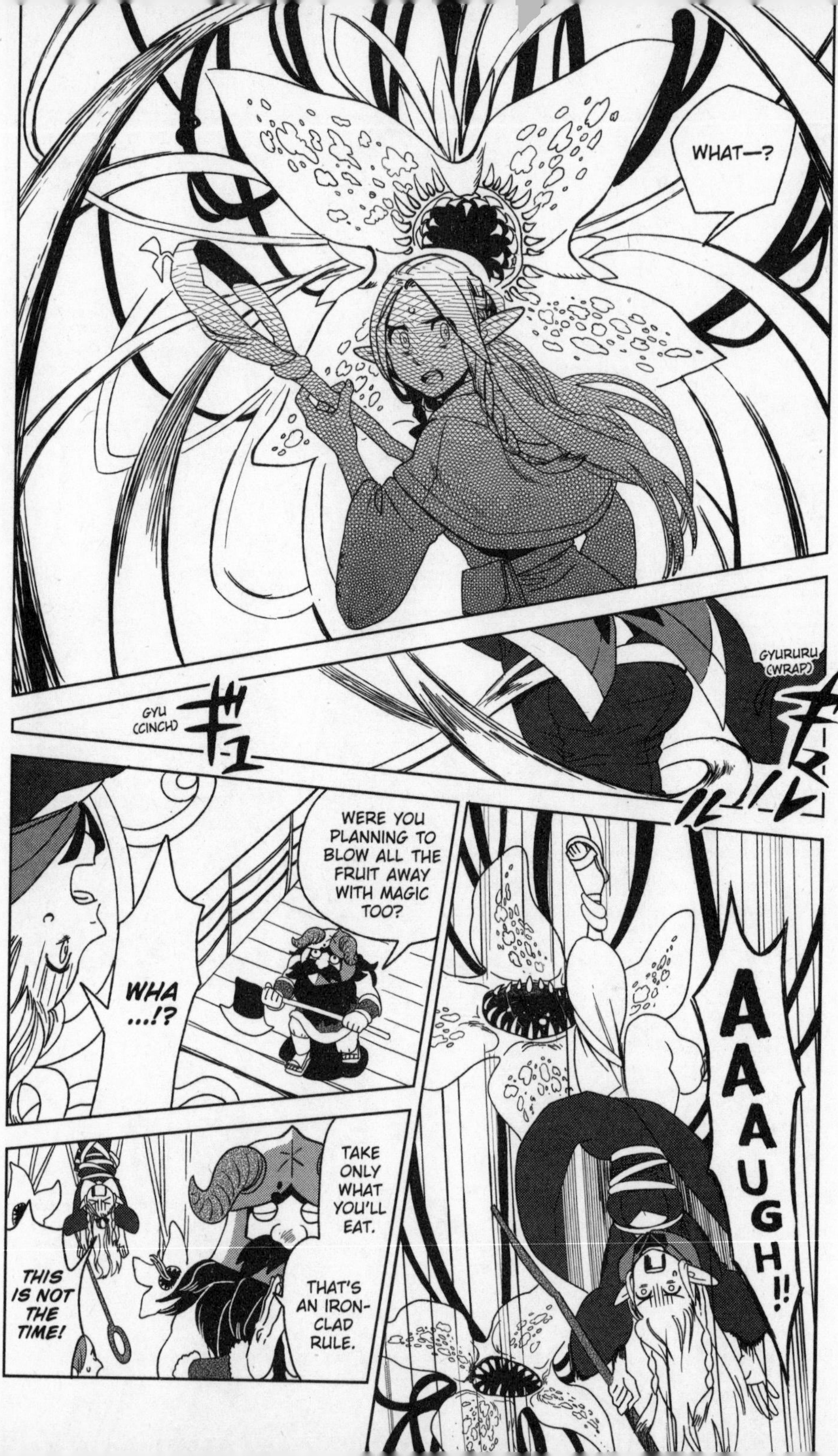
WHAT—?
GYURURU (WRAP)
ギュルル
GYU (CINCH)
ギュ
AAAUGH!!
WERE YOU PLANNING TO BLOW ALL THE FRUIT AWAY WITH MAGIC TOO?
WHA ...!?
TAKE ONLY WHAT YOU'LL EAT.
THAT'S AN IRON-CLAD RULE.
THIS IS NOT THE TIME!

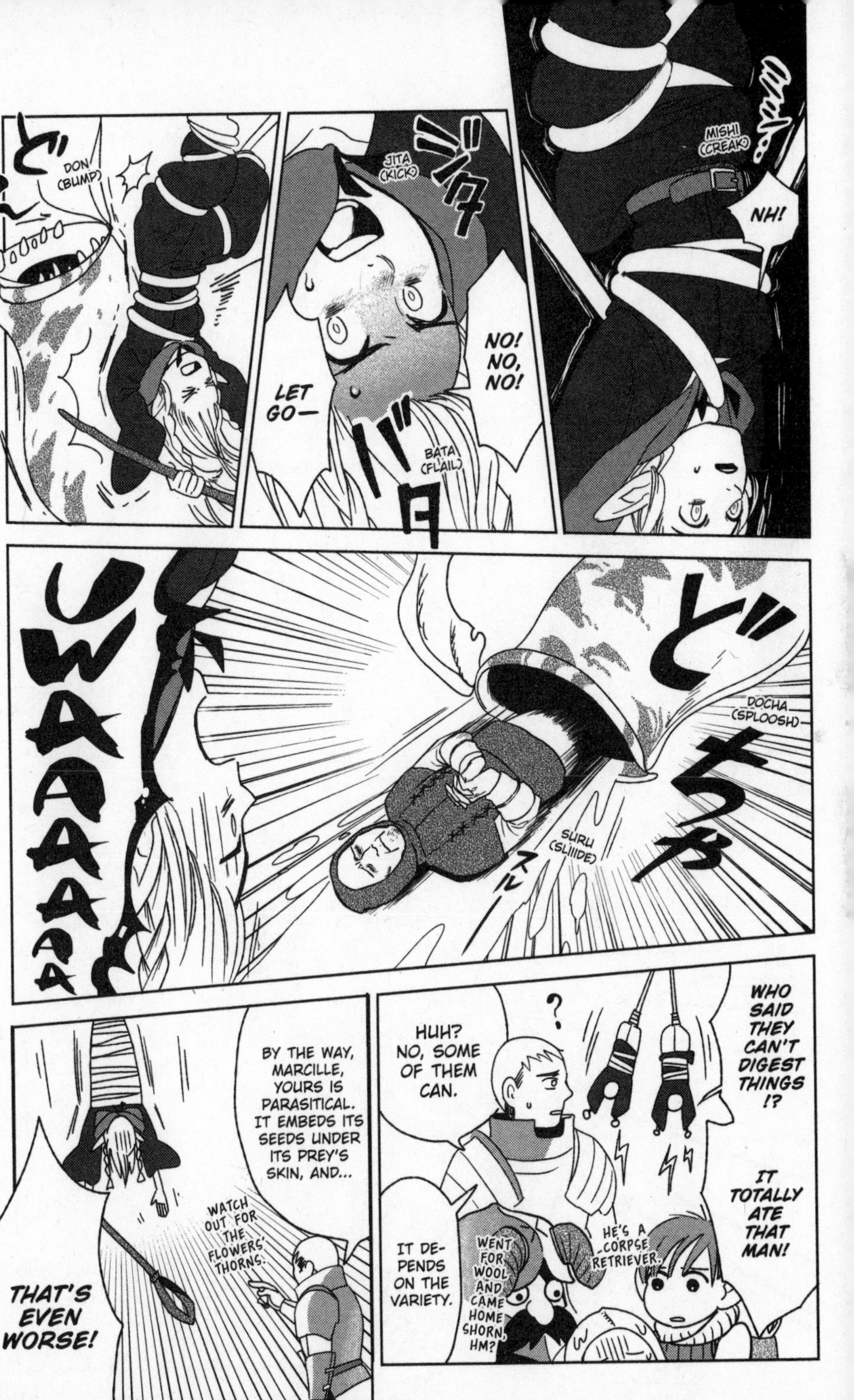
MISHI (CREAK)
NH!
ジタ
JITA (KICK)
NO! NO, NO!
LET GO—
バタ
BATA (FLAIL)
どん
DON (BUMP)
どちゃ
DOCHA (SPLOOSH)
スル
SURU (SLIIIDE)
UWAAAAAAA
WHO SAID THEY CAN'T DIGEST THINGS!?
?
HUH? NO, SOME OF THEM CAN.
IT TOTALLY ATE THAT MAN!
HE'S A CORPSE RETRIEVER.
WENT FOR WOOL AND CAME HOME SHORN, HM?
IT DEPENDS ON THE VARIETY.
BY THE WAY, MARCILLE, YOURS IS PARASITICAL. IT EMBEDS ITS SEEDS UNDER ITS PREY'S SKIN, AND...
WATCH OUT FOR THE FLOWERS' THORNS.
THAT'S EVEN WORSE!

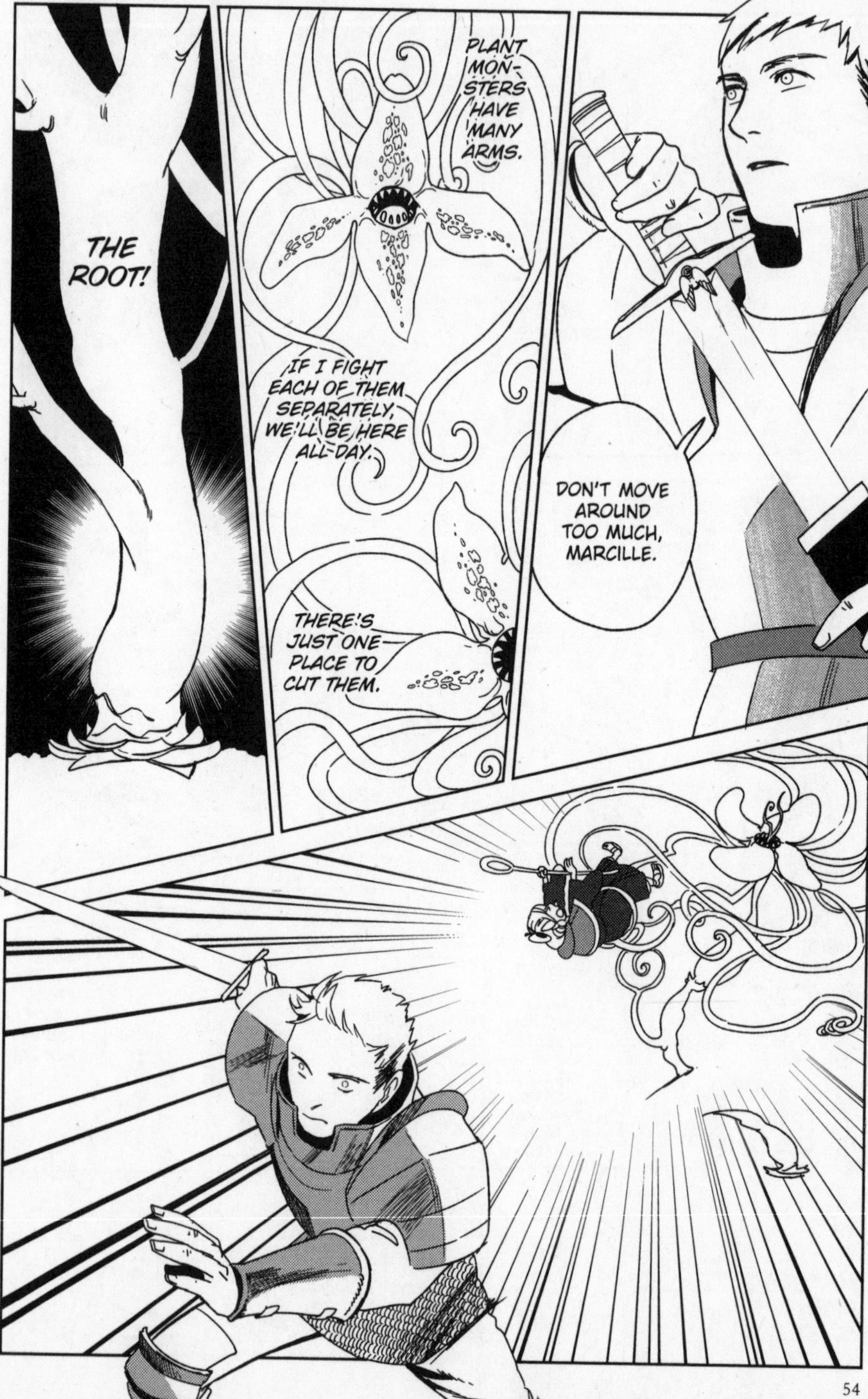
DON'T MOVE AROUND TOO MUCH, MARCILLE.
PLANT MONSTERS HAVE MANY ARMS.
IF I FIGHT EACH OF THEM SEPARATELY, WE'LL BE HERE ALL DAY.
THERE'S JUST ONE PLACE TO CUT THEM.
THE ROOT!

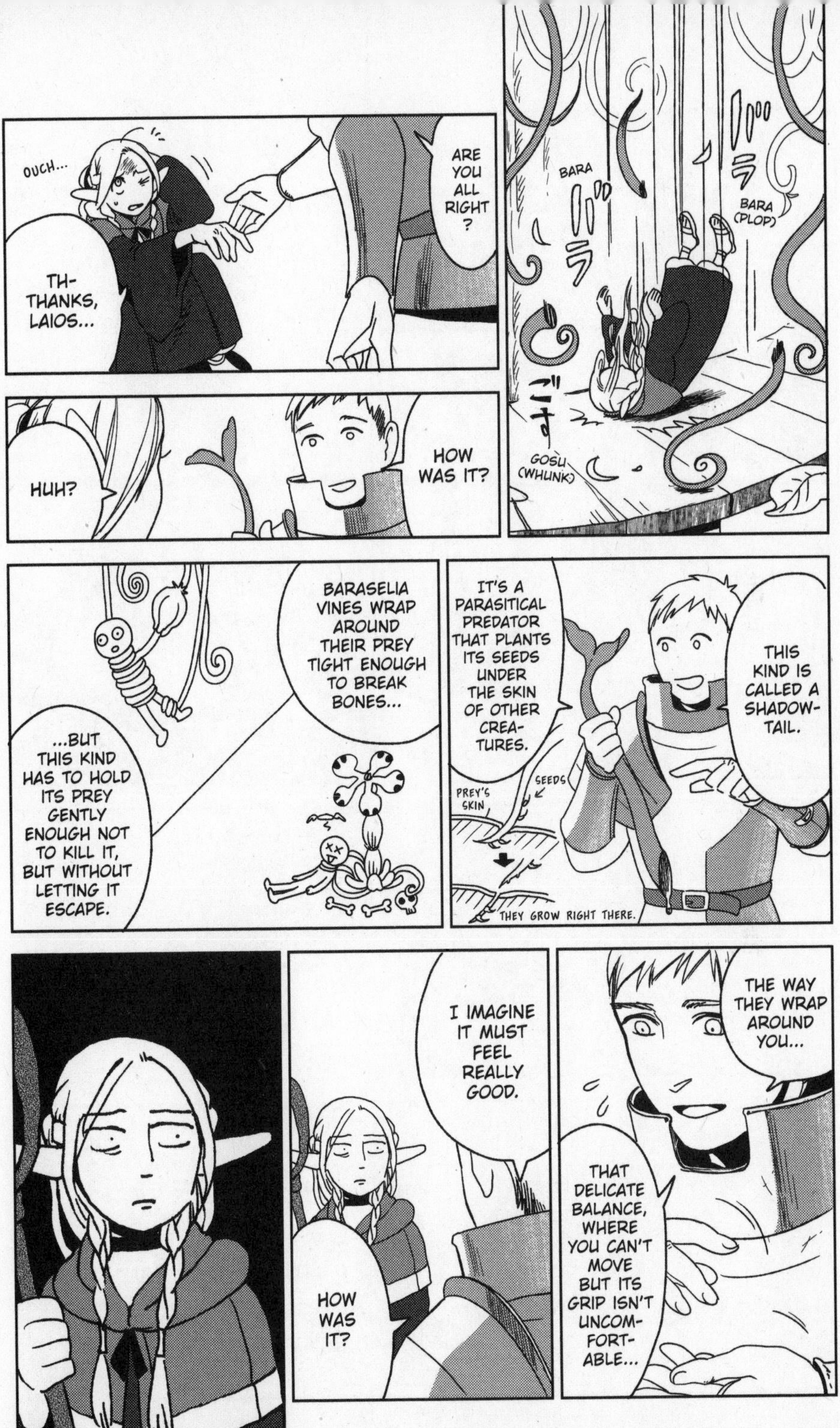
BARA (PLOP)
BARA
ごす
GOSU (WHUNK)
ARE YOU ALL RIGHT?
OUCH...
TH-THANKS, LAIOS...
HOW WAS IT?
HUH?
THIS KIND IS CALLED A SHADOW-TAIL.
IT'S A PARASITICAL PREDATOR THAT PLANTS ITS SEEDS UNDER THE SKIN OF OTHER CREATURES.
SEEDS
PREY'S SKIN
THEY GROW RIGHT THERE.
BARASELIA VINES WRAP AROUND THEIR PREY TIGHT ENOUGH TO BREAK BONES...
...BUT THIS KIND HAS TO HOLD ITS PREY GENTLY ENOUGH NOT TO KILL IT, BUT WITHOUT LETTING IT ESCAPE.
THE WAY THEY WRAP AROUND YOU...
THAT DELICATE BALANCE, WHERE YOU CAN'T MOVE BUT ITS GRIP ISN'T UNCOMFORTABLE...
I IMAGINE IT MUST FEEL REALLY GOOD.
HOW WAS IT?

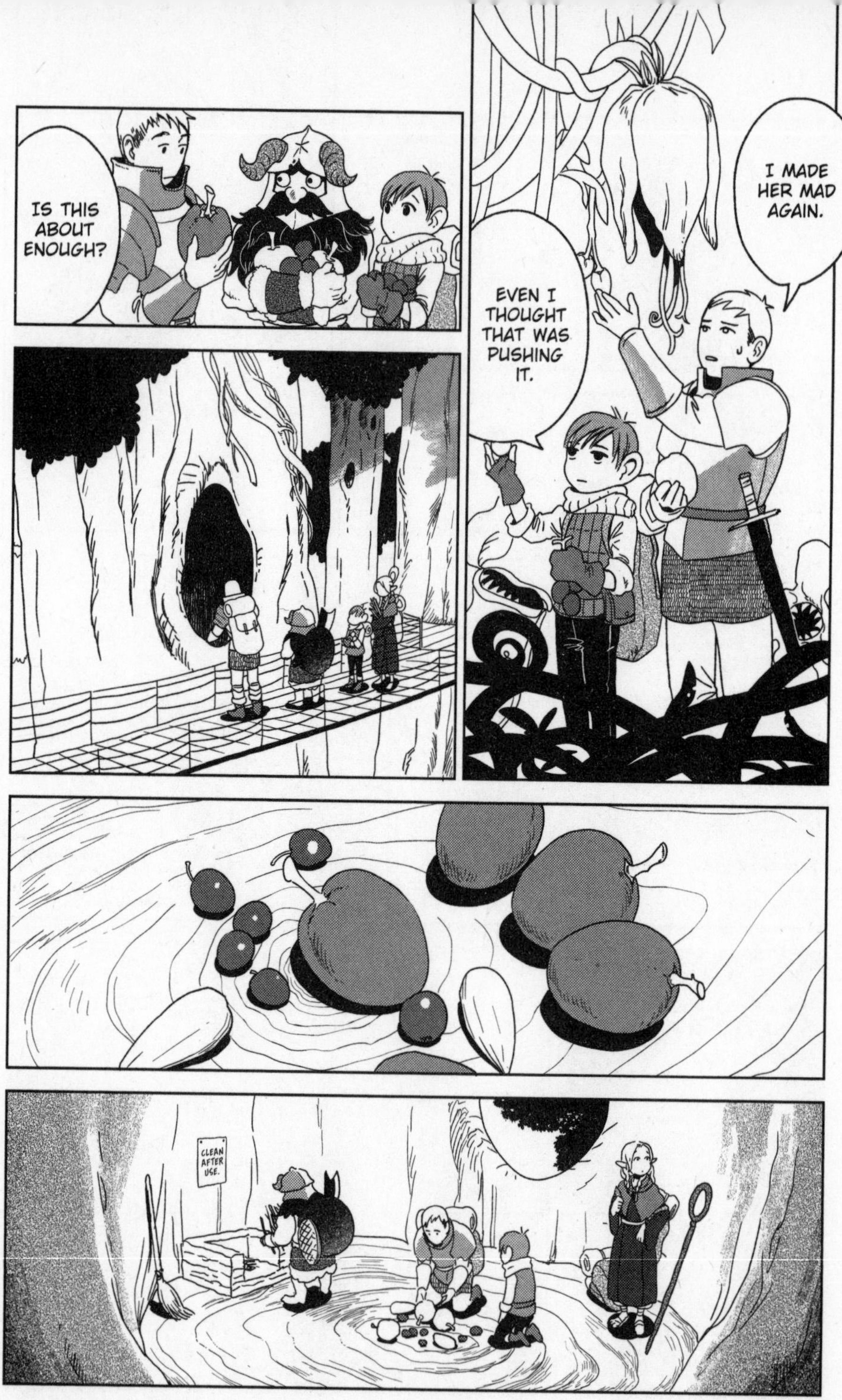
I MADE HER MAD AGAIN.
EVEN I THOUGHT THAT WAS PUSHING IT.
IS THIS ABOUT ENOUGH?
CLEAN AFTER USE.

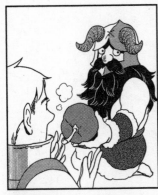

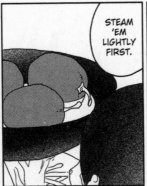

KFF! KFF!
STEAM 'EM LIGHTLY FIRST.
CUT AROUND THE STEM...
KURU (TURN)
...TWIST IT A BIT...
...THEN PULL.
ZURURU (SLIDE)
OOOH!
THE SEEDS COME RIGHT OUT THAT WAY.
HEY!
GOSO (RSTL)
GIVE ME WHAT YOU JUST PUT IN YOUR ARMOR!
I'LL TAKE GOOD CARE OF IT!
I WANT TO SEE IF THESE CAN GROW ABOVE-GROUND.
GOOO (FWOOM)
AAAUGH!

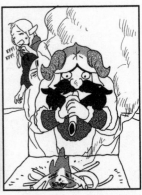

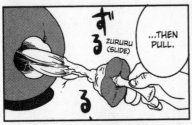

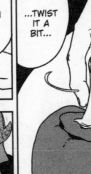

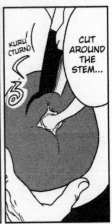

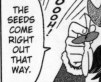

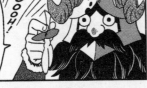

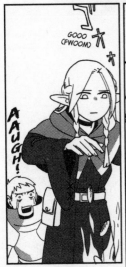

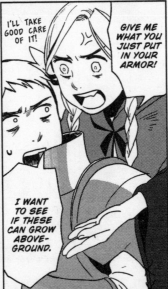

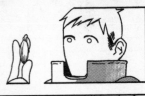

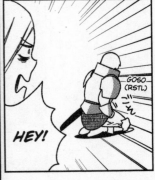

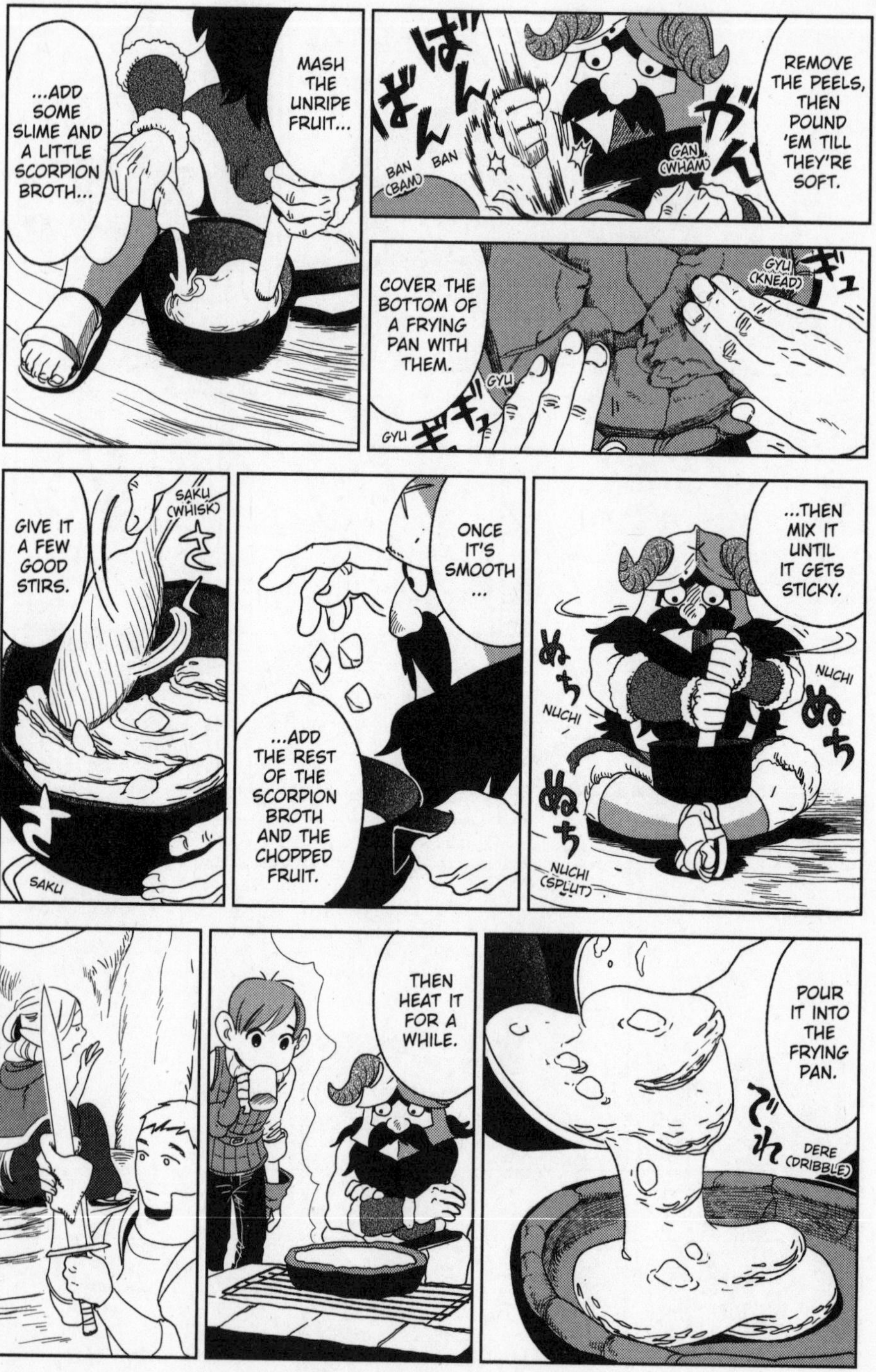
REMOVE THE PEELS, THEN POUND 'EM TILL THEY'RE SOFT.
がん
GAN (WHAM)
ばん ばん
BAN BAN (BAM)
ギュ
GYU (KNEAD)
COVER THE BOTTOM OF A FRYING PAN WITH THEM.
GYU
ギュ
GYU
MASH THE UNRIPE FRUIT...
...ADD SOME SLIME AND A LITTLE SCORPION BROTH...
...THEN MIX IT UNTIL IT GETS STICKY.
NUCHI
ぬち
ぬち
NUCHI
ぬち
NUCHI (SPLUT)
ONCE IT'S SMOOTH ...
...ADD THE REST OF THE SCORPION BROTH AND THE CHOPPED FRUIT.
SAKU (WHISK)
さ
GIVE IT A FEW GOOD STIRS.
さ
SAKU
POUR IT INTO THE FRYING PAN.
でれ
DERE (DRIBBLE)
THEN HEAT IT FOR A WHILE.

...PUT THE REST OF THE FRUIT ON TOP.

ONCE THE SURFACE STARTS TO BUBBLE...

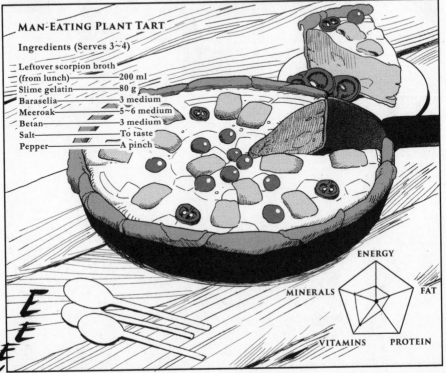

MAN-EATING PLANT TART

Ingredients (Serves 3~4)

Leftover scorpion broth (from lunch)	200 ml
Slime gelatin	80 g
Baraselia	3 medium
Meeroak	5~6 medium
Betan	3 medium
Salt	To taste
Pepper	A pinch

ENERGY

MINERALS   FAT

VITAMINS   PROTEIN

EEEK!

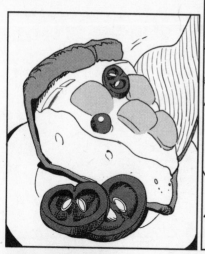

IT... IT'S A TART.
EVEN THOUGH YOU DIDN'T USE EGGS OR FLOUR...
IT ONLY LOOKS LIKE ONE.
ZAKU (SLICE)
THE PEELS WERE JUST TO KEEP IT FROM SCORCH-ING.
IT LOOKS RIGHT.
YOU CAN LEAVE 'EM. DON'T EAT 'EM.
IT'S SALTY.
IT'S NOT SWEET.
THAT'S NOT WHAT I EX-PECTED.
YEAH. IT'S GOOD.
TRY IT, MARCILLE.
I THINK YOU'LL LIKE THE FLAVOR.

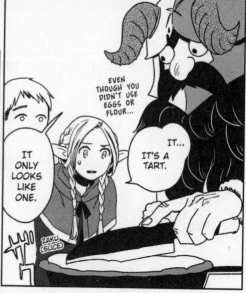

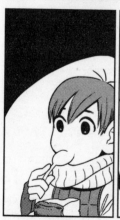

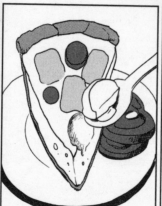

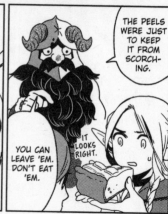

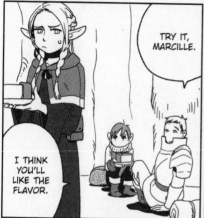

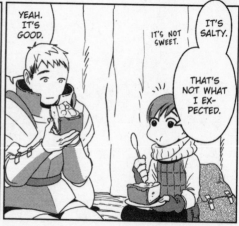

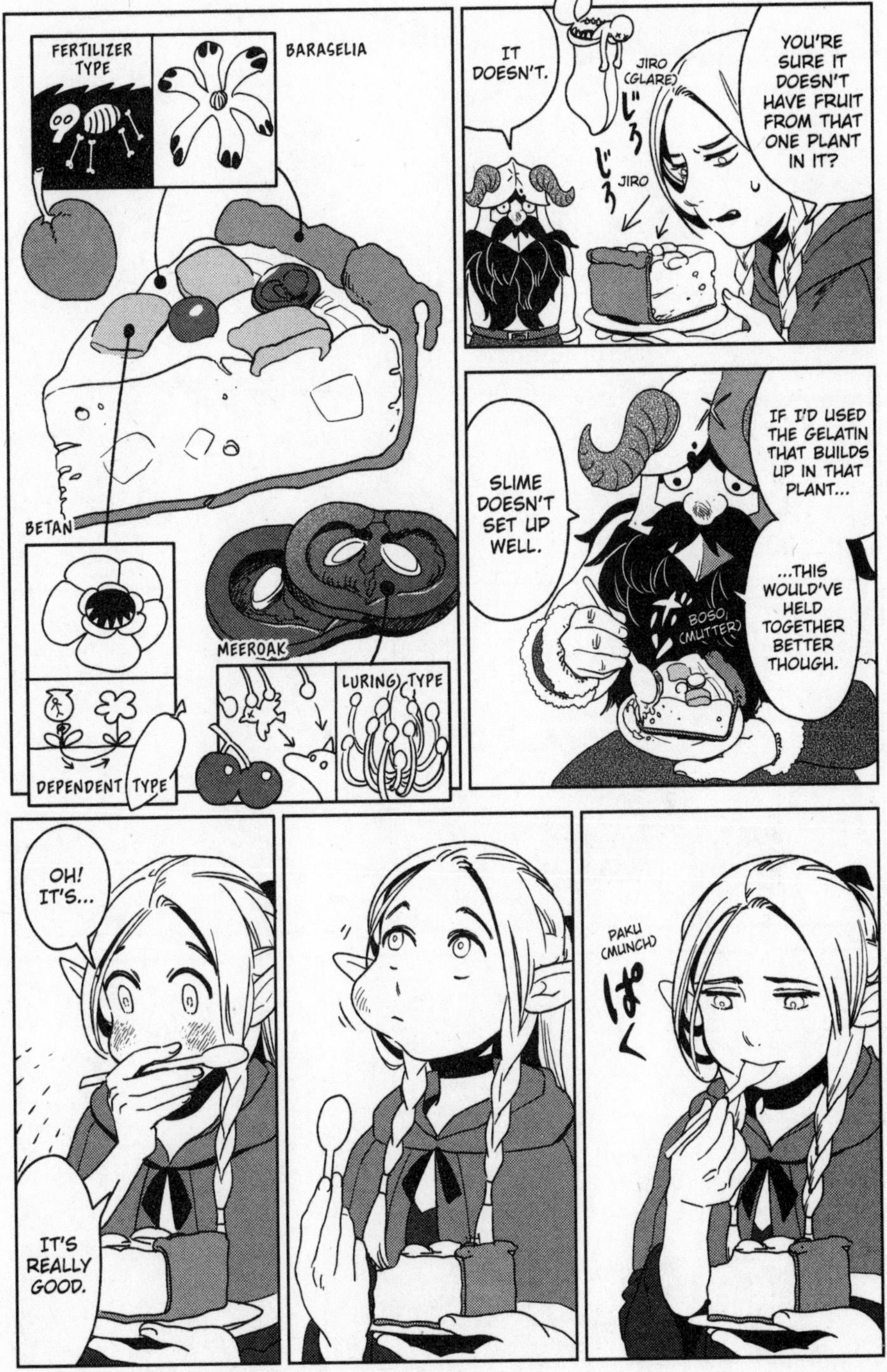
YOU'RE SURE IT DOESN'T HAVE FRUIT FROM THAT ONE PLANT IN IT?
JIRO (GLARE)
じろ
じろ
JIRO
IT DOESN'T.
IF I'D USED THE GELATIN THAT BUILDS UP IN THAT PLANT...
...THIS WOULD'VE HELD TOGETHER BETTER THOUGH.
BOSO (MUTTER)
SLIME DOESN'T SET UP WELL.
BARASELIA
FERTILIZER TYPE
BETAN
MEEROAK
LURING TYPE
DEPENDENT TYPE
PAKU (MUNCH)
ぱく
OH! IT'S...
IT'S REALLY GOOD.

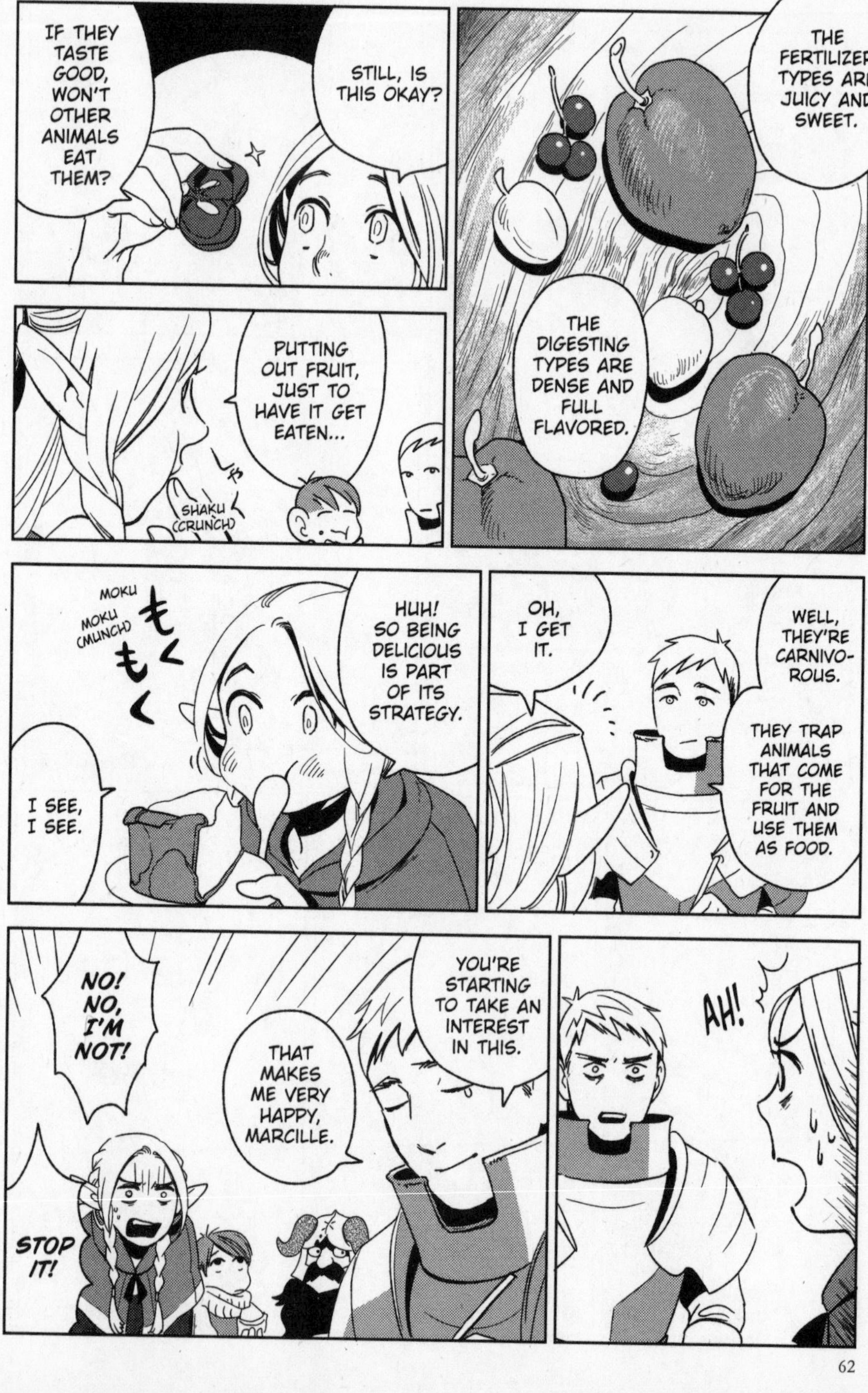
THE FERTILIZER TYPES ARE JUICY AND SWEET.
THE DIGESTING TYPES ARE DENSE AND FULL FLAVORED.
STILL, IS THIS OKAY?
IF THEY TASTE GOOD, WON'T OTHER ANIMALS EAT THEM?
PUTTING OUT FRUIT, JUST TO HAVE IT GET EATEN...
SHAKU (CRUNCH)
WELL, THEY'RE CARNIVO-ROUS.
THEY TRAP ANIMALS THAT COME FOR THE FRUIT AND USE THEM AS FOOD.
OH, I GET IT.
HUH! SO BEING DELICIOUS IS PART OF ITS STRATEGY.
MOKU MOKU (MUNCH)
I SEE, I SEE.
AH!
YOU'RE STARTING TO TAKE AN INTEREST IN THIS.
THAT MAKES ME VERY HAPPY, MARCILLE.
NO! NO, I'M NOT!
STOP IT!

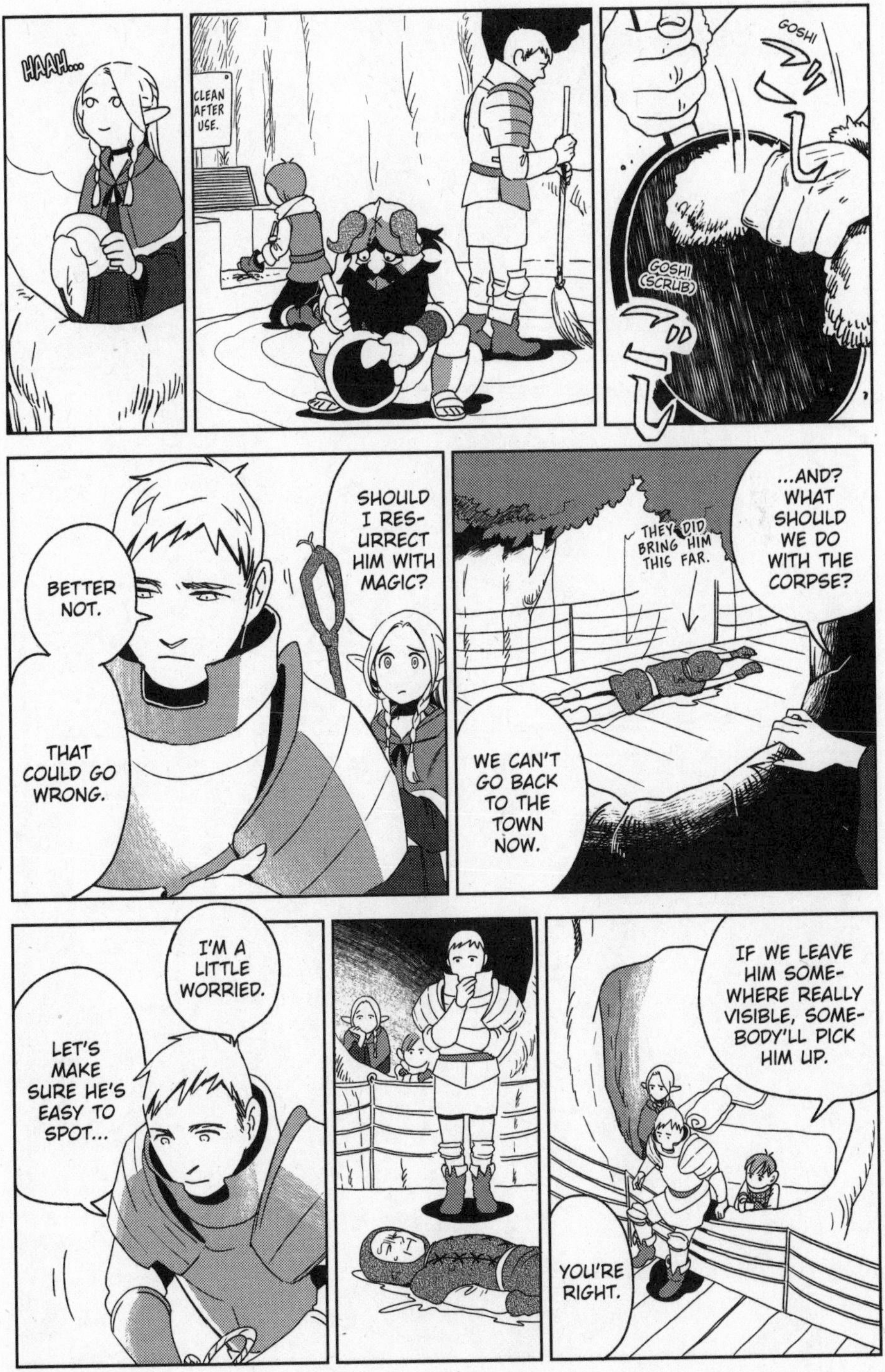
GOSHI
GOSHI (SCRUB)
CLEAN AFTER USE.
HAAAH...
...AND? WHAT SHOULD WE DO WITH THE CORPSE?
THEY DID BRING HIM THIS FAR.
WE CAN'T GO BACK TO THE TOWN NOW.
SHOULD I RES-URRECT HIM WITH MAGIC?
BETTER NOT.
THAT COULD GO WRONG.
IF WE LEAVE HIM SOME-WHERE REALLY VISIBLE, SOME-BODY'LL PICK HIM UP.
YOU'RE RIGHT.
I'M A LITTLE WORRIED.
LET'S MAKE SURE HE'S EASY TO SPOT...

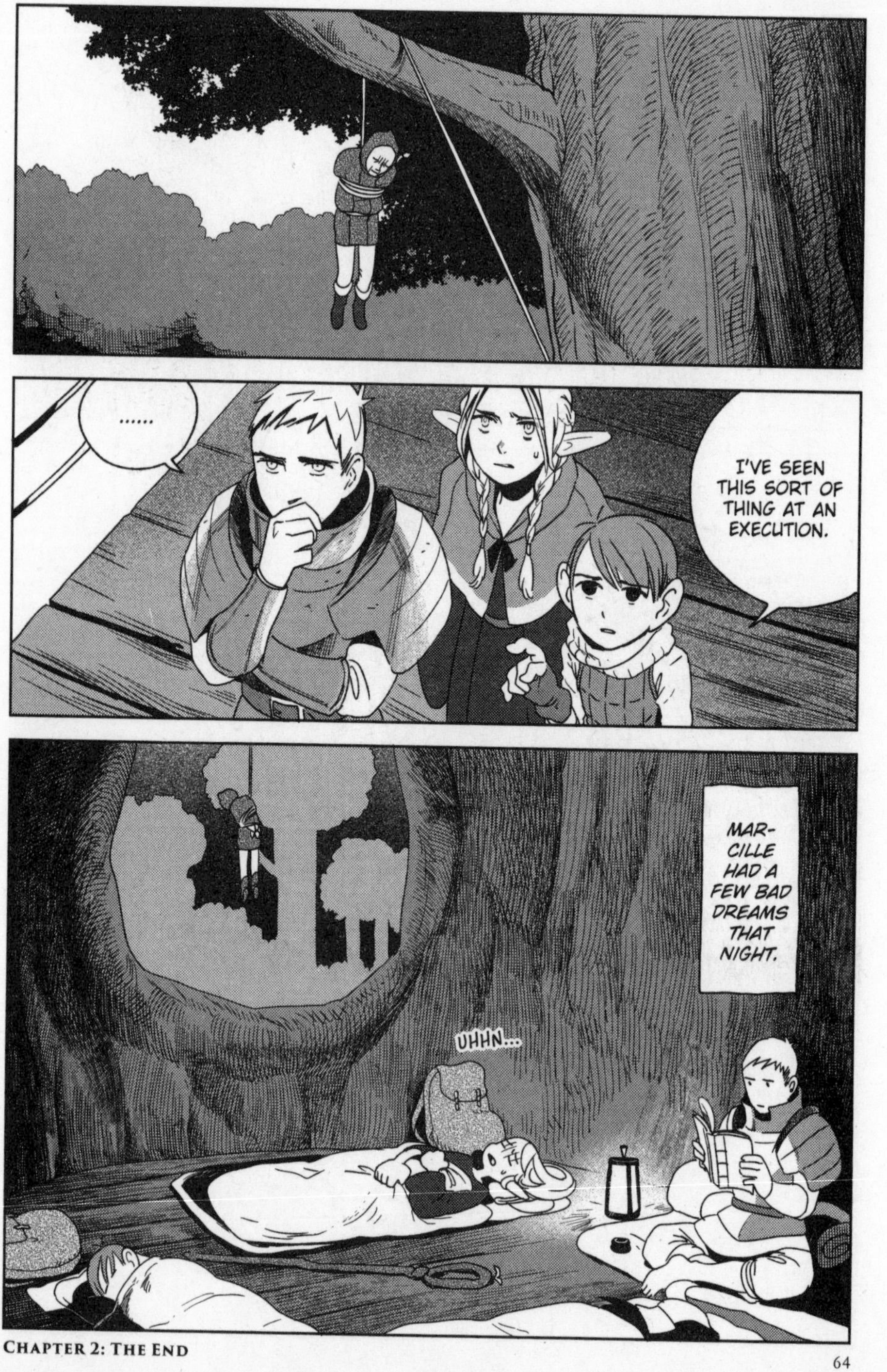
......
I'VE SEEN THIS SORT OF THING AT AN EXECUTION.
MAR-CILLE HAD A FEW BAD DREAMS THAT NIGHT.
UHHN...

Chapter 2: The End

3. Roast Basilisk

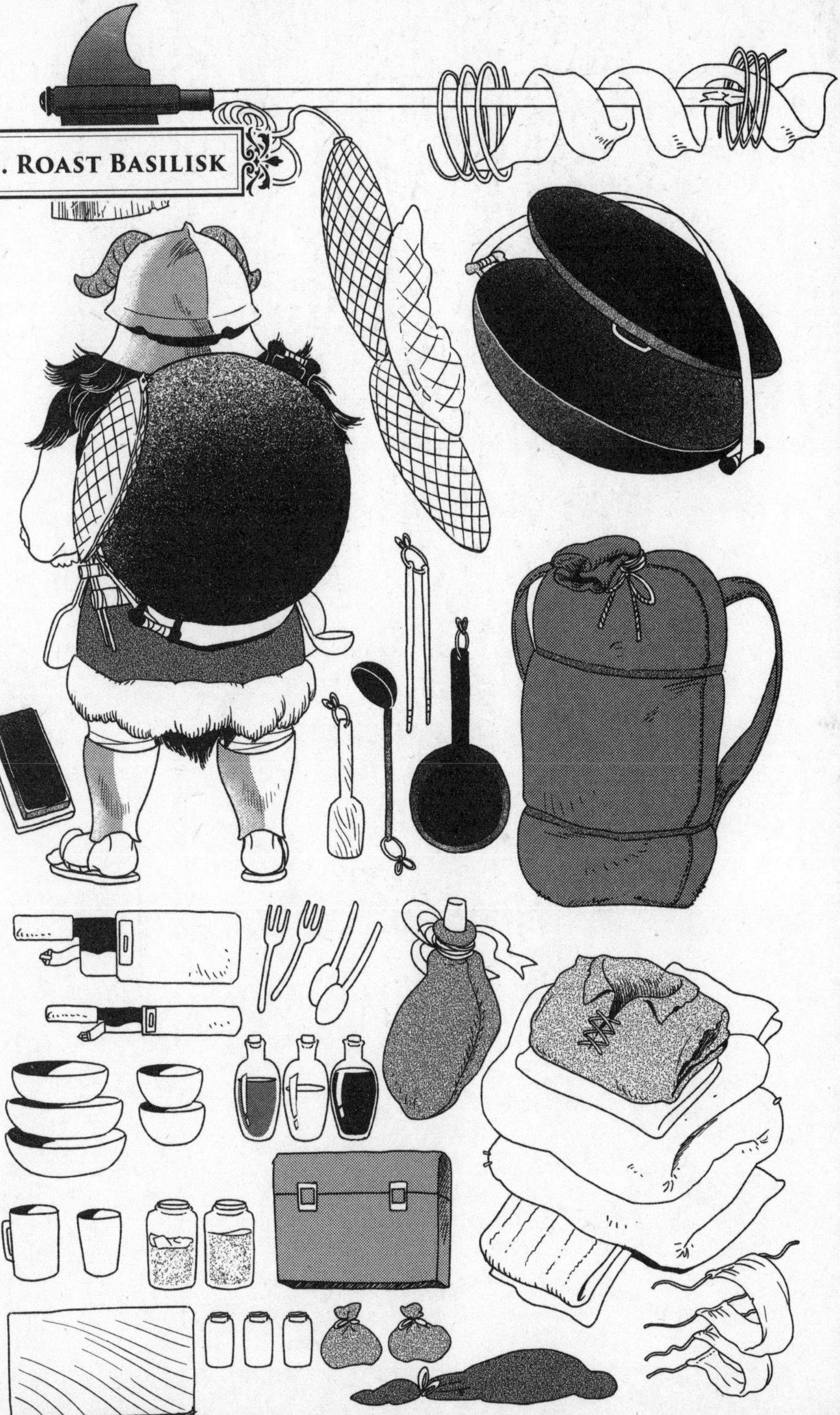

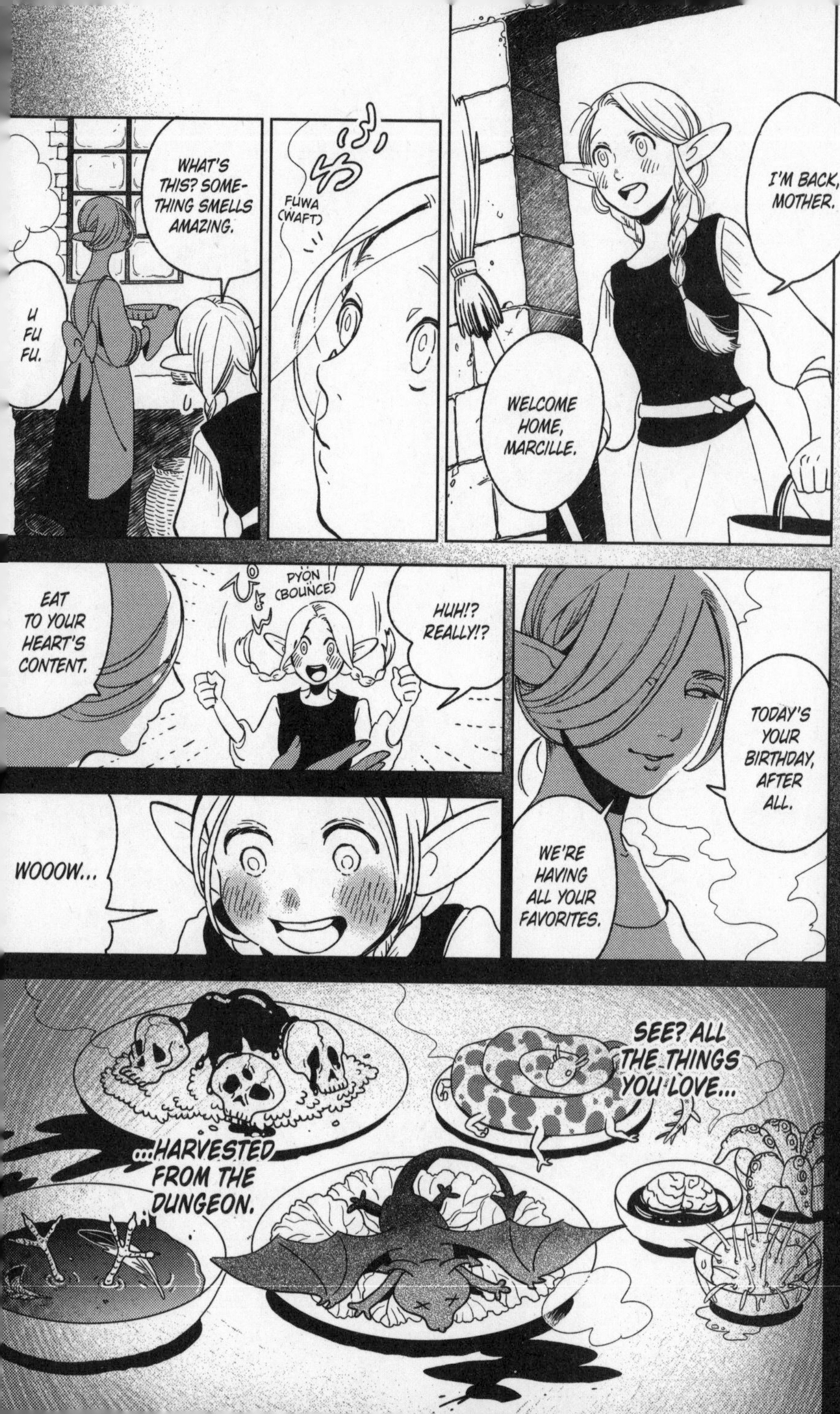
I'M BACK, MOTHER.
WELCOME HOME, MARCILLE.
FUWA (WAFT)
WHAT'S THIS? SOME-THING SMELLS AMAZING.
U FU FU.
TODAY'S YOUR BIRTHDAY, AFTER ALL.
WE'RE HAVING ALL YOUR FAVORITES.
HUH!? REALLY!?
PYON (BOUNCE)
EAT TO YOUR HEART'S CONTENT.
WOOOW...
SEE? ALL THE THINGS YOU LOVE...
...HARVESTED FROM THE DUNGEON.

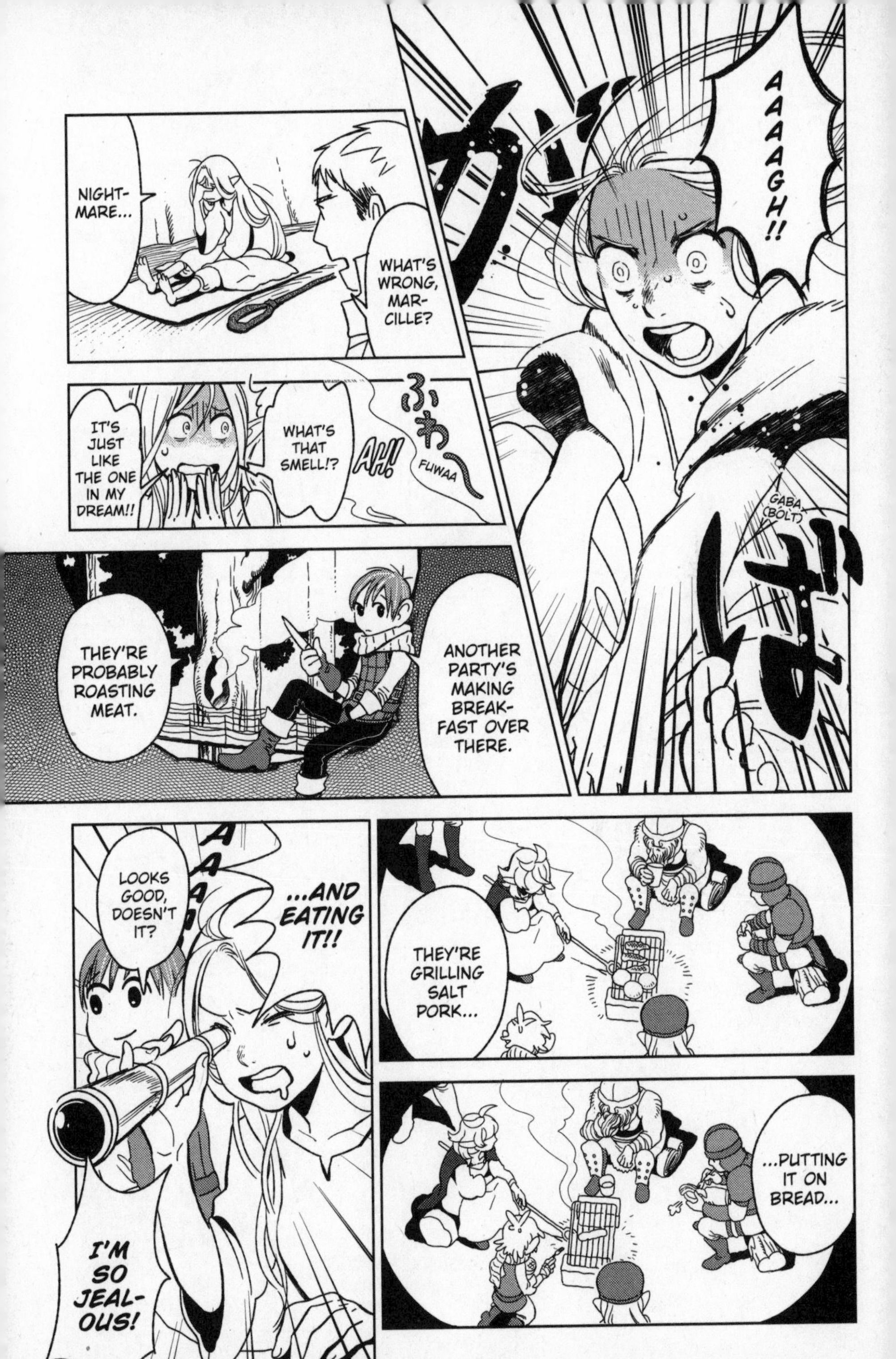
AAAAAGH!!
GABA (BOLT)
WHAT'S WRONG, MARCILLE?
NIGHT-MARE...
FUWAA
AH!
WHAT'S THAT SMELL!?
IT'S JUST LIKE THE ONE IN MY DREAM!!
ANOTHER PARTY'S MAKING BREAK-FAST OVER THERE.
THEY'RE PROBABLY ROASTING MEAT.
THEY'RE GRILLING SALT PORK...
...PUTTING IT ON BREAD...
...AND EATING IT!!
LOOKS GOOD, DOESN'T IT?
I'M SO JEAL-OUS!

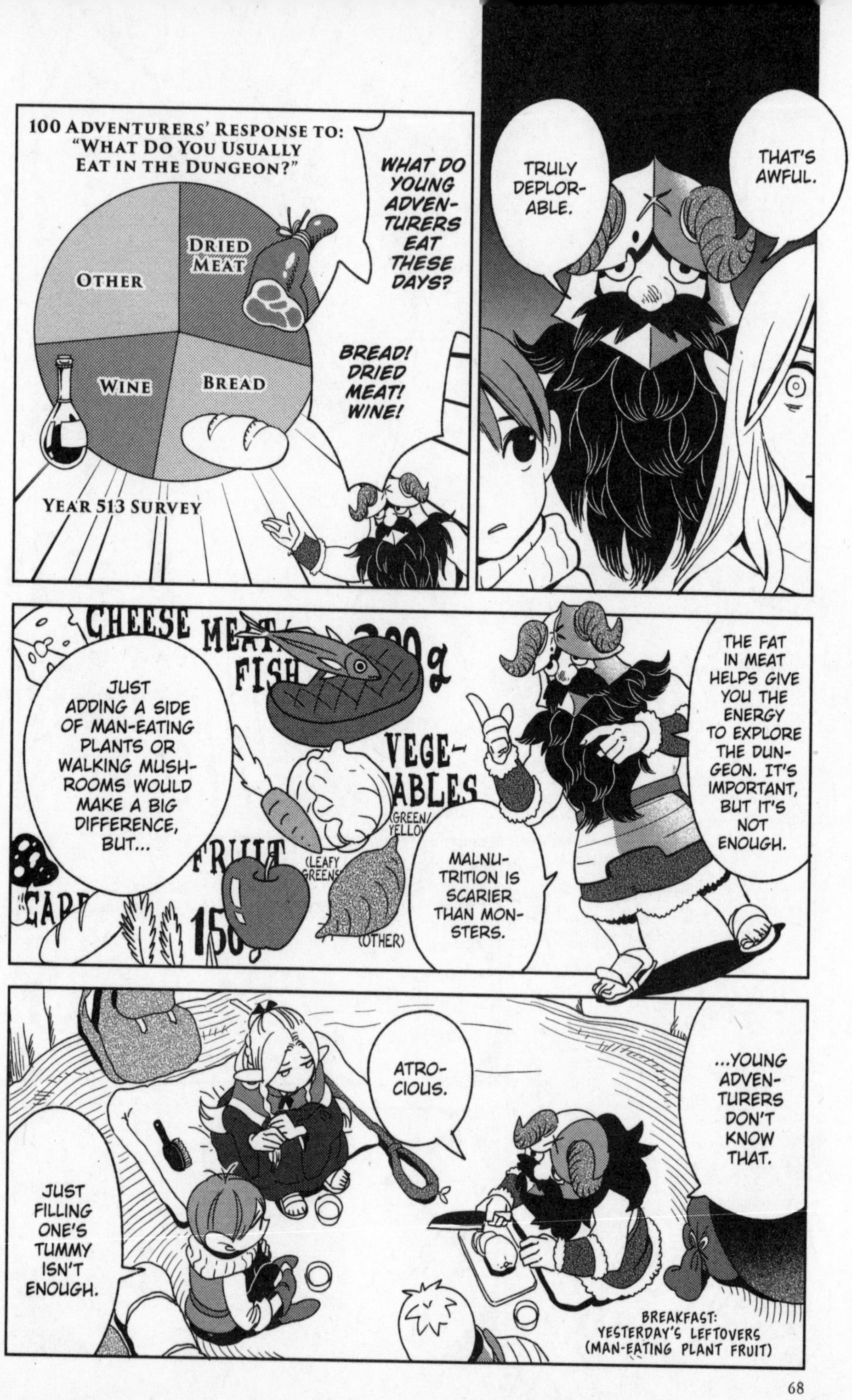
THAT'S AWFUL.
TRULY DEPLORABLE.
WHAT DO YOUNG ADVENTURERS EAT THESE DAYS?
BREAD! DRIED MEAT! WINE!
100 Adventurers' Response to: "What Do You Usually Eat in the Dungeon?"
Dried Meat
Other
Wine
Bread
Year 513 Survey
THE FAT IN MEAT HELPS GIVE YOU THE ENERGY TO EXPLORE THE DUNGEON. IT'S IMPORTANT, BUT IT'S NOT ENOUGH.
MALNUTRITION IS SCARIER THAN MONSTERS.
JUST ADDING A SIDE OF MAN-EATING PLANTS OR WALKING MUSHROOMS WOULD MAKE A BIG DIFFERENCE, BUT...
CHEESE
FRUIT
(OTHER)
...YOUNG ADVENTURERS DON'T KNOW THAT.
ATROCIOUS.
BREAKFAST: YESTERDAY'S LEFTOVERS (MAN-EATING PLANT FRUIT)
JUST FILLING ONE'S TUMMY ISN'T ENOUGH.

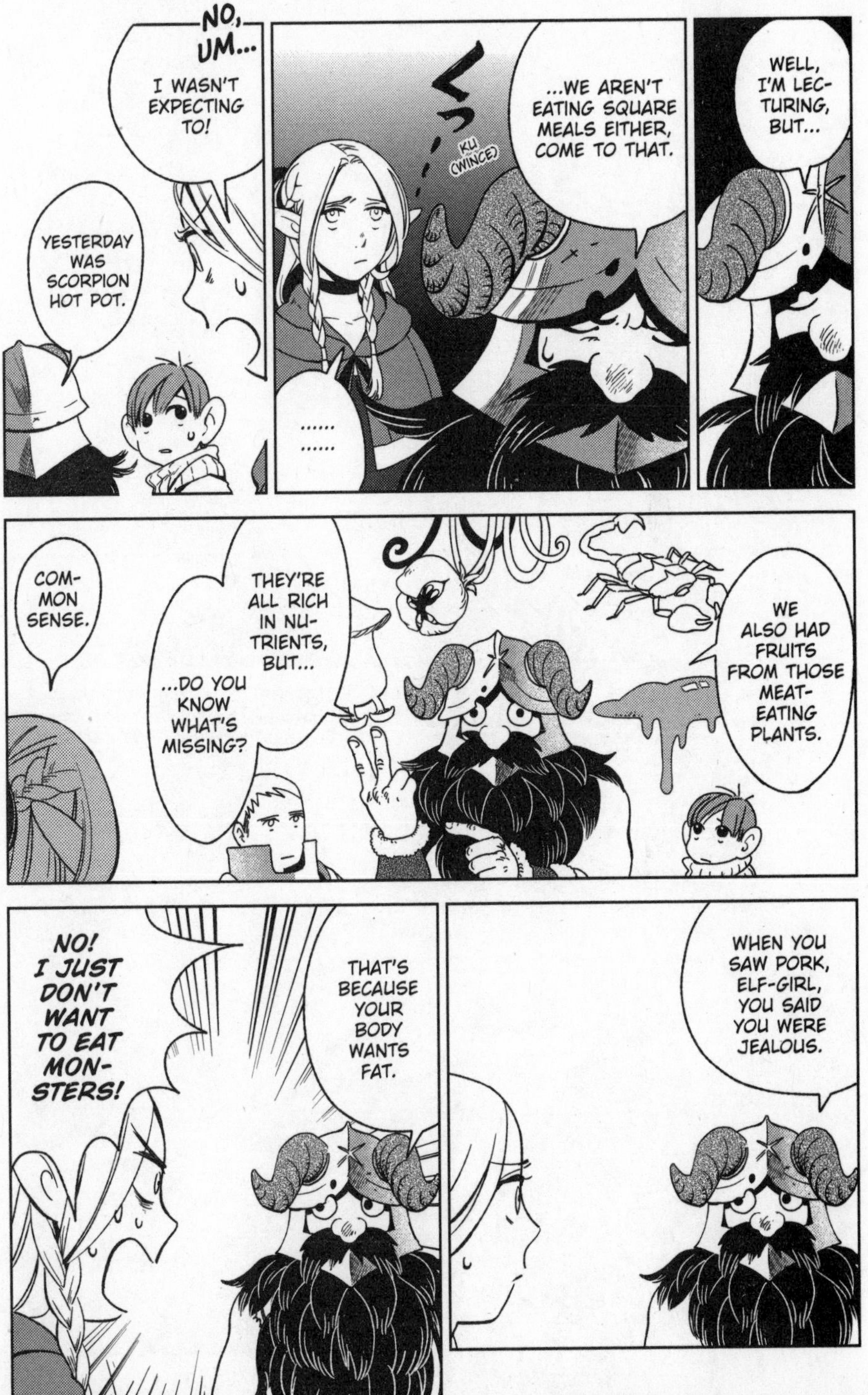
WELL, I'M LECTURING, BUT...
...WE AREN'T EATING SQUARE MEALS EITHER, COME TO THAT.
KU (WINCE)
......
......
NO, UM...
I WASN'T EXPECTING TO!
YESTERDAY WAS SCORPION HOT POT.
WE ALSO HAD FRUITS FROM THOSE MEAT-EATING PLANTS.
THEY'RE ALL RICH IN NUTRIENTS, BUT...
...DO YOU KNOW WHAT'S MISSING?
COMMON SENSE.
WHEN YOU SAW PORK, ELF-GIRL, YOU SAID YOU WERE JEALOUS.
THAT'S BECAUSE YOUR BODY WANTS FAT.
NO! I JUST DON'T WANT TO EAT MONSTERS!

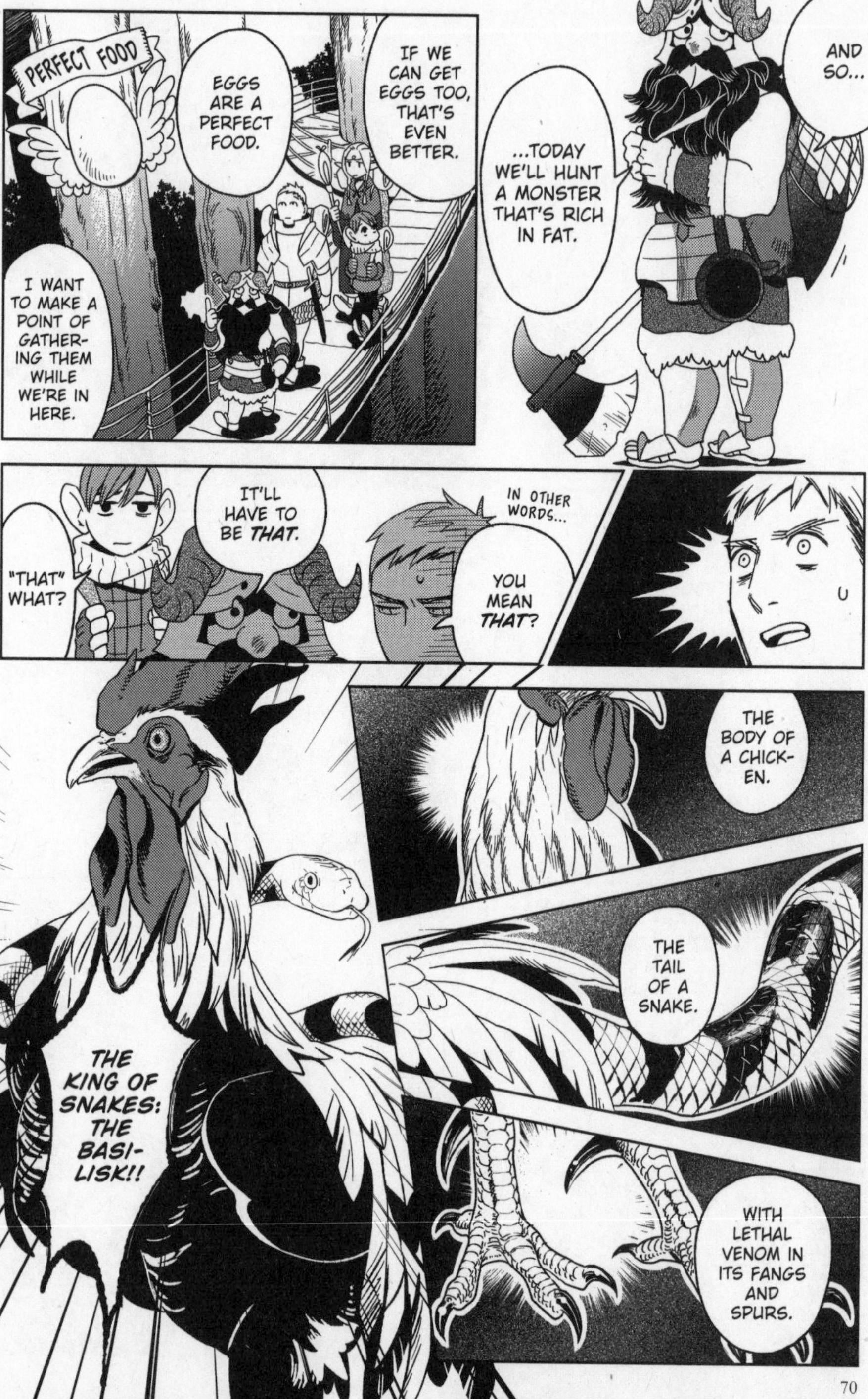
AND SO...
...TODAY WE'LL HUNT A MONSTER THAT'S RICH IN FAT.
IF WE CAN GET EGGS TOO, THAT'S EVEN BETTER.
EGGS ARE A PERFECT FOOD.
PERFECT FOOD
I WANT TO MAKE A POINT OF GATHERING THEM WHILE WE'RE IN HERE.
IN OTHER WORDS...
YOU MEAN *THAT*?
IT'LL HAVE TO BE *THAT*.
"THAT" WHAT?
THE BODY OF A CHICKEN.
THE TAIL OF A SNAKE.
WITH LETHAL VENOM IN ITS FANGS AND SPURS.
THE KING OF SNAKES: THE BASILISK!!

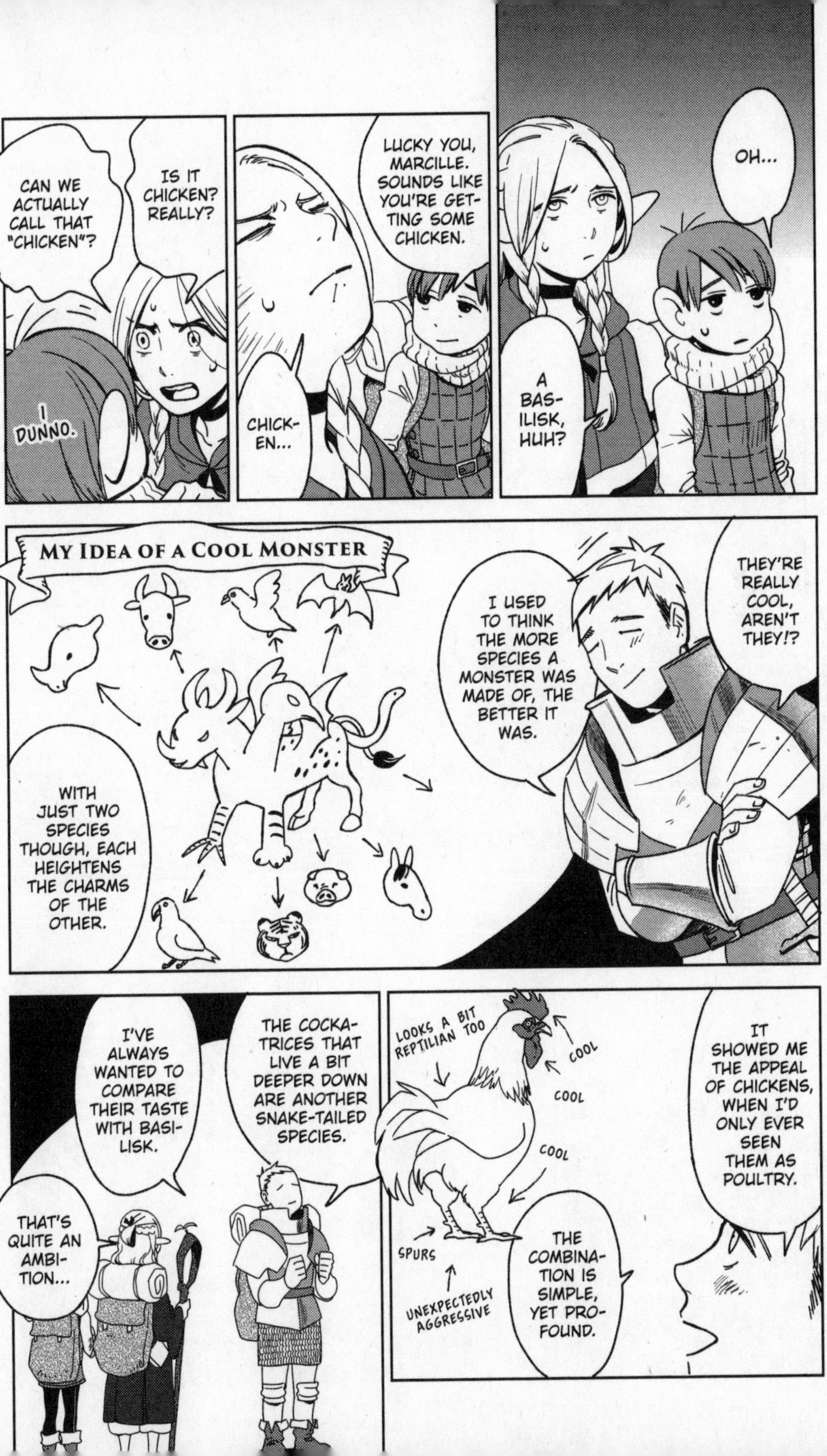
OH...
A BAS-ILISK, HUH?
LUCKY YOU, MARCILLE. SOUNDS LIKE YOU'RE GET-TING SOME CHICKEN.
CHICK-EN...
IS IT CHICKEN? REALLY?
CAN WE ACTUALLY CALL THAT "CHICKEN"?
I DUNNO.
THEY'RE REALLY COOL, AREN'T THEY!?
I USED TO THINK THE MORE SPECIES A MONSTER WAS MADE OF, THE BETTER IT WAS.
MY IDEA OF A COOL MONSTER
WITH JUST TWO SPECIES THOUGH, EACH HEIGHTENS THE CHARMS OF THE OTHER.
IT SHOWED ME THE APPEAL OF CHICKENS, WHEN I'D ONLY EVER SEEN THEM AS POULTRY.
LOOKS A BIT REPTILIAN TOO
COOL
COOL
COOL
SPURS
UNEXPECTEDLY AGGRESSIVE
THE COMBINA-TION IS SIMPLE, YET PRO-FOUND.
THE COCKA-TRICES THAT LIVE A BIT DEEPER DOWN ARE ANOTHER SNAKE-TAILED SPECIES.
I'VE ALWAYS WANTED TO COMPARE THEIR TASTE WITH BASI-LISK.
THAT'S QUITE AN AMBI-TION...

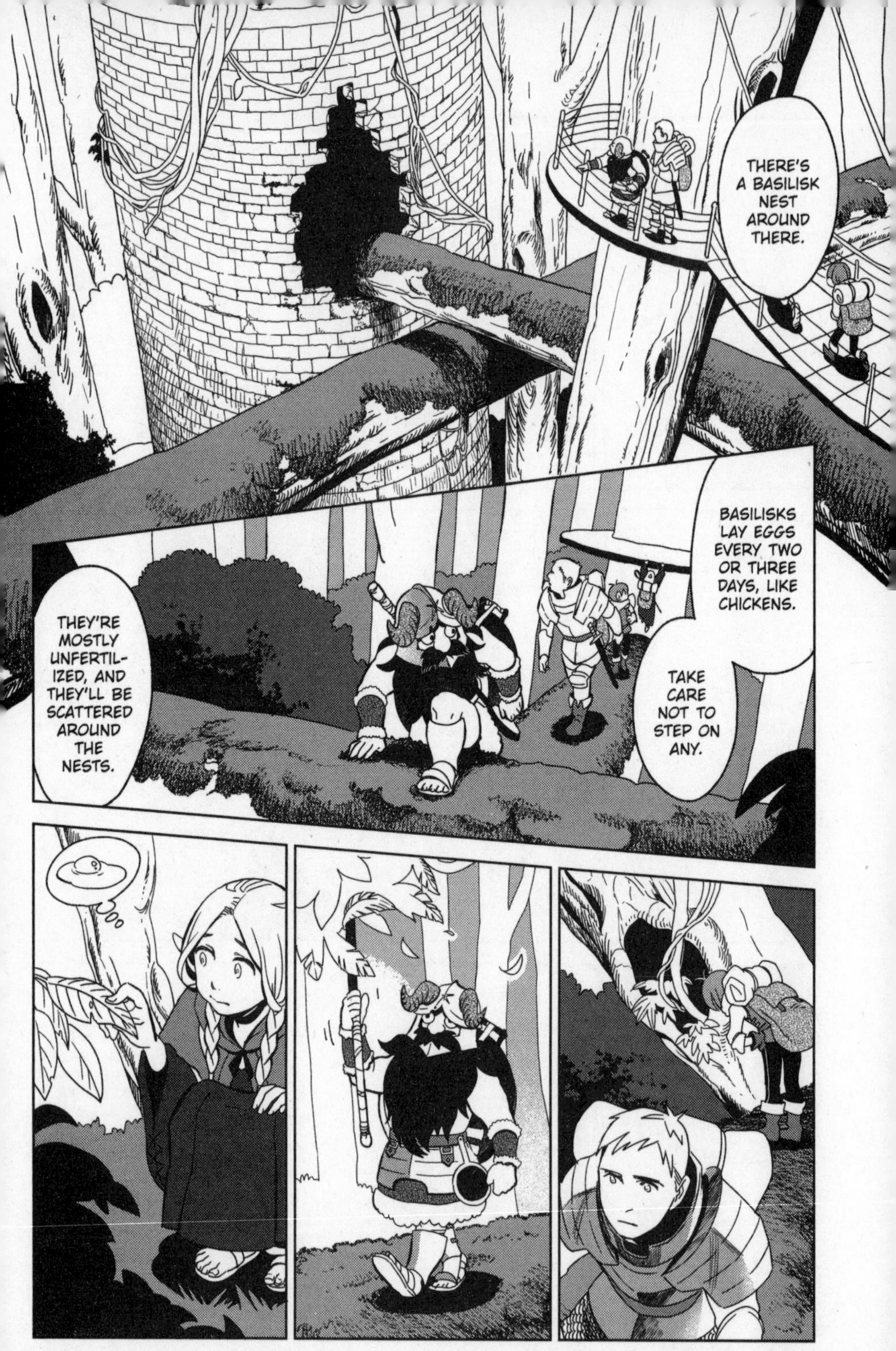
THERE'S A BASILISK NEST AROUND THERE.
BASILISKS LAY EGGS EVERY TWO OR THREE DAYS, LIKE CHICKENS.
TAKE CARE NOT TO STEP ON ANY.
THEY'RE MOSTLY UNFERTIL-IZED, AND THEY'LL BE SCATTERED AROUND THE NESTS.

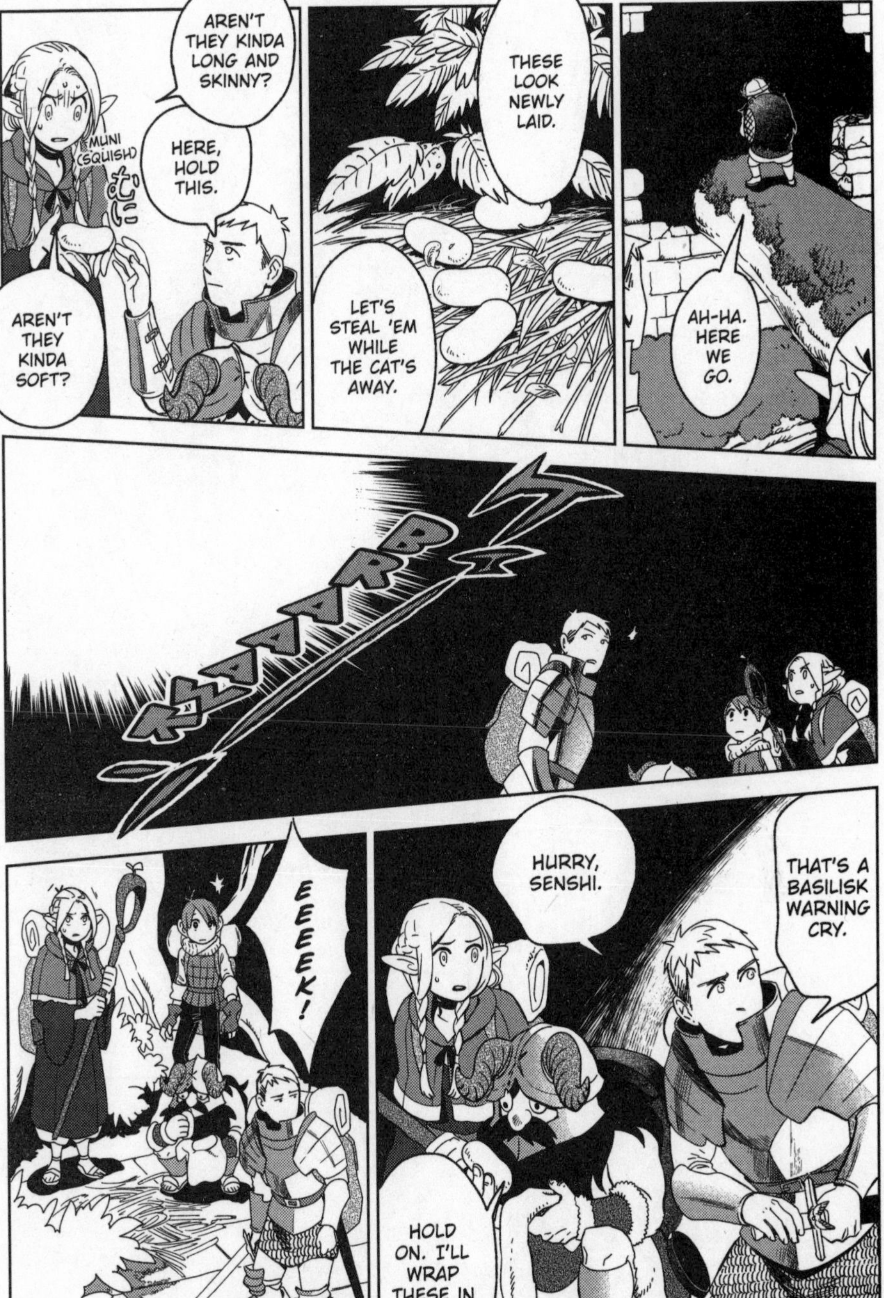
AH-HA. HERE WE GO.
THESE LOOK NEWLY LAID.
LET'S STEAL 'EM WHILE THE CAT'S AWAY.
AREN'T THEY KINDA LONG AND SKINNY?
HERE, HOLD THIS.
MUNI (SQUISH)
むに
AREN'T THEY KINDA SOFT?
KWAAARB
THAT'S A BASILISK WARNING CRY.
HURRY, SENSHI.
HOLD ON. I'LL WRAP THESE IN CLOTH.
EEEEEK!

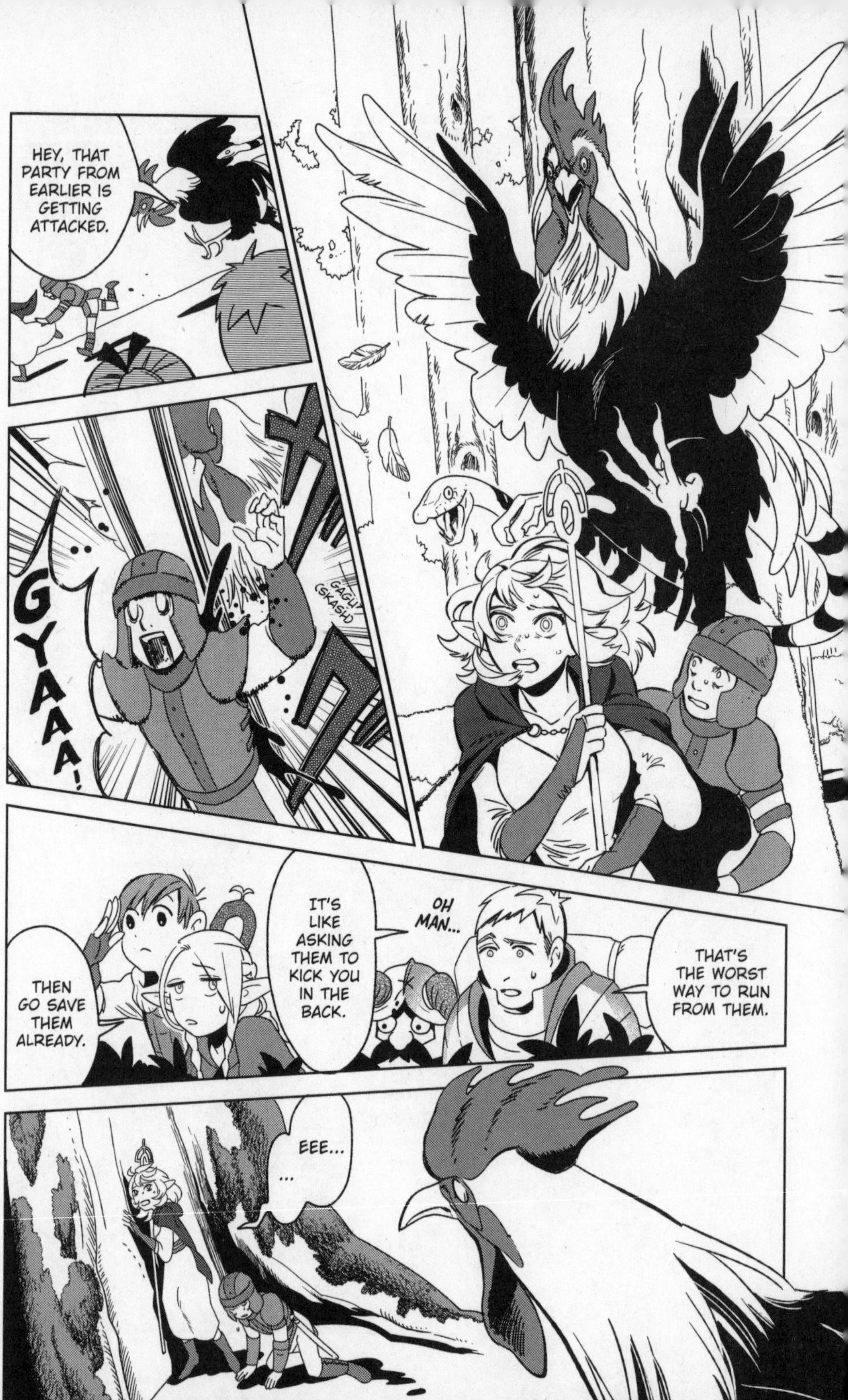

HEY, THAT PARTY FROM EARLIER IS GETTING ATTACKED.
GYAAA!
GAGU (SKASH)
THAT'S THE WORST WAY TO RUN FROM THEM.
OH MAN...
IT'S LIKE ASKING THEM TO KICK YOU IN THE BACK.
THEN GO SAVE THEM ALREADY.
EEE...
...

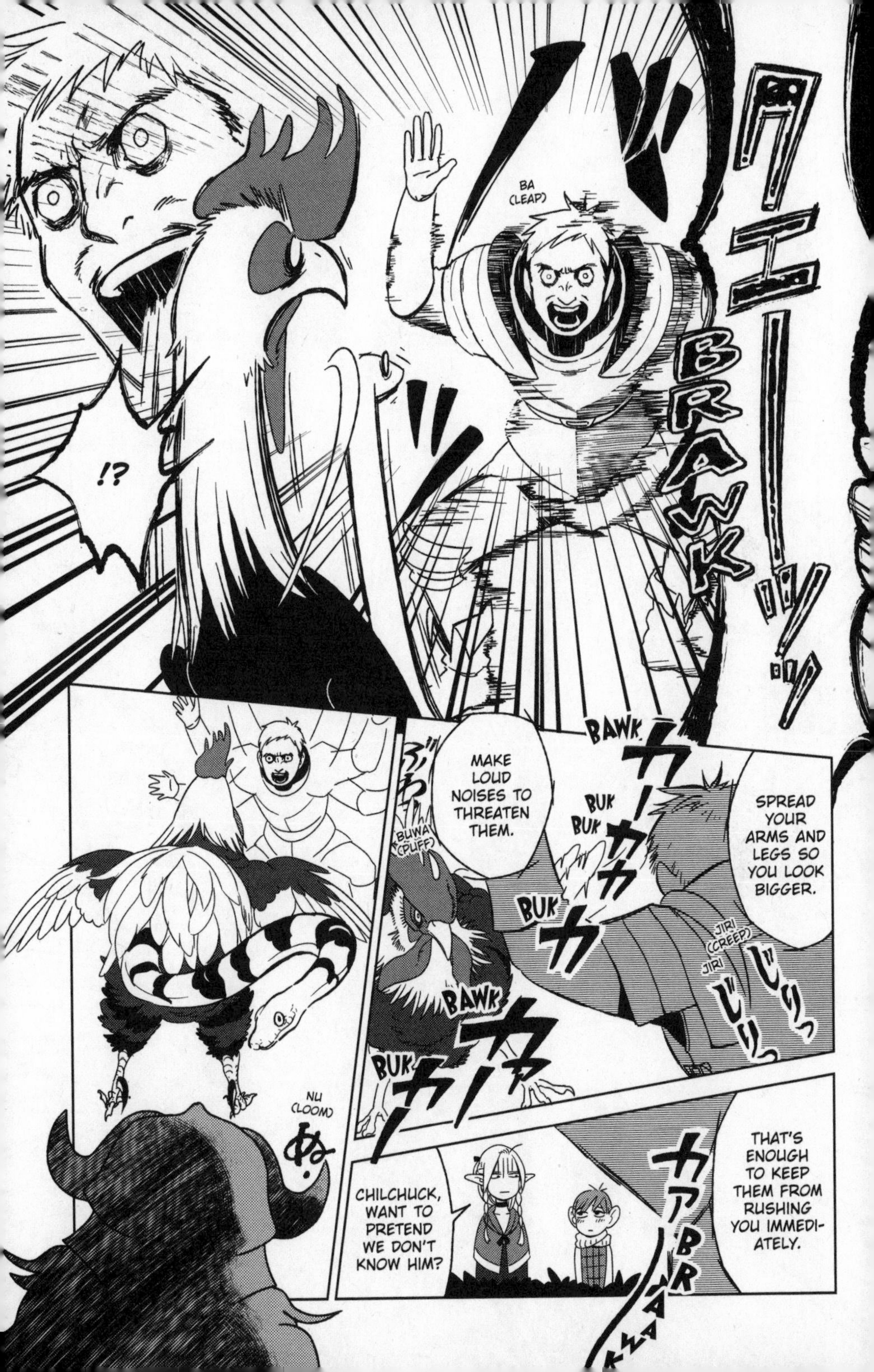
BRAWK
BA (LEAP)
!?
SPREAD YOUR ARMS AND LEGS SO YOU LOOK BIGGER.
JIRI (CREEP) JIRI
BAWK
BUK BUK
BUK
MAKE LOUD NOISES TO THREATEN THEM.
BUWA (PUFF)
BAWK
BUK
THAT'S ENOUGH TO KEEP THEM FROM RUSHING YOU IMMEDIATELY.
BRAWK
CHILCHUCK, WANT TO PRETEND WE DON'T KNOW HIM?
NU (LOOM)

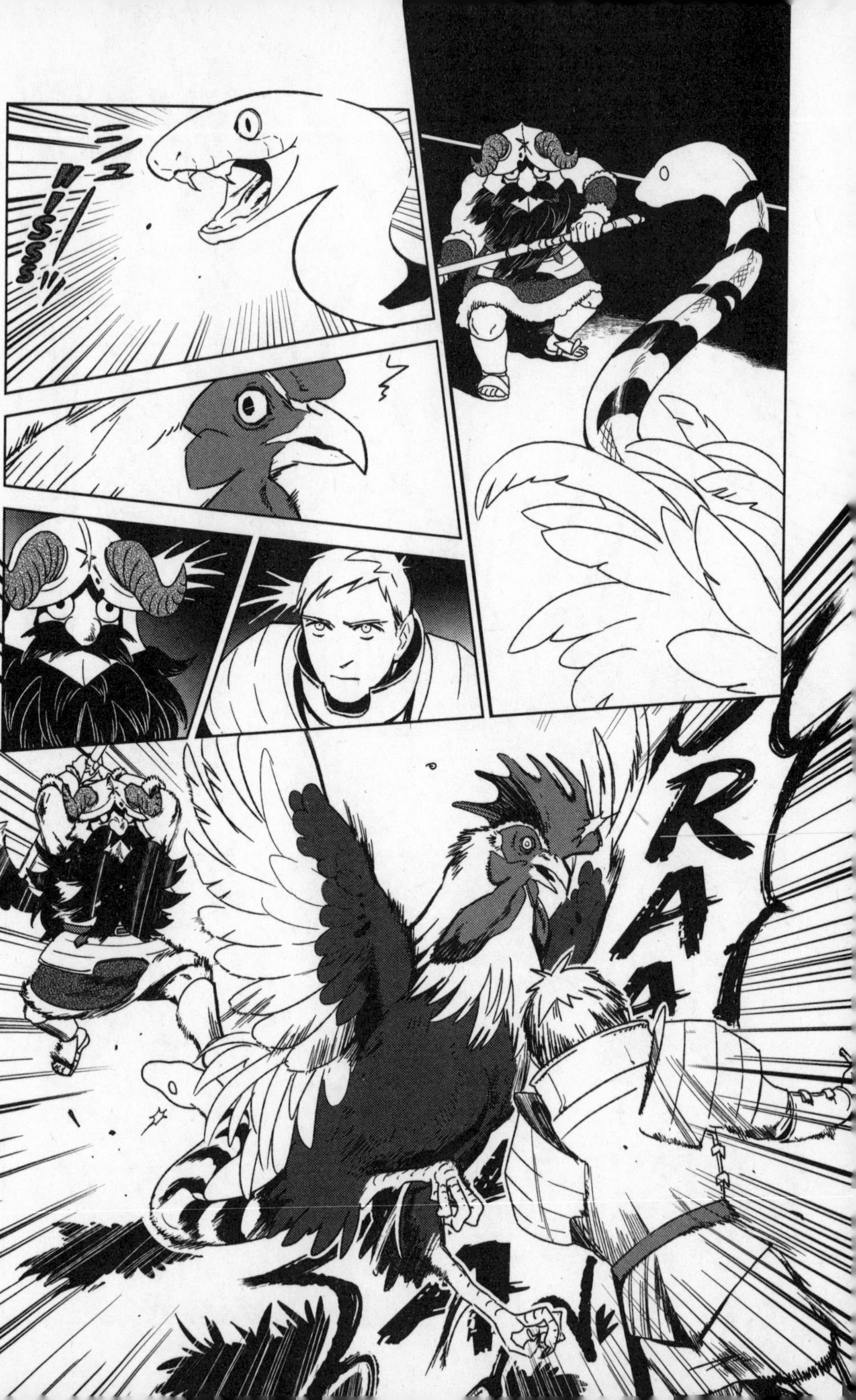

HISSS!!
RAA

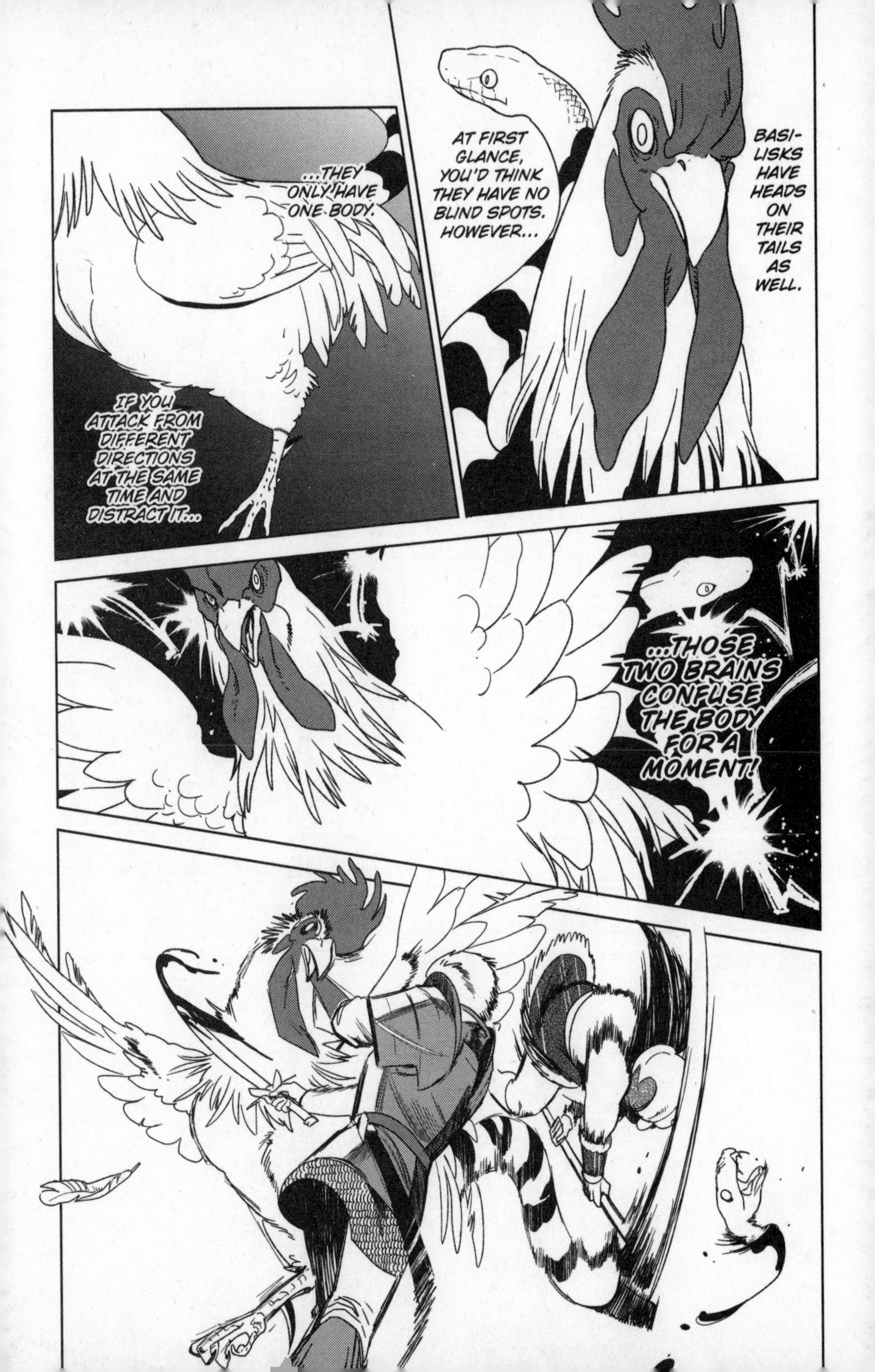
BASI-LISKS HAVE HEADS ON THEIR TAILS AS WELL.
AT FIRST GLANCE, YOU'D THINK THEY HAVE NO BLIND SPOTS. HOWEVER...
...THEY ONLY HAVE ONE BODY.
IF YOU ATTACK FROM DIFFERENT DIRECTIONS AT THE SAME TIME AND DISTRACT IT...
...THOSE TWO BRAINS CONFUSE THE BODY FOR A MOMENT!

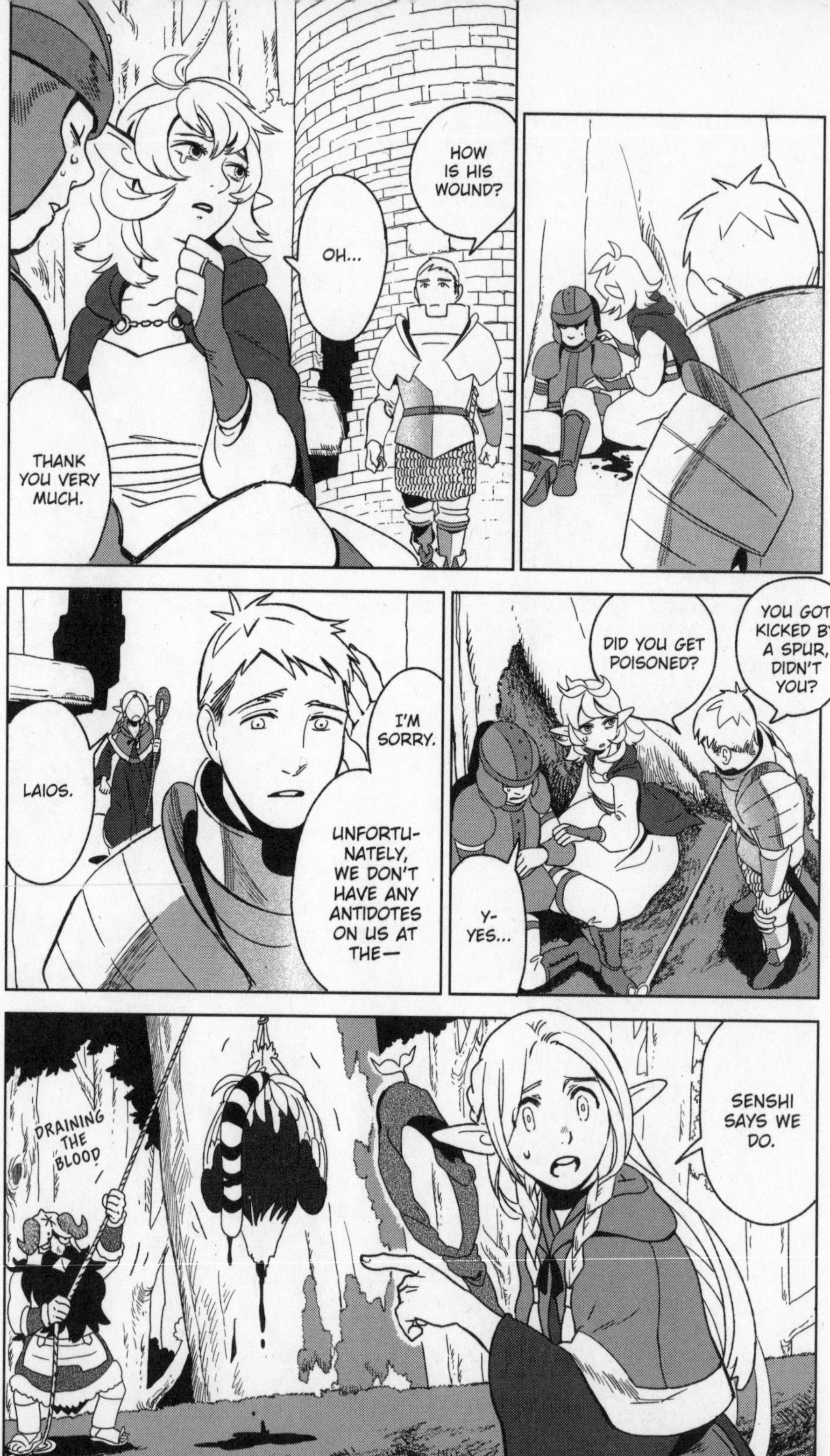
HOW IS HIS WOUND?
OH...
THANK YOU VERY MUCH.
YOU GOT KICKED BY A SPUR, DIDN'T YOU?
DID YOU GET POISONED?
Y- YES...
I'M SORRY.
UNFORTU- NATELY, WE DON'T HAVE ANY ANTIDOTES ON US AT THE—
LAIOS.
SENSHI SAYS WE DO.
DRAINING THE BLOOD

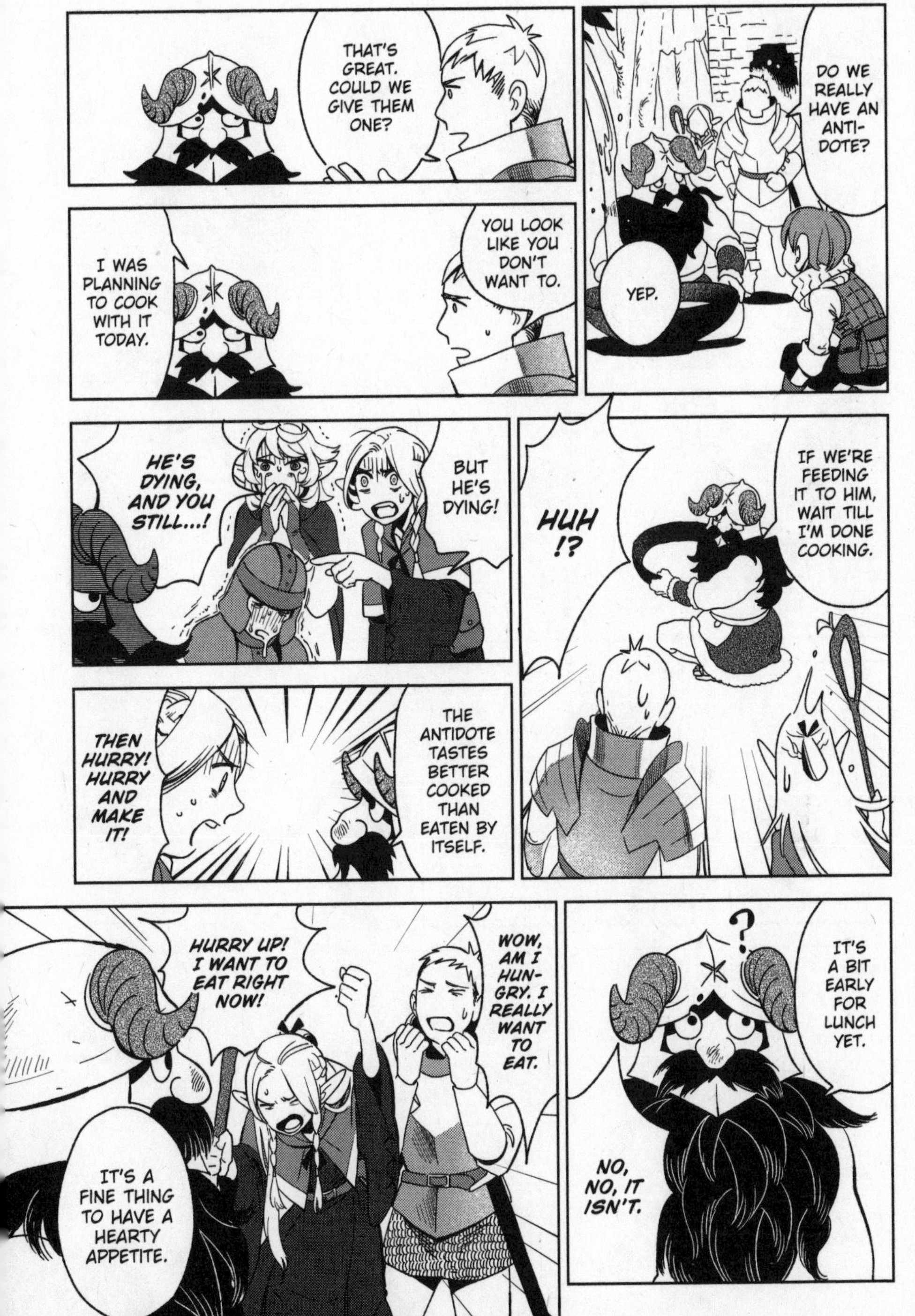
DO WE REALLY HAVE AN ANTIDOTE?
YEP.
THAT'S GREAT. COULD WE GIVE THEM ONE?
YOU LOOK LIKE YOU DON'T WANT TO.
I WAS PLANNING TO COOK WITH IT TODAY.
IF WE'RE FEEDING IT TO HIM, WAIT TILL I'M DONE COOKING.
HUH!?
BUT HE'S DYING!
HE'S DYING, AND YOU STILL...!
THE ANTIDOTE TASTES BETTER COOKED THAN EATEN BY ITSELF.
THEN HURRY! HURRY AND MAKE IT!
?
IT'S A BIT EARLY FOR LUNCH YET.
NO, NO, IT ISN'T.
WOW, AM I HUNGRY. I REALLY WANT TO EAT.
HURRY UP! I WANT TO EAT RIGHT NOW!
IT'S A FINE THING TO HAVE A HEARTY APPETITE.

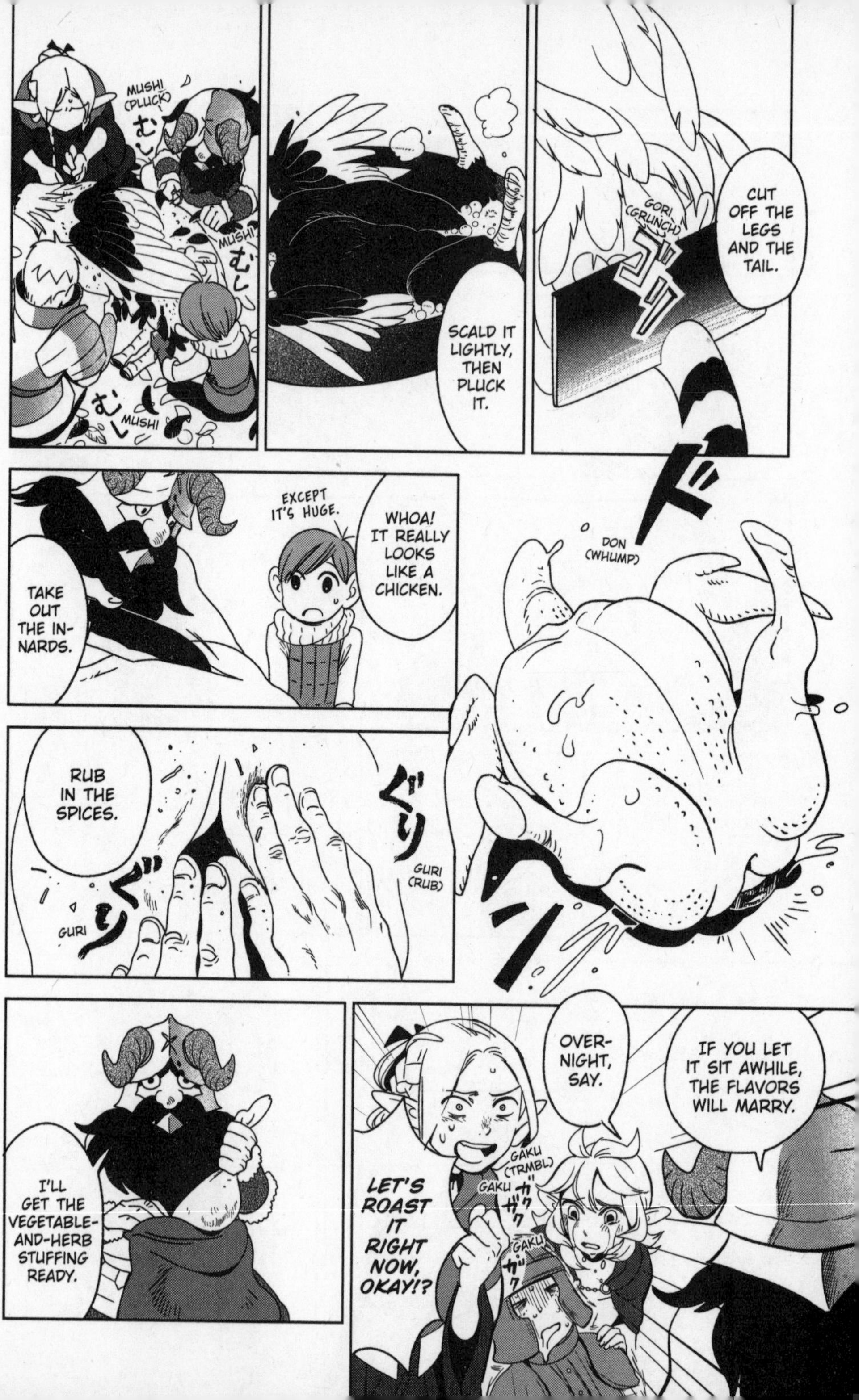
CUT OFF THE LEGS AND THE TAIL.
GORI (GRUNCH)
SCALD IT LIGHTLY, THEN PLUCK IT.
MUSHI (PLUCK)
MUSHI
MUSHI
DON (WHUMP)
WHOA! IT REALLY LOOKS LIKE A CHICKEN.
EXCEPT IT'S HUGE.
TAKE OUT THE IN-NARDS.
RUB IN THE SPICES.
GURI (RUB)
GURI
IF YOU LET IT SIT AWHILE, THE FLAVORS WILL MARRY.
OVER-NIGHT, SAY.
GAKU (TRMBL)
GAKU
GAKU
LET'S ROAST IT RIGHT NOW, OKAY!?
I'LL GET THE VEGETABLE-AND-HERB STUFFING READY.

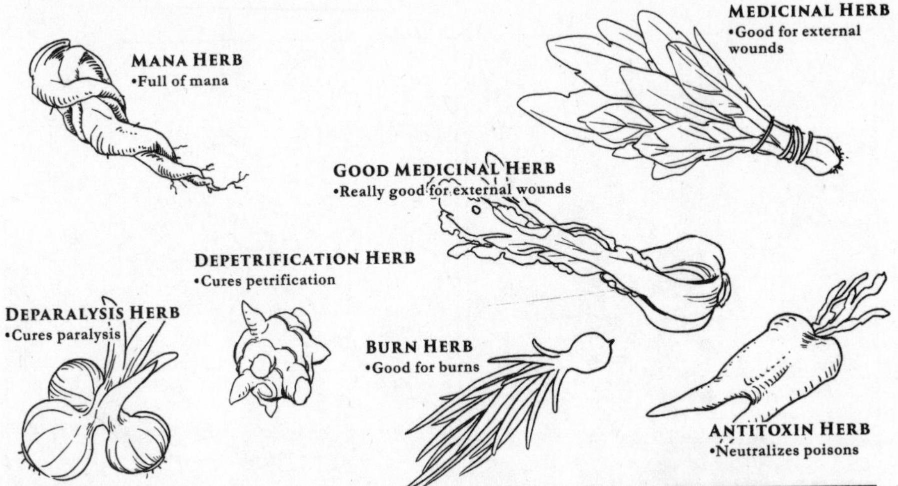
MEDICINAL HERB
•Good for external wounds
MANA HERB
•Full of mana
GOOD MEDICINAL HERB
•Really good for external wounds
DEPETRIFICATION HERB
•Cures petrification
DEPARALYSIS HERB
•Cures paralysis
BURN HERB
•Good for burns
ANTITOXIN HERB
•Neutralizes poisons

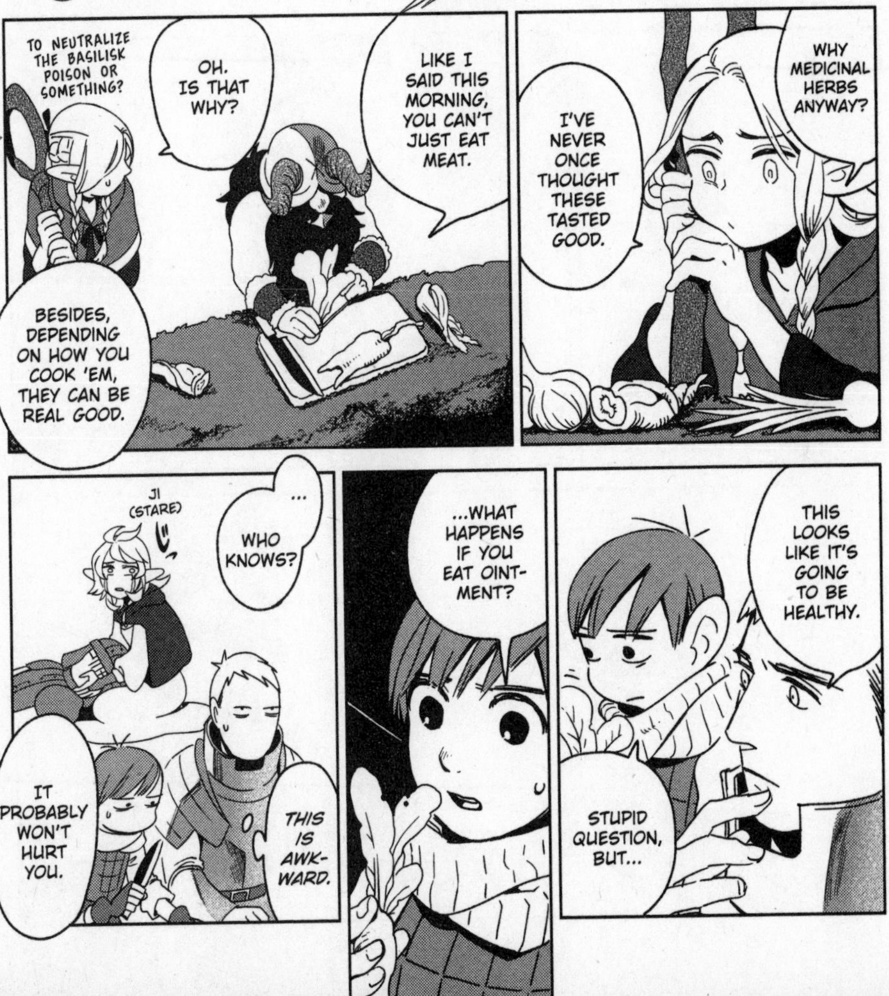
WHY MEDICINAL HERBS ANYWAY?
I'VE NEVER ONCE THOUGHT THESE TASTED GOOD.
LIKE I SAID THIS MORNING, YOU CAN'T JUST EAT MEAT.
OH. IS THAT WHY?
TO NEUTRALIZE THE BASILISK POISON OR SOMETHING?
BESIDES, DEPENDING ON HOW YOU COOK 'EM, THEY CAN BE REAL GOOD.
THIS LOOKS LIKE IT'S GOING TO BE HEALTHY.
STUPID QUESTION, BUT...
...WHAT HAPPENS IF YOU EAT OINT-MENT?
...
WHO KNOWS?
JI (STARE)
IT PROBABLY WON'T HURT YOU.
THIS IS AWK-WARD.

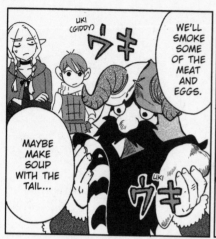

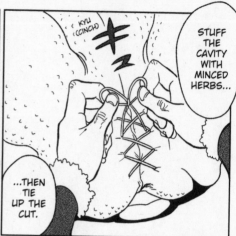

KYU (CINCH)
キュ
STUFF THE CAVITY WITH MINCED HERBS...
...THEN TIE UP THE CUT.
UKI (GIDDY)
ヴキ
WE'LL SMOKE SOME OF THE MEAT AND EGGS.
MAYBE MAKE SOUP WITH THE TAIL...
UKI
ウキ
RUN A SKEWER THROUGH THE MEAT.
GASHA (CLANK)
ガしゃ
THEN ROAST IT WELL.

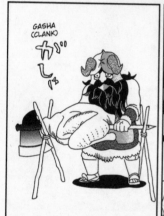

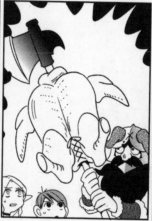

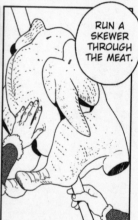

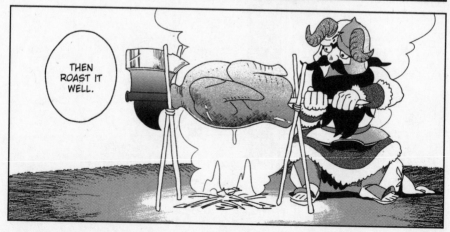

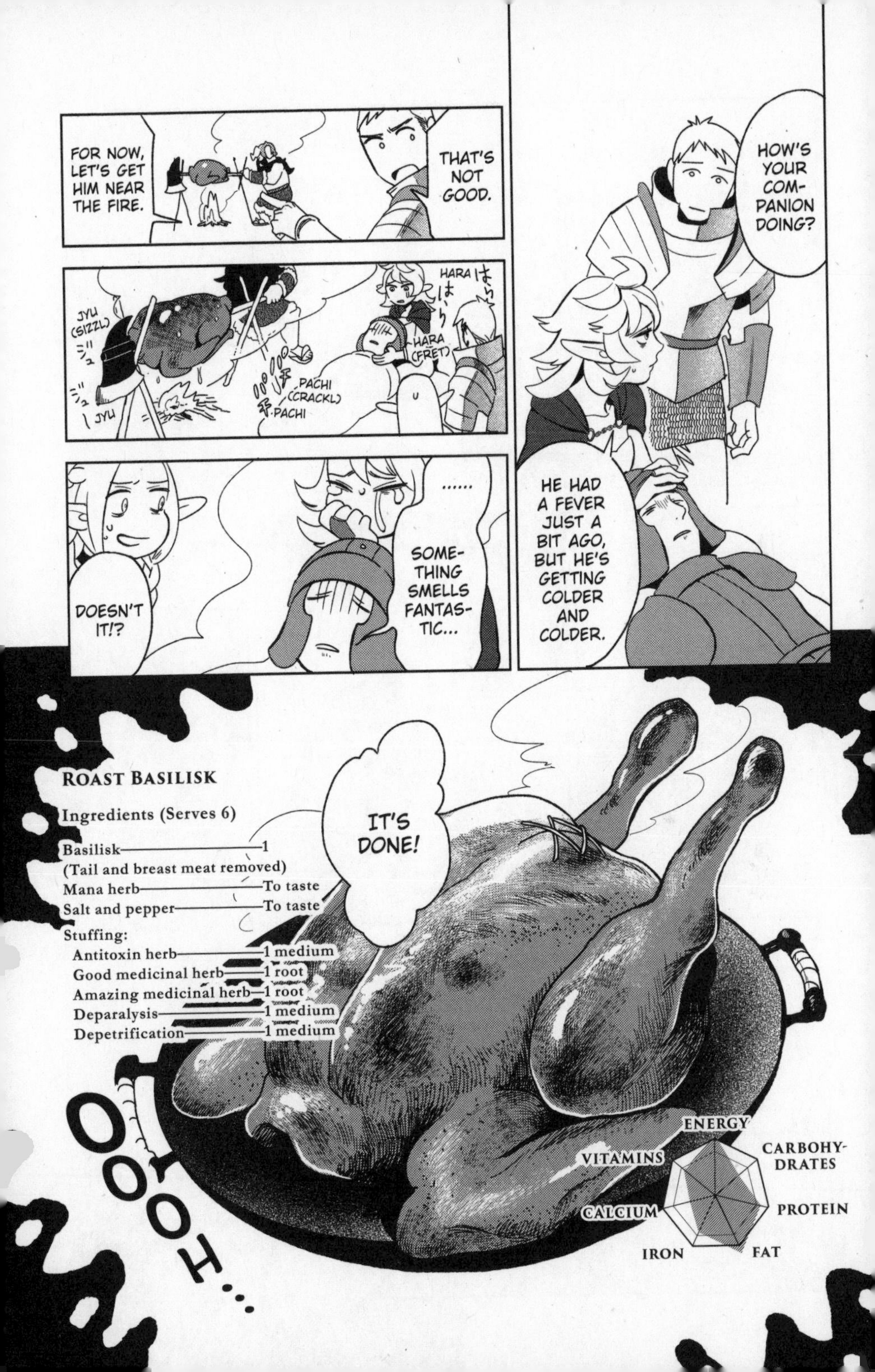
HOW'S YOUR COMPANION DOING?
HE HAD A FEVER JUST A BIT AGO, BUT HE'S GETTING COLDER AND COLDER.
THAT'S NOT GOOD.
FOR NOW, LET'S GET HIM NEAR THE FIRE.
HARA はらはら HARA (FRET)
PACHI (CRACKL) パチパチ PACHI
JYU (SIZZL) ジュジュ JYU
......
SOMETHING SMELLS FANTASTIC...
DOESN'T IT!?
IT'S DONE!
OOOOH...
ROAST BASILISK
Ingredients (Serves 6)
Basilisk—1
(Tail and breast meat removed)
Mana herb—To taste
Salt and pepper—To taste
Stuffing:
Antitoxin herb—1 medium
Good medicinal herb—1 root
Amazing medicinal herb—1 root
Deparalysis—1 medium
Depetrification—1 medium
ENERGY
CARBOHYDRATES
PROTEIN
FAT
IRON
CALCIUM
VITAMINS

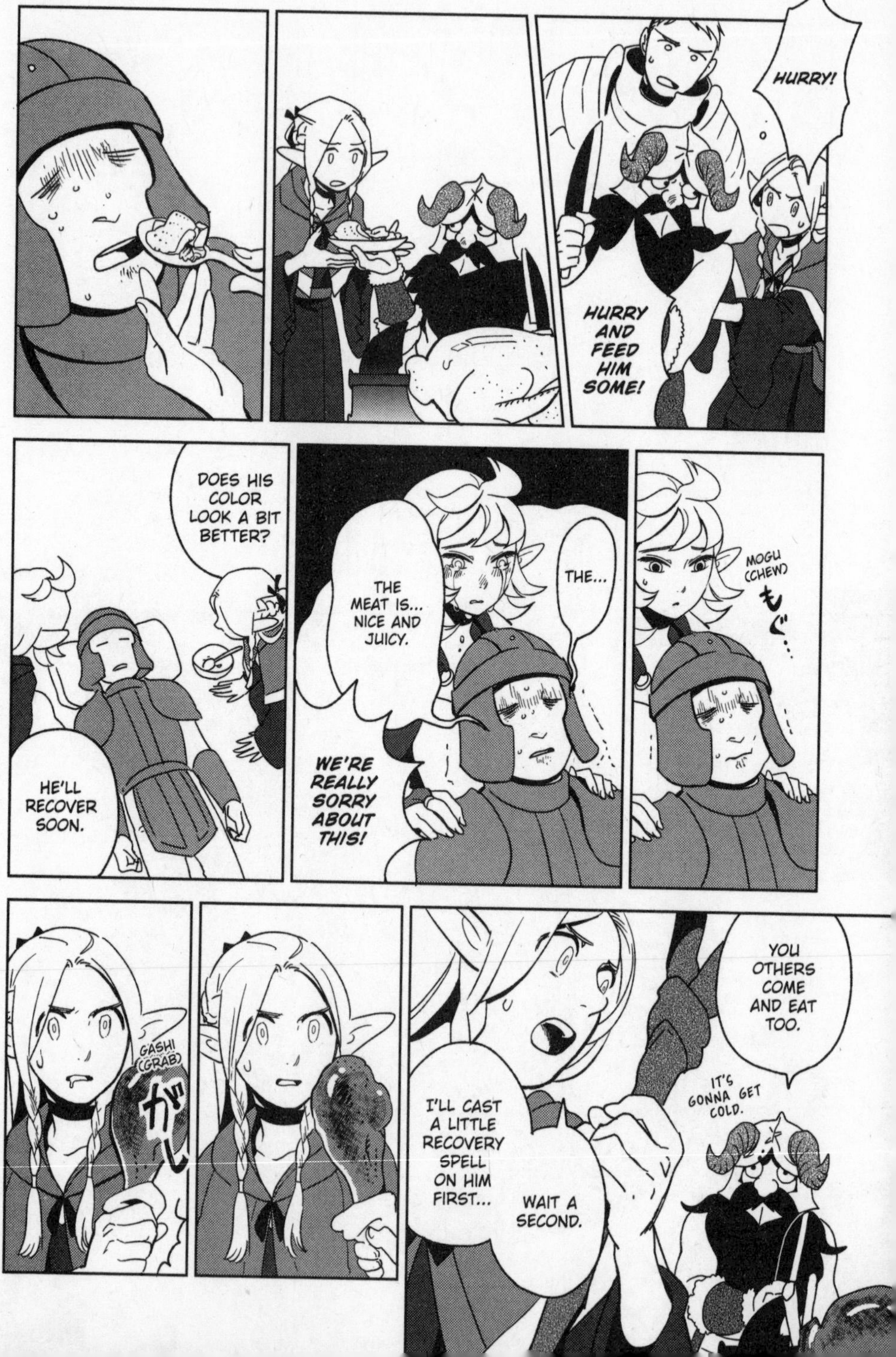
HURRY!
HURRY AND FEED HIM SOME!
MOGU (CHEW)
もぐ...
THE...
THE MEAT IS... NICE AND JUICY.
WE'RE REALLY SORRY ABOUT THIS!
DOES HIS COLOR LOOK A BIT BETTER?
HE'LL RECOVER SOON.
YOU OTHERS COME AND EAT TOO.
IT'S GONNA GET COLD.
WAIT A SECOND.
I'LL CAST A LITTLE RECOVERY SPELL ON HIM FIRST...
GASHI (GRAB)
ガし

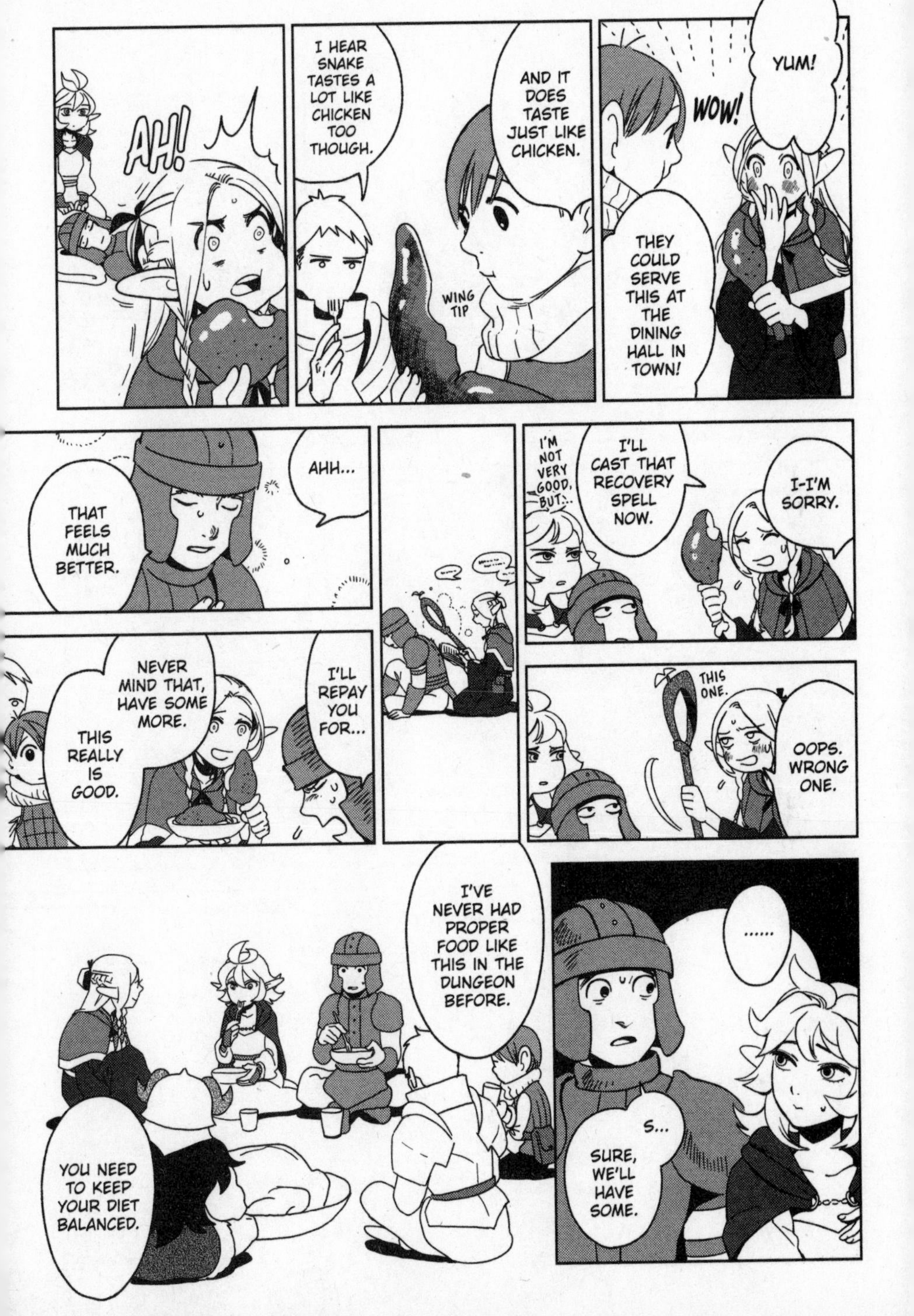
YUM!
WOW!
THEY COULD SERVE THIS AT THE DINING HALL IN TOWN!
AND IT DOES TASTE JUST LIKE CHICKEN.
I HEAR SNAKE TASTES A LOT LIKE CHICKEN TOO THOUGH.
WING TIP
AH!
I-I'M SORRY.
I'LL CAST THAT RECOVERY SPELL NOW.
I'M NOT VERY GOOD, BUT...
OOPS. WRONG ONE.
THIS ONE.
AHH...
THAT FEELS MUCH BETTER.
I'LL REPAY YOU FOR...
NEVER MIND THAT, HAVE SOME MORE.
THIS REALLY IS GOOD.
......
S...
SURE, WE'LL HAVE SOME.
I'VE NEVER HAD PROPER FOOD LIKE THIS IN THE DUNGEON BEFORE.
YOU NEED TO KEEP YOUR DIET BALANCED.

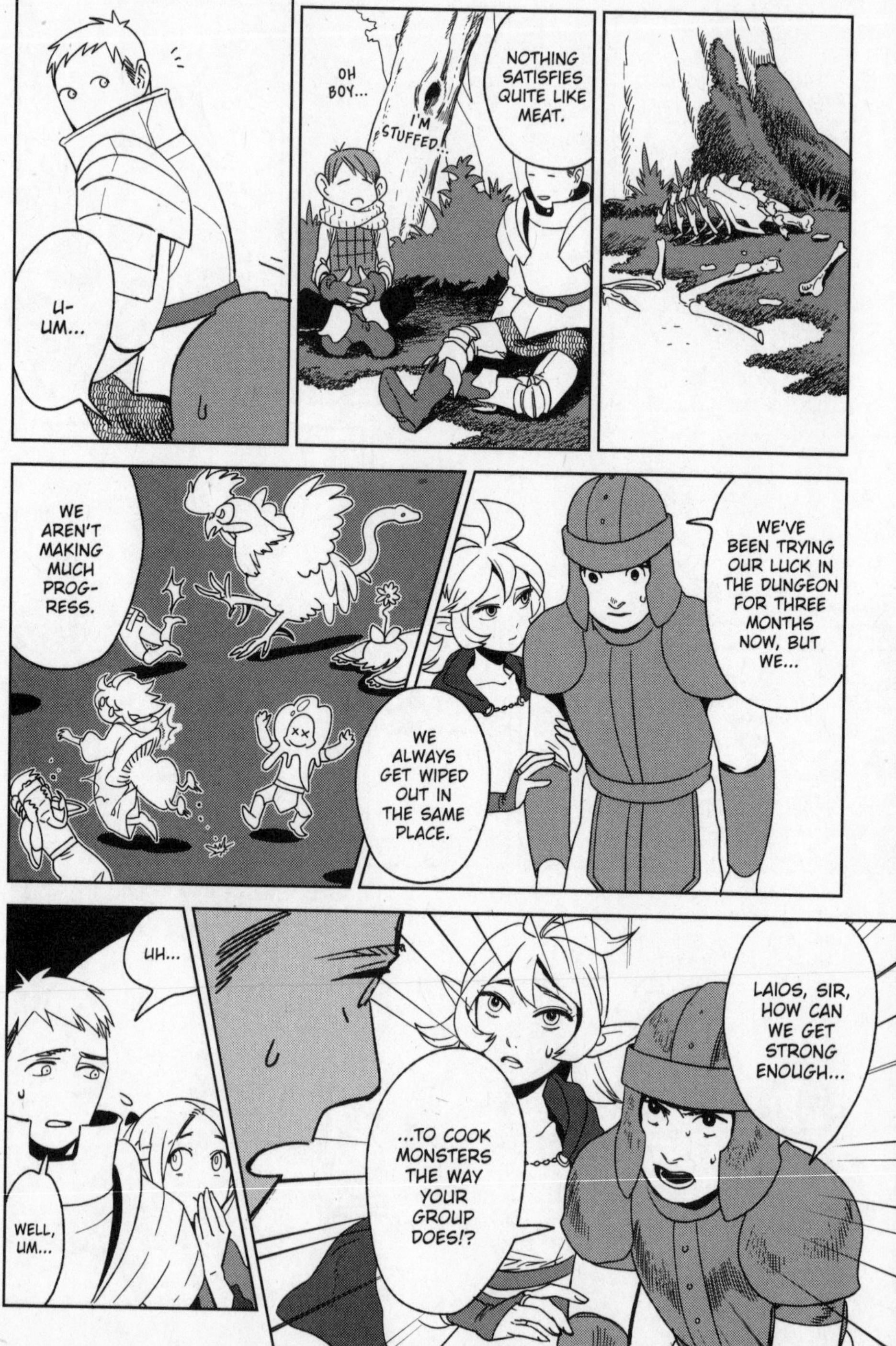
NOTHING SATISFIES QUITE LIKE MEAT.
OH BOY...
I'M STUFFED...
U-UM...
WE'VE BEEN TRYING OUR LUCK IN THE DUNGEON FOR THREE MONTHS NOW, BUT WE...
WE ALWAYS GET WIPED OUT IN THE SAME PLACE.
WE AREN'T MAKING MUCH PROG-RESS.
LAIOS, SIR, HOW CAN WE GET STRONG ENOUGH...
...TO COOK MONSTERS THE WAY YOUR GROUP DOES!?
UH...
WELL, UM...

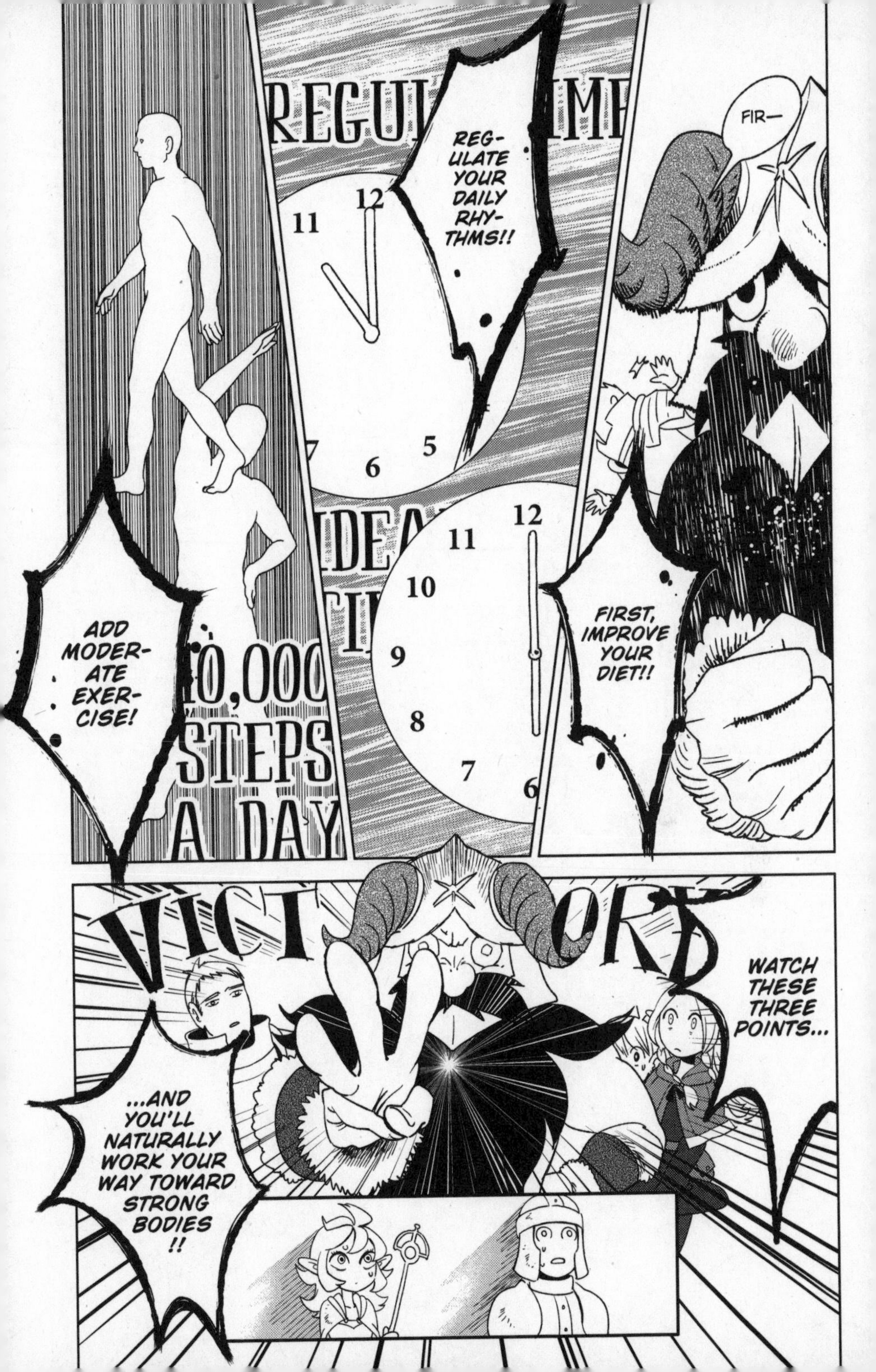

FIR—
FIRST, IMPROVE YOUR DIET!!
REGULATE YOUR DAILY RHYTHMS!!
10,000 STEPS A DAY
ADD MODERATE EXERCISE!
WATCH THESE THREE POINTS...
...AND YOU'LL NATURALLY WORK YOUR WAY TOWARD STRONG BODIES!!

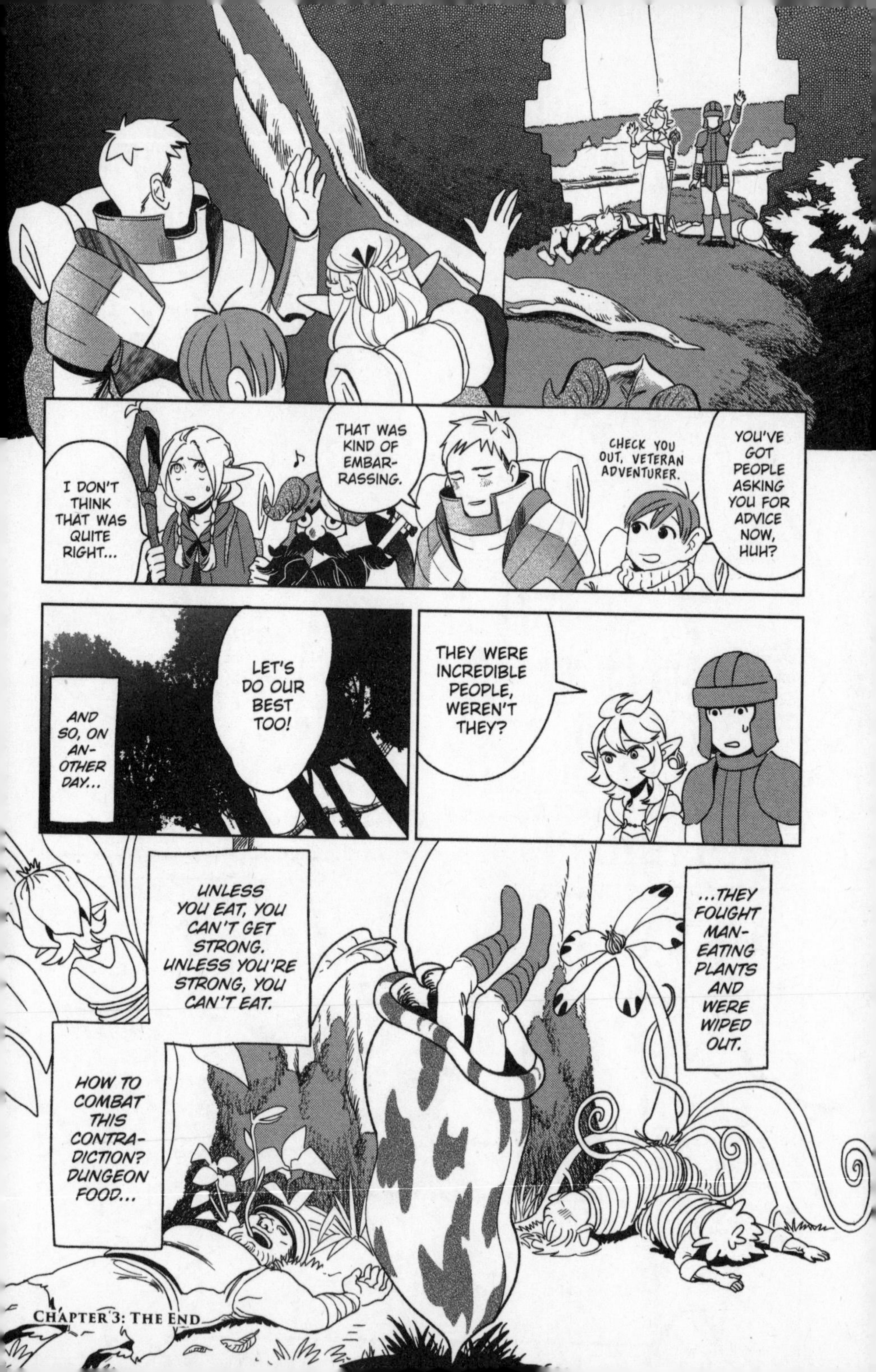
YOU'VE GOT PEOPLE ASKING YOU FOR ADVICE NOW, HUH?
CHECK YOU OUT, VETERAN ADVENTURER.
THAT WAS KIND OF EMBARRASSING.
I DON'T THINK THAT WAS QUITE RIGHT...
THEY WERE INCREDIBLE PEOPLE, WEREN'T THEY?
LET'S DO OUR BEST TOO!
AND SO, ON ANOTHER DAY...
...THEY FOUGHT MAN-EATING PLANTS AND WERE WIPED OUT.
UNLESS YOU EAT, YOU CAN'T GET STRONG. UNLESS YOU'RE STRONG, YOU CAN'T EAT.
HOW TO COMBAT THIS CONTRADICTION? DUNGEON FOOD...
CHAPTER 3: THE END

4. Omelet

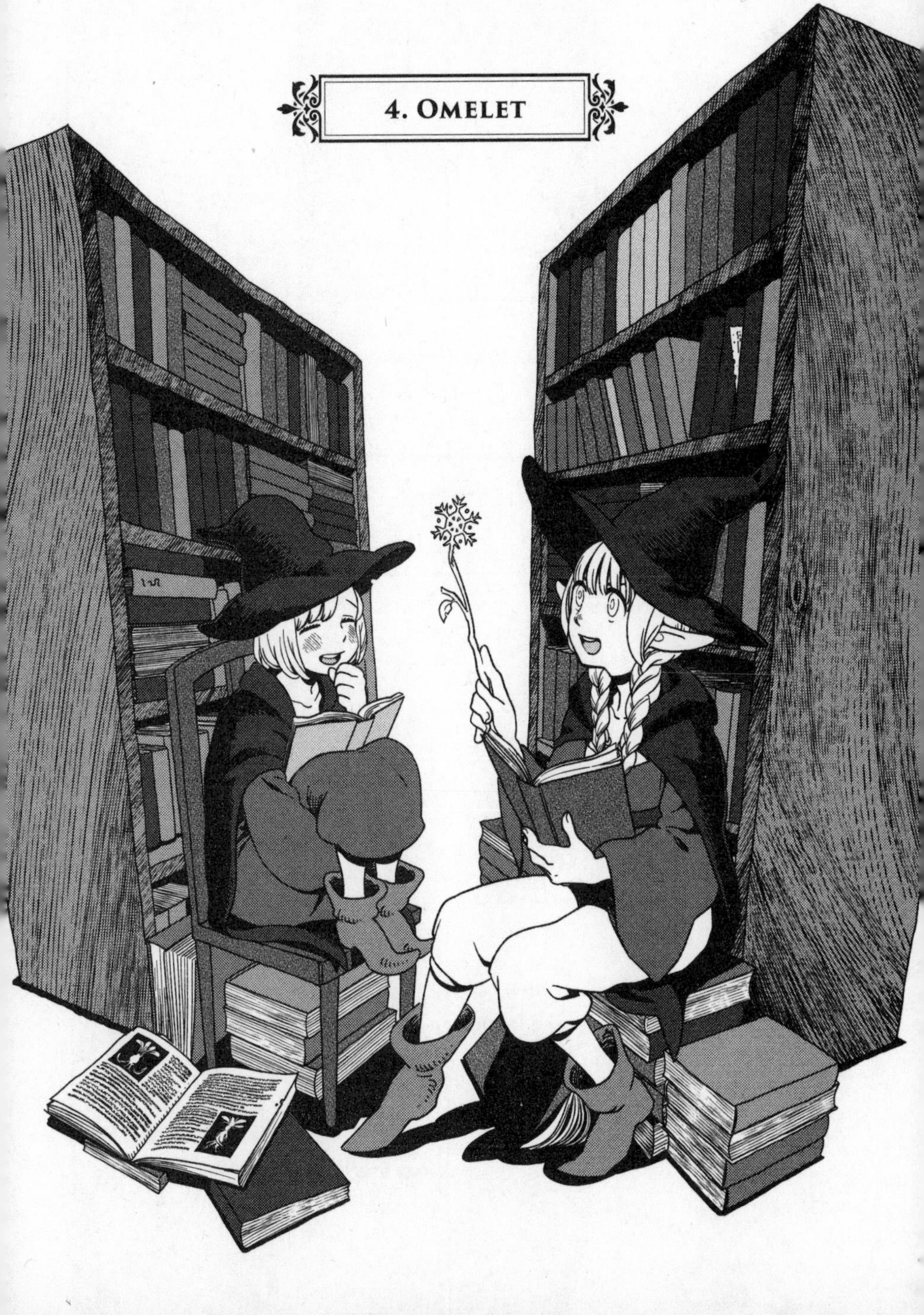

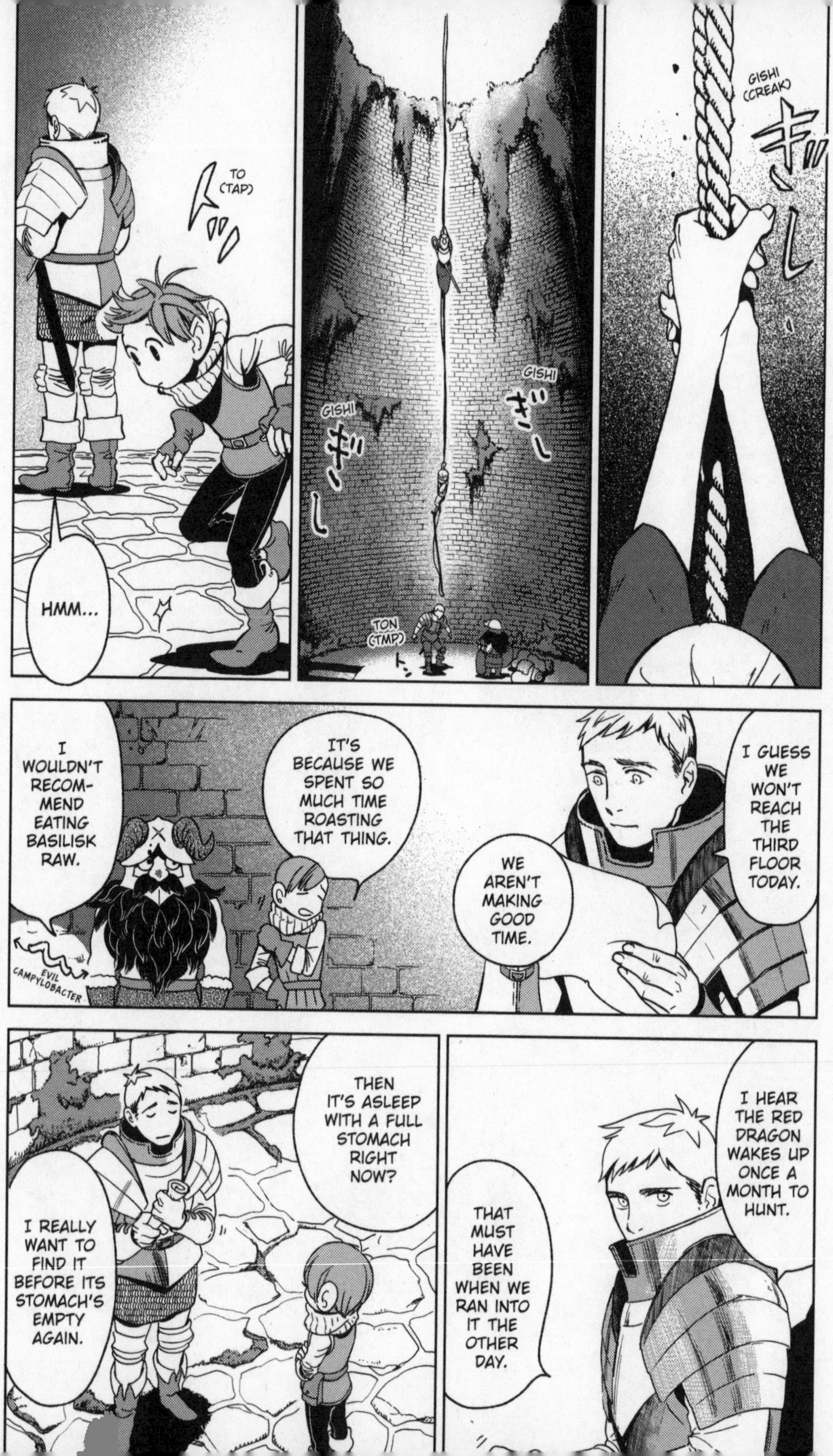
GISHI (CREAK)
GISHI
ぎし
GISHI
ぎし
TON (TMP)
TO (TAP)
HMM...
I GUESS WE WON'T REACH THE THIRD FLOOR TODAY.
WE AREN'T MAKING GOOD TIME.
IT'S BECAUSE WE SPENT SO MUCH TIME ROASTING THAT THING.
I WOULDN'T RECOM-MEND EATING BASILISK RAW.
EVIL CAMPYLOBACTER
I HEAR THE RED DRAGON WAKES UP ONCE A MONTH TO HUNT.
THAT MUST HAVE BEEN WHEN WE RAN INTO IT THE OTHER DAY.
THEN IT'S ASLEEP WITH A FULL STOMACH RIGHT NOW?
I REALLY WANT TO FIND IT BEFORE ITS STOMACH'S EMPTY AGAIN.

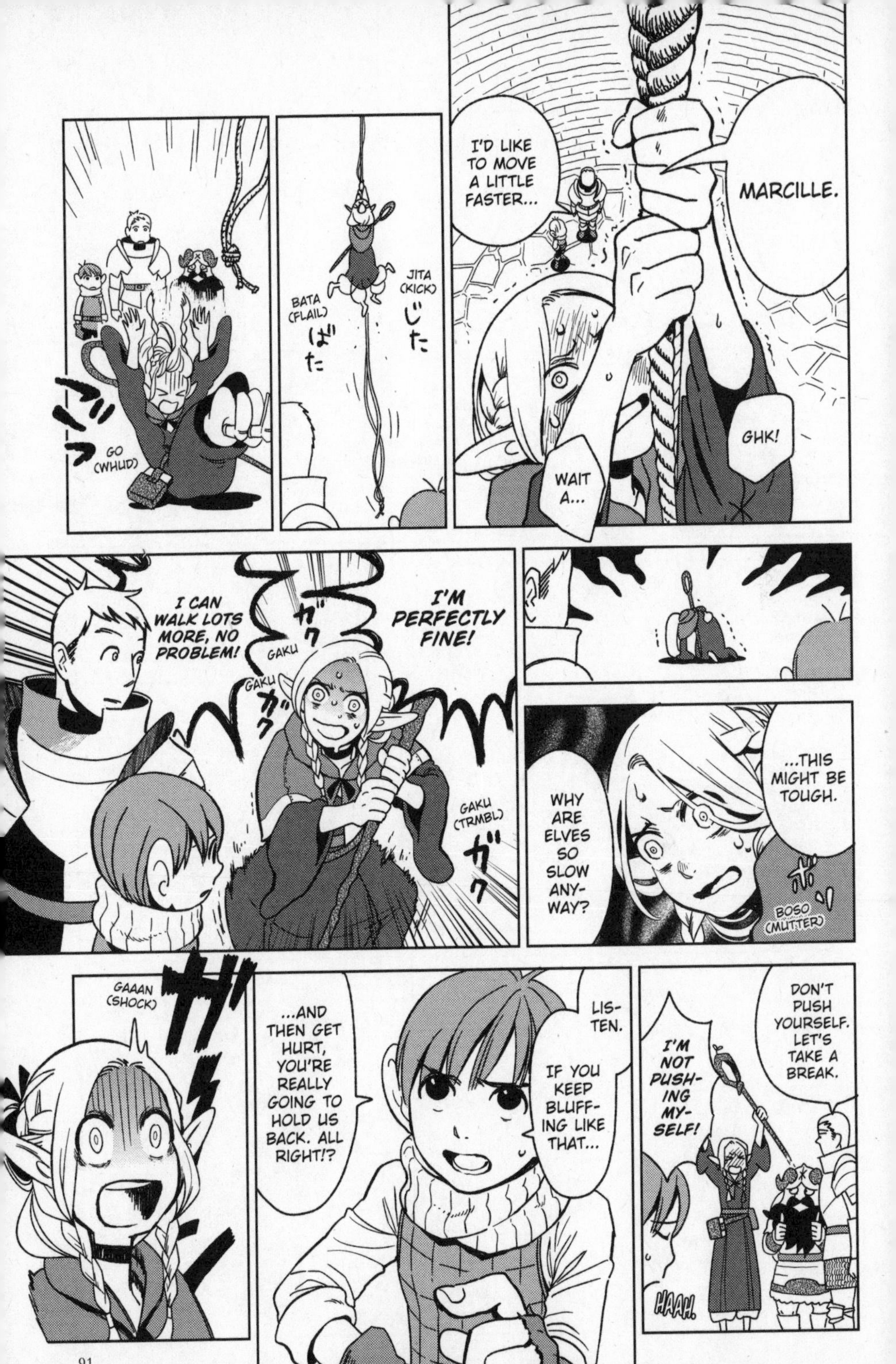
MARCILLE.
I'D LIKE TO MOVE A LITTLE FASTER...
GHK!
WAIT A...
JITA (KICK)
じた
BATA (FLAIL)
ばた
GO (WHUD)
...THIS MIGHT BE TOUGH.
WHY ARE ELVES SO SLOW ANY-WAY?
BOSO (MUTTER)
I'M PERFECTLY FINE!
GAKU
ガク
I CAN WALK LOTS MORE, NO PROBLEM!
GAKU
ガク
GAKU (TRMBL)
ガク
DON'T PUSH YOURSELF. LET'S TAKE A BREAK.
I'M NOT PUSH-ING MY-SELF!
HAAH.
LIS-TEN.
IF YOU KEEP BLUFF-ING LIKE THAT...
...AND THEN GET HURT, YOU'RE REALLY GOING TO HOLD US BACK. ALL RIGHT!?
GAAAN (SHOCK)

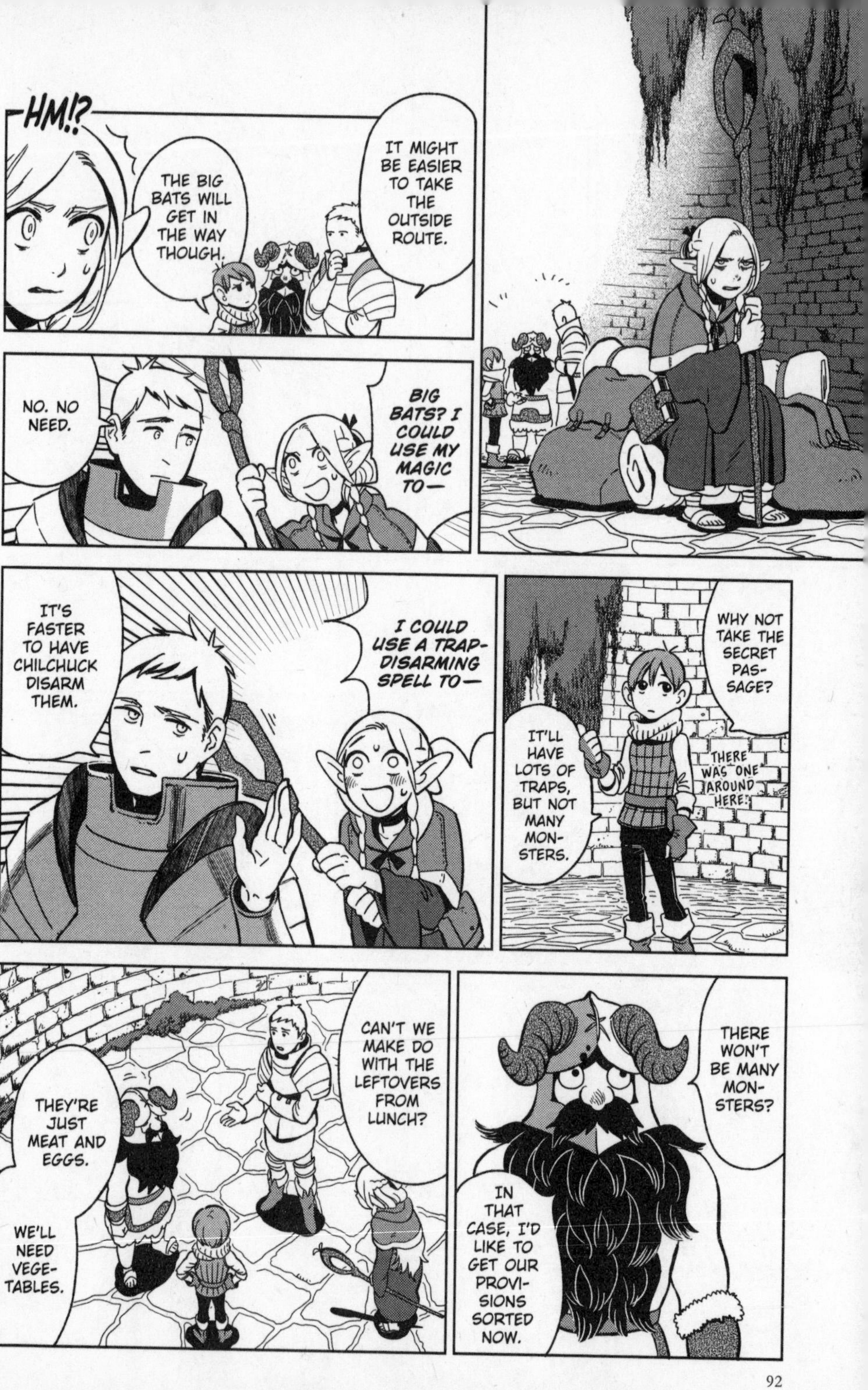
IT MIGHT BE EASIER TO TAKE THE OUTSIDE ROUTE.
THE BIG BATS WILL GET IN THE WAY THOUGH.
HM!?
BIG BATS? I COULD USE MY MAGIC TO—
NO. NO NEED.
WHY NOT TAKE THE SECRET PASSAGE?
IT'LL HAVE LOTS OF TRAPS, BUT NOT MANY MONSTERS.
THERE WAS ONE AROUND HERE.
I COULD USE A TRAP-DISARMING SPELL TO—
IT'S FASTER TO HAVE CHILCHUCK DISARM THEM.
THERE WON'T BE MANY MONSTERS?
IN THAT CASE, I'D LIKE TO GET OUR PROVISIONS SORTED NOW.
CAN'T WE MAKE DO WITH THE LEFTOVERS FROM LUNCH?
THEY'RE JUST MEAT AND EGGS.
WE'LL NEED VEGETABLES.

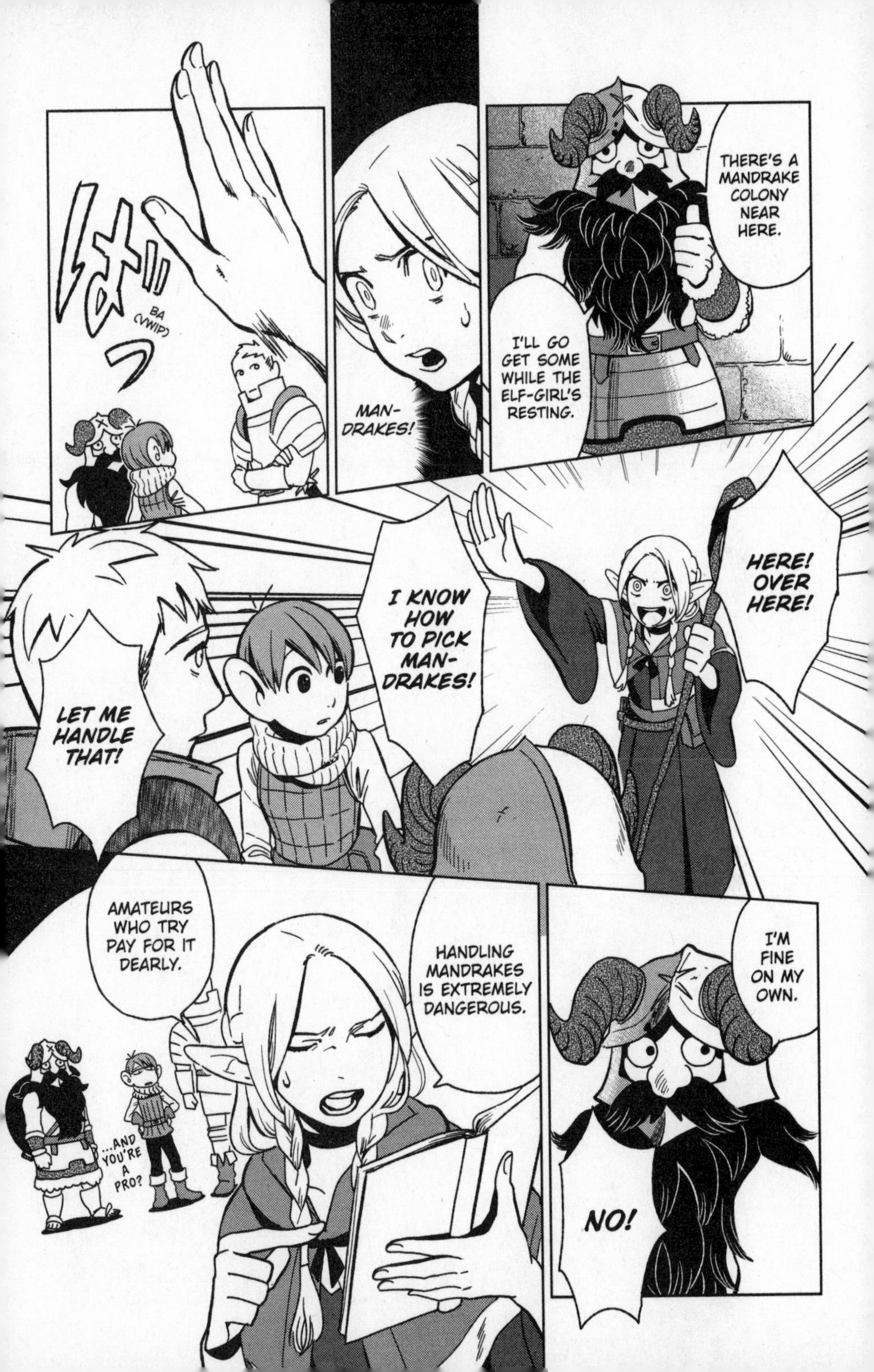
THERE'S A MANDRAKE COLONY NEAR HERE.
I'LL GO GET SOME WHILE THE ELF-GIRL'S RESTING.
MAN-DRAKES!
はっ
BA (VWIP)
HERE! OVER HERE!
I KNOW HOW TO PICK MAN-DRAKES!
LET ME HANDLE THAT!
I'M FINE ON MY OWN.
NO!
HANDLING MANDRAKES IS EXTREMELY DANGEROUS.
AMATEURS WHO TRY PAY FOR IT DEARLY.
...AND YOU'RE A PRO?

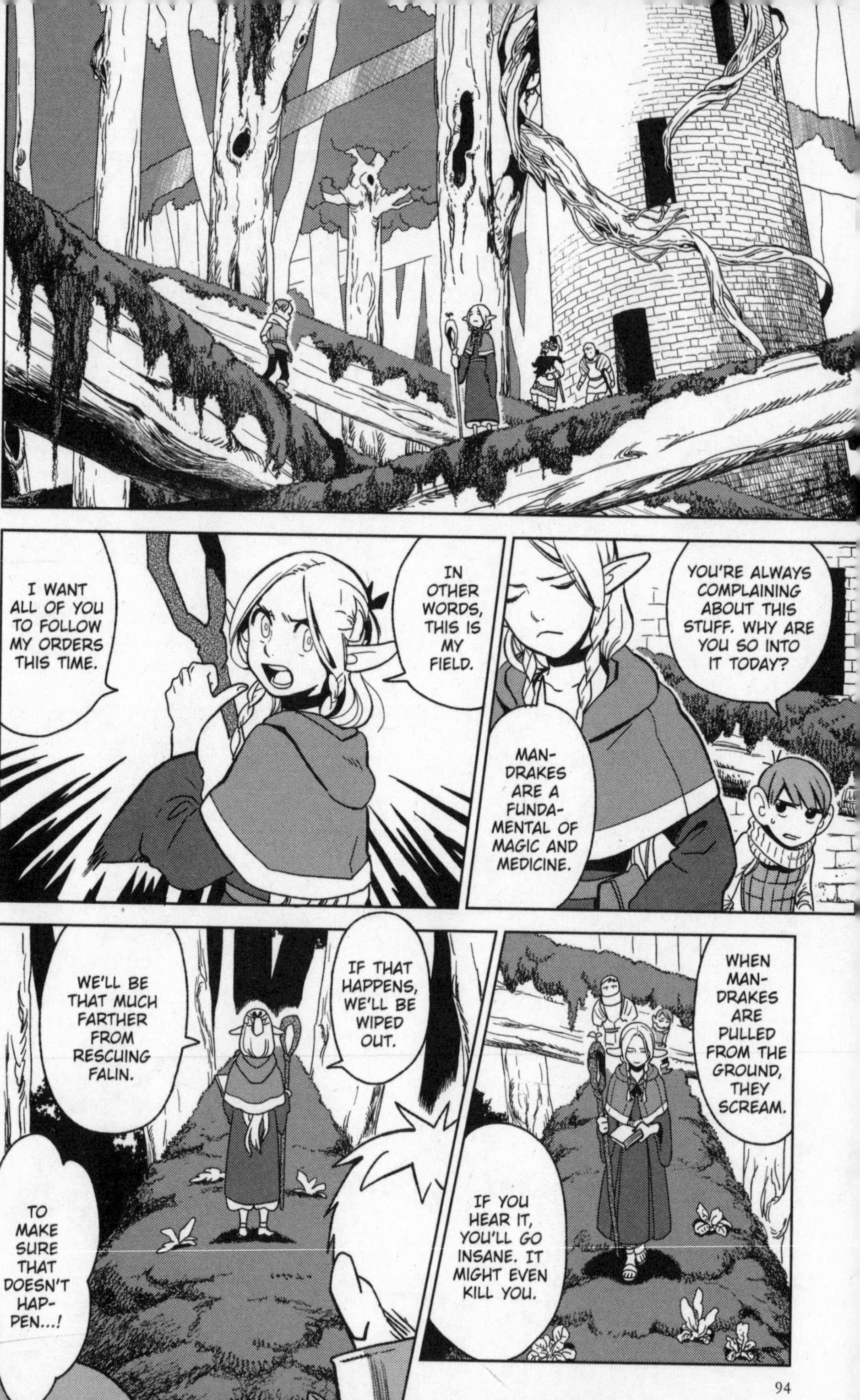
YOU'RE ALWAYS COMPLAINING ABOUT THIS STUFF. WHY ARE YOU SO INTO IT TODAY?
MANDRAKES ARE A FUNDAMENTAL OF MAGIC AND MEDICINE.
IN OTHER WORDS, THIS IS MY FIELD.
I WANT ALL OF YOU TO FOLLOW MY ORDERS THIS TIME.
WHEN MANDRAKES ARE PULLED FROM THE GROUND, THEY SCREAM.
IF YOU HEAR IT, YOU'LL GO INSANE. IT MIGHT EVEN KILL YOU.
IF THAT HAPPENS, WE'LL BE WIPED OUT.
WE'LL BE THAT MUCH FARTHER FROM RESCUING FALIN.
TO MAKE SURE THAT DOESN'T HAPPEN...!

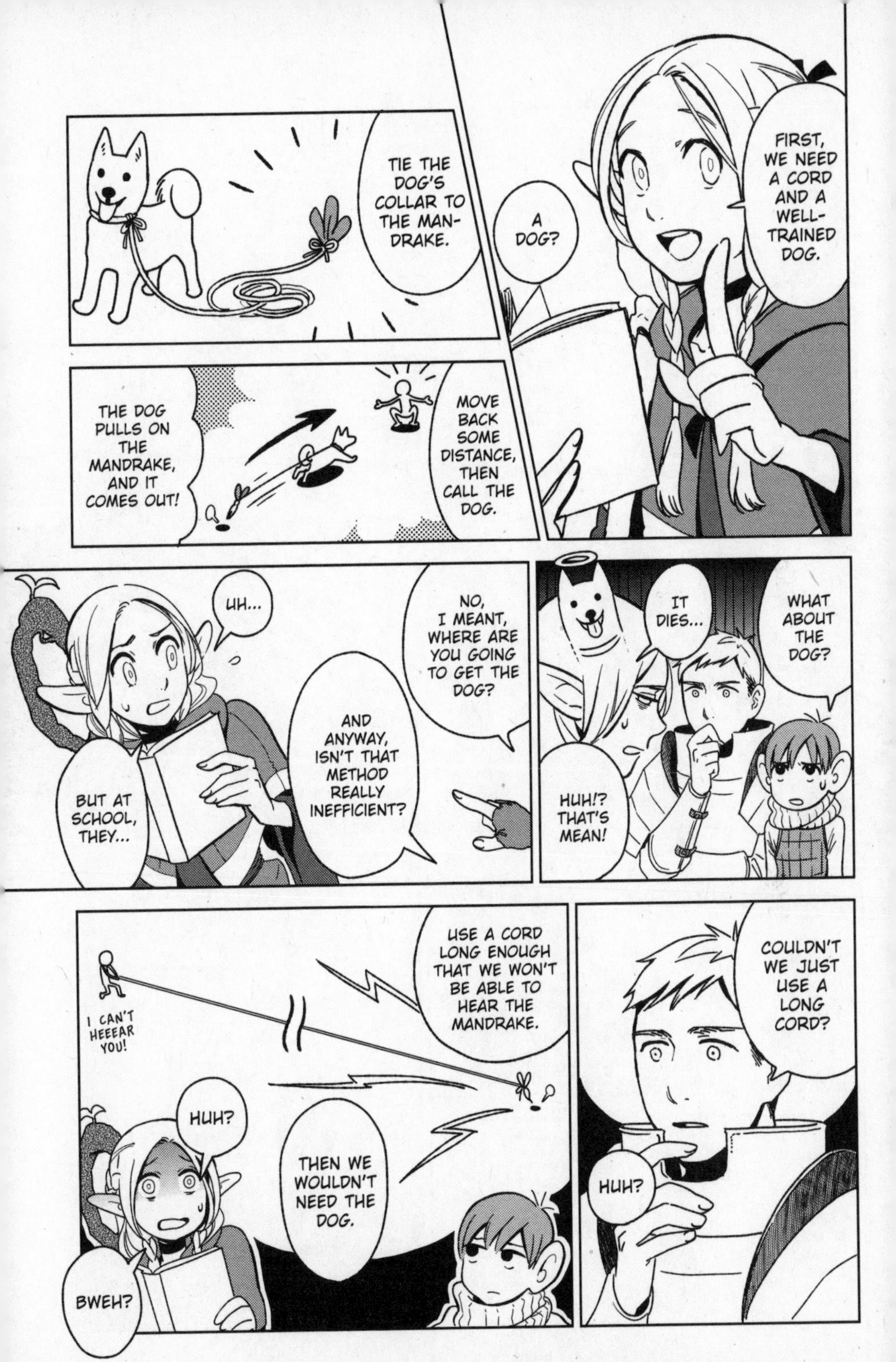
FIRST, WE NEED A CORD AND A WELL-TRAINED DOG.
A DOG?
TIE THE DOG'S COLLAR TO THE MAN-DRAKE.
MOVE BACK SOME DISTANCE, THEN CALL THE DOG.
THE DOG PULLS ON THE MANDRAKE, AND IT COMES OUT!
WHAT ABOUT THE DOG?
IT DIES...
HUH!? THAT'S MEAN!
NO, I MEANT, WHERE ARE YOU GOING TO GET THE DOG?
AND ANYWAY, ISN'T THAT METHOD REALLY INEFFICIENT?
UH...
BUT AT SCHOOL, THEY...
COULDN'T WE JUST USE A LONG CORD?
HUH?
USE A CORD LONG ENOUGH THAT WE WON'T BE ABLE TO HEAR THE MANDRAKE.
I CAN'T HEEEAR YOU!
HUH?
THEN WE WOULDN'T NEED THE DOG.
BWEH?

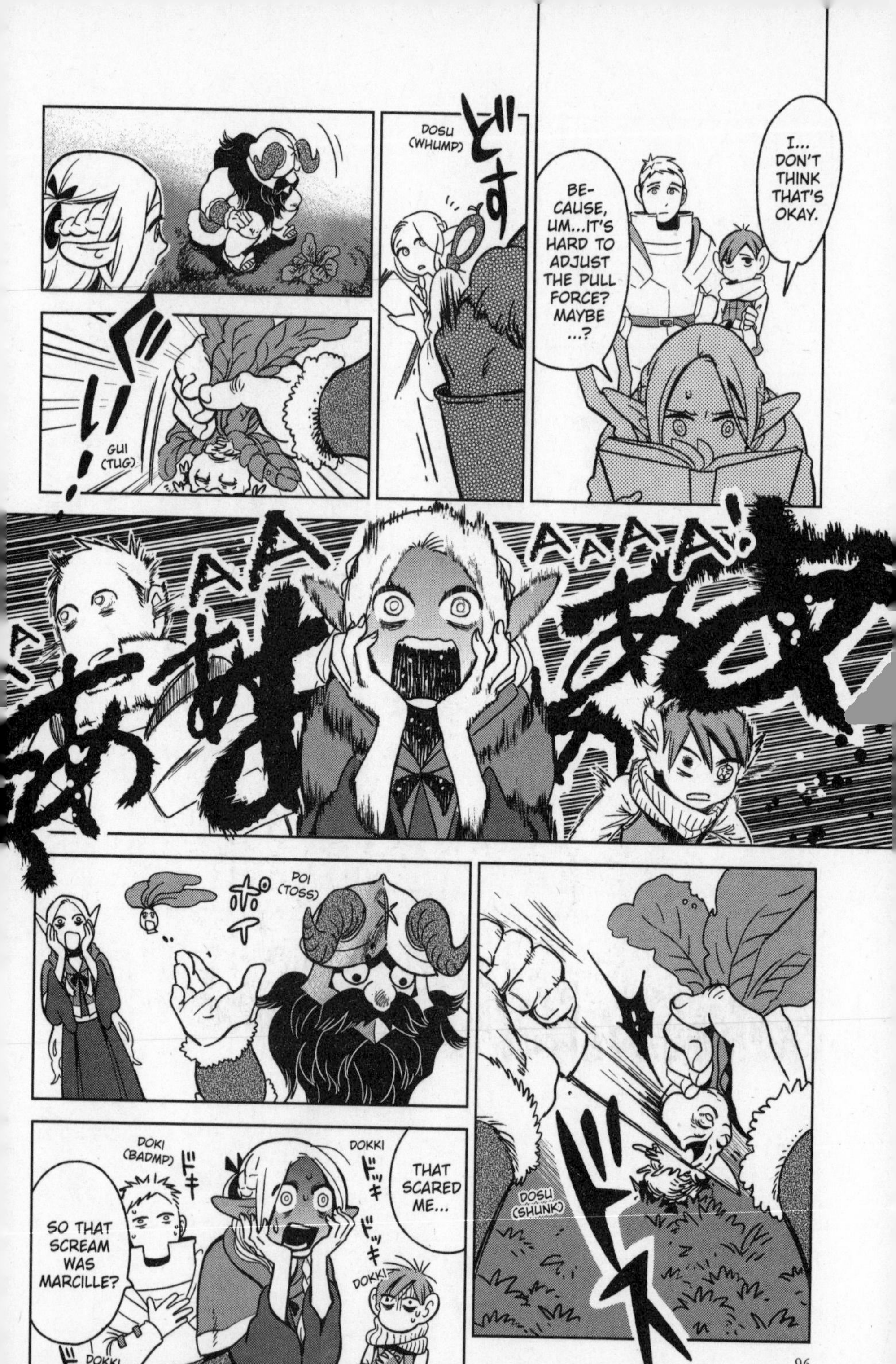

I... DON'T THINK THAT'S OKAY.
BE-CAUSE, UM...IT'S HARD TO ADJUST THE PULL FORCE? MAYBE ...?
どす
DOSU (WHUMP)
ぐい!
GUI (TUG)
AAAAAAAAA!
ドス
DOSU (SHUNK)
ポイ
POI (TOSS)
THAT SCARED ME...
ドッキ
DOKKI
ドキ
DOKI (BADMP)
SO THAT SCREAM WAS MARCILLE?
ドッキ
DOKKI
ドッキ
DOKKI

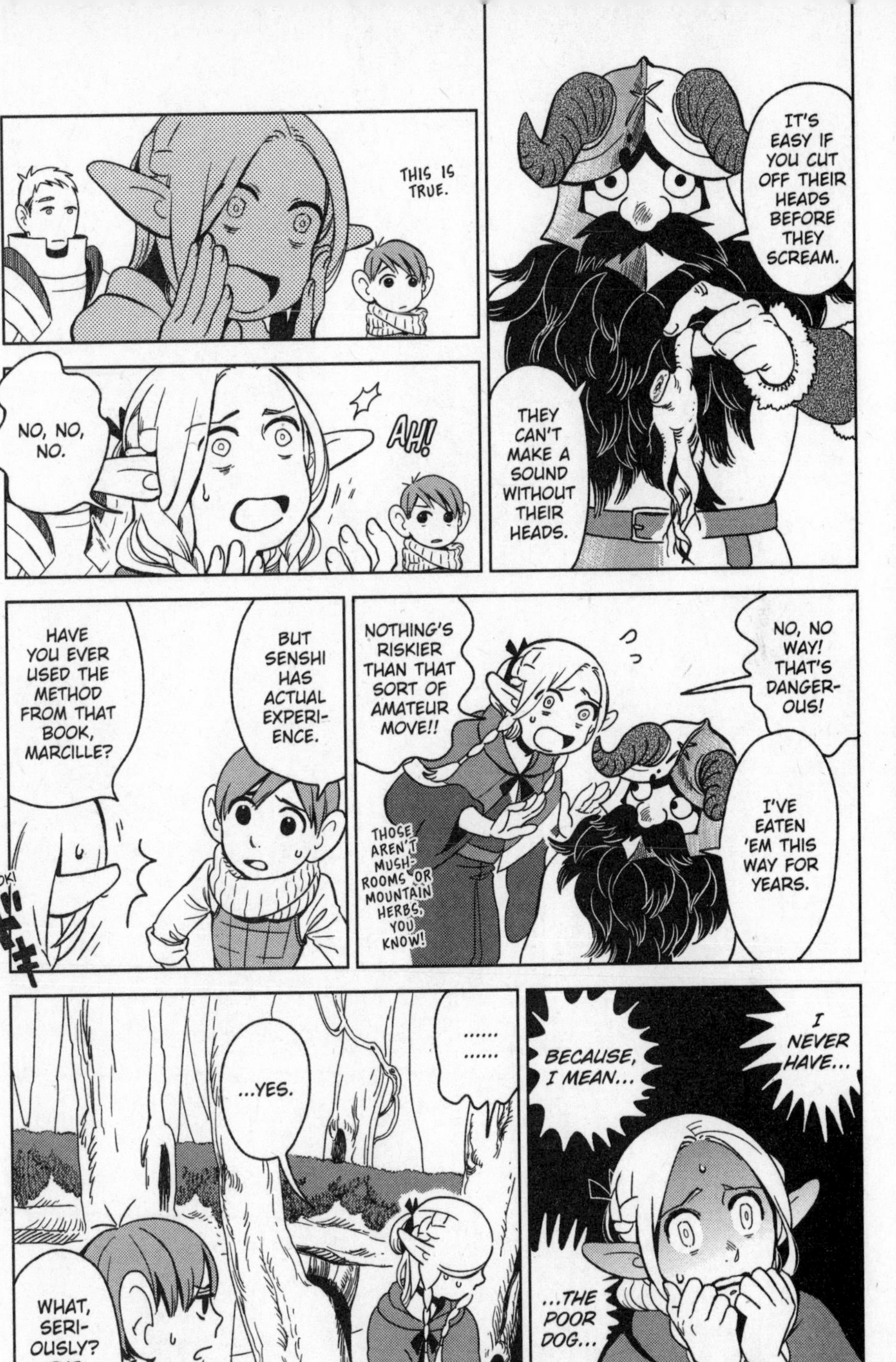
IT'S EASY IF YOU CUT OFF THEIR HEADS BEFORE THEY SCREAM.
THEY CAN'T MAKE A SOUND WITHOUT THEIR HEADS.
THIS IS TRUE.
AH!
NO, NO, NO.
NO, NO WAY! THAT'S DANGER-OUS!
I'VE EATEN 'EM THIS WAY FOR YEARS.
NOTHING'S RISKIER THAN THAT SORT OF AMATEUR MOVE!!
THOSE AREN'T MUSH-ROOMS OR MOUNTAIN HERBS, YOU KNOW!
BUT SENSHI HAS ACTUAL EXPERI-ENCE.
HAVE YOU EVER USED THE METHOD FROM THAT BOOK, MARCILLE?
DOKI
I NEVER HAVE...
BECAUSE, I MEAN...
...THE POOR DOG...
......
......
...YES.
WHAT, SERI-OUSLY? THE POOR DOG.

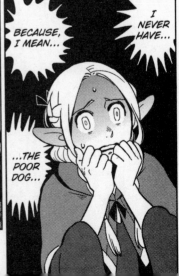

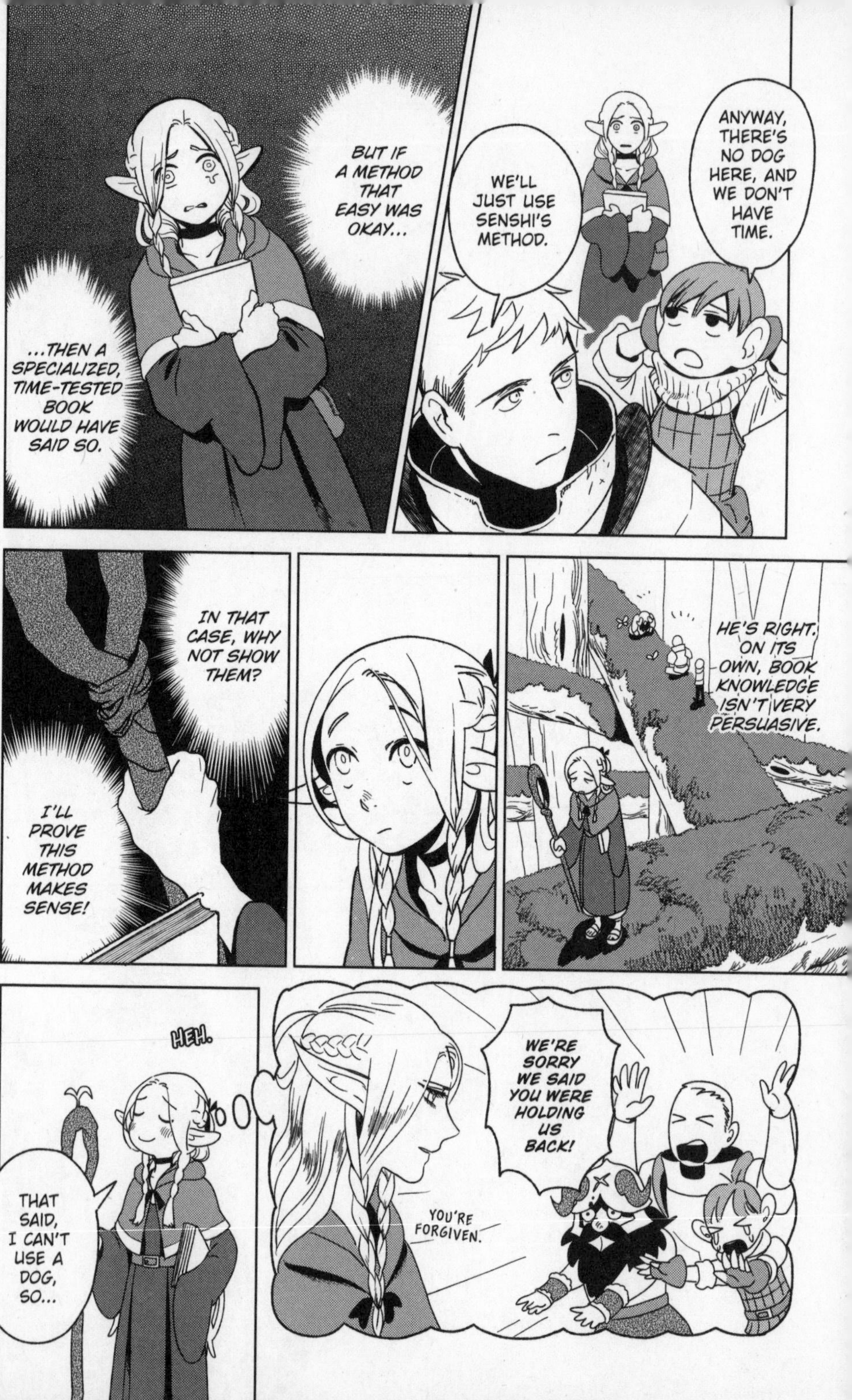
ANYWAY, THERE'S NO DOG HERE, AND WE DON'T HAVE TIME.
WE'LL JUST USE SENSHI'S METHOD.
BUT IF A METHOD THAT EASY WAS OKAY...
...THEN A SPECIALIZED, TIME-TESTED BOOK WOULD HAVE SAID SO.
HE'S RIGHT. ON ITS OWN, BOOK KNOWLEDGE ISN'T VERY PERSUASIVE.
IN THAT CASE, WHY NOT SHOW THEM?
I'LL PROVE THIS METHOD MAKES SENSE!
WE'RE SORRY WE SAID YOU WERE HOLDING US BACK!
YOU'RE FORGIVEN.
HEH.
THAT SAID, I CAN'T USE A DOG, SO...

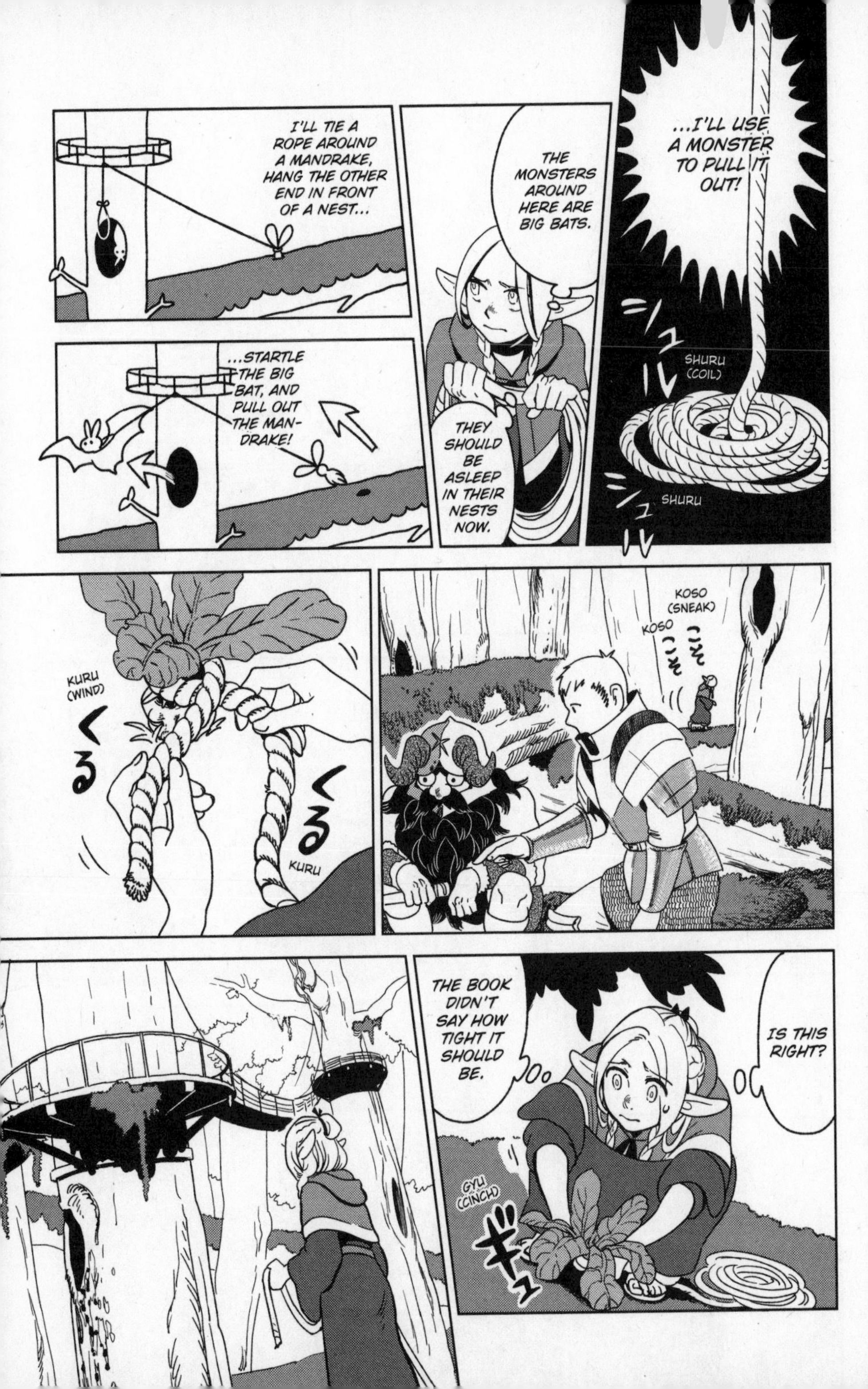
...I'LL USE A MONSTER TO PULL IT OUT!
シュル
SHURU (COIL)
シュル
SHURU
THE MONSTERS AROUND HERE ARE BIG BATS.
THEY SHOULD BE ASLEEP IN THEIR NESTS NOW.
I'LL TIE A ROPE AROUND A MANDRAKE, HANG THE OTHER END IN FRONT OF A NEST...
...STARTLE THE BIG BAT, AND PULL OUT THE MAN-DRAKE!
KOSO (SNEAK)
こそ
KOSO
こそ
KURU (WIND)
くる
くる
KURU
THE BOOK DIDN'T SAY HOW TIGHT IT SHOULD BE.
IS THIS RIGHT?
GYU (CINCH)
ギュ

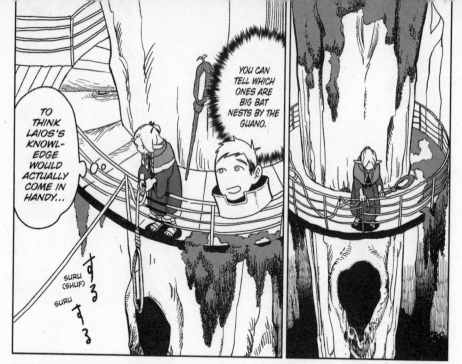

YOU CAN TELL WHICH ONES ARE BIG BAT NESTS BY THE GUANO.
TO THINK LAIOS'S KNOWL-EDGE WOULD ACTUALLY COME IN HANDY...
SURU (SHUF) する
SURU する
SO...
...WHERE CAN I GO TO AVOID HEARING THE SCREAM?
THAT TOWER!
HUFF!
HUFF!
HYOKO (POKE) ひょこ

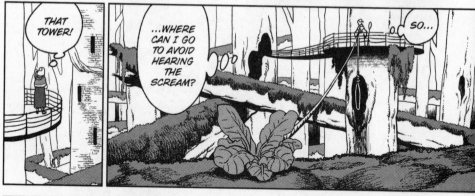

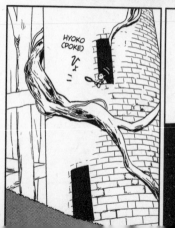

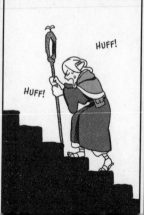

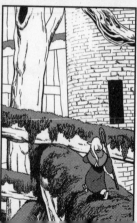

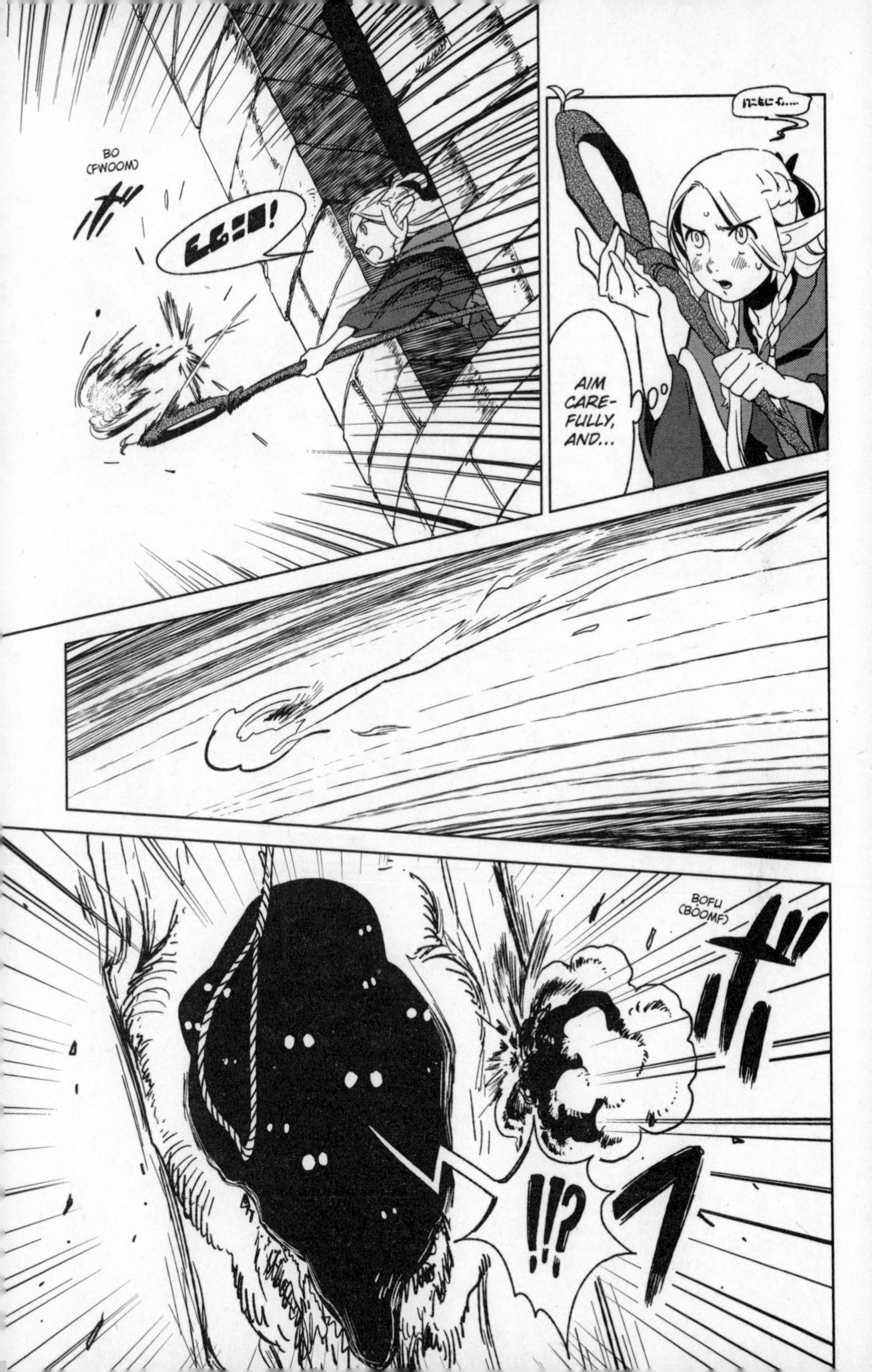
AIM CAREFULLY, AND...
BO (FWOOM)
BOFU (BOOMF)
!!?

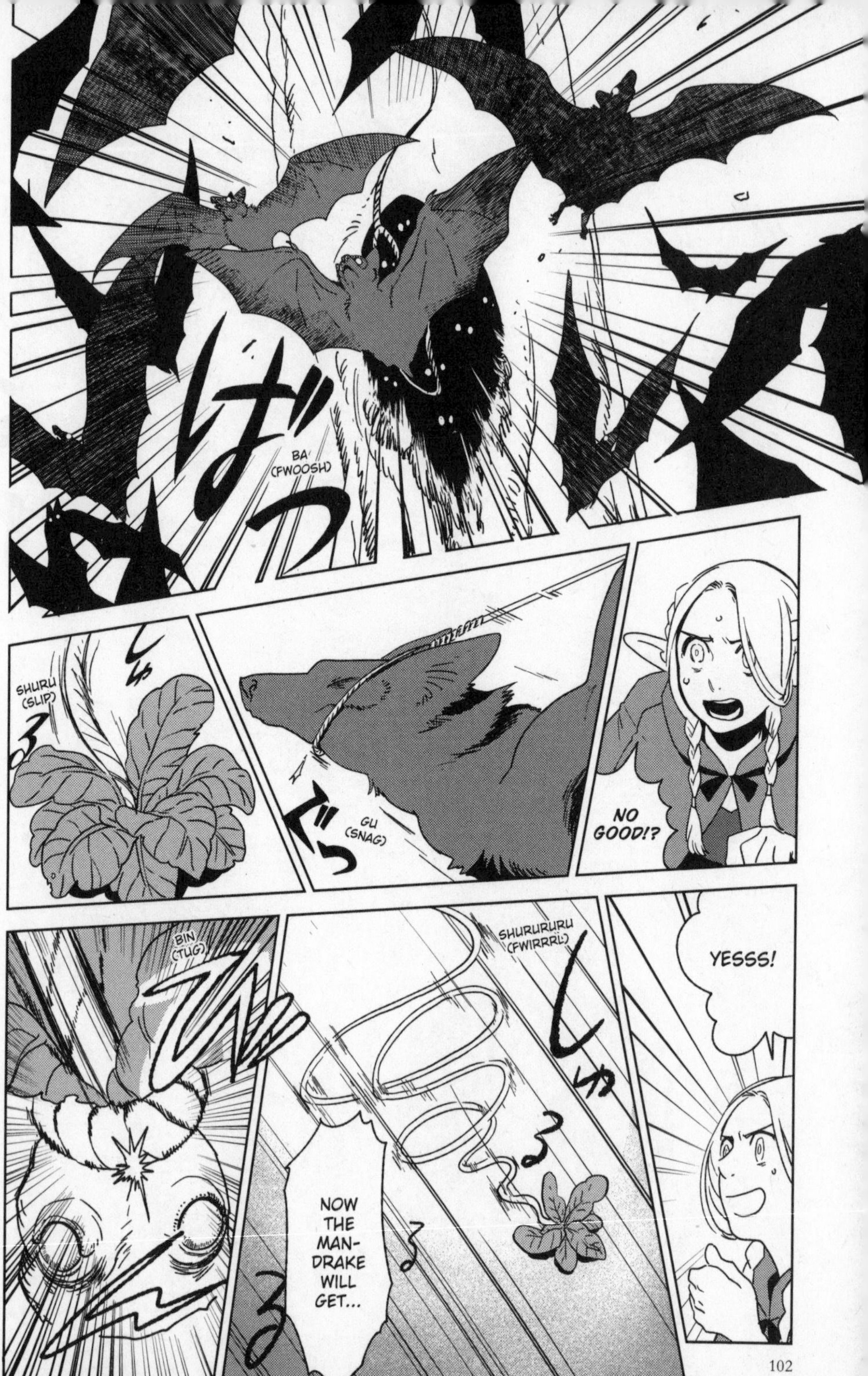
BA
(FWOOSH)
NO GOOD!?
GU
(SNAG)
SHURU
(SLIP)
YESSS!
SHURURURU
(FWIRRRL!)
NOW THE MAN-DRAKE WILL GET...
BIN
(TUG)

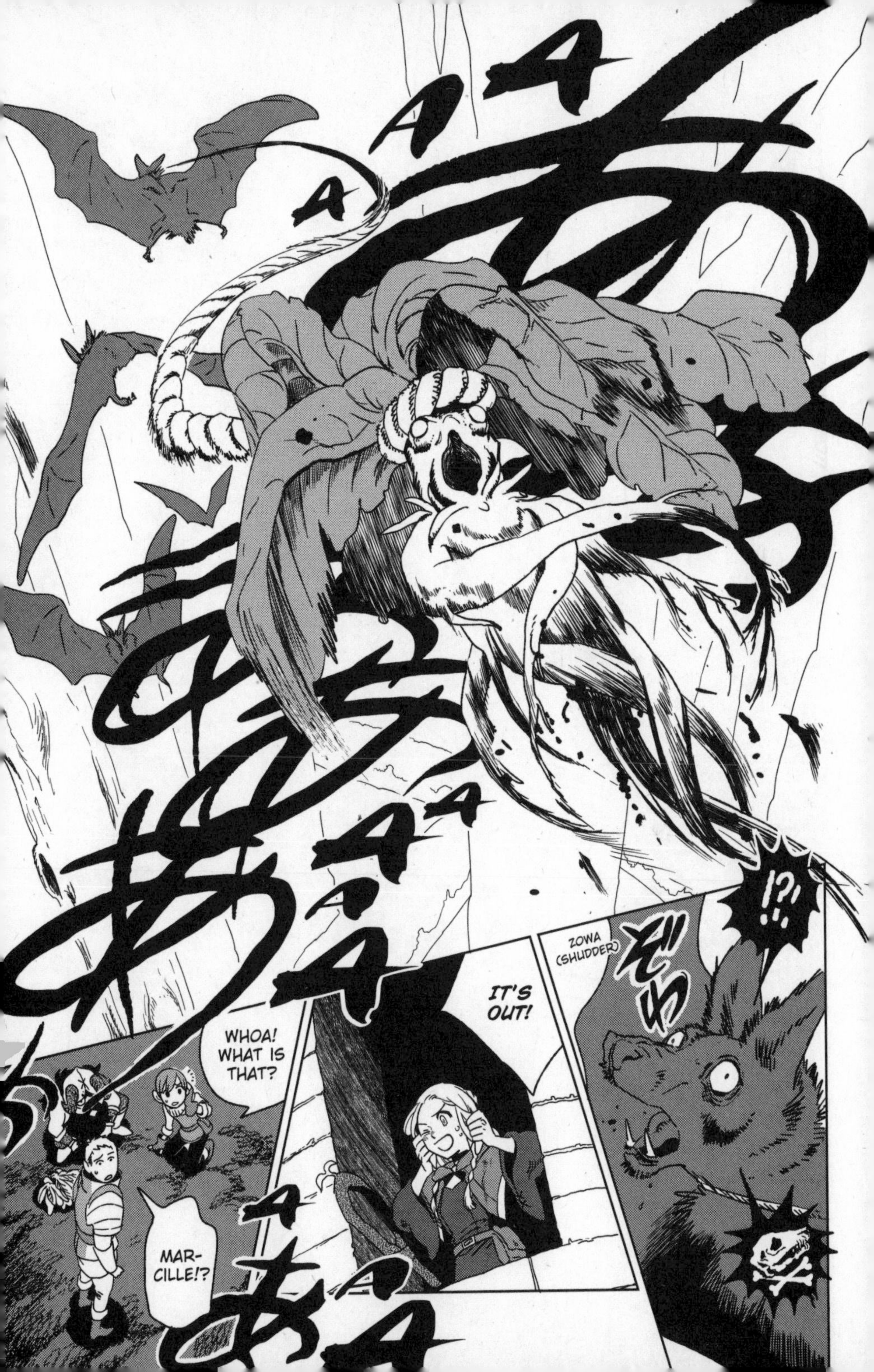

AAAA
AAAA
!?!
ZOWA (SHUDDER)
IT'S OUT!
WHOA! WHAT IS THAT?
MAR-CILLE!?
AAA

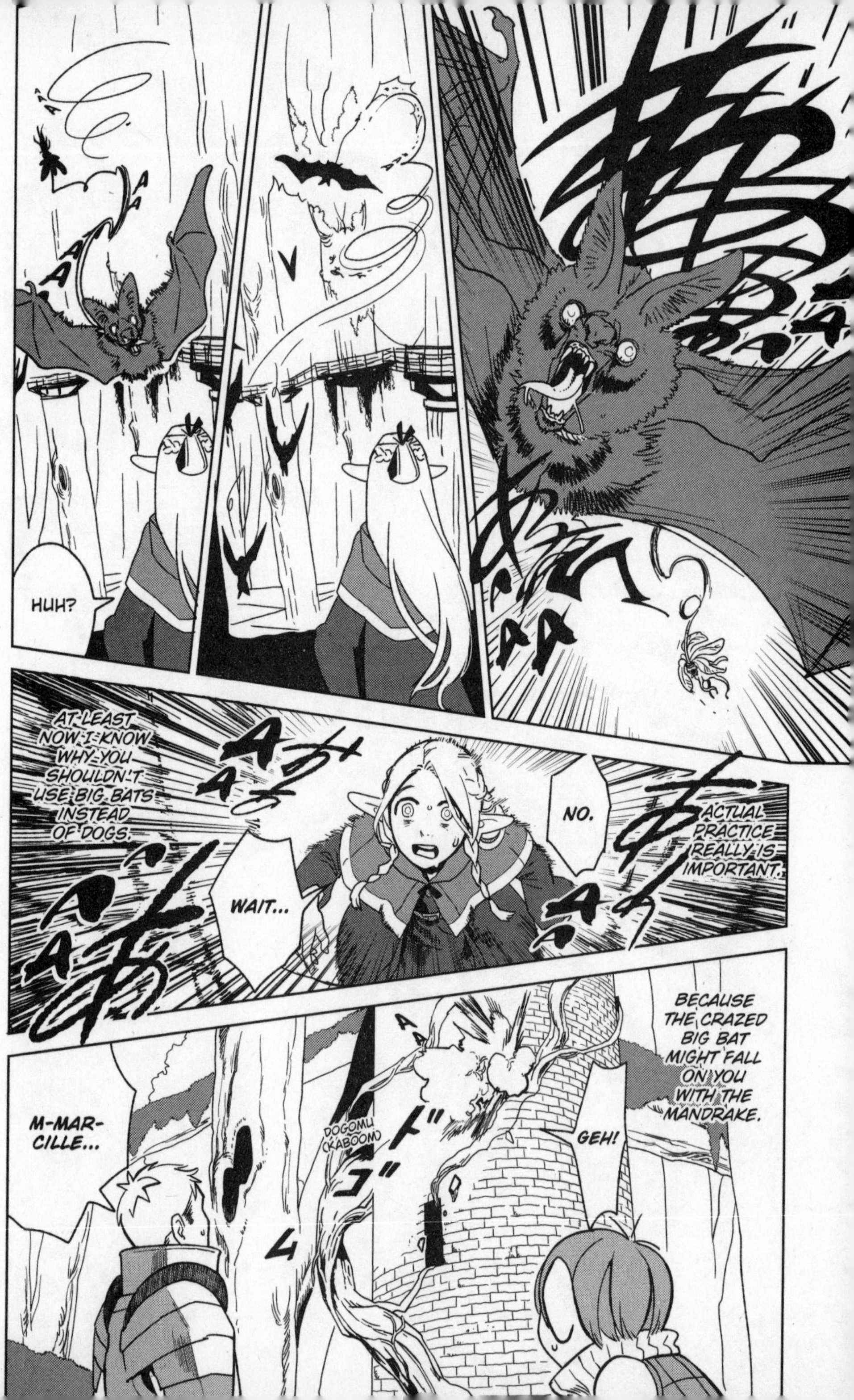
HUH?
ACTUAL PRACTICE REALLY IS IMPORTANT.
NO.
WAIT...
AT LEAST NOW I KNOW WHY YOU SHOULDN'T USE BIG BATS INSTEAD OF DOGS.
BECAUSE THE CRAZED BIG BAT MIGHT FALL ON YOU WITH THE MANDRAKE.
GEH!
DOGOMU (KABOOM)
M-MARCILLE...

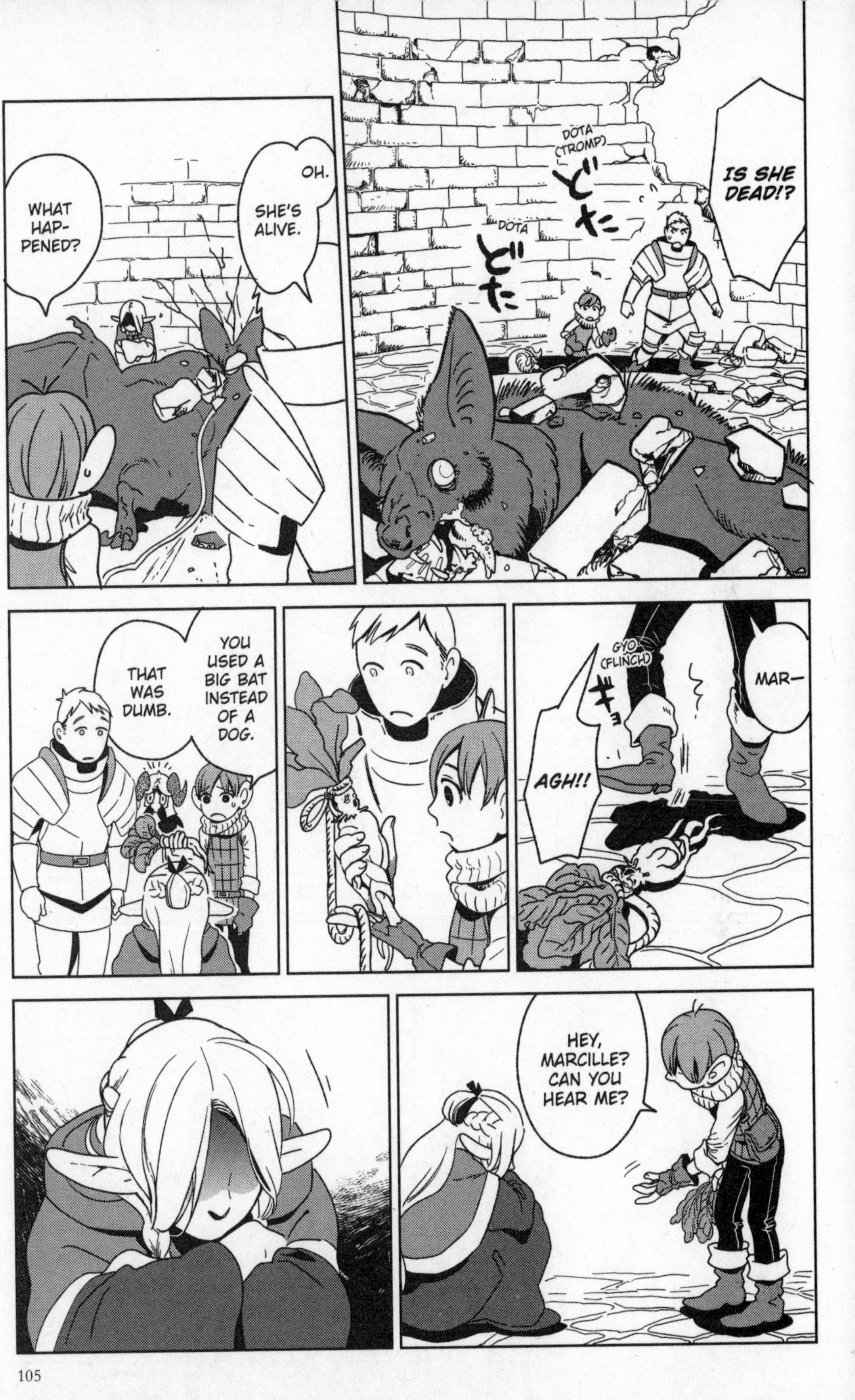
IS SHE DEAD!?
DOTA (TROMP)
どた
DOTA
どた
OH. SHE'S ALIVE.
WHAT HAP-PENED?
MAR—
GYO (FLINCH)
ギョ
AGH!!
YOU USED A BIG BAT INSTEAD OF A DOG.
THAT WAS DUMB.
HEY, MARCILLE? CAN YOU HEAR ME?

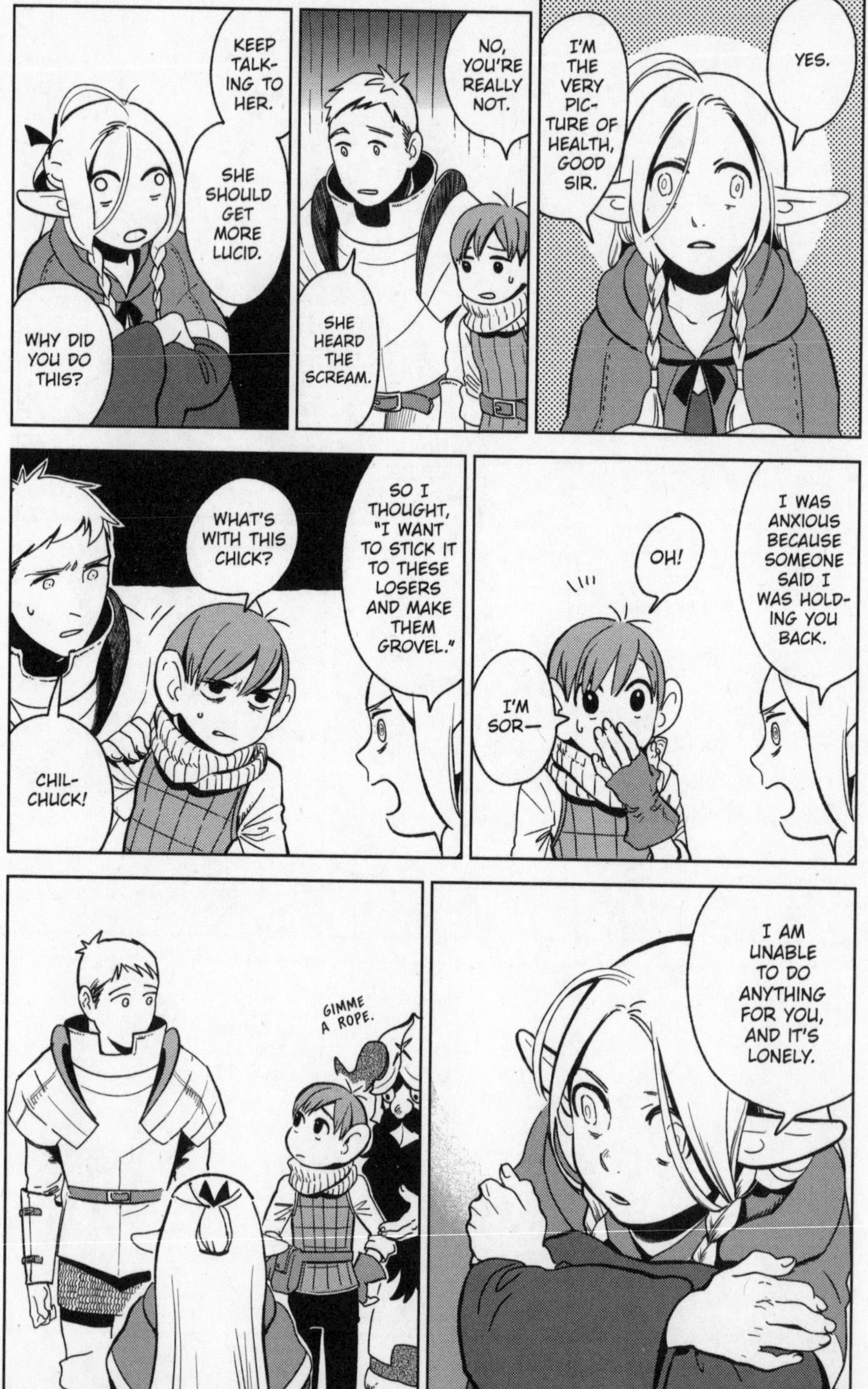
YES.
I'M THE VERY PICTURE OF HEALTH, GOOD SIR.
NO, YOU'RE REALLY NOT.
SHE HEARD THE SCREAM.
KEEP TALKING TO HER.
SHE SHOULD GET MORE LUCID.
WHY DID YOU DO THIS?
I WAS ANXIOUS BECAUSE SOMEONE SAID I WAS HOLDING YOU BACK.
OH!
I'M SOR—
SO I THOUGHT, "I WANT TO STICK IT TO THESE LOSERS AND MAKE THEM GROVEL."
WHAT'S WITH THIS CHICK?
CHILCHUCK!
I AM UNABLE TO DO ANYTHING FOR YOU, AND IT'S LONELY.
GIMME A ROPE.

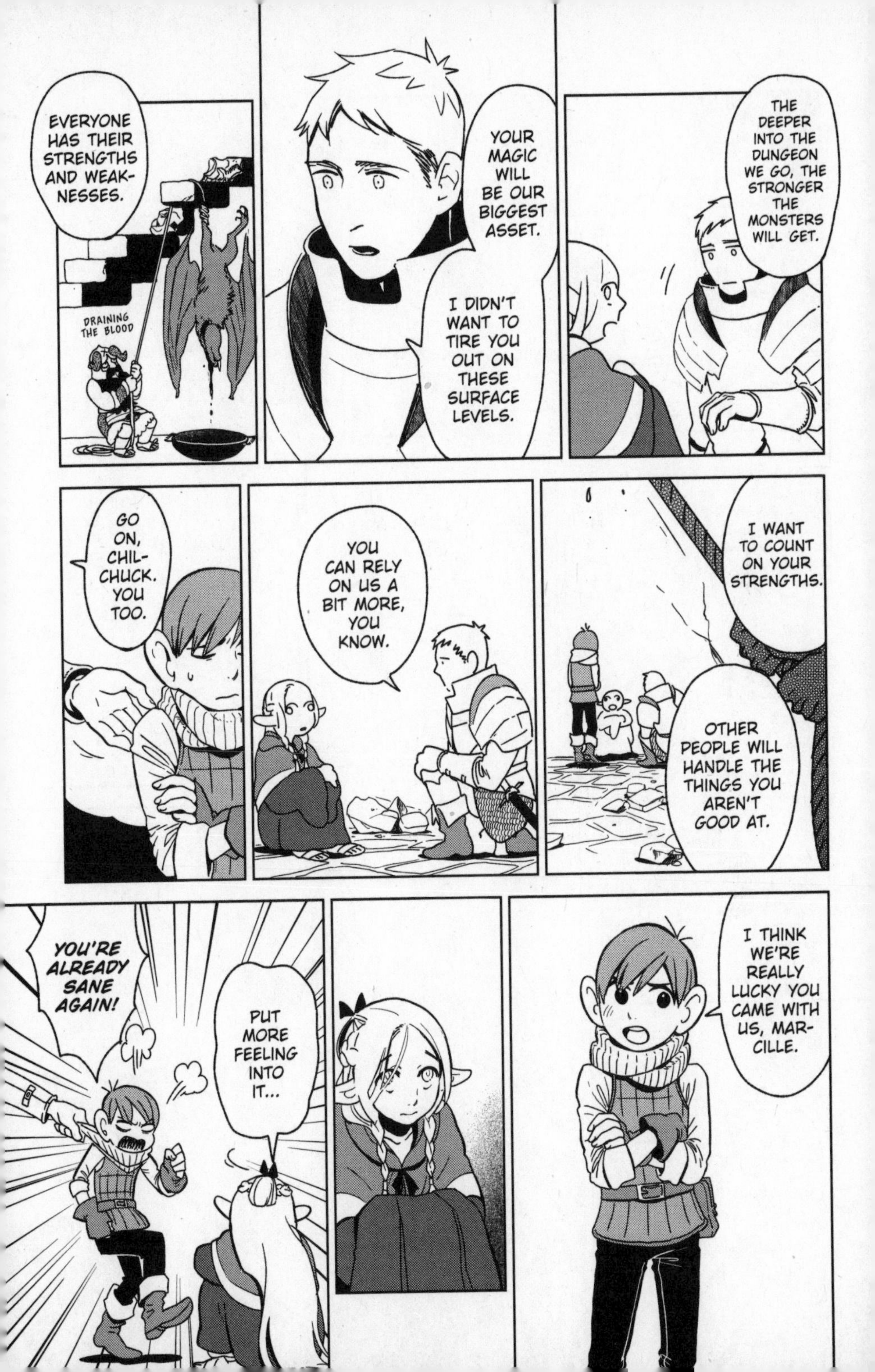
THE DEEPER INTO THE DUNGEON WE GO, THE STRONGER THE MONSTERS WILL GET.
YOUR MAGIC WILL BE OUR BIGGEST ASSET.
I DIDN'T WANT TO TIRE YOU OUT ON THESE SURFACE LEVELS.
EVERYONE HAS THEIR STRENGTHS AND WEAK-NESSES.
DRAINING THE BLOOD
I WANT TO COUNT ON YOUR STRENGTHS.
OTHER PEOPLE WILL HANDLE THE THINGS YOU AREN'T GOOD AT.
YOU CAN RELY ON US A BIT MORE, YOU KNOW.
GO ON, CHIL-CHUCK. YOU TOO.
I THINK WE'RE REALLY LUCKY YOU CAME WITH US, MAR-CILLE.
PUT MORE FEELING INTO IT...
YOU'RE ALREADY SANE AGAIN!

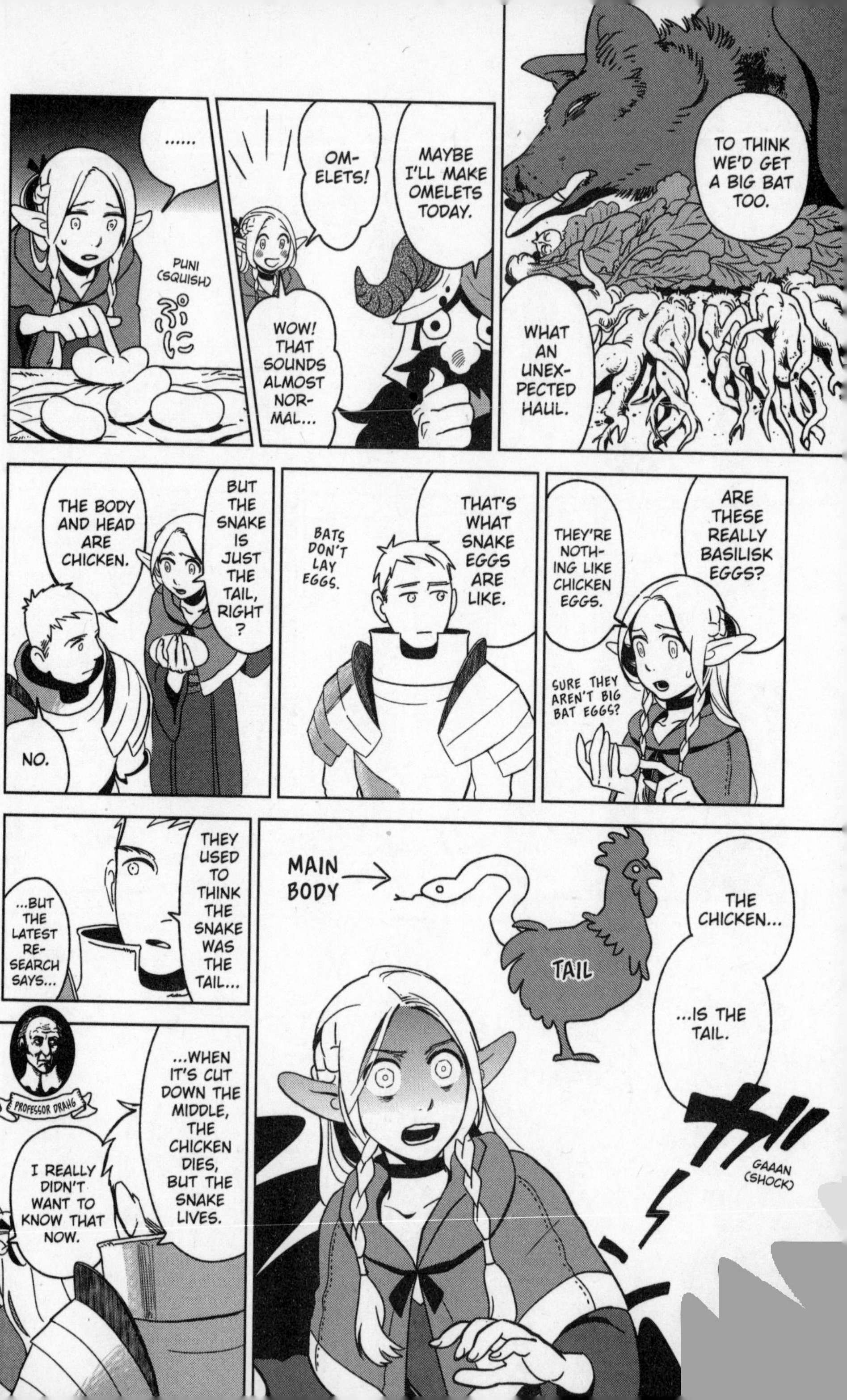
TO THINK WE'D GET A BIG BAT TOO.
WHAT AN UNEXPECTED HAUL.
MAYBE I'LL MAKE OMELETS TODAY.
OM-ELETS!
WOW! THAT SOUNDS ALMOST NOR-MAL...
......
PUNI (SQUISH)
ぷに
ARE THESE REALLY BASILISK EGGS?
THEY'RE NOTH-ING LIKE CHICKEN EGGS.
SURE THEY AREN'T BIG BAT EGGS?
THAT'S WHAT SNAKE EGGS ARE LIKE.
BATS DON'T LAY EGGS.
BUT THE SNAKE IS JUST THE TAIL, RIGHT?
THE BODY AND HEAD ARE CHICKEN.
NO.
THEY USED TO THINK THE SNAKE WAS THE TAIL...
...BUT THE LATEST RE-SEARCH SAYS...
MAIN BODY
TAIL
THE CHICKEN...
...IS THE TAIL.
GAAAN (SHOCK)
PROFESSOR DRAHG
...WHEN IT'S CUT DOWN THE MIDDLE, THE CHICKEN DIES, BUT THE SNAKE LIVES.
I REALLY DIDN'T WANT TO KNOW THAT NOW.

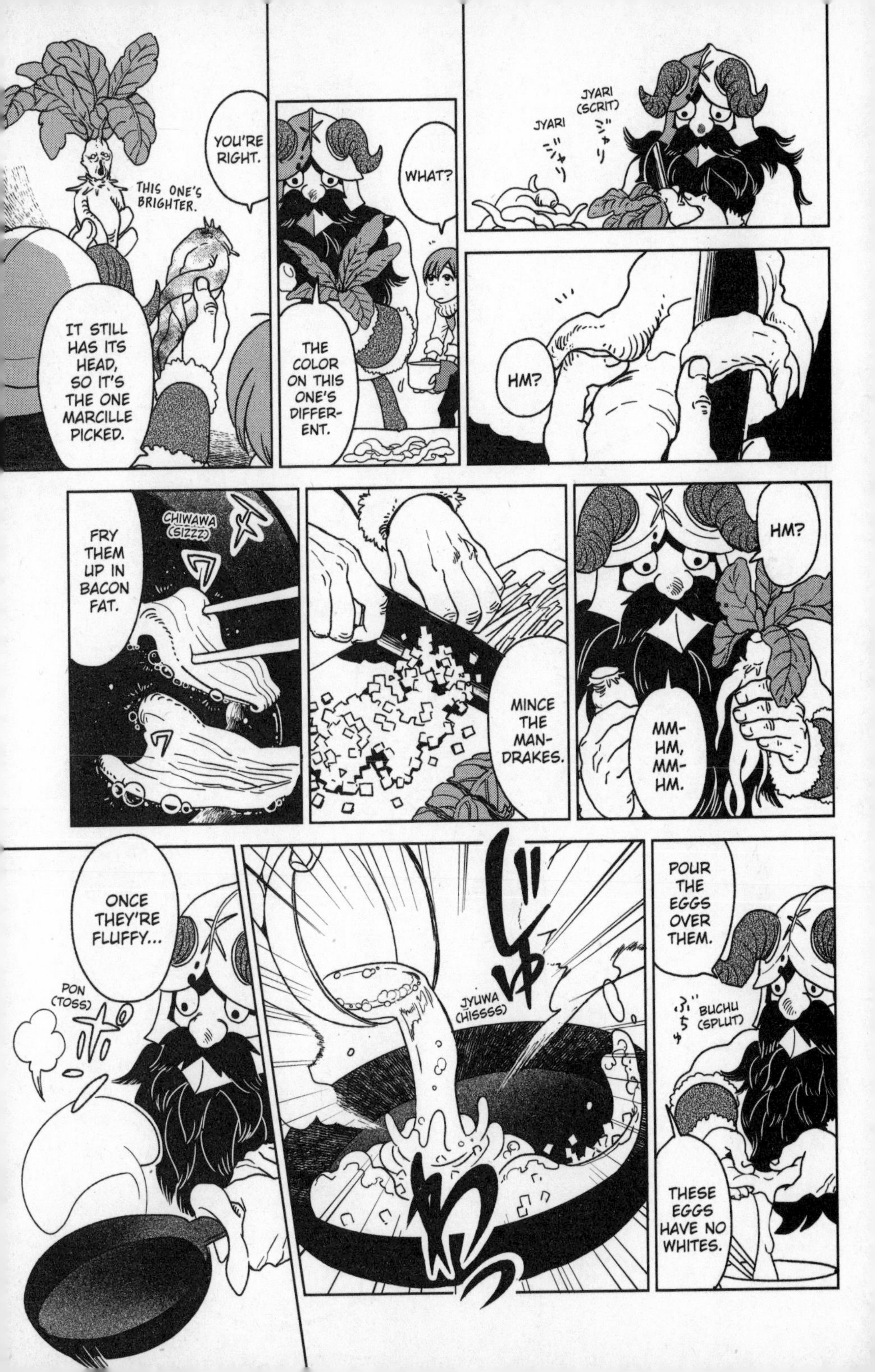
JYARI (SCRIT)
JYARI
ジャリ
ジャリ
HM?
WHAT?
THE COLOR ON THIS ONE'S DIFFER-ENT.
YOU'RE RIGHT.
THIS ONE'S BRIGHTER.
IT STILL HAS ITS HEAD, SO IT'S THE ONE MARCILLE PICKED.
HM?
MM-HM, MM-HM.
MINCE THE MAN-DRAKES.
CHIWAWA (SIZZZ)
FRY THEM UP IN BACON FAT.
POUR THE EGGS OVER THEM.
BUCHU (SPLUT)
THESE EGGS HAVE NO WHITES.
JYUWA (HISSSS)
ONCE THEY'RE FLUFFY...
PON (TOSS)

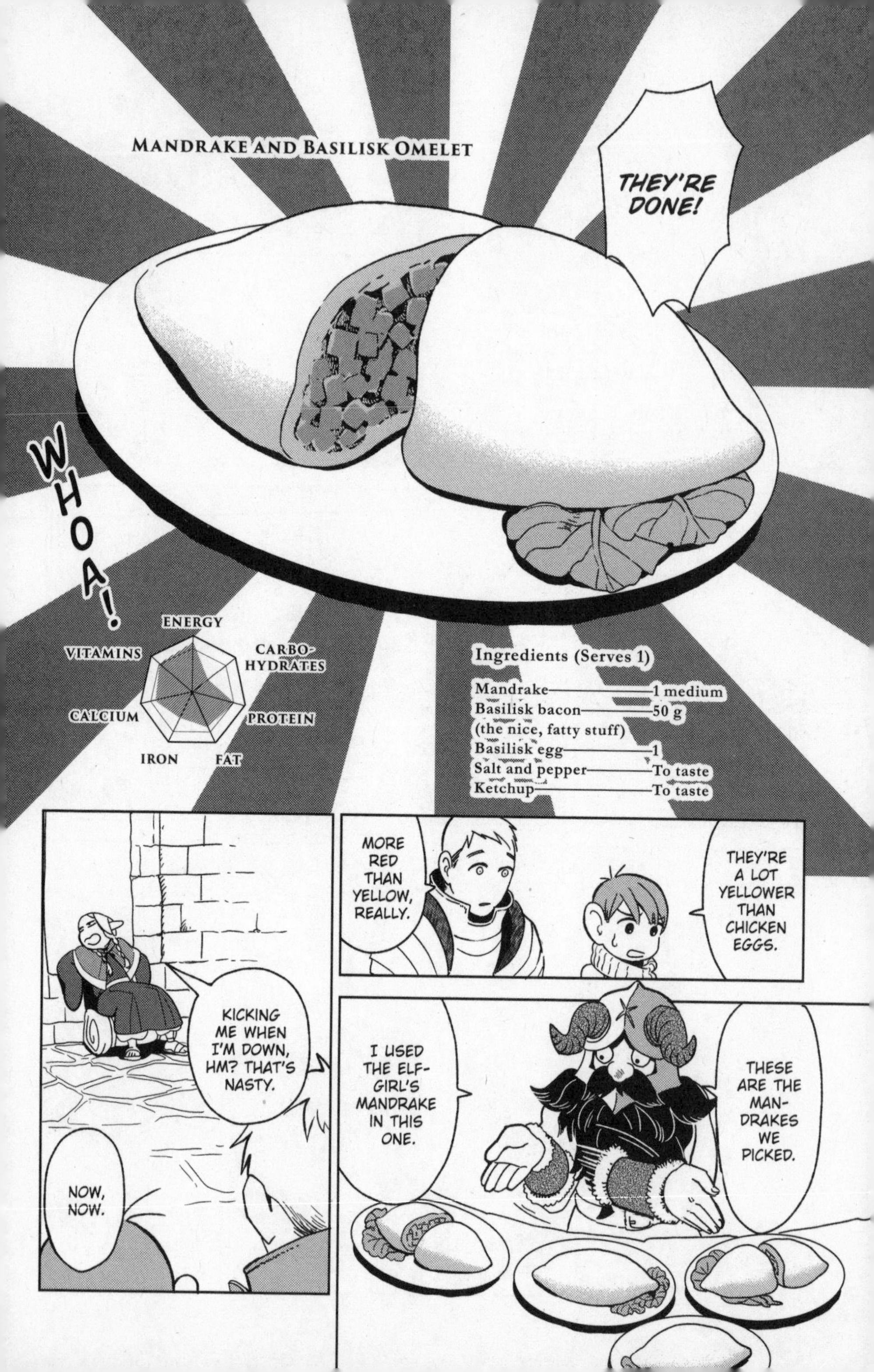
THEY'RE DONE!
MANDRAKE AND BASILISK OMELET
WHOA!
ENERGY
CARBO-HYDRATES
PROTEIN
FAT
IRON
CALCIUM
VITAMINS
Ingredients (Serves 1)
Mandrake—1 medium
Basilisk bacon—50 g
(the nice, fatty stuff)
Basilisk egg—1
Salt and pepper—To taste
Ketchup—To taste
THEY'RE A LOT YELLOWER THAN CHICKEN EGGS.
MORE RED THAN YELLOW, REALLY.
THESE ARE THE MAN-DRAKES WE PICKED.
I USED THE ELF-GIRL'S MANDRAKE IN THIS ONE.
KICKING ME WHEN I'M DOWN, HM? THAT'S NASTY.
NOW, NOW.

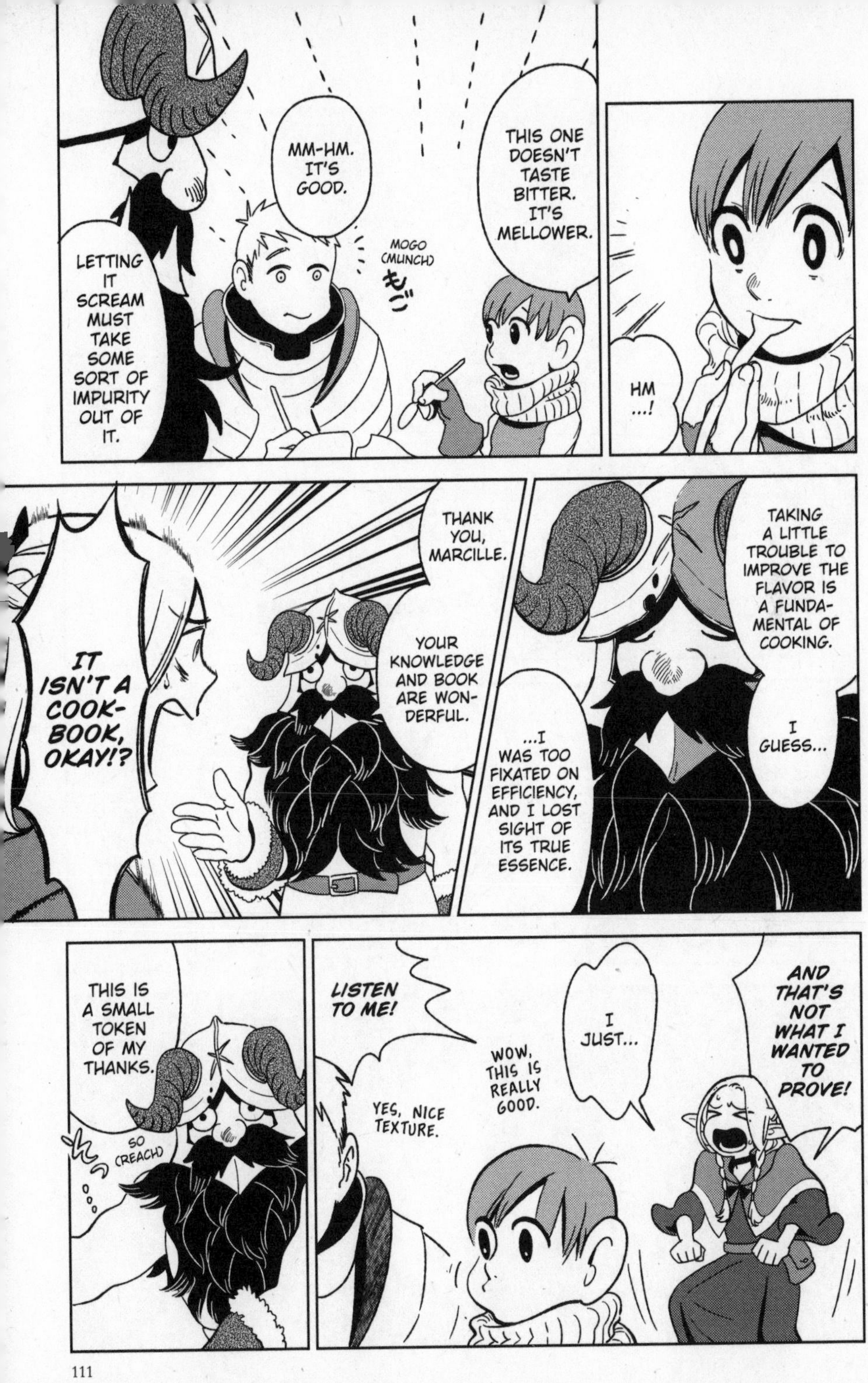
HM ...!
THIS ONE DOESN'T TASTE BITTER. IT'S MELLOWER.
MM-HM. IT'S GOOD.
MOGO (MUNCH)
もご
LETTING IT SCREAM MUST TAKE SOME SORT OF IMPURITY OUT OF IT.
TAKING A LITTLE TROUBLE TO IMPROVE THE FLAVOR IS A FUNDA-MENTAL OF COOKING.
I GUESS...
...I WAS TOO FIXATED ON EFFICIENCY, AND I LOST SIGHT OF ITS TRUE ESSENCE.
THANK YOU, MARCILLE.
YOUR KNOWLEDGE AND BOOK ARE WON-DERFUL.
IT ISN'T A COOK-BOOK, OKAY!?
AND THAT'S NOT WHAT I WANTED TO PROVE!
I JUST...
WOW, THIS IS REALLY GOOD.
LISTEN TO ME!
YES, NICE TEXTURE.
THIS IS A SMALL TOKEN OF MY THANKS.
SO (REACH)

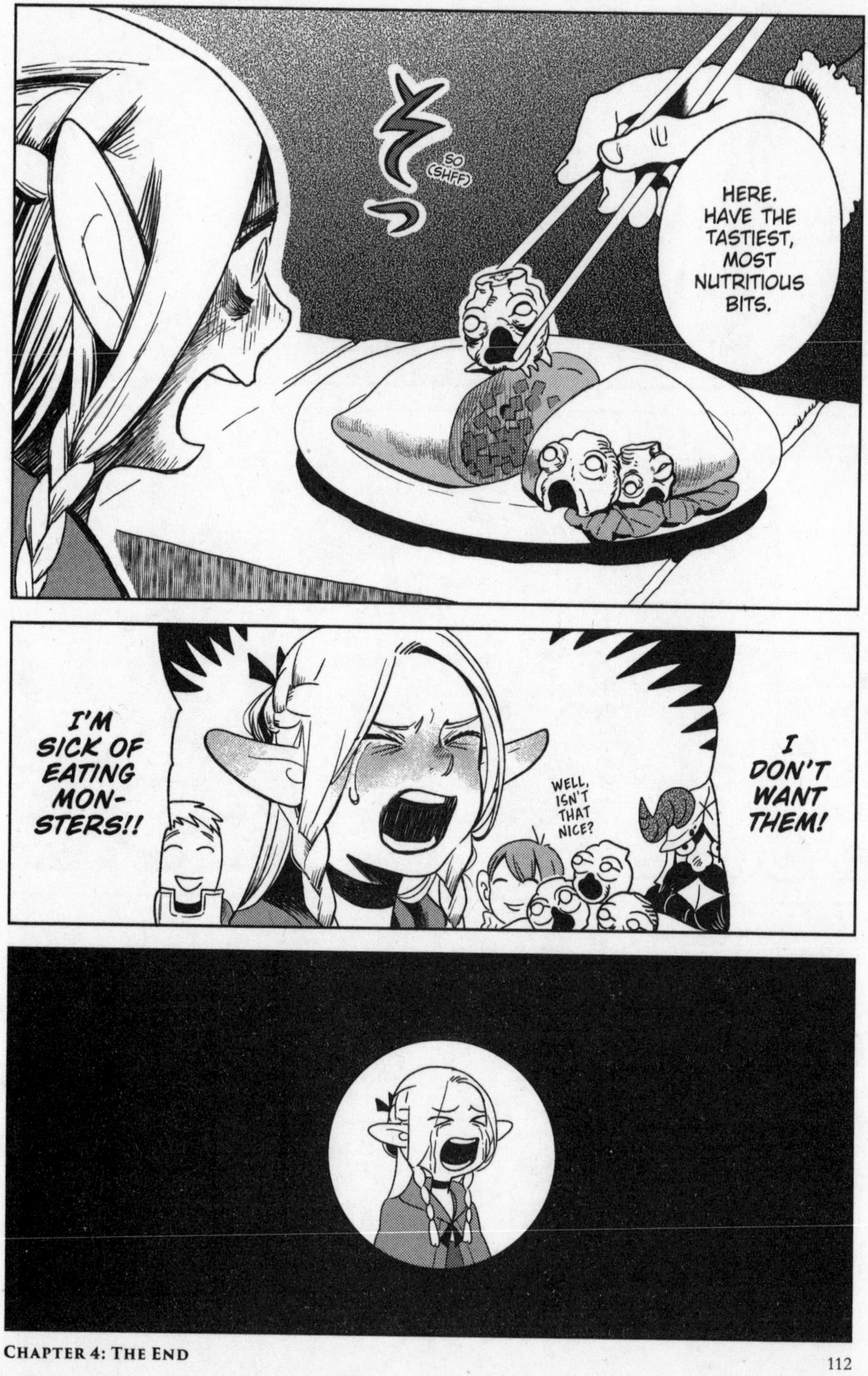
HERE. HAVE THE TASTIEST, MOST NUTRITIOUS BITS.
そっ
SO (SHFF)
I DON'T WANT THEM!
WELL, ISN'T THAT NICE?
I'M SICK OF EATING MON-STERS!!

Chapter 4: The End

5. Kakiage

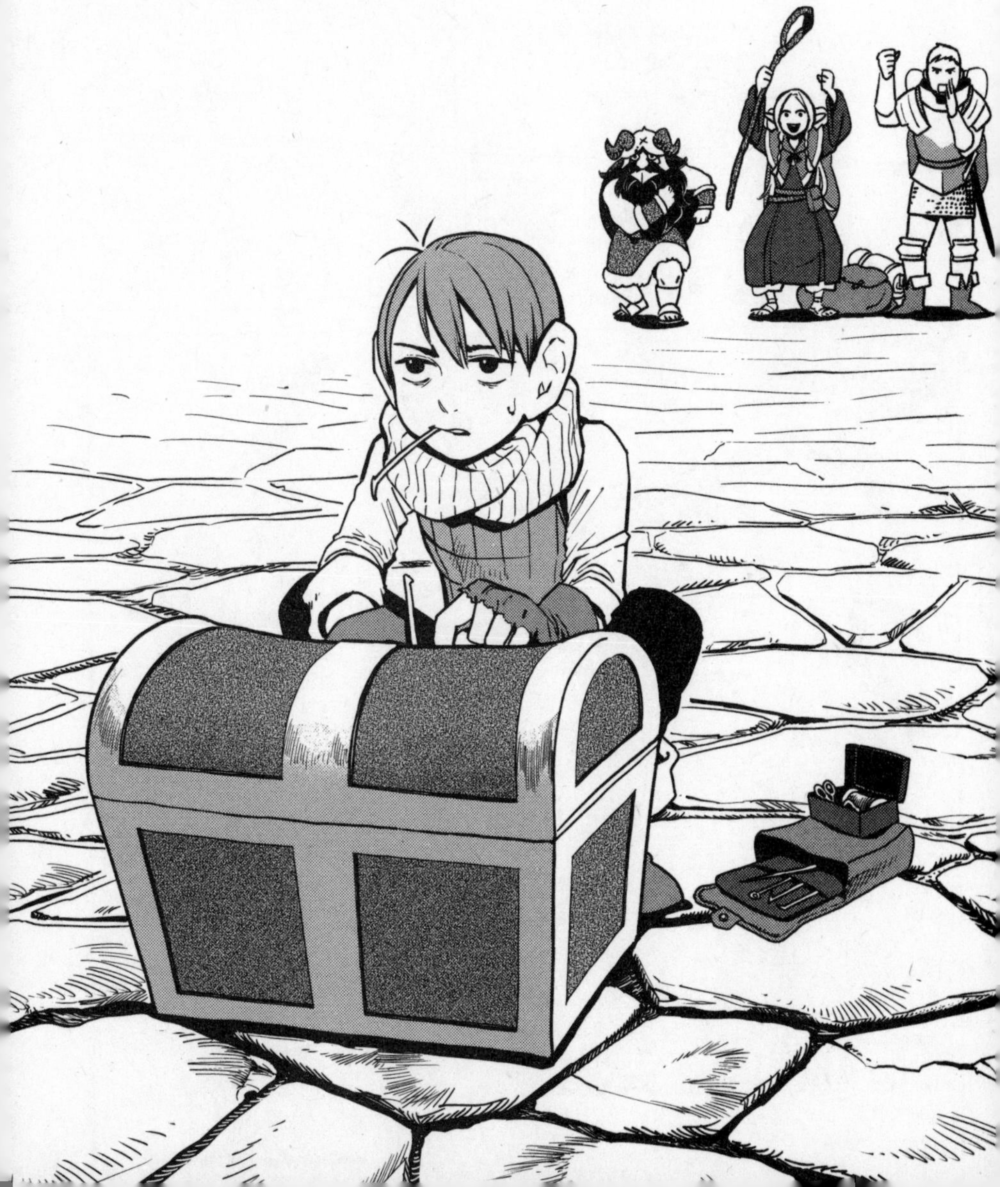

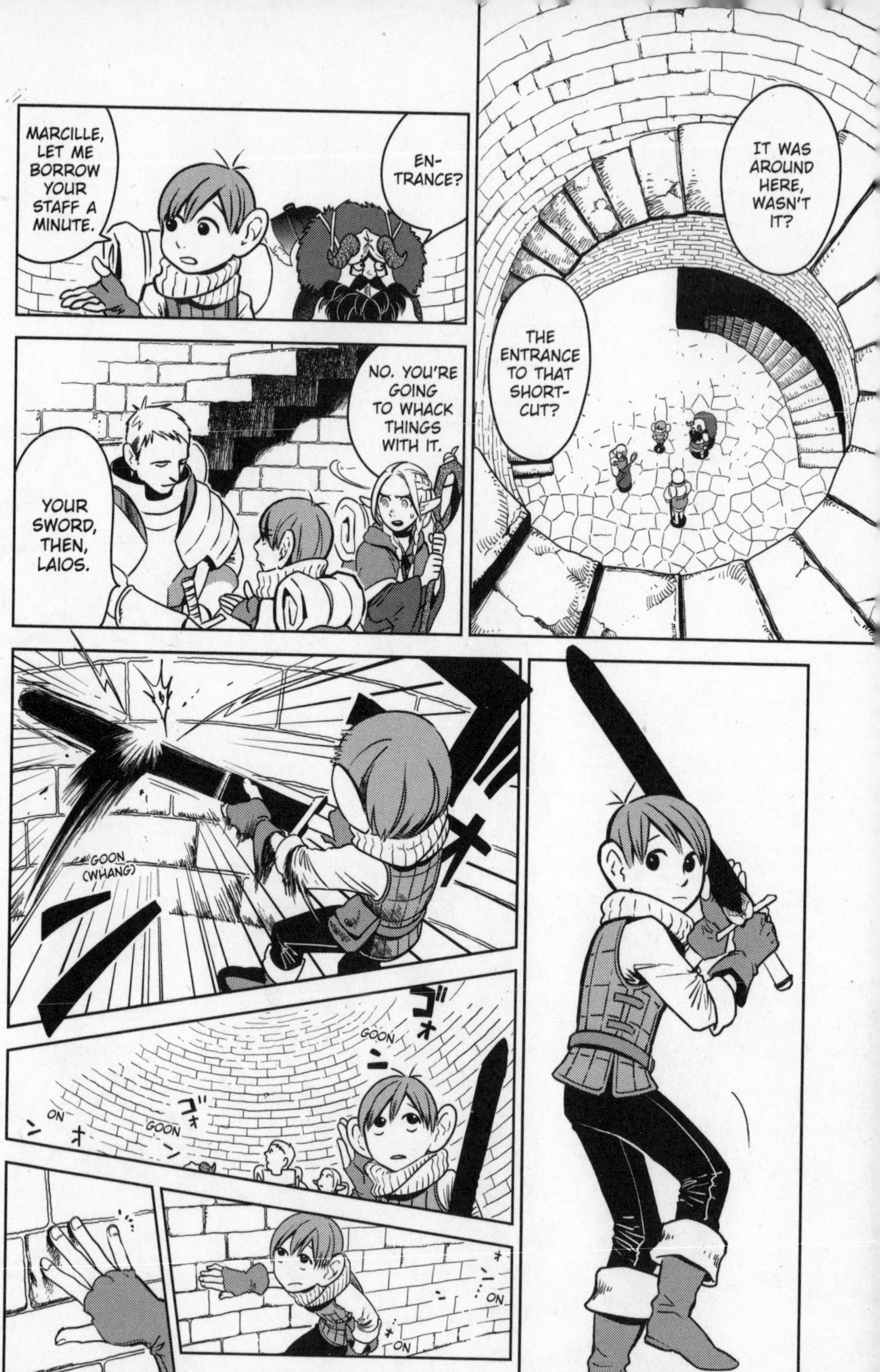
IT WAS AROUND HERE, WASN'T IT?
THE ENTRANCE TO THAT SHORTCUT?
EN-TRANCE?
MARCILLE, LET ME BORROW YOUR STAFF A MINUTE.
NO. YOU'RE GOING TO WHACK THINGS WITH IT.
YOUR SWORD, THEN, LAIOS.
GOON (WHANG)
GOON
GOON
ON
ON
ON

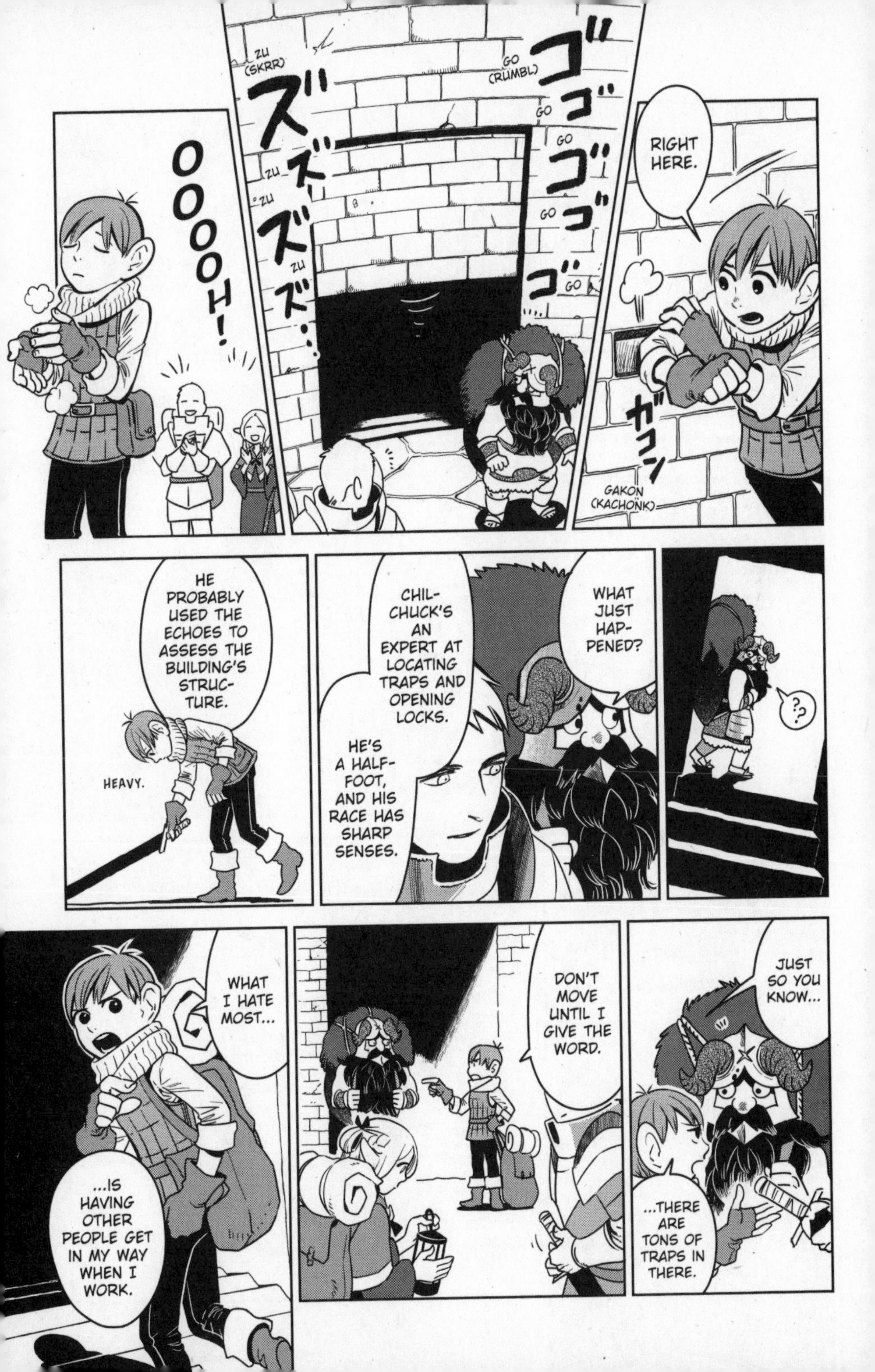
RIGHT HERE.
ガコン
GAKON (KACHÖNK)
ゴゴゴゴ
GO (RUMBL)
GO
GO
GO
GO
ズズズズ
ZU (SKRR)
ZU
ZU
ZU
OOOOH!
WHAT JUST HAPPENED?
??
CHIL-CHUCK'S AN EXPERT AT LOCATING TRAPS AND OPENING LOCKS.
HE'S A HALF-FOOT, AND HIS RACE HAS SHARP SENSES.
HE PROBABLY USED THE ECHOES TO ASSESS THE BUILDING'S STRUCTURE.
HEAVY.
JUST SO YOU KNOW...
...THERE ARE TONS OF TRAPS IN THERE.
DON'T MOVE UNTIL I GIVE THE WORD.
WHAT I HATE MOST...
...IS HAVING OTHER PEOPLE GET IN MY WAY WHEN I WORK.

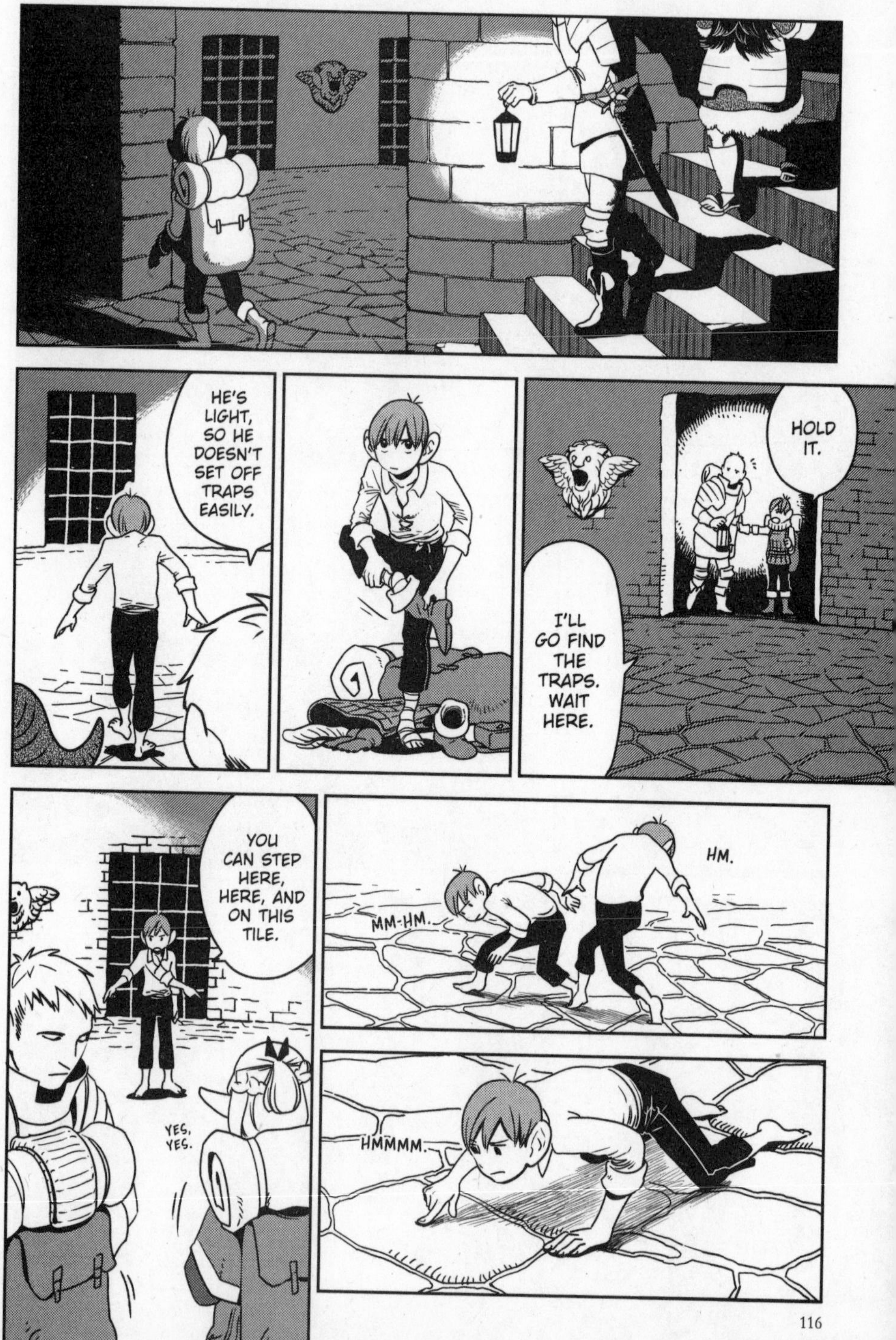

HOLD IT.
I'LL GO FIND THE TRAPS. WAIT HERE.
HE'S LIGHT, SO HE DOESN'T SET OFF TRAPS EASILY.
HM.
MM-HM.
HMMMM.
YOU CAN STEP HERE, HERE, AND ON THIS TILE.
YES, YES.

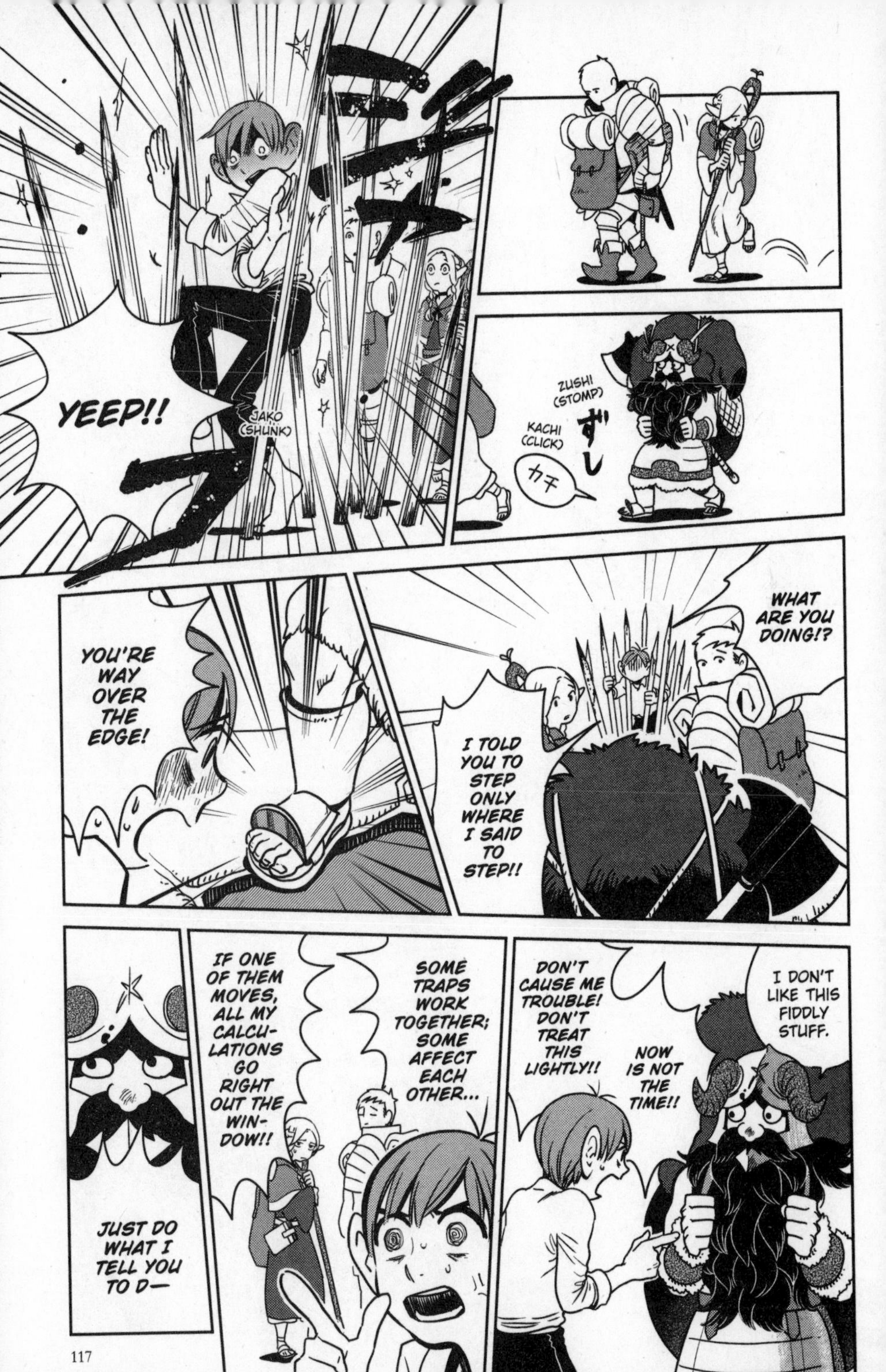
ZUSHI (STOMP)
ずし
KACHI (CLICK)
カチ
JAKO (SHUNK)
YEEP!!
WHAT ARE YOU DOING!?
I TOLD YOU TO STEP ONLY WHERE I SAID TO STEP!!
YOU'RE WAY OVER THE EDGE!
I DON'T LIKE THIS FIDDLY STUFF.
NOW IS NOT THE TIME!!
DON'T CAUSE ME TROUBLE! DON'T TREAT THIS LIGHTLY!!
SOME TRAPS WORK TOGETHER; SOME AFFECT EACH OTHER...
IF ONE OF THEM MOVES, ALL MY CALCULATIONS GO RIGHT OUT THE WINDOW!!
JUST DO WHAT I TELL YOU TO D—

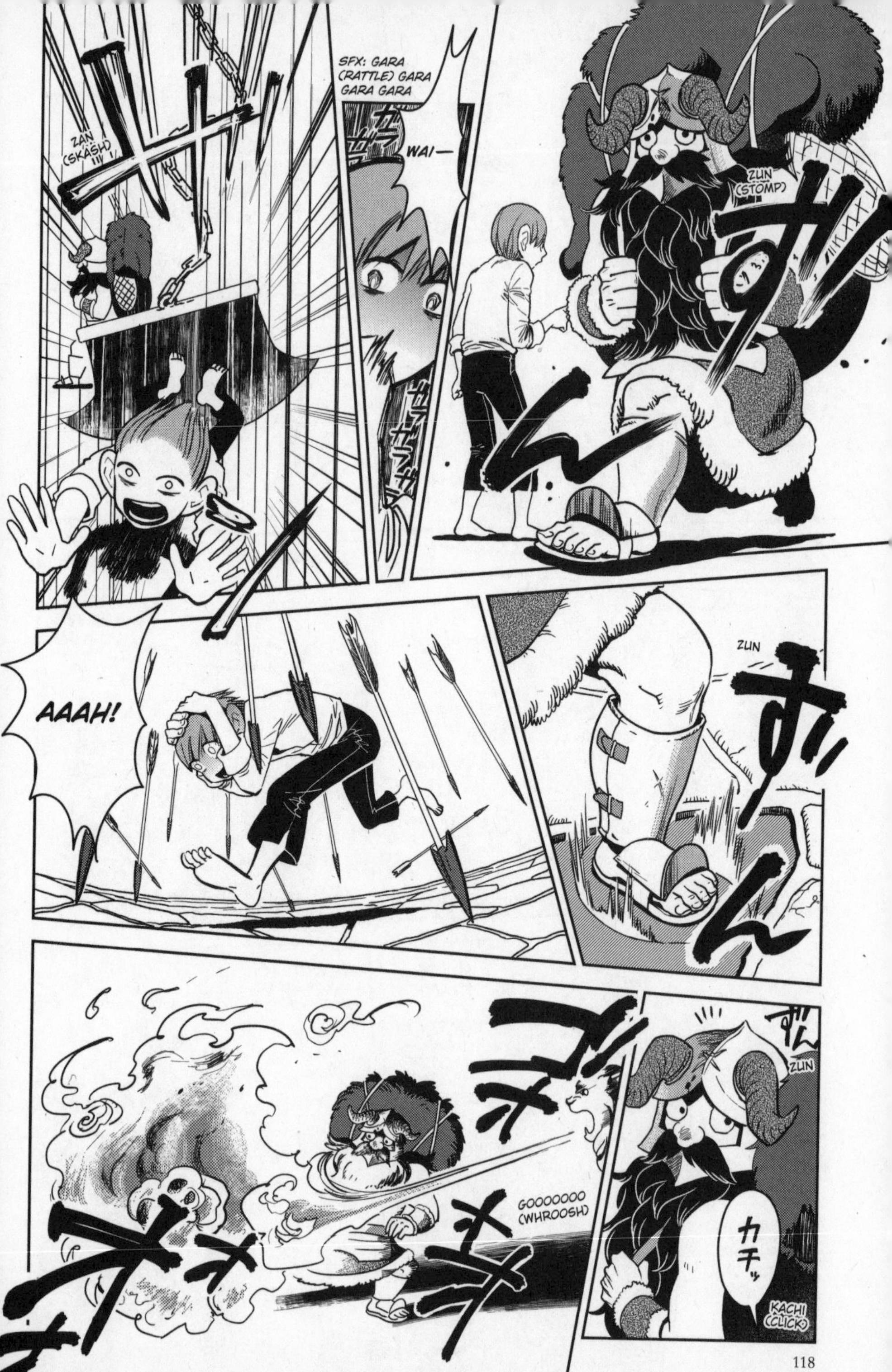
ZUN
(STOMP)
SFX: GARA
(RATTLE) GARA
GARA GARA
WAI—
ZAN
(SKASH)
ZUN
AAAH!
ZUN
カチッ
KACHI
(CLICK)
GOOOOOOO
(WHROOSH)

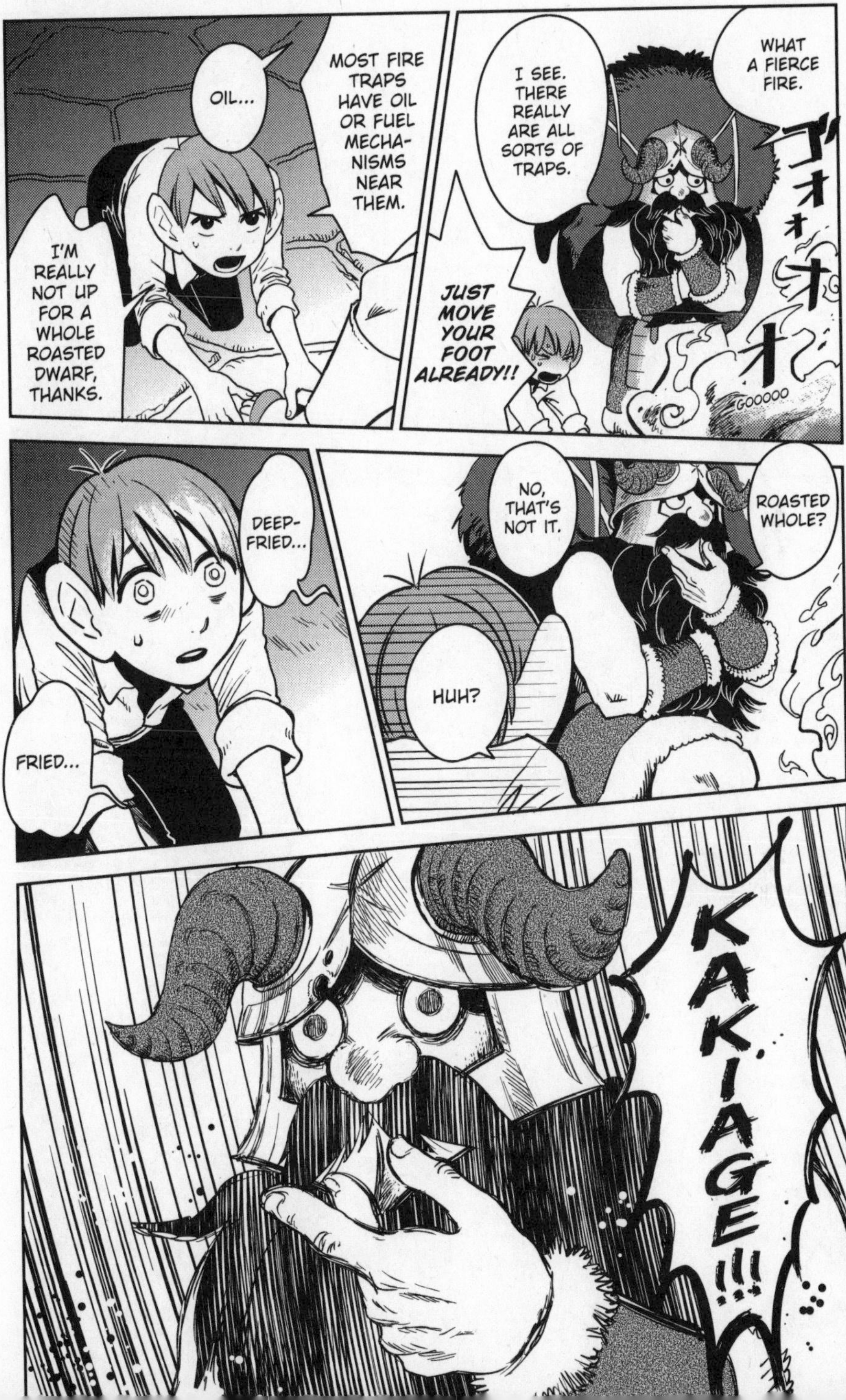
WHAT A FIERCE FIRE.
GOOOOO
I SEE. THERE REALLY ARE ALL SORTS OF TRAPS.
JUST MOVE YOUR FOOT ALREADY!!
MOST FIRE TRAPS HAVE OIL OR FUEL MECHA-NISMS NEAR THEM.
OIL...
I'M REALLY NOT UP FOR A WHOLE ROASTED DWARF, THANKS.
ROASTED WHOLE?
NO, THAT'S NOT IT.
HUH?
DEEP-FRIED...
FRIED...
KAKIAGE!!!

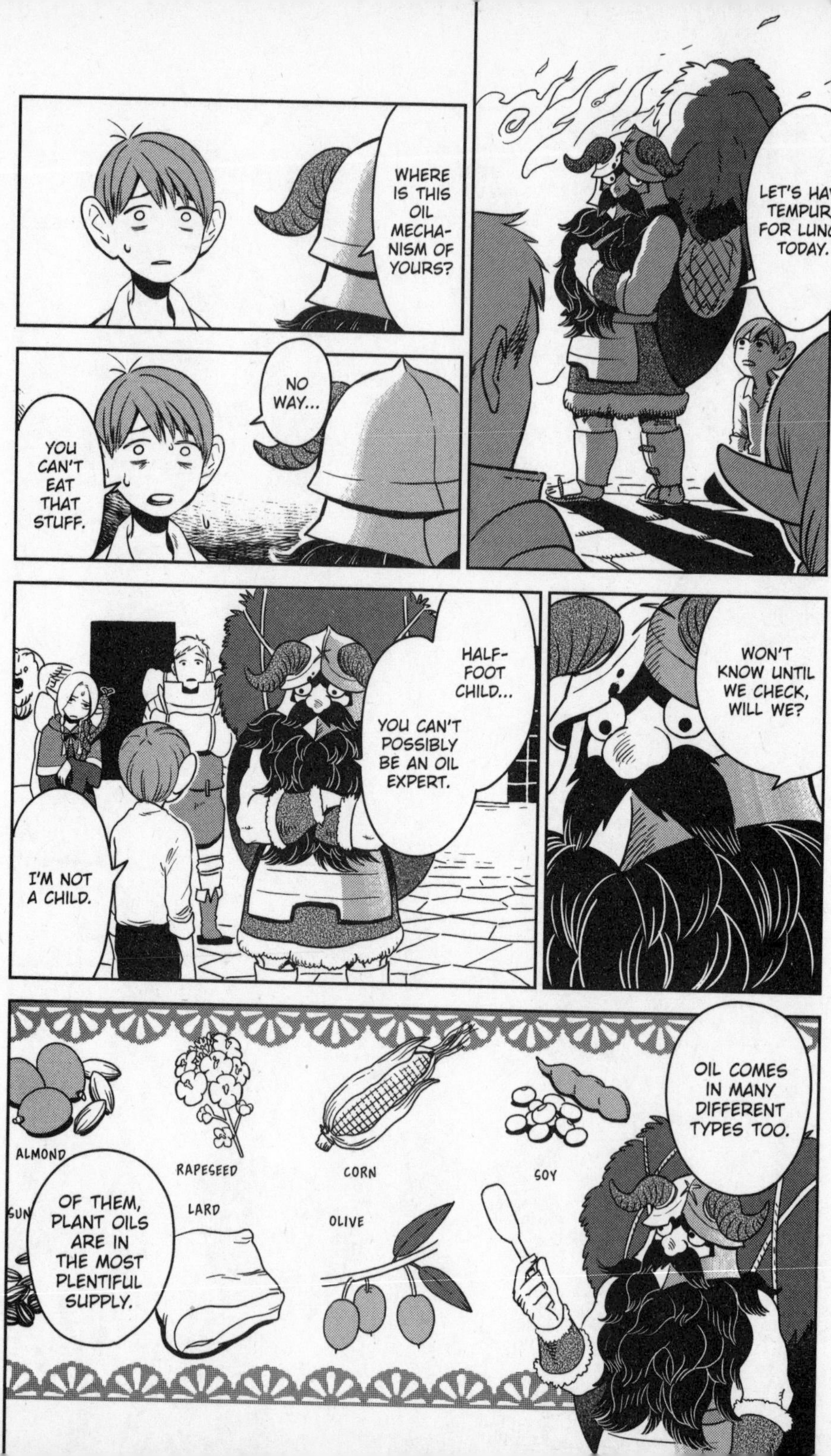
LET'S HAVE TEMPURA FOR LUNCH TODAY.
WHERE IS THIS OIL MECHA-NISM OF YOURS?
NO WAY...
YOU CAN'T EAT THAT STUFF.
WON'T KNOW UNTIL WE CHECK, WILL WE?
HALF-FOOT CHILD...
YOU CAN'T POSSIBLY BE AN OIL EXPERT.
I'M NOT A CHILD.
OIL COMES IN MANY DIFFERENT TYPES TOO.
SOY
CORN
RAPESEED
ALMOND
OLIVE
LARD
SUN
OF THEM, PLANT OILS ARE IN THE MOST PLENTIFUL SUPPLY.

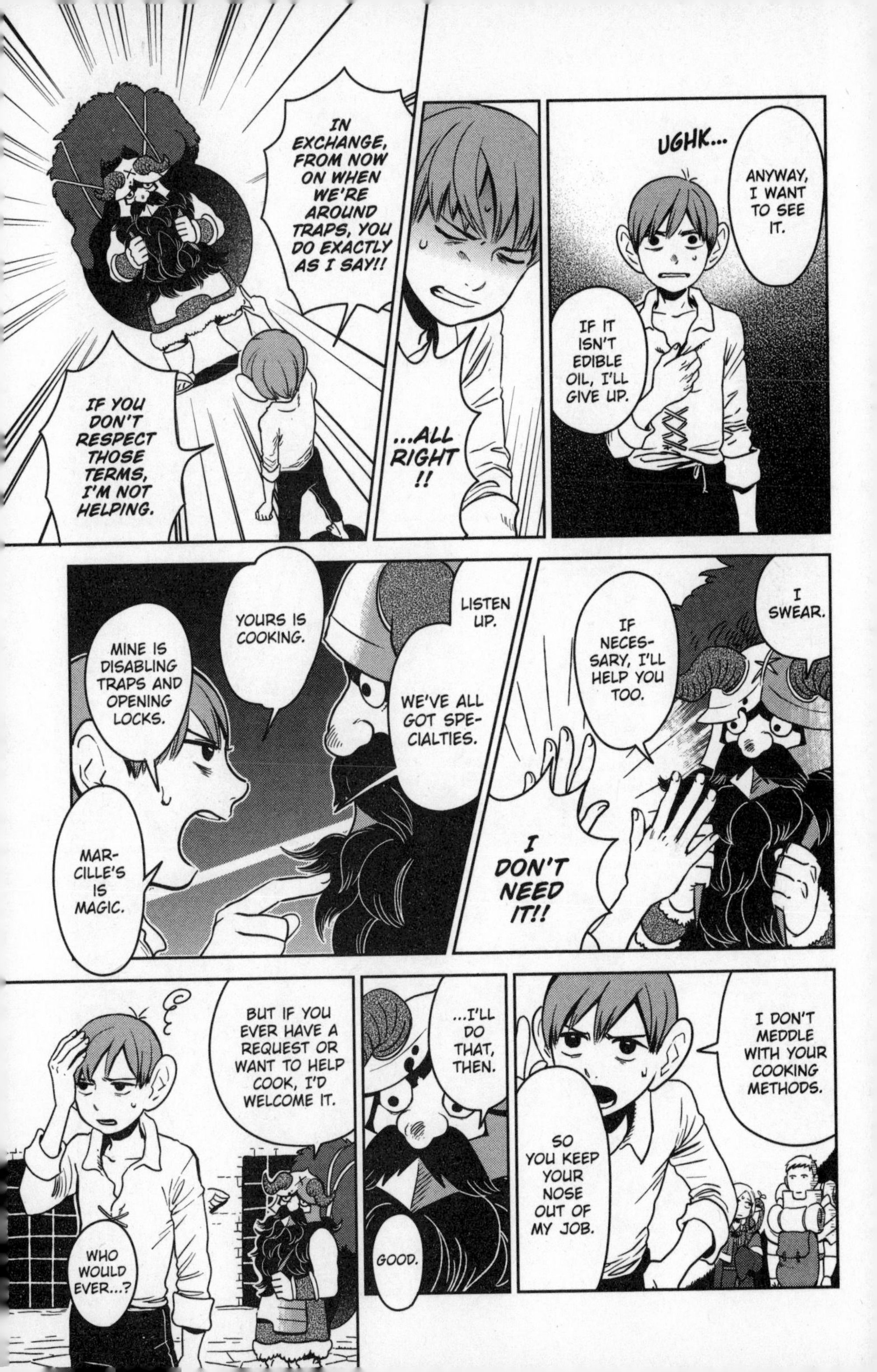
UGHK...
ANYWAY, I WANT TO SEE IT.
IF IT ISN'T EDIBLE OIL, I'LL GIVE UP.
...ALL RIGHT!!
IN EXCHANGE, FROM NOW ON WHEN WE'RE AROUND TRAPS, YOU DO EXACTLY AS I SAY!!
IF YOU DON'T RESPECT THOSE TERMS, I'M NOT HELPING.
I SWEAR.
IF NECESSARY, I'LL HELP YOU TOO.
I DON'T NEED IT!!
LISTEN UP.
WE'VE ALL GOT SPECIALTIES.
YOURS IS COOKING.
MINE IS DISABLING TRAPS AND OPENING LOCKS.
MARCILLE'S IS MAGIC.
I DON'T MEDDLE WITH YOUR COOKING METHODS.
SO YOU KEEP YOUR NOSE OUT OF MY JOB.
...I'LL DO THAT, THEN.
GOOD.
BUT IF YOU EVER HAVE A REQUEST OR WANT TO HELP COOK, I'D WELCOME IT.
WHO WOULD EVER...?

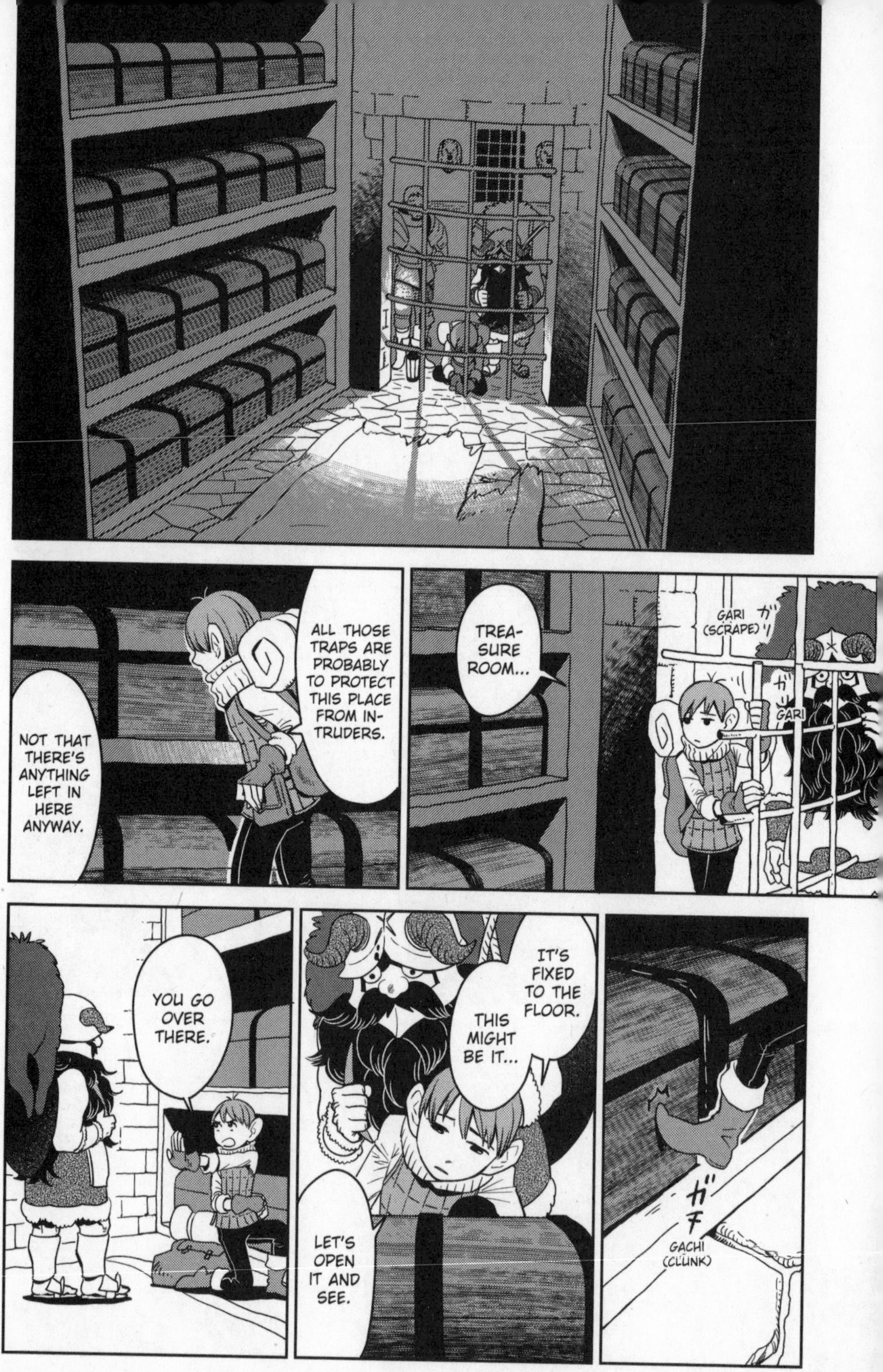
GARI ガリ (SCRAPE)
ガリ GARI
TREA-SURE ROOM...
ALL THOSE TRAPS ARE PROBABLY TO PROTECT THIS PLACE FROM IN-TRUDERS.
NOT THAT THERE'S ANYTHING LEFT IN HERE ANYWAY.
ガチ GACHI (CLUNK)
IT'S FIXED TO THE FLOOR.
THIS MIGHT BE IT...
LET'S OPEN IT AND SEE.
YOU GO OVER THERE.

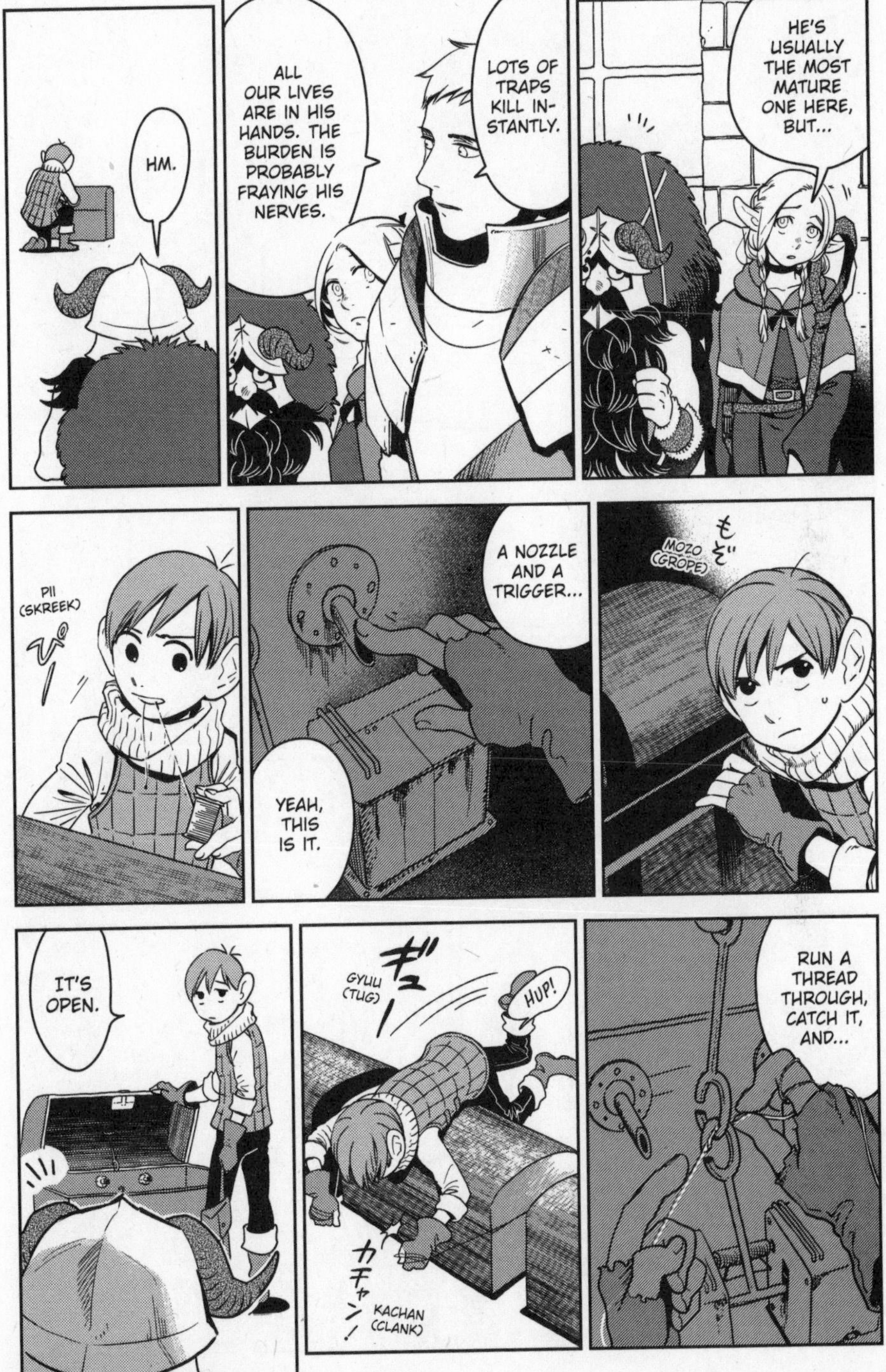
HE'S USUALLY THE MOST MATURE ONE HERE, BUT...
LOTS OF TRAPS KILL IN-STANTLY.
ALL OUR LIVES ARE IN HIS HANDS. THE BURDEN IS PROBABLY FRAYING HIS NERVES.
HM.
もぞ
MOZO (GROPE)
A NOZZLE AND A TRIGGER...
YEAH, THIS IS IT.
ぴ
PII (SKREEK)
RUN A THREAD THROUGH, CATCH IT, AND...
HUP!
ギュ
GYUU (TUG)
カチャン!
KACHAN (CLANK)
IT'S OPEN.

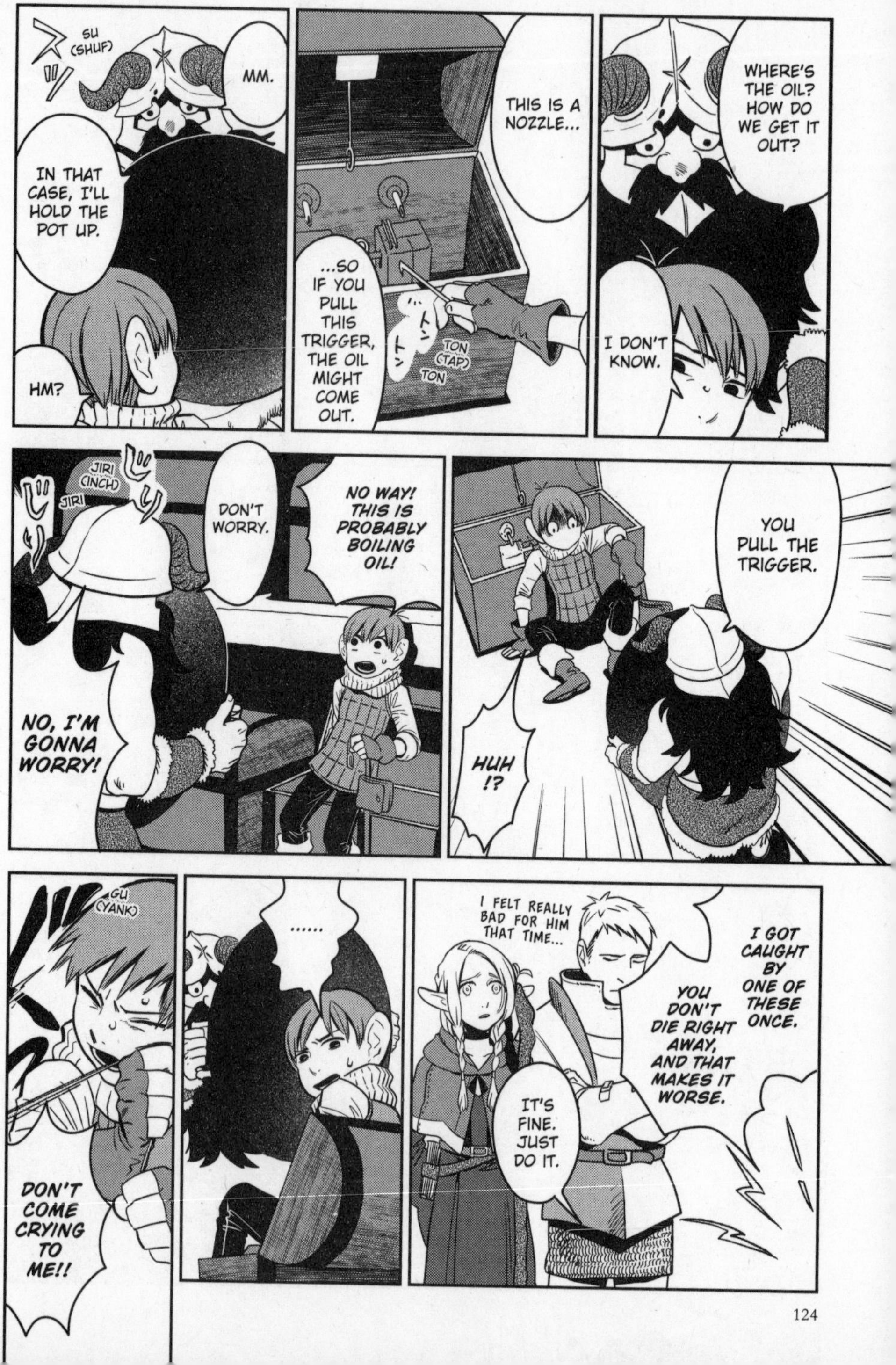
WHERE'S THE OIL? HOW DO WE GET IT OUT?
I DON'T KNOW.
THIS IS A NOZZLE...
...SO IF YOU PULL THIS TRIGGER, THE OIL MIGHT COME OUT.
TON (TAP) TON
SU (SHUF)
MM.
IN THAT CASE, I'LL HOLD THE POT UP.
HM?
YOU PULL THE TRIGGER.
HUH!?
NO WAY! THIS IS PROBABLY BOILING OIL!
DON'T WORRY.
JIRI (INCH) JIRI
NO, I'M GONNA WORRY!
I GOT CAUGHT BY ONE OF THESE ONCE.
YOU DON'T DIE RIGHT AWAY, AND THAT MAKES IT WORSE.
I FELT REALLY BAD FOR HIM THAT TIME...
IT'S FINE. JUST DO IT.
......
GU (YANK)
DON'T COME CRYING TO ME!!

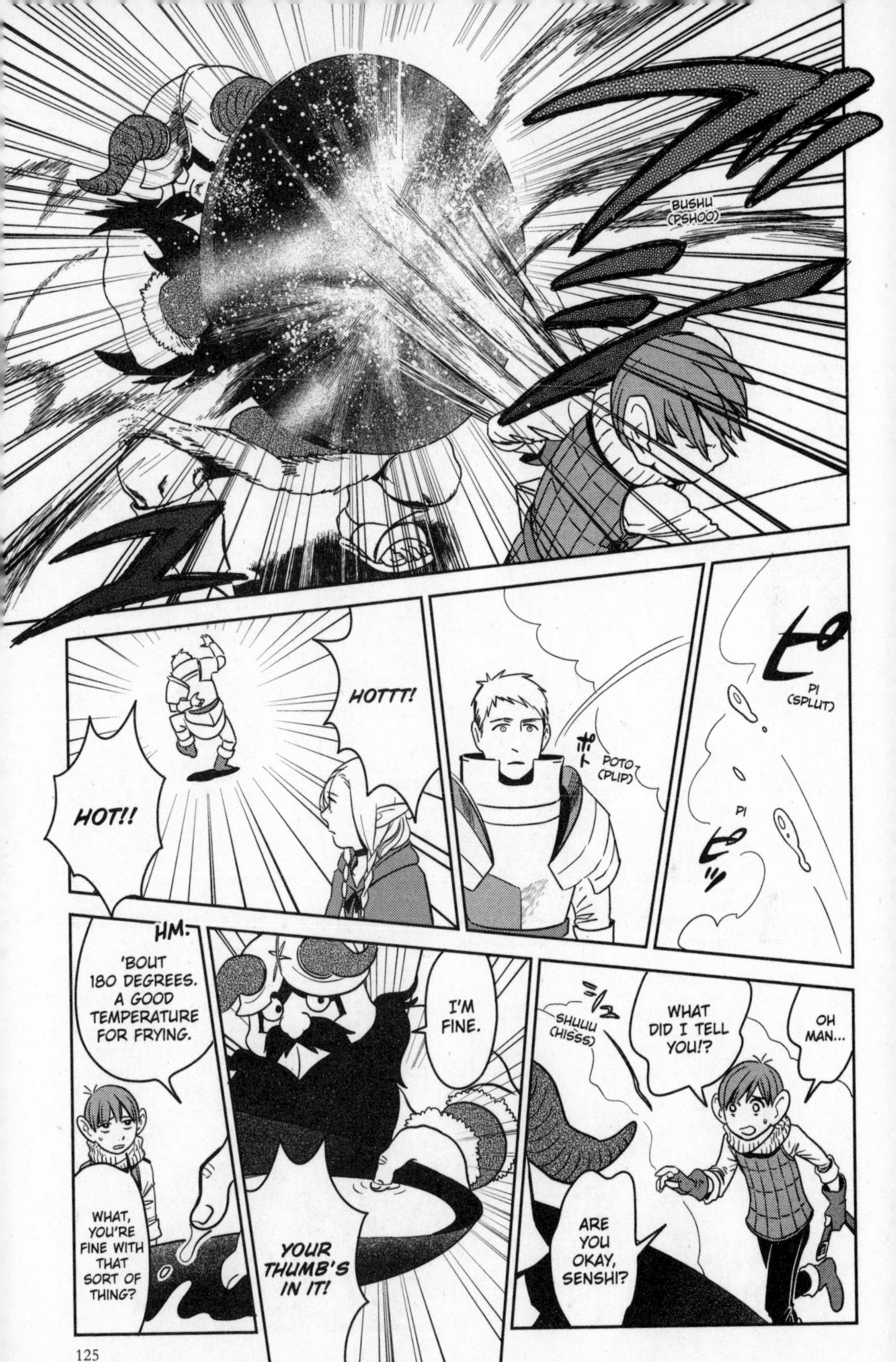
BUSHU (PSHOO)
PI (SPLUT)
PI
POTO (PLIP)
HOTTT!
HOT!!
OH MAN...
WHAT DID I TELL YOU!?
SHUUU (HISSS)
ARE YOU OKAY, SENSHI?
I'M FINE.
YOUR THUMB'S IN IT!
HM.
'BOUT 180 DEGREES. A GOOD TEMPERATURE FOR FRYING.
WHAT, YOU'RE FINE WITH THAT SORT OF THING?

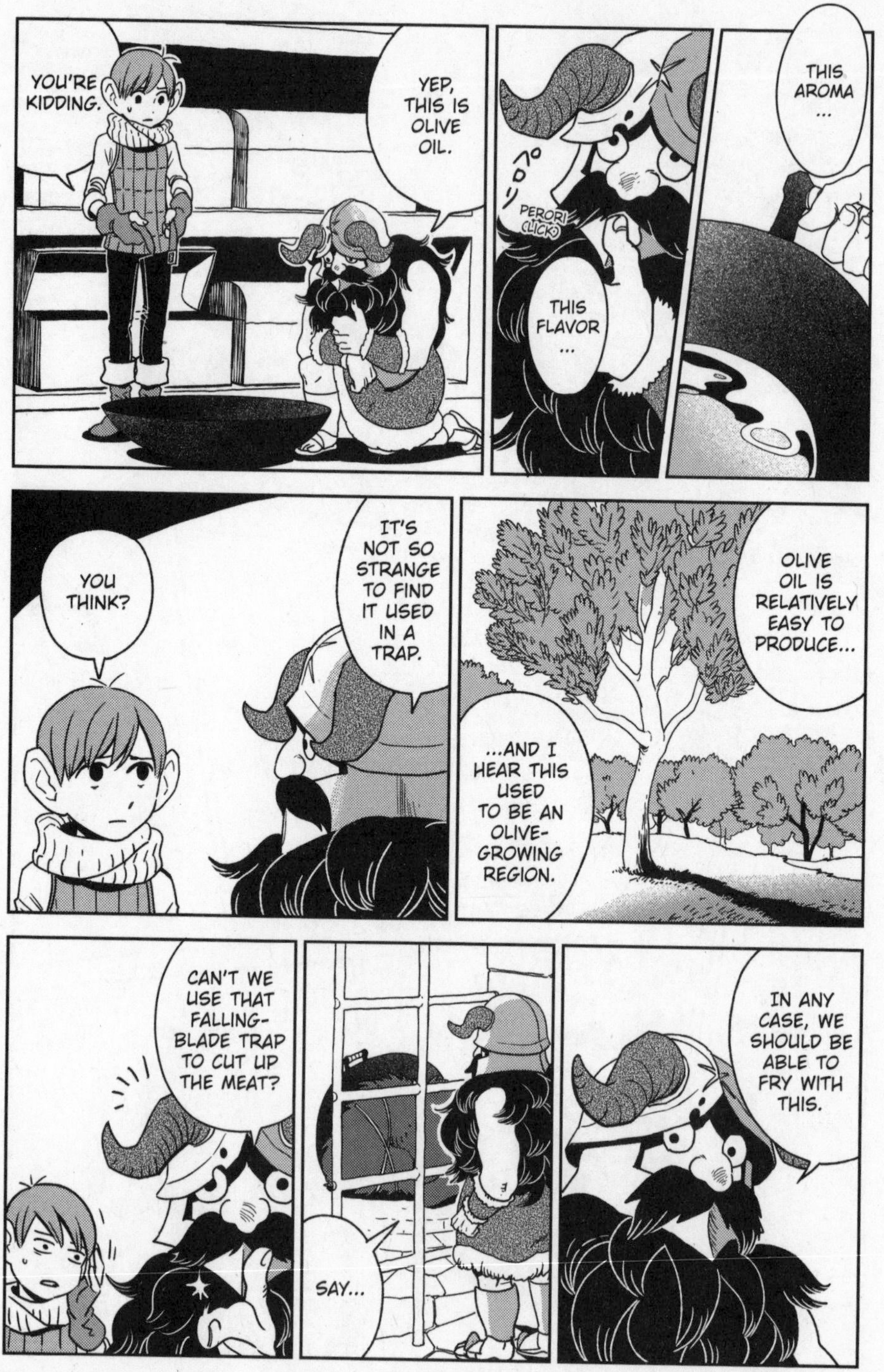
THIS AROMA ...
ペロリ
PERORI (CLICK)
THIS FLAVOR ...
YEP, THIS IS OLIVE OIL.
YOU'RE KIDDING.
OLIVE OIL IS RELATIVELY EASY TO PRODUCE...
...AND I HEAR THIS USED TO BE AN OLIVE-GROWING REGION.
IT'S NOT SO STRANGE TO FIND IT USED IN A TRAP.
YOU THINK?
IN ANY CASE, WE SHOULD BE ABLE TO FRY WITH THIS.
SAY...
CAN'T WE USE THAT FALLING-BLADE TRAP TO CUT UP THE MEAT?

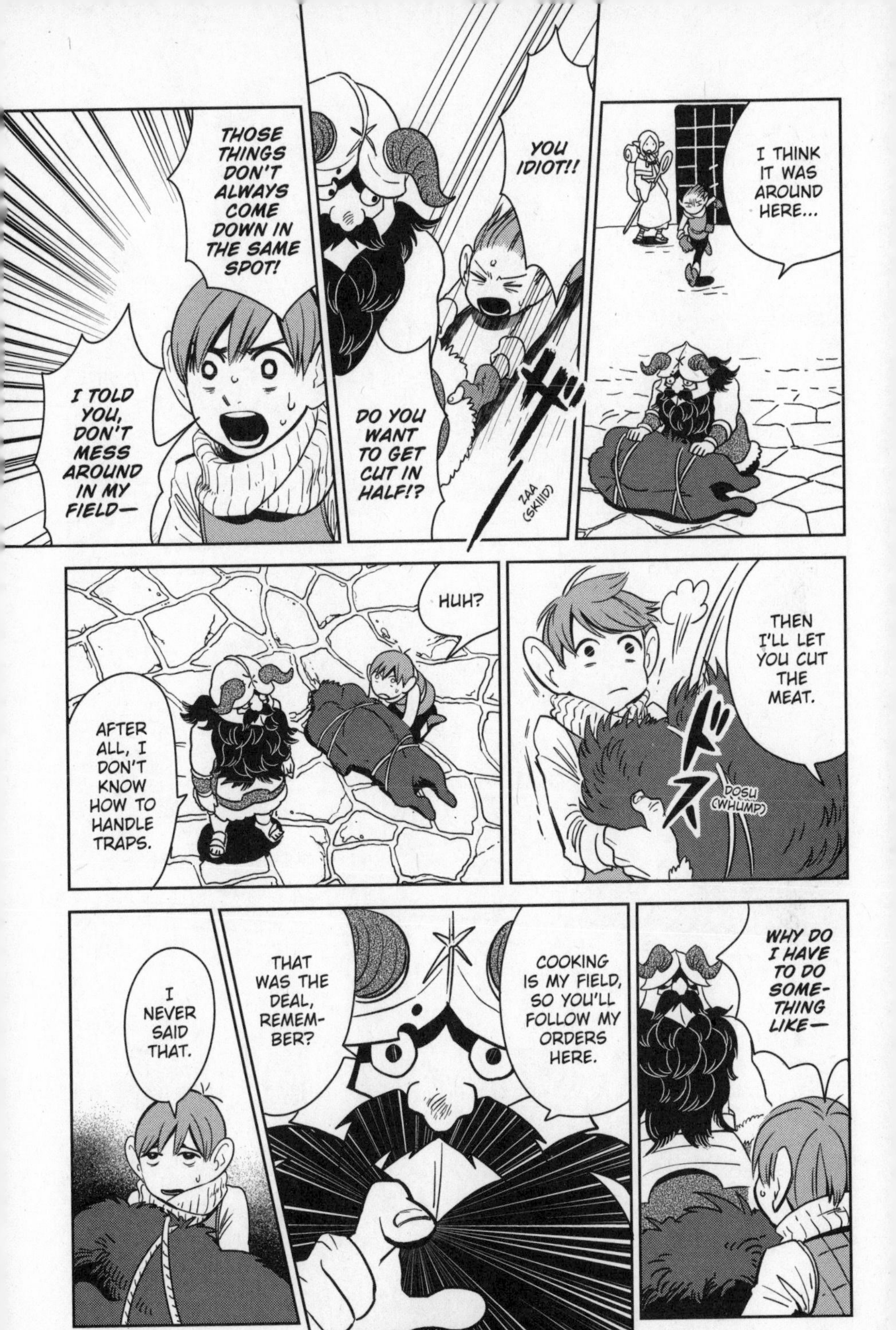
I THINK IT WAS AROUND HERE...
YOU IDIOT!!
DO YOU WANT TO GET CUT IN HALF!?
ZAA (SKIIID)
THOSE THINGS DON'T ALWAYS COME DOWN IN THE SAME SPOT!
I TOLD YOU, DON'T MESS AROUND IN MY FIELD—
THEN I'LL LET YOU CUT THE MEAT.
DOSU (WHUMP)
HUH?
AFTER ALL, I DON'T KNOW HOW TO HANDLE TRAPS.
WHY DO I HAVE TO DO SOME-THING LIKE—
COOKING IS MY FIELD, SO YOU'LL FOLLOW MY ORDERS HERE.
THAT WAS THE DEAL, REMEMBER?
I NEVER SAID THAT.

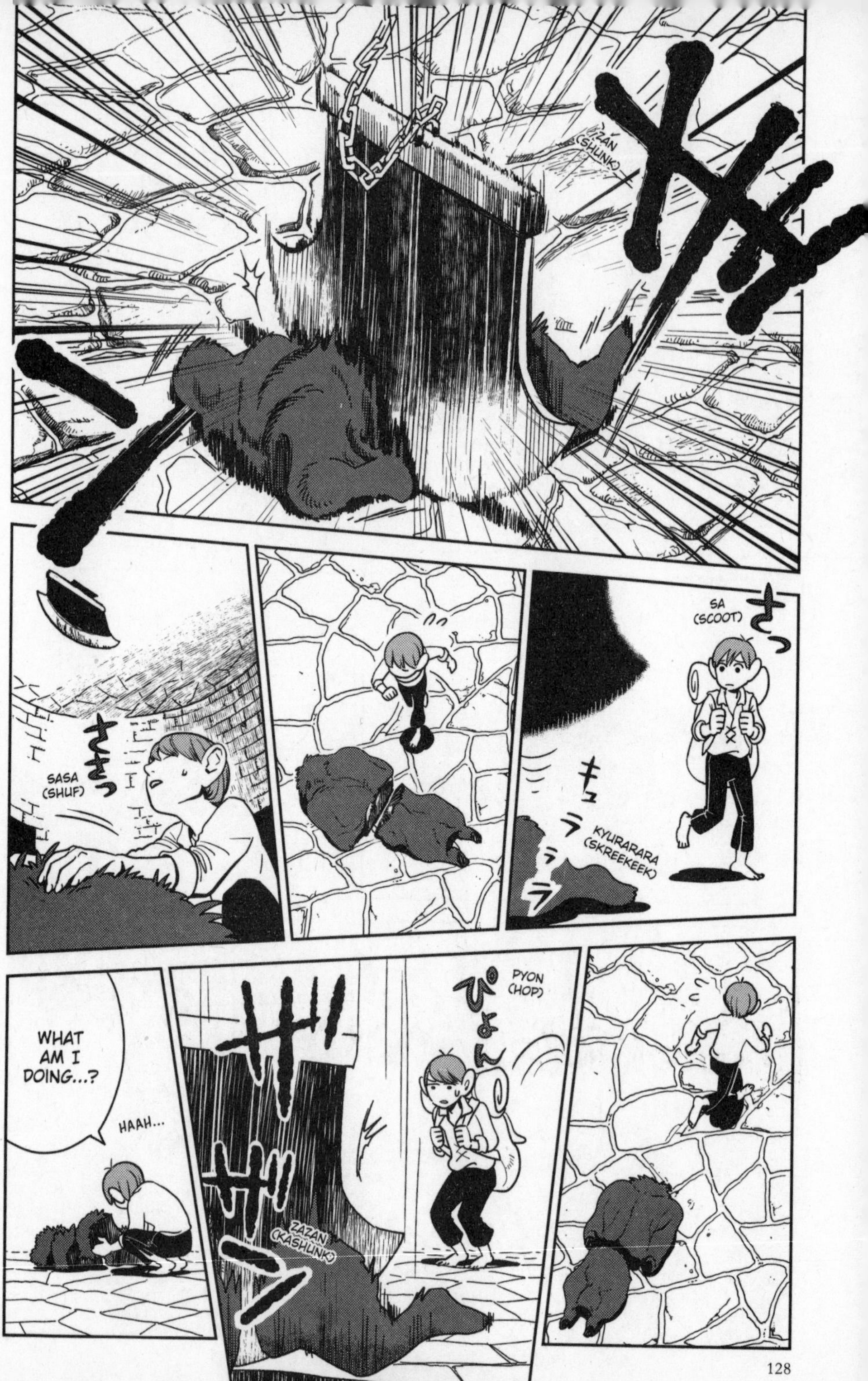
ZAN
(SHUNK)
SA
(SCOOT)
KYURARARA
(SKREEKEEK)
SASA
(SHUF)
PYON
(HOP)
ZAZAN
(KASHUNK)
WHAT AM I DOING...?
HAAH...

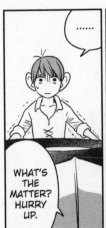

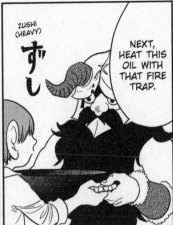

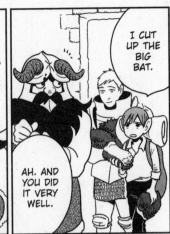

I CUT UP THE BIG BAT.
AH. AND YOU DID IT VERY WELL.
NEXT, HEAT THIS OIL WITH THAT FIRE TRAP.
ZUSHI (HEAVY)
ずし
......
WHAT'S THE MATTER? HURRY UP.
SKIN THE BIG BAT MEAT, THEN CHOP IT THICK.
SCORE IT LIGHTLY...
SUU (SLIT)
ス
...KNEAD THE SEA-SONINGS IN...
NYU
にゅっ
GUNYU (SQUISH)
ぐにゅ
...THEN LET IT REST A BIT.
ZZZ...
WHILE WE'RE WAITING, I'LL GET THE MANDRAKE KAKIAGE READY.

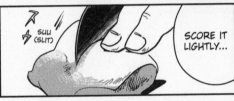

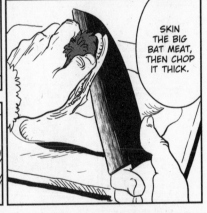

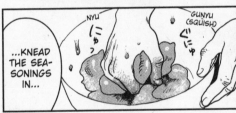

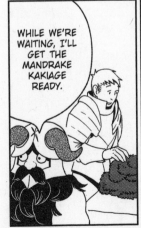

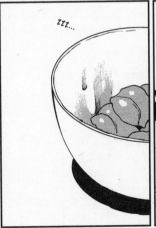

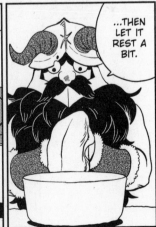

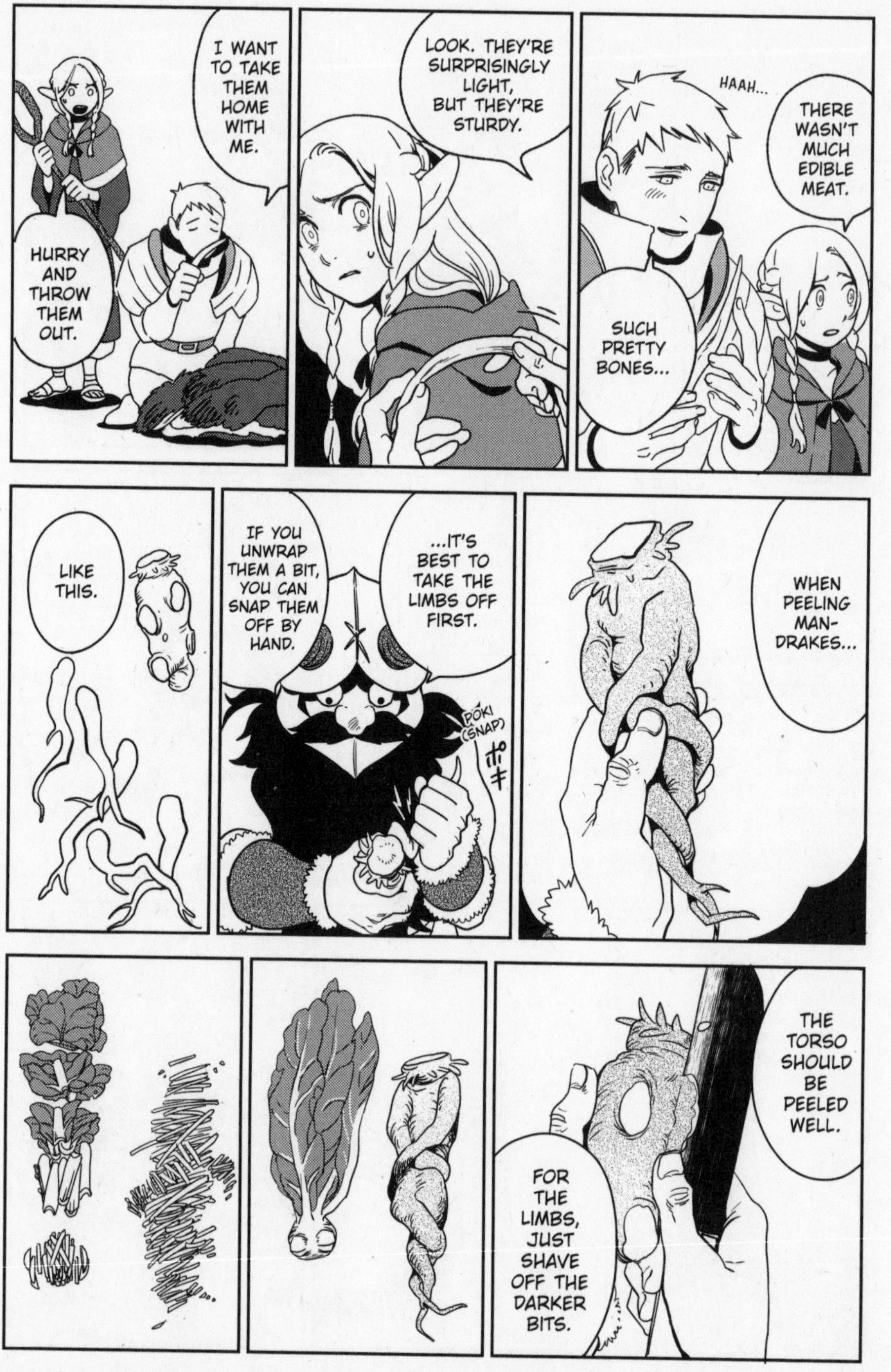
HAAH...
THERE WASN'T MUCH EDIBLE MEAT.
SUCH PRETTY BONES...
LOOK. THEY'RE SURPRISINGLY LIGHT, BUT THEY'RE STURDY.
I WANT TO TAKE THEM HOME WITH ME.
HURRY AND THROW THEM OUT.
WHEN PEELING MAN-DRAKES...
...IT'S BEST TO TAKE THE LIMBS OFF FIRST.
IF YOU UNWRAP THEM A BIT, YOU CAN SNAP THEM OFF BY HAND.
POKI (SNAP)
LIKE THIS.
THE TORSO SHOULD BE PEELED WELL.
FOR THE LIMBS, JUST SHAVE OFF THE DARKER BITS.

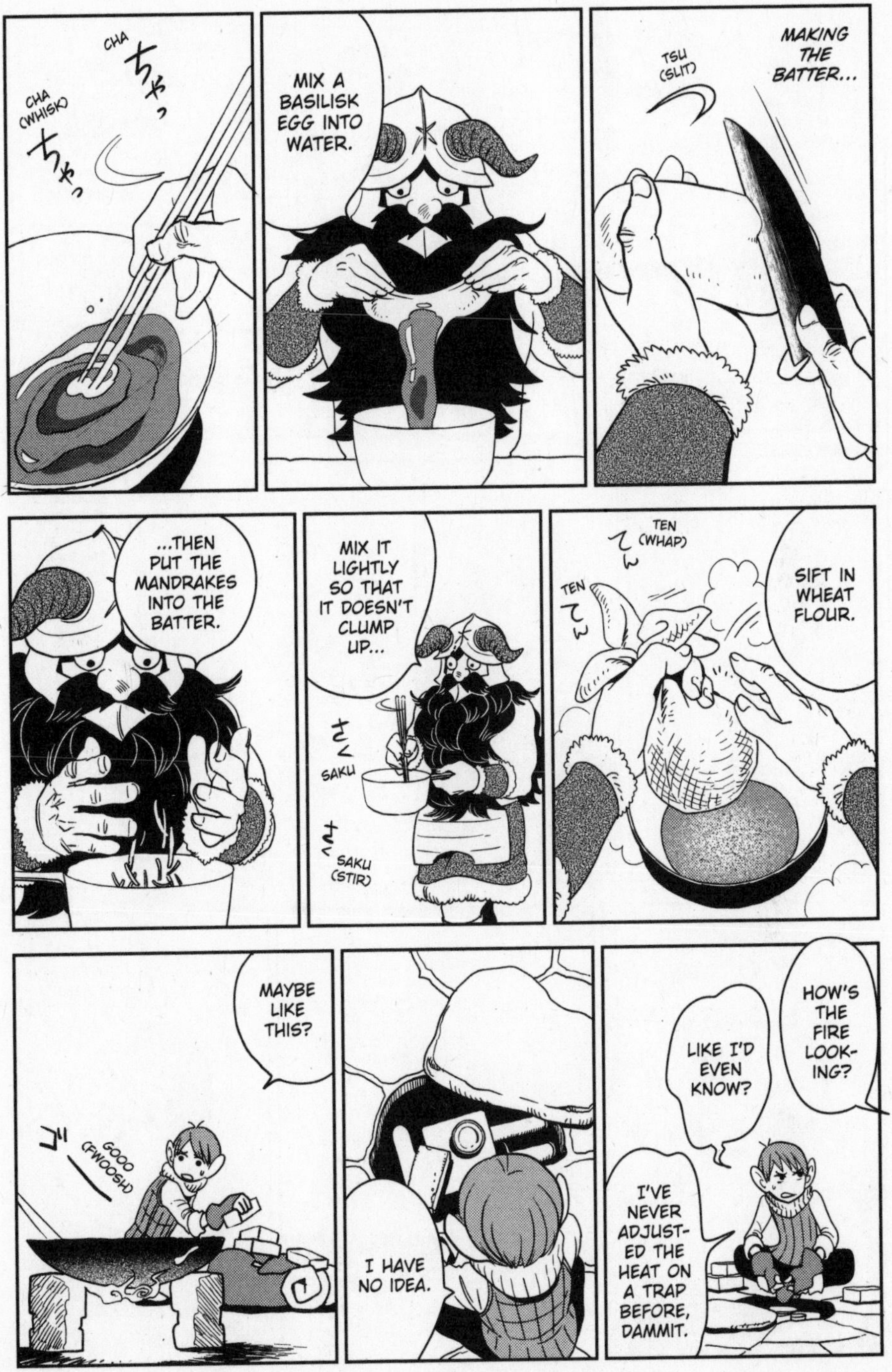
MAKING THE BATTER...
TSU (SLIT)
MIX A BASILISK EGG INTO WATER.
CHA
ちゃっ
CHA (WHISK)
ちゃっ
SIFT IN WHEAT FLOUR.
てん
TEN (WHAP)
てん
TEN
MIX IT LIGHTLY SO THAT IT DOESN'T CLUMP UP...
さく
SAKU
さく
SAKU (STIR)
...THEN PUT THE MANDRAKES INTO THE BATTER.
HOW'S THE FIRE LOOKING?
LIKE I'D EVEN KNOW?
I'VE NEVER ADJUSTED THE HEAT ON A TRAP BEFORE, DAMMIT.
I HAVE NO IDEA.
MAYBE LIKE THIS?
ゴー
GOOO (FWOOSH)

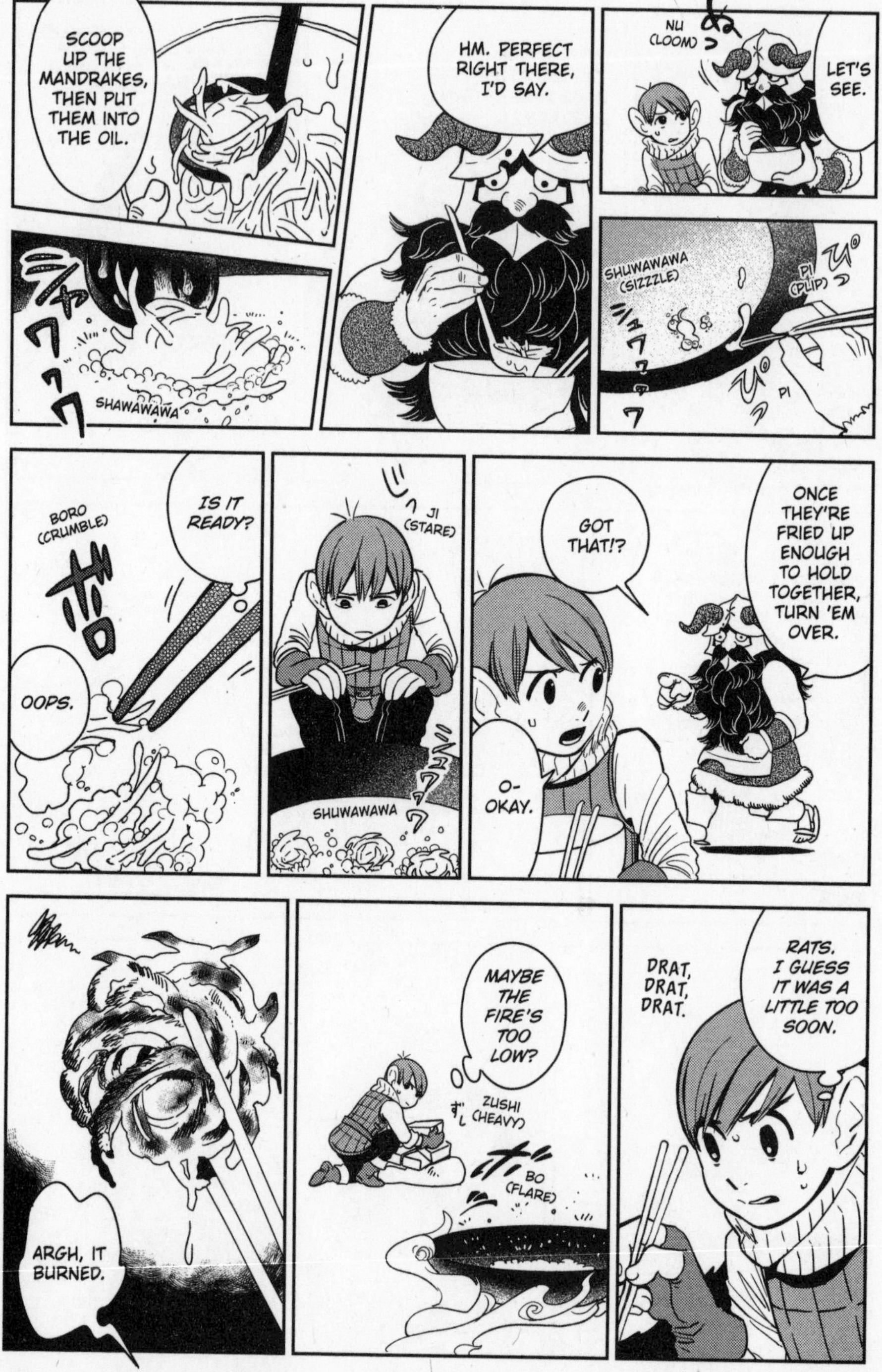
NU (LOOM)
LET'S SEE.
SHUWAWAWA (SIZZZLE)
PI (PLIP)
PI
HM. PERFECT RIGHT THERE, I'D SAY.
SCOOP UP THE MANDRAKES, THEN PUT THEM INTO THE OIL.
SHAWAWAWA
ONCE THEY'RE FRIED UP ENOUGH TO HOLD TOGETHER, TURN 'EM OVER.
GOT THAT!?
O-OKAY.
JI (STARE)
SHUWAWAWA
IS IT READY?
BORO (CRUMBLE)
OOPS.
RATS. I GUESS IT WAS A LITTLE TOO SOON.
DRAT, DRAT, DRAT.
MAYBE THE FIRE'S TOO LOW?
ZUSHI (HEAVY)
BO (FLARE)
ARGH, IT BURNED.

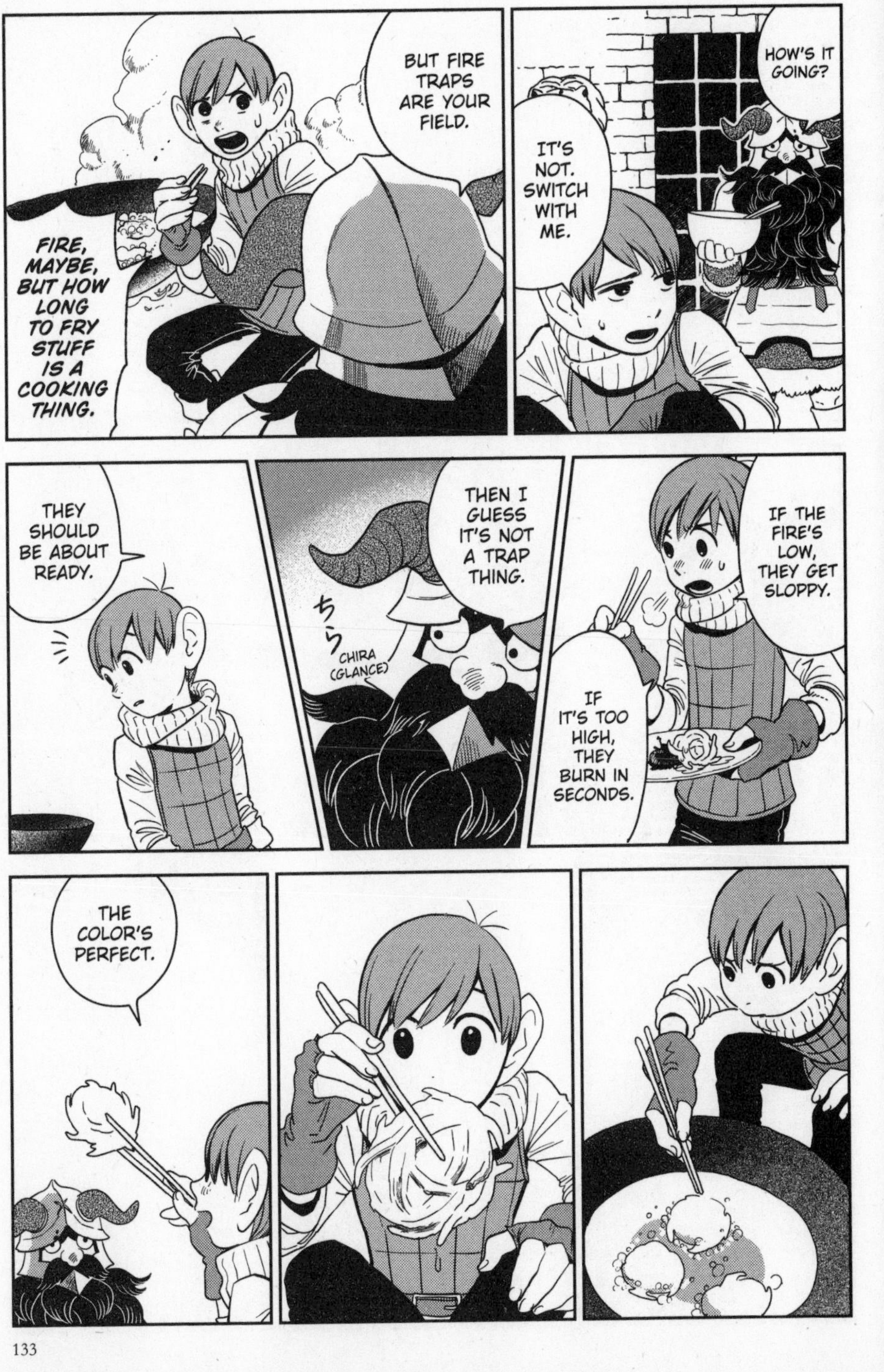
HOW'S IT GOING?
IT'S NOT. SWITCH WITH ME.
BUT FIRE TRAPS ARE YOUR FIELD.
FIRE, MAYBE, BUT HOW LONG TO FRY STUFF IS A COOKING THING.
IF THE FIRE'S LOW, THEY GET SLOPPY.
IF IT'S TOO HIGH, THEY BURN IN SECONDS.
THEN I GUESS IT'S NOT A TRAP THING.
ちら
CHIRA (GLANCE)
THEY SHOULD BE ABOUT READY.
THE COLOR'S PERFECT.

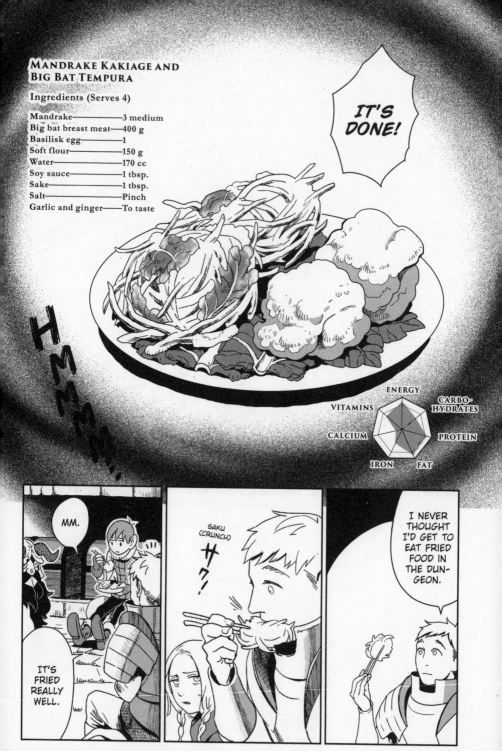

MANDRAKE KAKIAGE AND BIG BAT TEMPURA

Ingredients (Serves 4)

Mandrake	3 medium
Big bat breast meat	400 g
Basilisk egg	1
Soft flour	150 g
Water	170 cc
Soy sauce	1 tbsp.
Sake	1 tbsp.
Salt	Pinch
Garlic and ginger	To taste

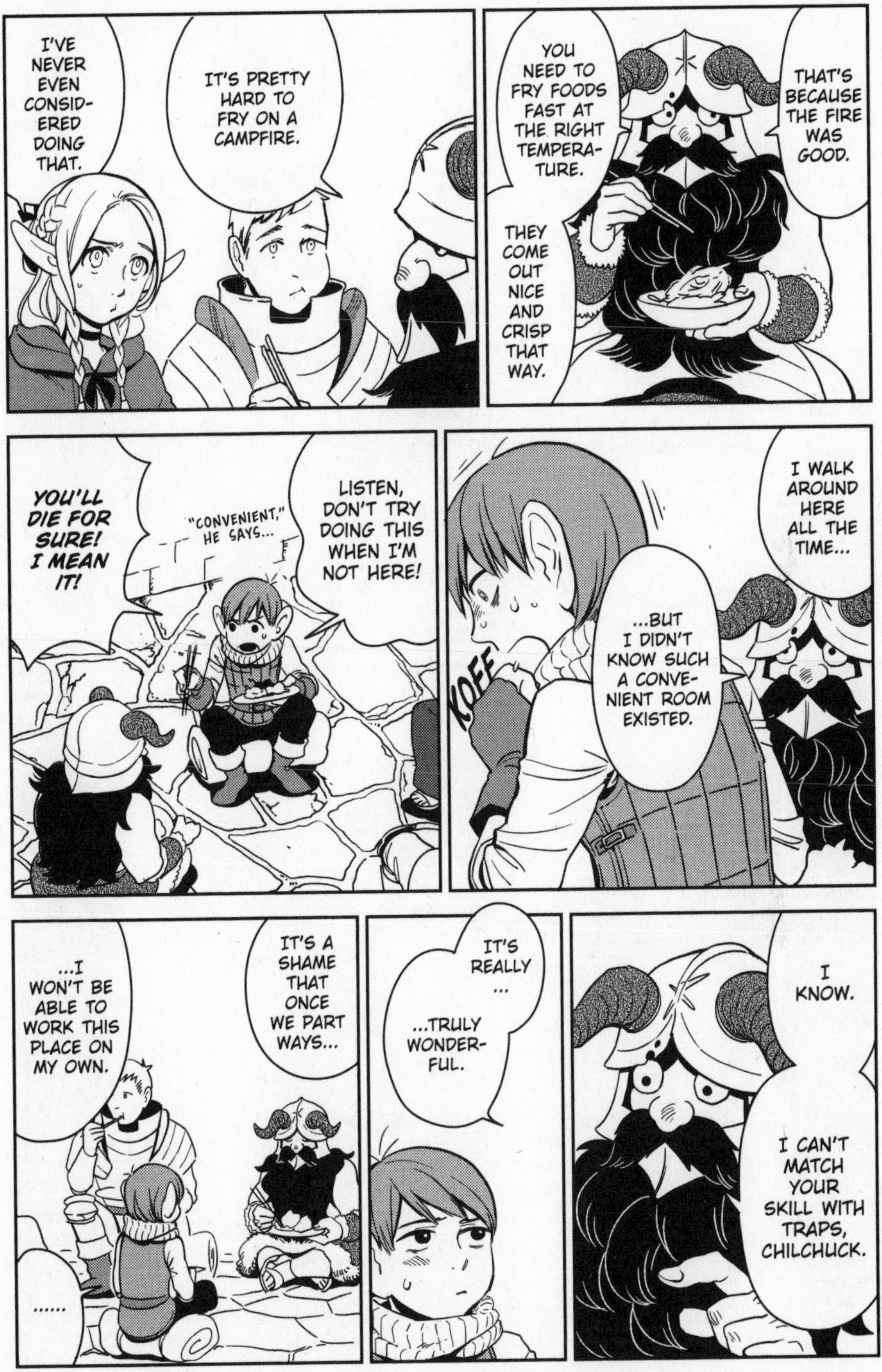
THAT'S BECAUSE THE FIRE WAS GOOD.
YOU NEED TO FRY FOODS FAST AT THE RIGHT TEMPERATURE.
THEY COME OUT NICE AND CRISP THAT WAY.
IT'S PRETTY HARD TO FRY ON A CAMPFIRE.
I'VE NEVER EVEN CONSIDERED DOING THAT.
I WALK AROUND HERE ALL THE TIME...
KOFF
...BUT I DIDN'T KNOW SUCH A CONVENIENT ROOM EXISTED.
LISTEN, DON'T TRY DOING THIS WHEN I'M NOT HERE!
"CONVENIENT," HE SAYS...
YOU'LL DIE FOR SURE! I MEAN IT!
I KNOW.
I CAN'T MATCH YOUR SKILL WITH TRAPS, CHILCHUCK.
IT'S REALLY...
...TRULY WONDERFUL.
IT'S A SHAME THAT ONCE WE PART WAYS...
...I WON'T BE ABLE TO WORK THIS PLACE ON MY OWN.
......

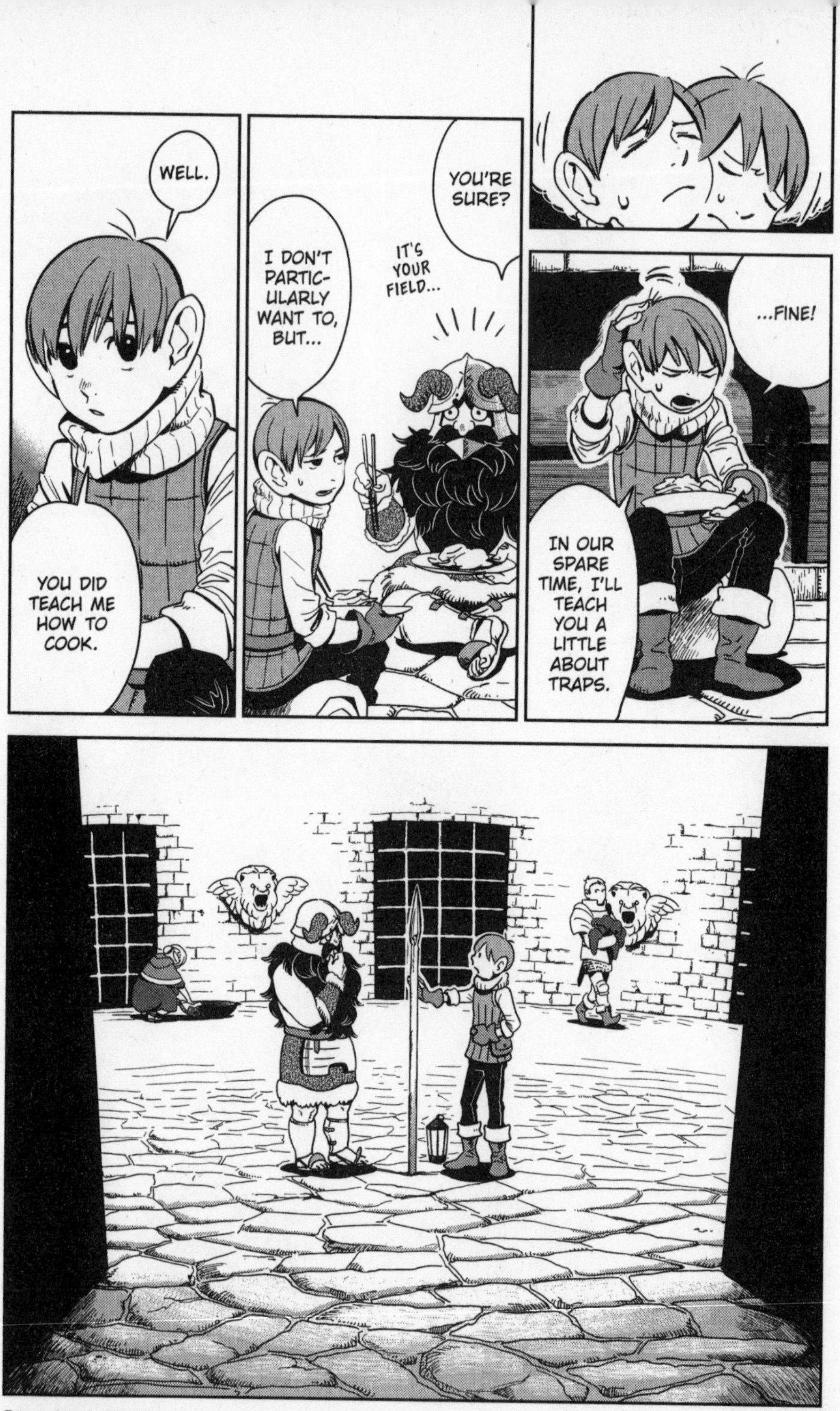
...FINE!
IN OUR SPARE TIME, I'LL TEACH YOU A LITTLE ABOUT TRAPS.
YOU'RE SURE?
IT'S YOUR FIELD...
I DON'T PARTICULARLY WANT TO, BUT...
WELL.
YOU DID TEACH ME HOW TO COOK.

CHAPTER 5: THE END

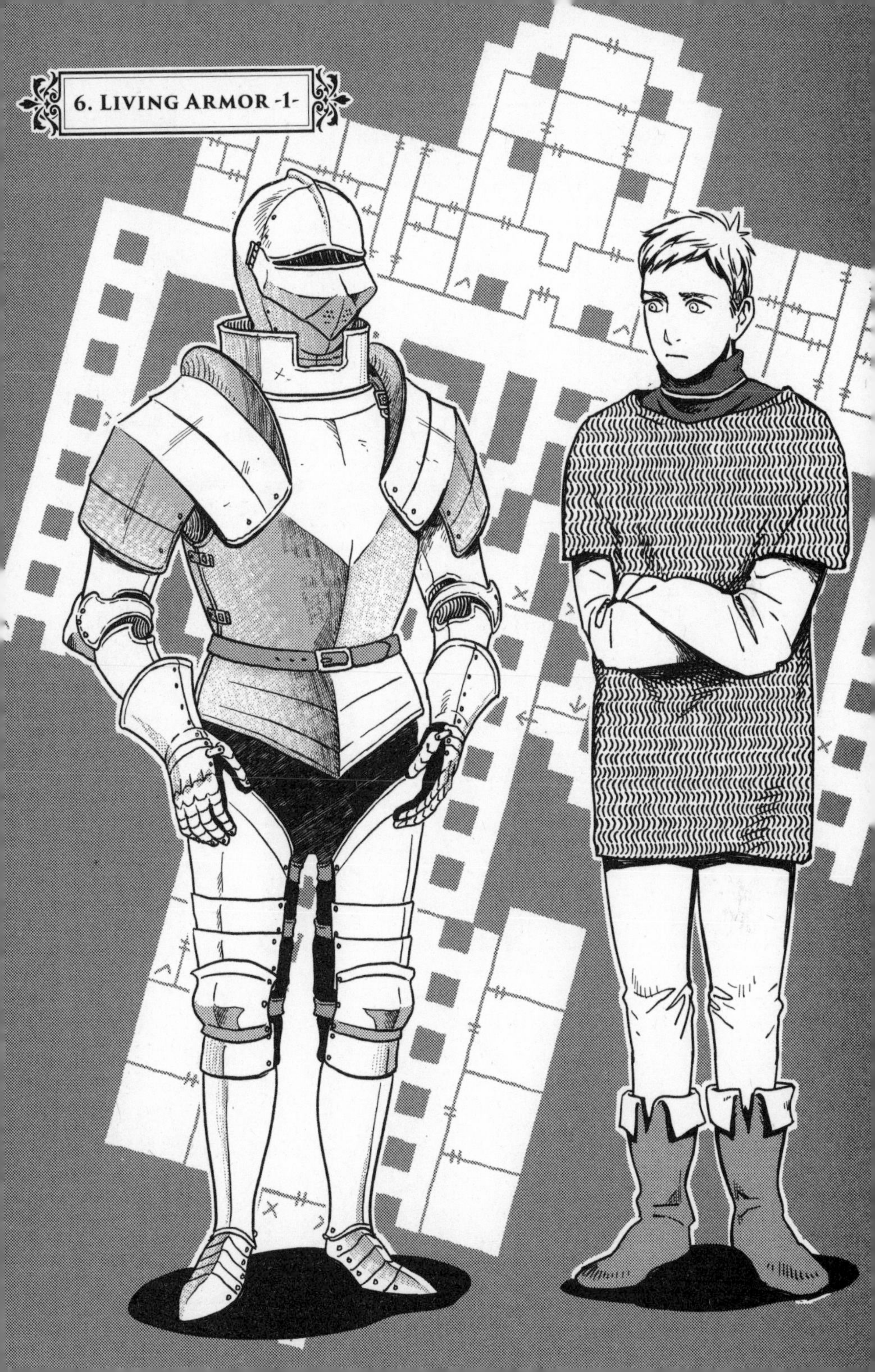
6. LIVING ARMOR -1-

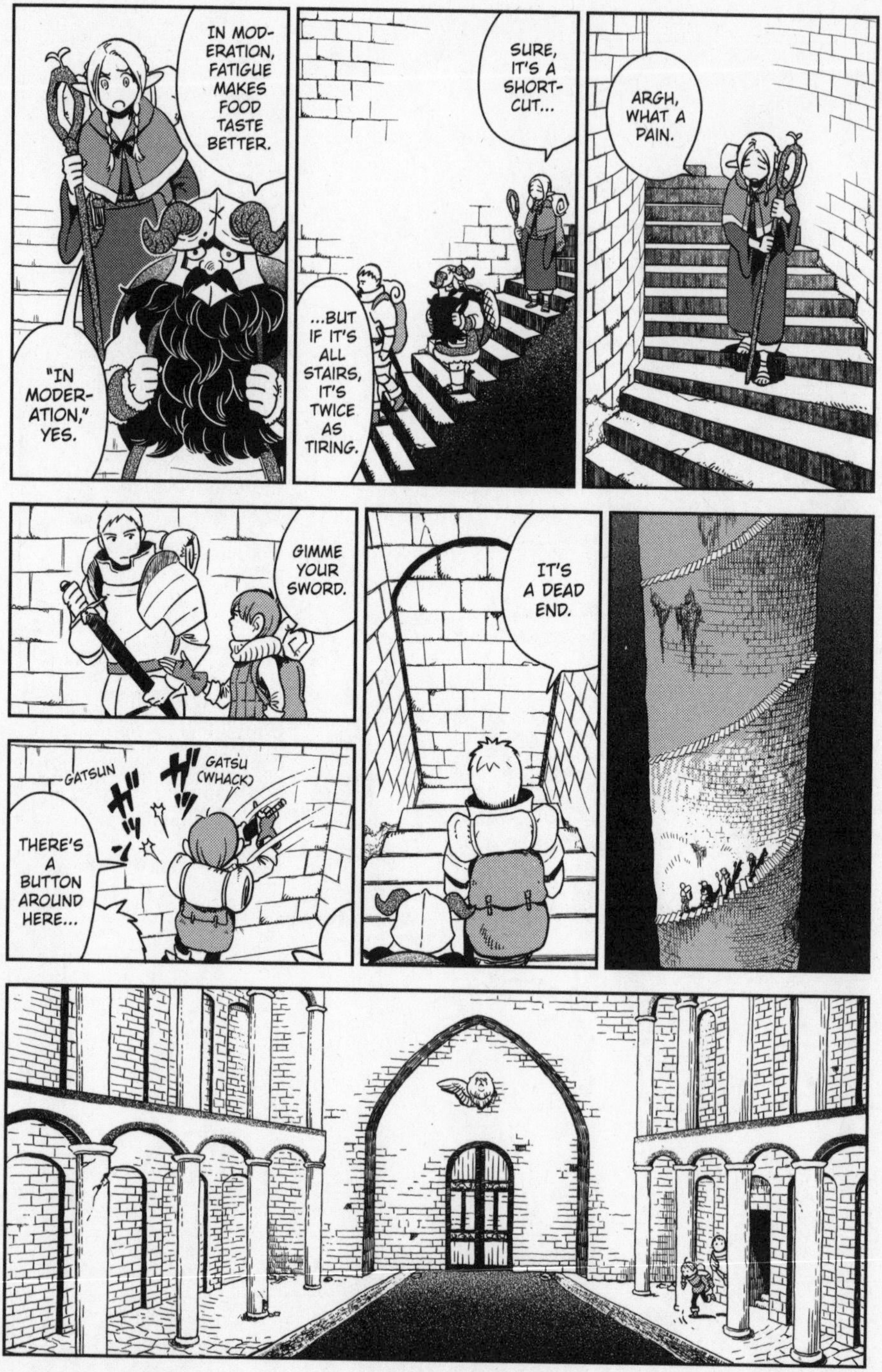
ARGH, WHAT A PAIN.
SURE, IT'S A SHORT-CUT...
...BUT IF IT'S ALL STAIRS, IT'S TWICE AS TIRING.
IN MOD-ERATION, FATIGUE MAKES FOOD TASTE BETTER.
"IN MODER-ATION," YES.
IT'S A DEAD END.
GIMME YOUR SWORD.
GATSU (WHACK)
GATSUN
THERE'S A BUTTON AROUND HERE...

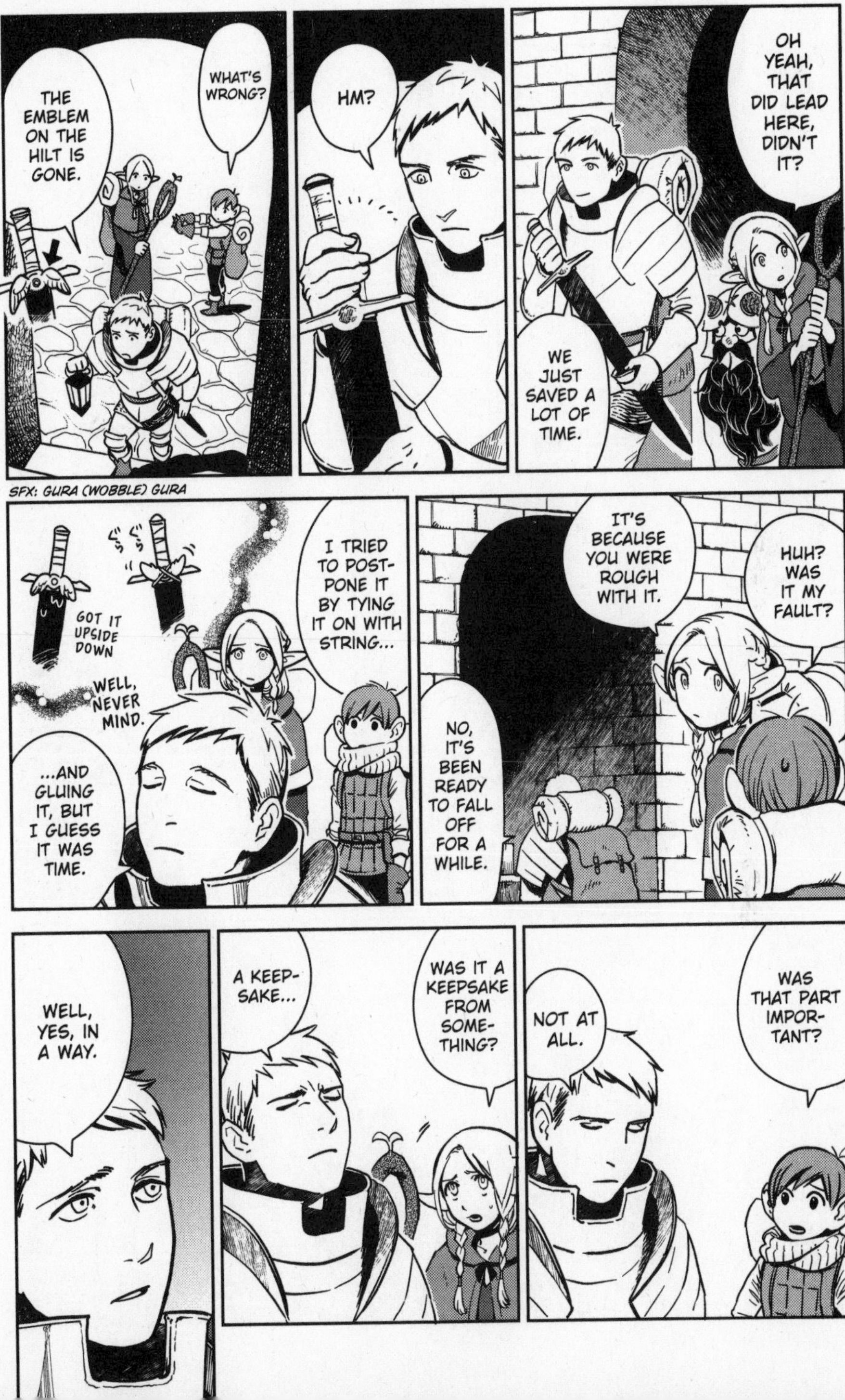
OH YEAH, THAT DID LEAD HERE, DIDN'T IT?
WE JUST SAVED A LOT OF TIME.
HM?
WHAT'S WRONG?
THE EMBLEM ON THE HILT IS GONE.
SFX: GURA (WOBBLE) GURA
HUH? WAS IT MY FAULT?
IT'S BECAUSE YOU WERE ROUGH WITH IT.
NO, IT'S BEEN READY TO FALL OFF FOR A WHILE.
I TRIED TO POST-PONE IT BY TYING IT ON WITH STRING...
GOT IT UPSIDE DOWN
WELL, NEVER MIND.
...AND GLUING IT, BUT I GUESS IT WAS TIME.
WAS THAT PART IMPOR-TANT?
NOT AT ALL.
WAS IT A KEEPSAKE FROM SOME-THING?
A KEEP-SAKE...
WELL, YES, IN A WAY.

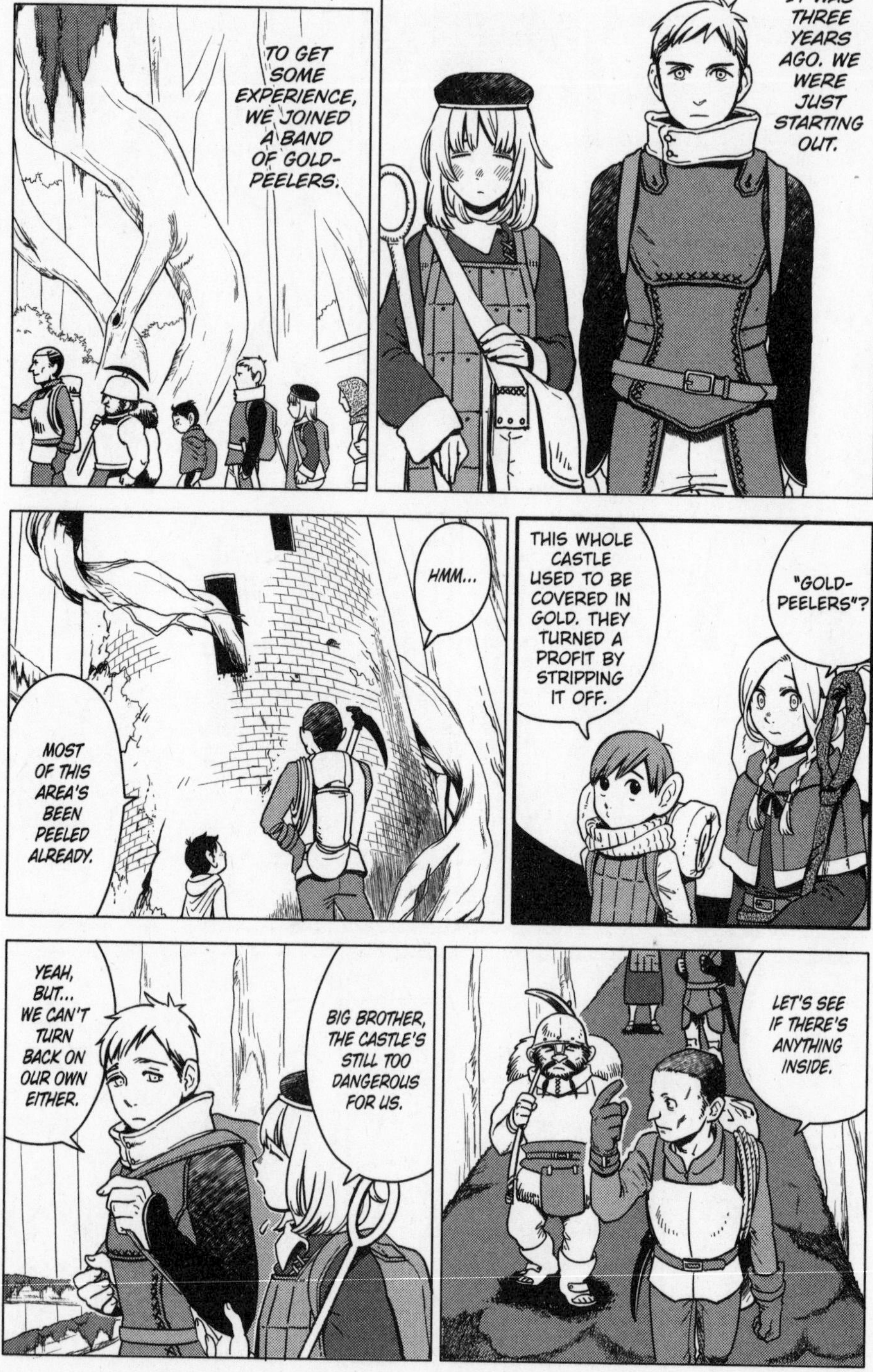
IT WAS THREE YEARS AGO. WE WERE JUST STARTING OUT.
TO GET SOME EXPERIENCE, WE JOINED A BAND OF GOLD-PEELERS.
"GOLD-PEELERS"?
THIS WHOLE CASTLE USED TO BE COVERED IN GOLD. THEY TURNED A PROFIT BY STRIPPING IT OFF.
HMM...
MOST OF THIS AREA'S BEEN PEELED ALREADY.
LET'S SEE IF THERE'S ANYTHING INSIDE.
BIG BROTHER, THE CASTLE'S STILL TOO DANGEROUS FOR US.
YEAH, BUT... WE CAN'T TURN BACK ON OUR OWN EITHER.

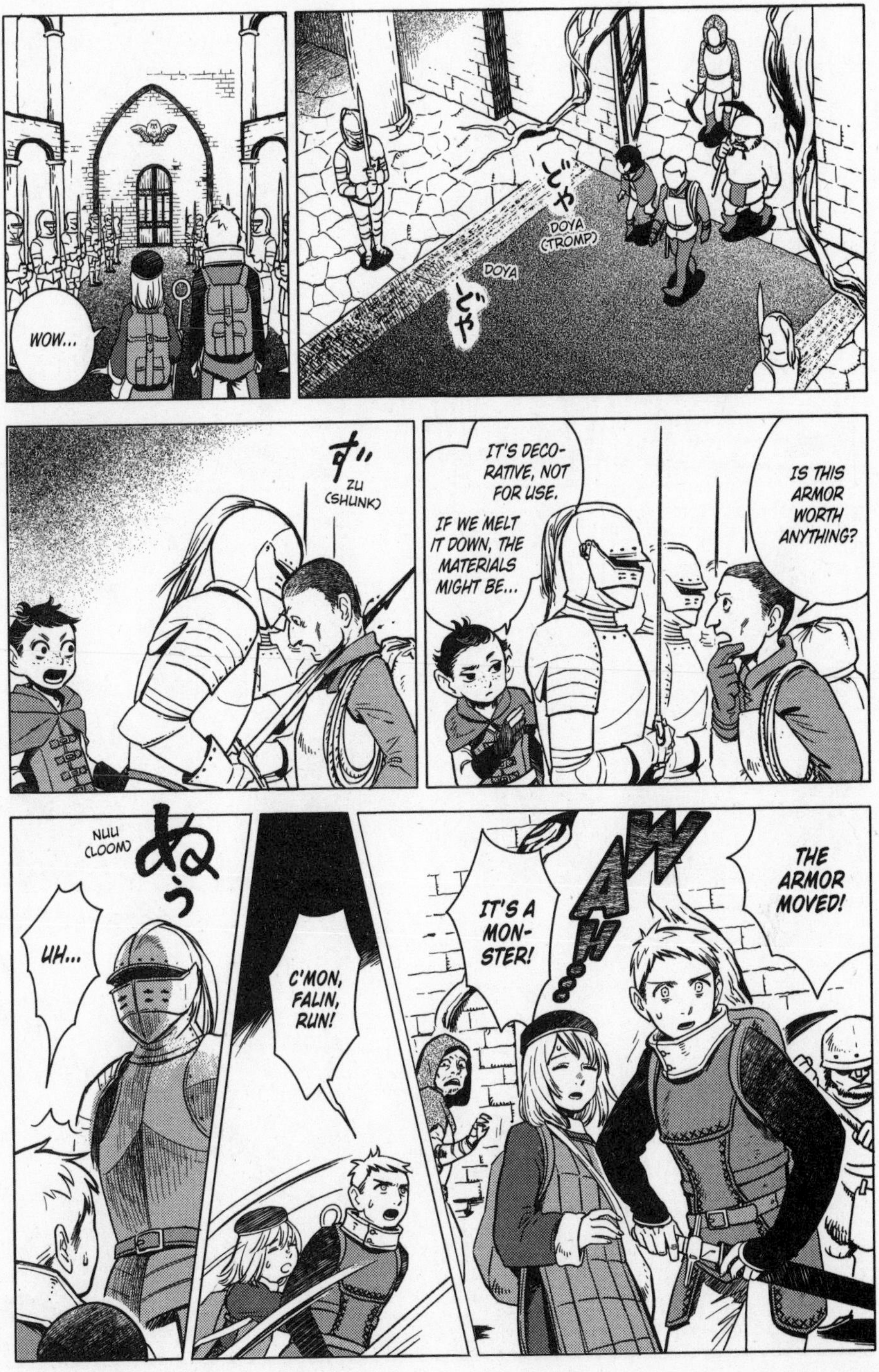
どや
DOYA
(TROMP)
DOYA
どや
WOW...
IS THIS ARMOR WORTH ANYTHING?
IT'S DECORATIVE, NOT FOR USE.
IF WE MELT IT DOWN, THE MATERIALS MIGHT BE...
ずい
ZU
(SHUNK)
THE ARMOR MOVED!
WAH!!
IT'S A MONSTER!
C'MON, FALIN, RUN!
NUU
(LOOM)
ぬう
UH...

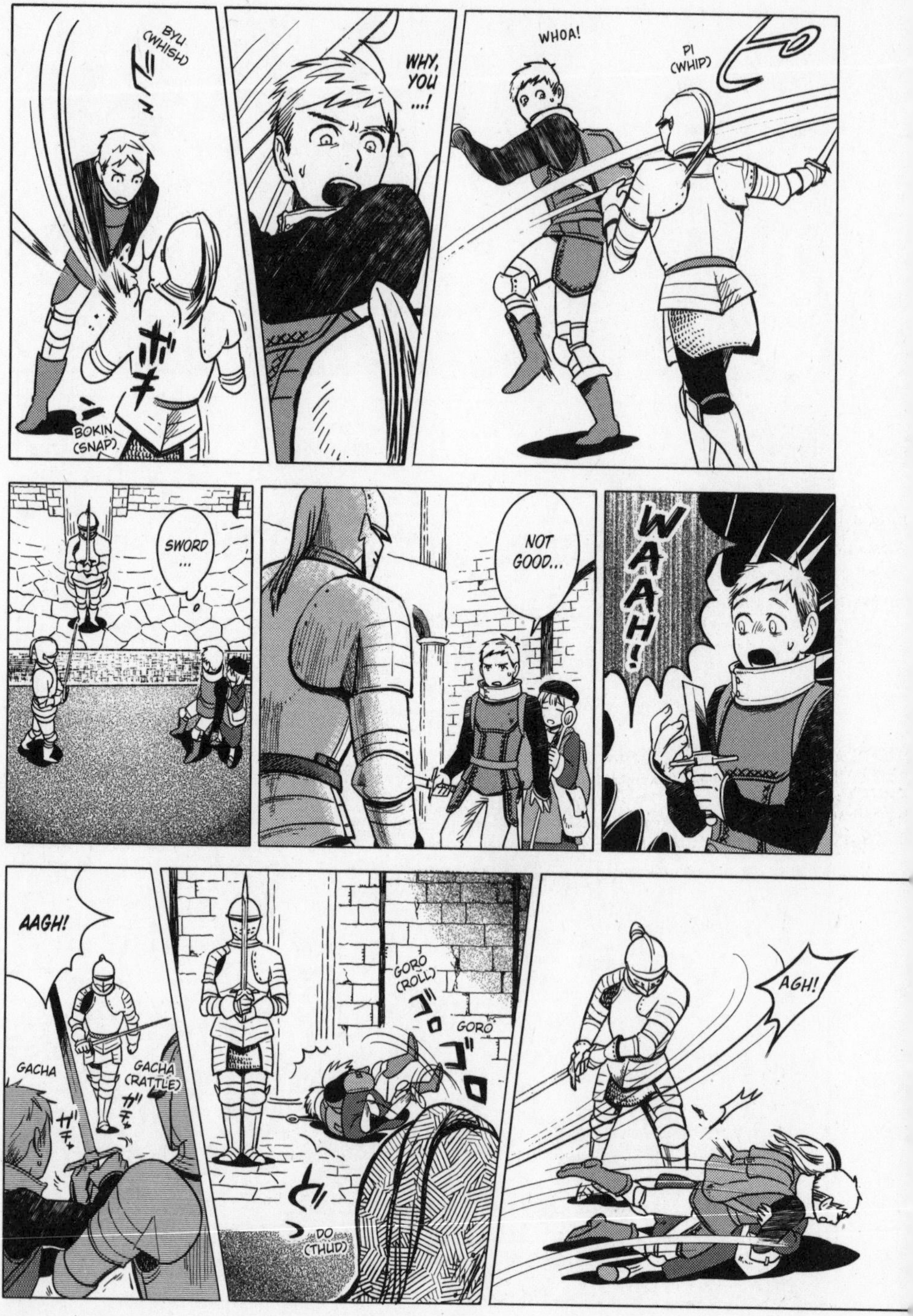
WHOA!
PI (WHIP)
WHY, YOU ...!
BYU (WHISH)
BOKIN (SNAP)
WAAAH!
NOT GOOD...
SWORD ...
AGH!
GORO (ROLL)
GORO
DO (THUD)
AAGH!
GACHA
GACHA (RATTLE)

AH!
AAAAH!

SURUN
(SLIP)

GUWA
(LUNGE)

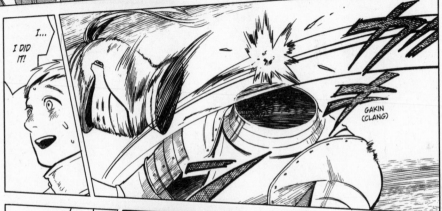

I....
I DID
IT!

GAKIN
(CLANG)

BIG
BRO!

HUH
...?

DO
(SHUNK)

143

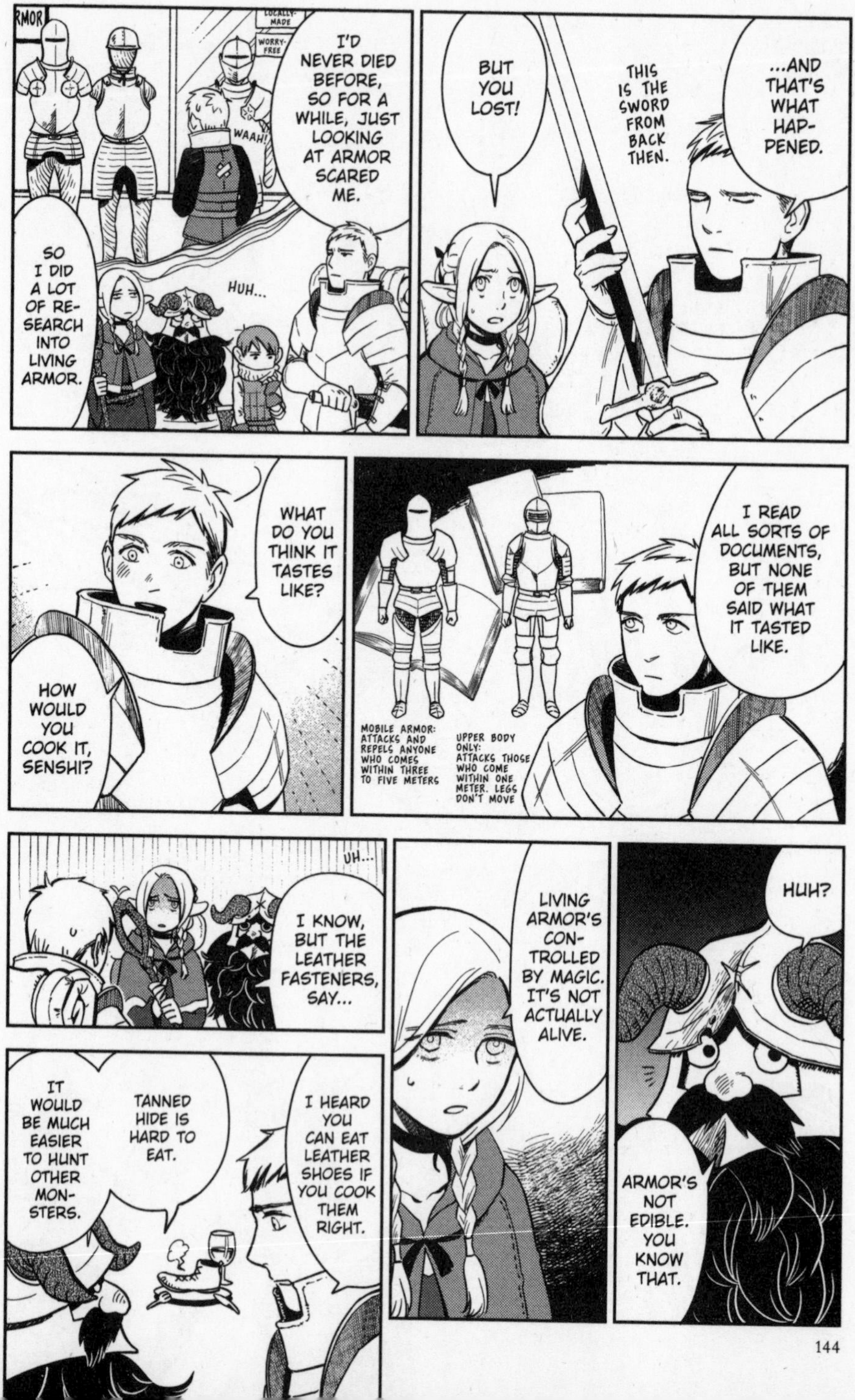
...AND THAT'S WHAT HAP-PENED.
THIS IS THE SWORD FROM BACK THEN.
BUT YOU LOST!
ARMOR
LOCALLY-MADE
WORRY-FREE
I'D NEVER DIED BEFORE, SO FOR A WHILE, JUST LOOKING AT ARMOR SCARED ME.
WAAH!
SO I DID A LOT OF RE-SEARCH INTO LIVING ARMOR.
HUH...
I READ ALL SORTS OF DOCUMENTS, BUT NONE OF THEM SAID WHAT IT TASTED LIKE.
MOBILE ARMOR: ATTACKS AND REPELS ANYONE WHO COMES WITHIN THREE TO FIVE METERS
UPPER BODY ONLY: ATTACKS THOSE WHO COME WITHIN ONE METER. LEGS DON'T MOVE
WHAT DO YOU THINK IT TASTES LIKE?
HOW WOULD YOU COOK IT, SENSHI?
HUH?
ARMOR'S NOT EDIBLE. YOU KNOW THAT.
LIVING ARMOR'S CON-TROLLED BY MAGIC. IT'S NOT ACTUALLY ALIVE.
UH...
I KNOW, BUT THE LEATHER FASTENERS, SAY...
I HEARD YOU CAN EAT LEATHER SHOES IF YOU COOK THEM RIGHT.
TANNED HIDE IS HARD TO EAT.
IT WOULD BE MUCH EASIER TO HUNT OTHER MON-STERS.

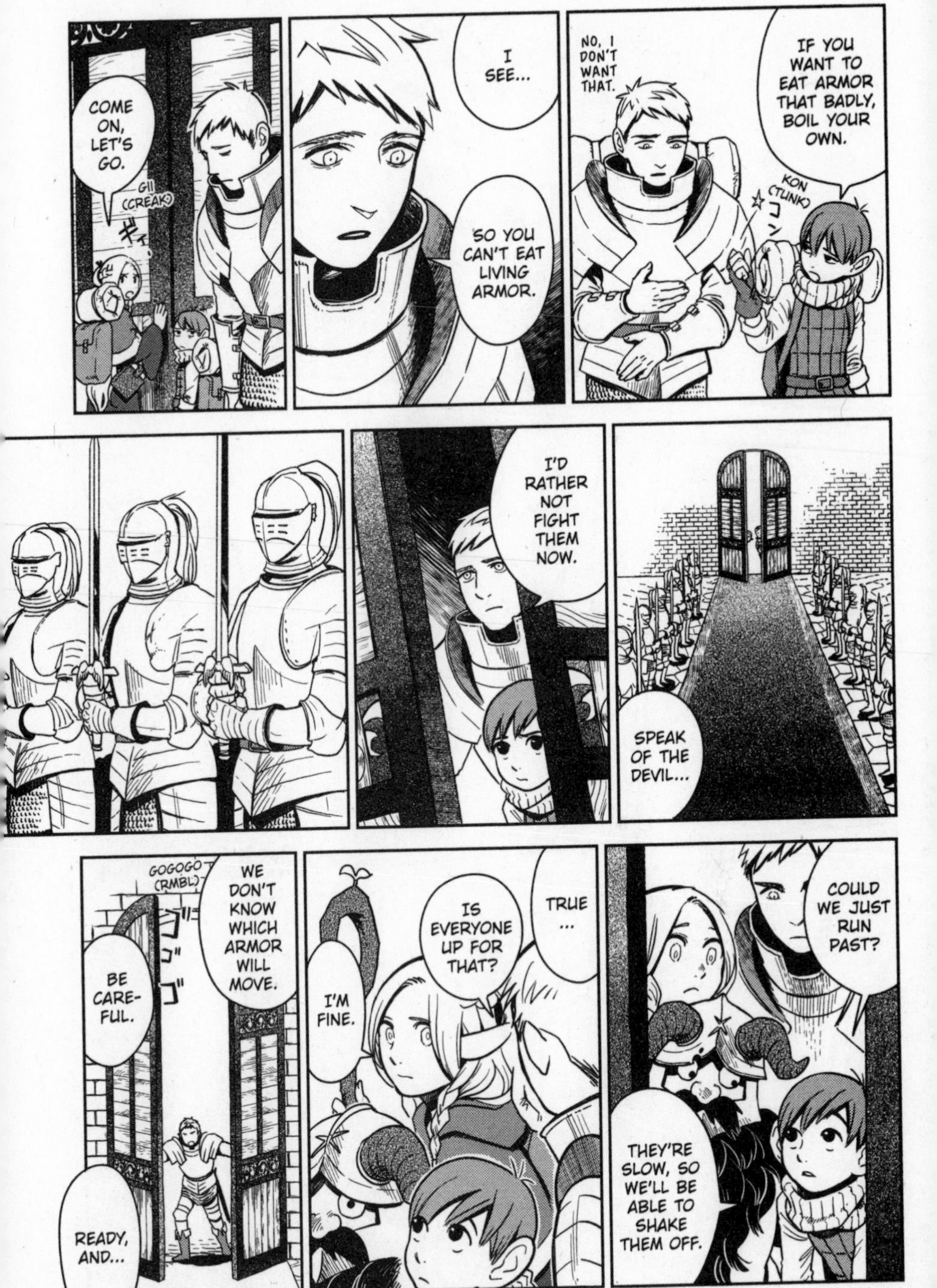

IF YOU WANT TO EAT ARMOR THAT BADLY, BOIL YOUR OWN.
KON (TUNK)
NO, I DON'T WANT THAT.
I SEE...
SO YOU CAN'T EAT LIVING ARMOR.
COME ON, LET'S GO.
GII (CREAK)
SPEAK OF THE DEVIL...
I'D RATHER NOT FIGHT THEM NOW.
COULD WE JUST RUN PAST?
THEY'RE SLOW, SO WE'LL BE ABLE TO SHAKE THEM OFF.
TRUE ...
IS EVERYONE UP FOR THAT?
I'M FINE.
WE DON'T KNOW WHICH ARMOR WILL MOVE.
GOGOGO (RMBL)
BE CARE-FUL.
READY, AND...

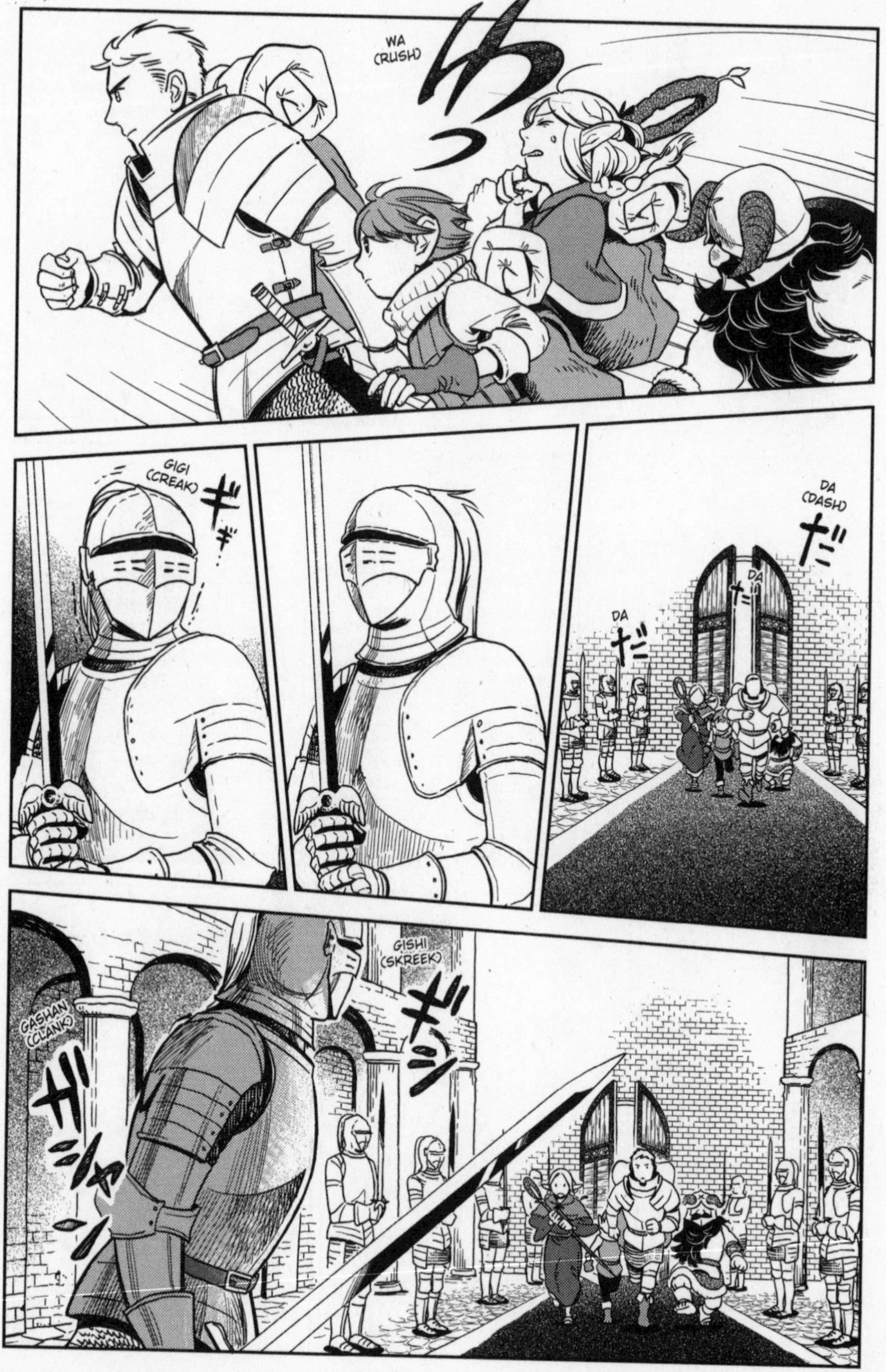
WA (RUSH)
DA (DASH)
DA
DA
GIGI (CREAK)
GISHI (SKREEK)
GASHAN (CLANK)

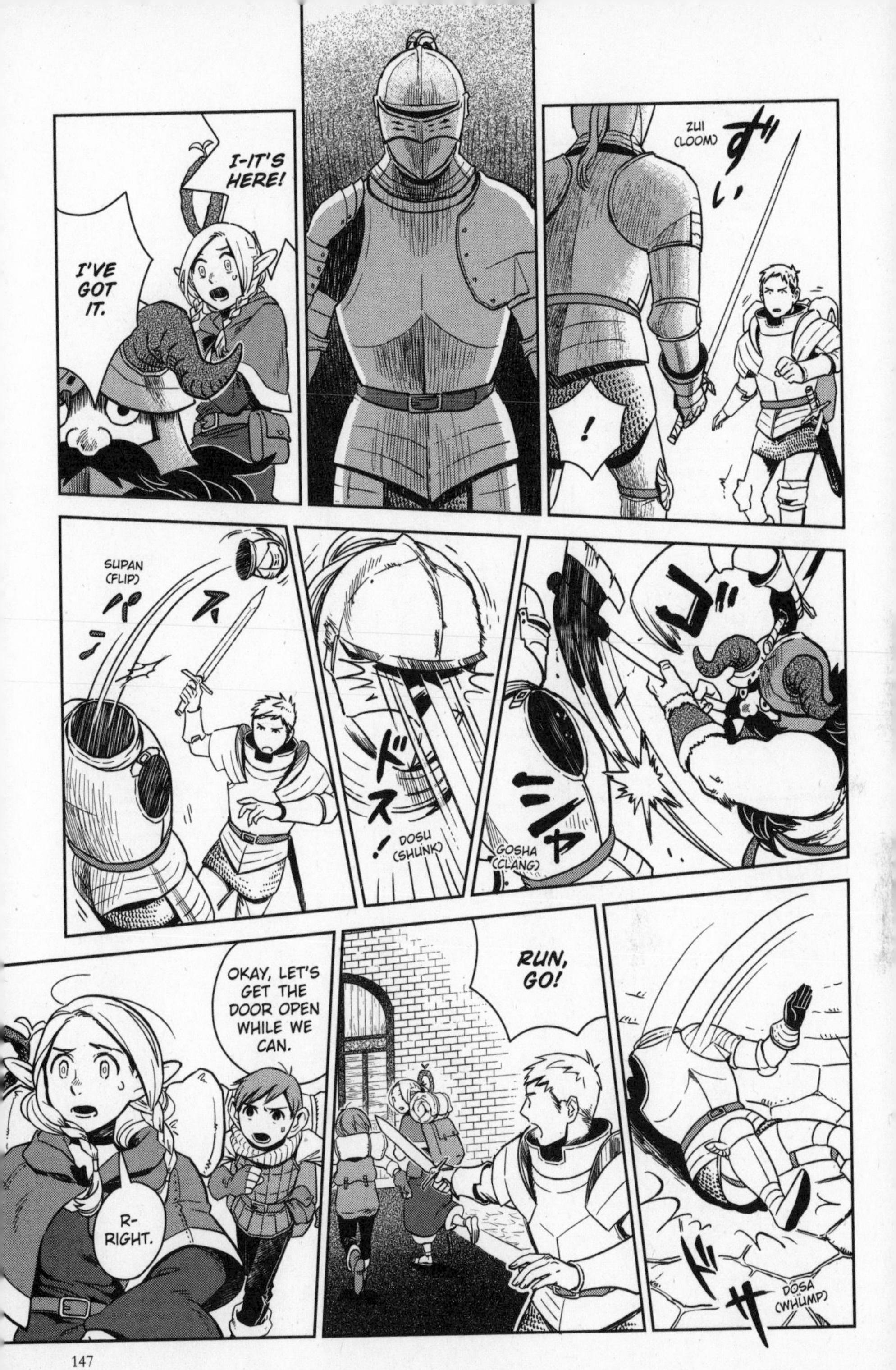
ZUI
(LOOM)
!
I-IT'S HERE!
I'VE GOT IT.
GOSHA
(CLANG)
DOSU
(SHUNK)
SUPAN
(FLIP)
DOSA
(WHUMP)
RUN, GO!
OKAY, LET'S GET THE DOOR OPEN WHILE WE CAN.
R-RIGHT.

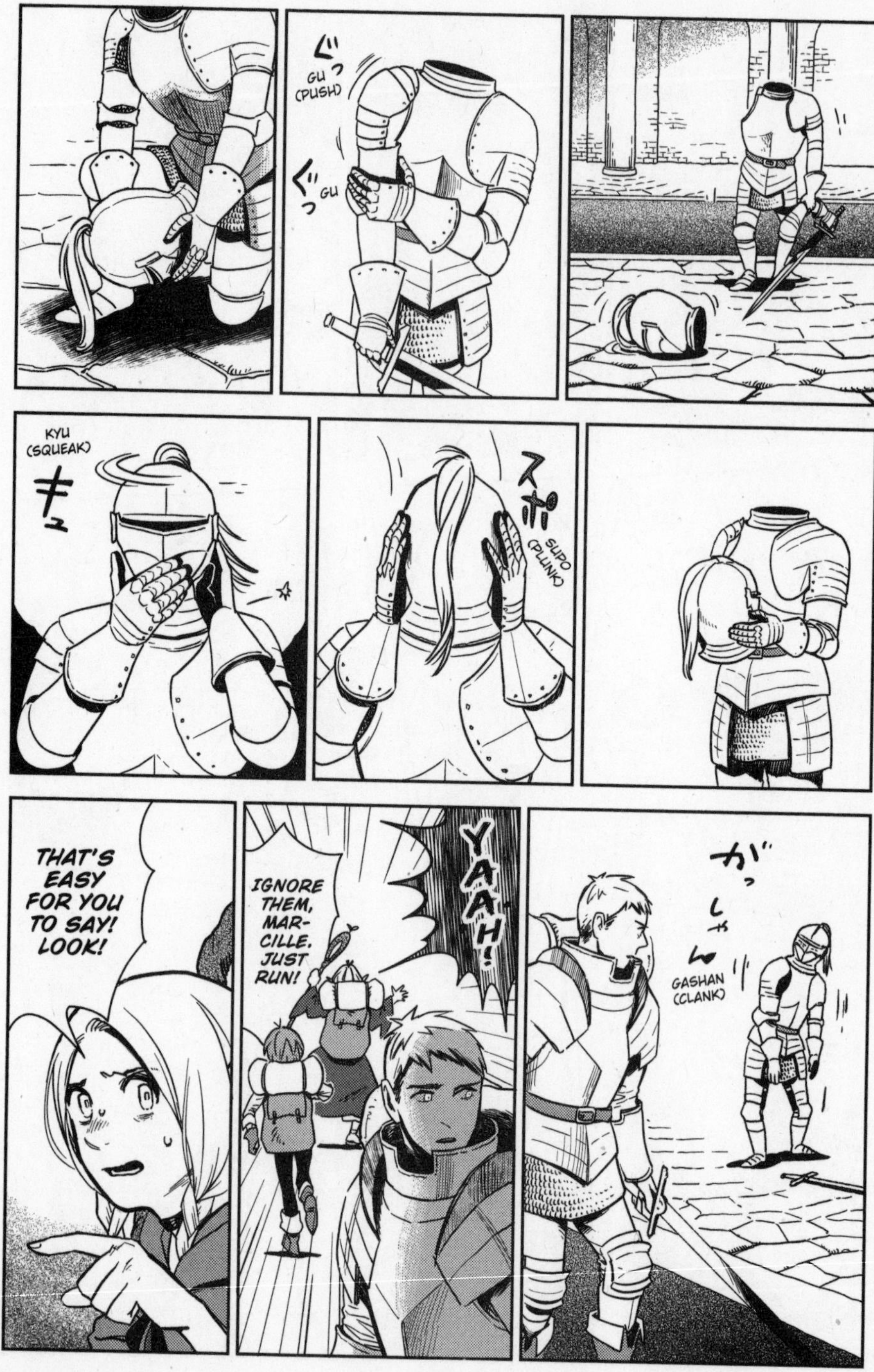
ぐっ
GU (PUSH)
ぐっ
GU
スポ
SUPO (PLINK)
KYU (SQUEAK)
キュ
がっしゃん
GASHAN (CLANK)
YAAH!
IGNORE THEM, MAR-CILLE. JUST RUN!
THAT'S EASY FOR YOU TO SAY! LOOK!

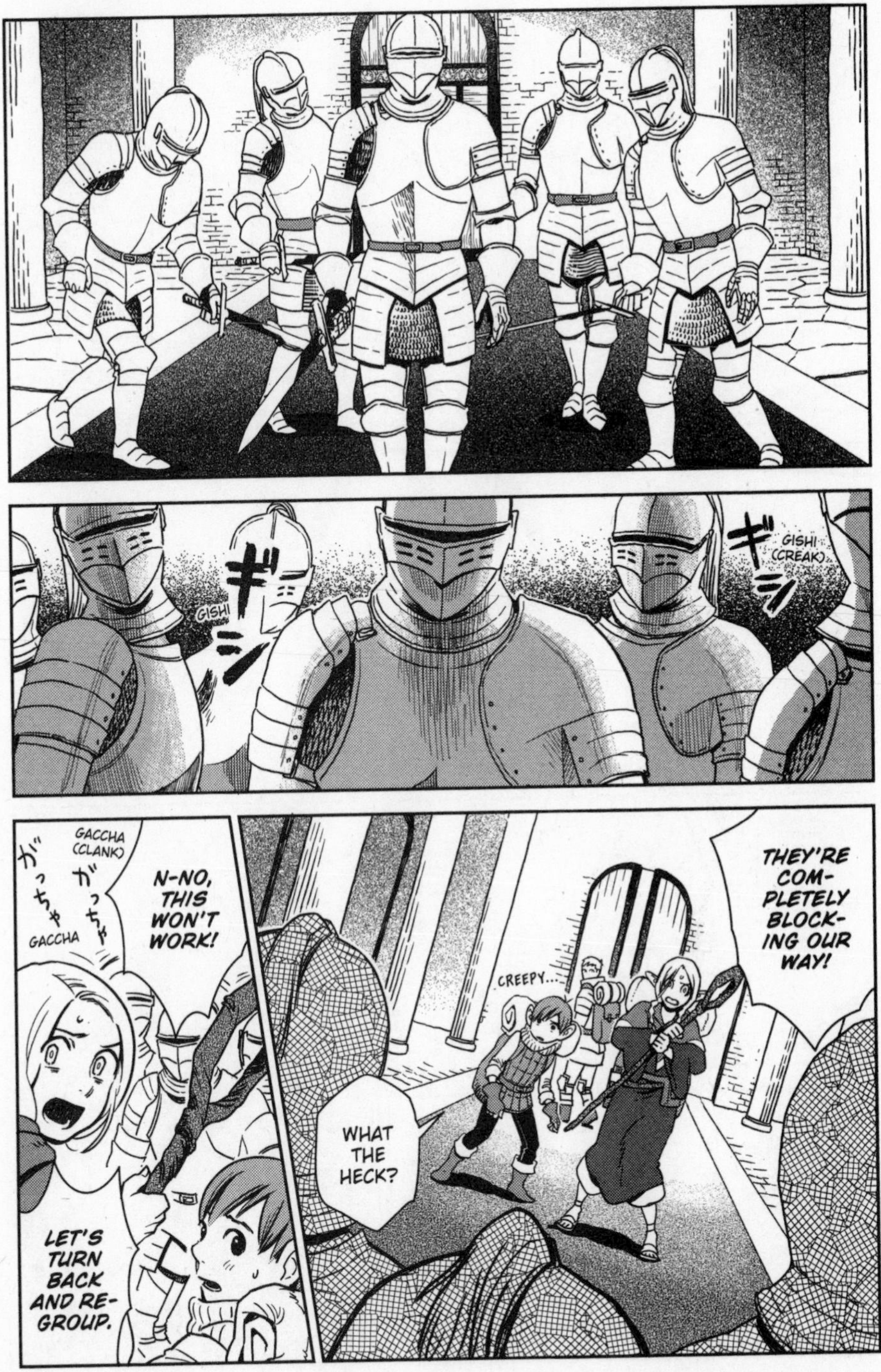
ギシ
GISHI (CREAK)
ギシ
GISHI
THEY'RE COM-PLETELY BLOCK-ING OUR WAY!
CREEPY...
WHAT THE HECK?
N-NO, THIS WON'T WORK!
がっちゃ
GACCHA (CLANK)
がっちゃ
GACCHA
LET'S TURN BACK AND RE-GROUP.

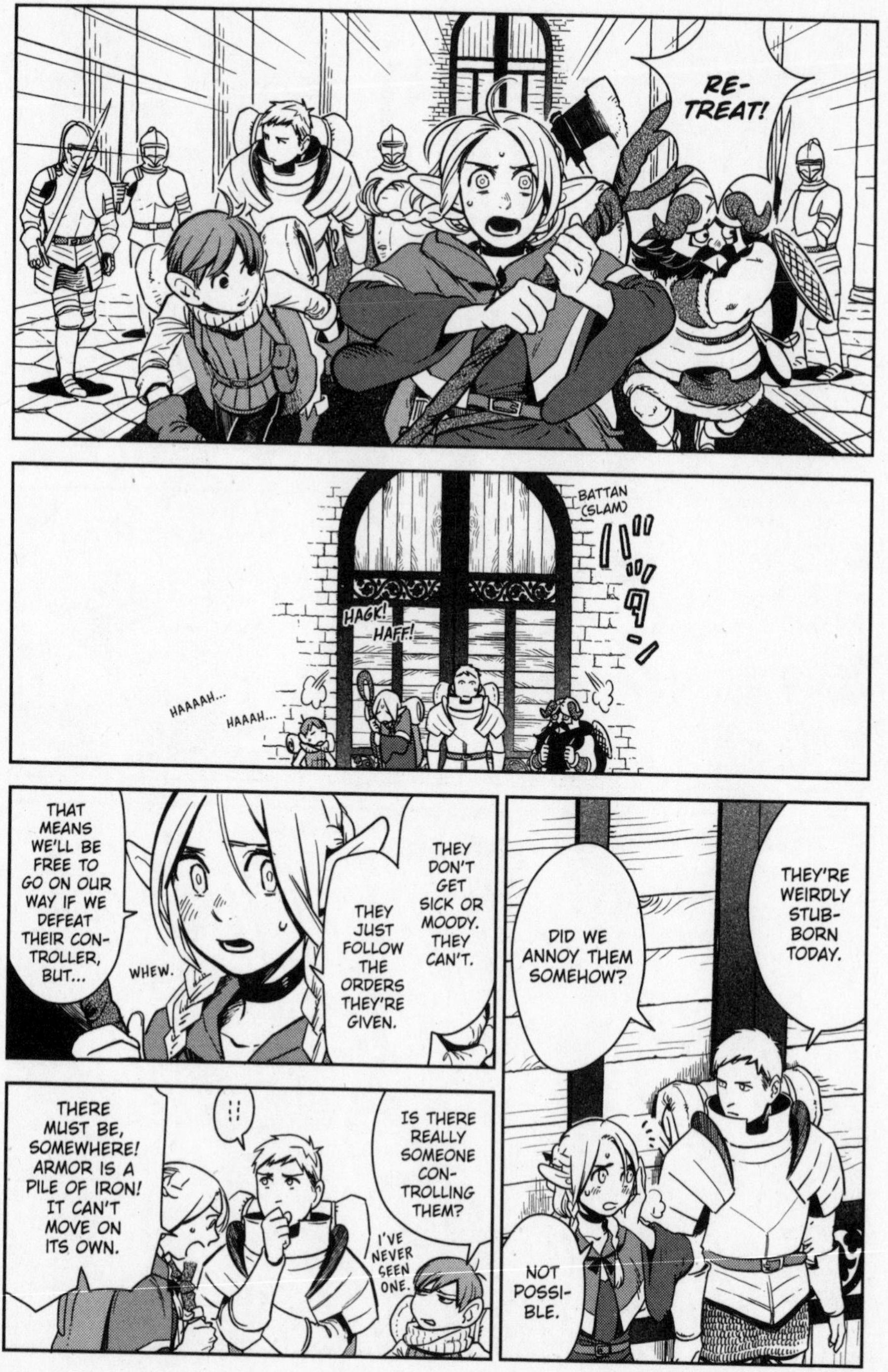
RE-TREAT!
BATTAN (SLAM)
HAGK! HAFF!
HAAAAH... HAAAH...
THEY'RE WEIRDLY STUB-BORN TODAY.
DID WE ANNOY THEM SOMEHOW?
NOT POSSI-BLE.
THEY DON'T GET SICK OR MOODY. THEY CAN'T.
THEY JUST FOLLOW THE ORDERS THEY'RE GIVEN.
THAT MEANS WE'LL BE FREE TO GO ON OUR WAY IF WE DEFEAT THEIR CON-TROLLER, BUT...
WHEW.
IS THERE REALLY SOMEONE CON-TROLLING THEM?
I'VE NEVER SEEN ONE.
!!
THERE MUST BE, SOMEWHERE! ARMOR IS A PILE OF IRON! IT CAN'T MOVE ON ITS OWN.

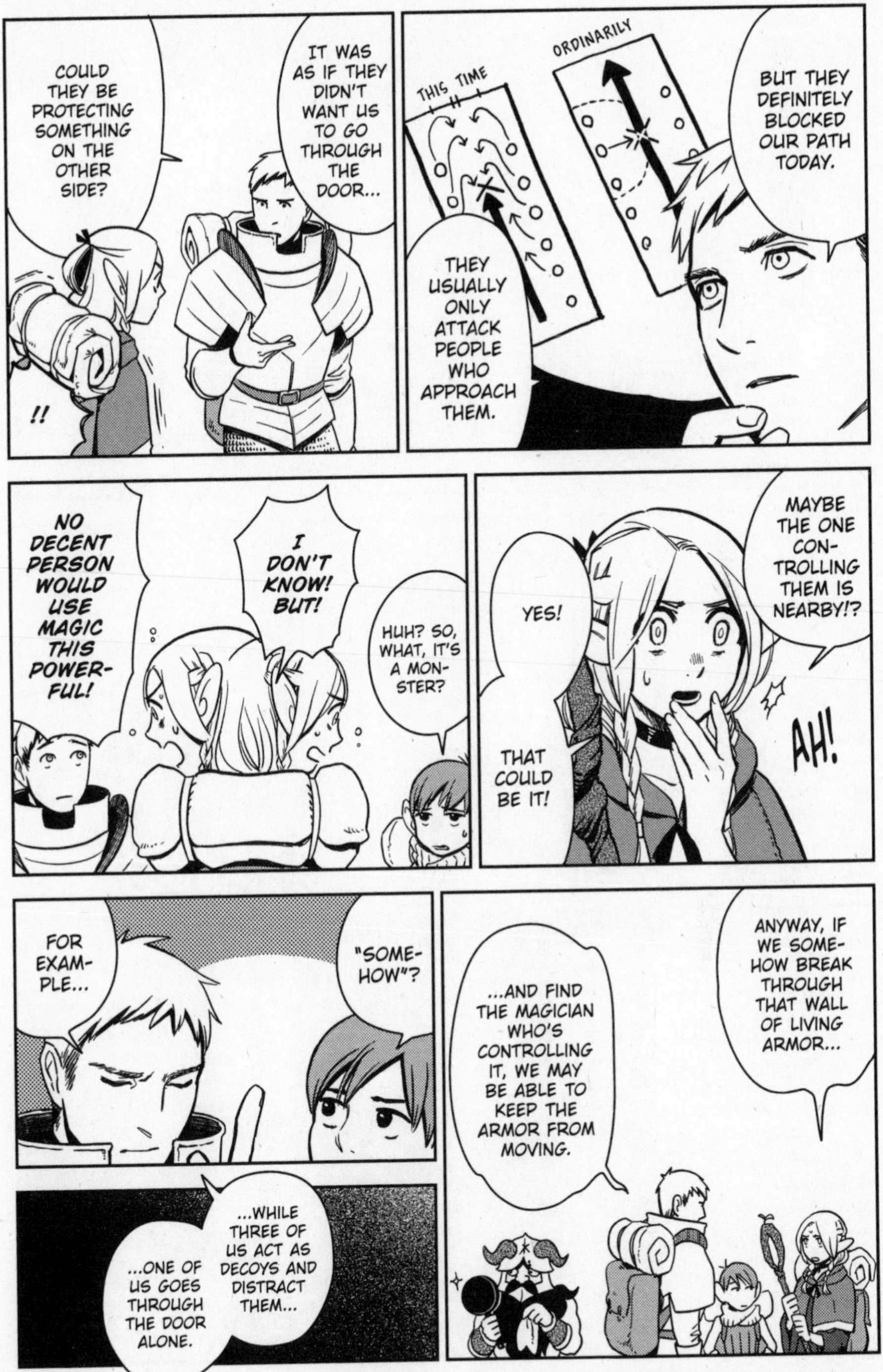
BUT THEY DEFINITELY BLOCKED OUR PATH TODAY.
ORDINARILY
THIS TIME
THEY USUALLY ONLY ATTACK PEOPLE WHO APPROACH THEM.
IT WAS AS IF THEY DIDN'T WANT US TO GO THROUGH THE DOOR...
COULD THEY BE PROTECTING SOMETHING ON THE OTHER SIDE?
!!
MAYBE THE ONE CONTROLLING THEM IS NEARBY!?
AH!
YES!
THAT COULD BE IT!
HUH? SO, WHAT, IT'S A MONSTER?
I DON'T KNOW! BUT!
NO DECENT PERSON WOULD USE MAGIC THIS POWERFUL!
ANYWAY, IF WE SOMEHOW BREAK THROUGH THAT WALL OF LIVING ARMOR...
...AND FIND THE MAGICIAN WHO'S CONTROLLING IT, WE MAY BE ABLE TO KEEP THE ARMOR FROM MOVING.
"SOMEHOW"?
FOR EXAMPLE...
...WHILE THREE OF US ACT AS DECOYS AND DISTRACT THEM...
...ONE OF US GOES THROUGH THE DOOR ALONE.

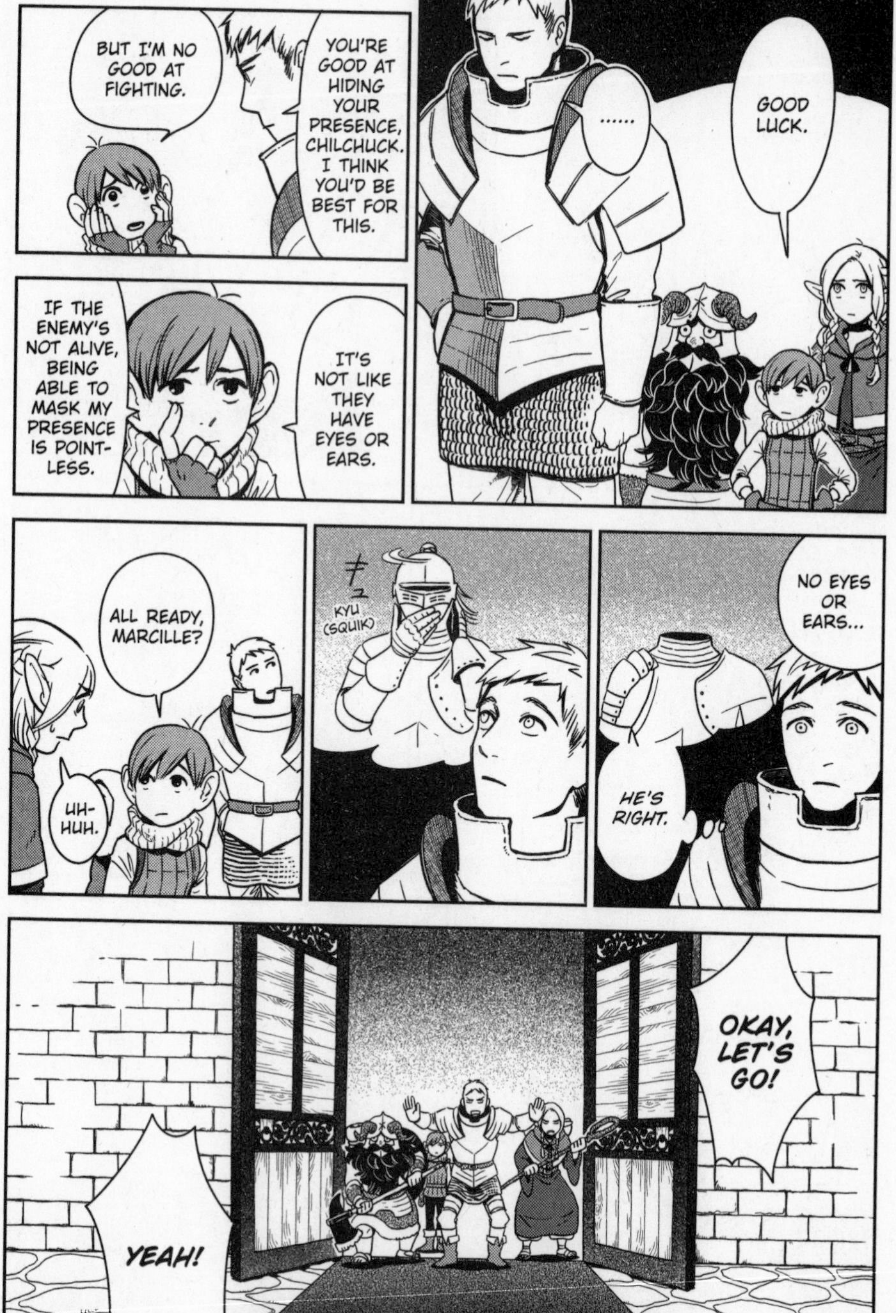
GOOD LUCK.
......
YOU'RE GOOD AT HIDING YOUR PRESENCE, CHILCHUCK. I THINK YOU'D BE BEST FOR THIS.
BUT I'M NO GOOD AT FIGHTING.
IT'S NOT LIKE THEY HAVE EYES OR EARS.
IF THE ENEMY'S NOT ALIVE, BEING ABLE TO MASK MY PRESENCE IS POINTLESS.
NO EYES OR EARS...
HE'S RIGHT.
KYU (SQUIK)
ALL READY, MARCILLE?
UH-HUH.
OKAY, LET'S GO!
YEAH!

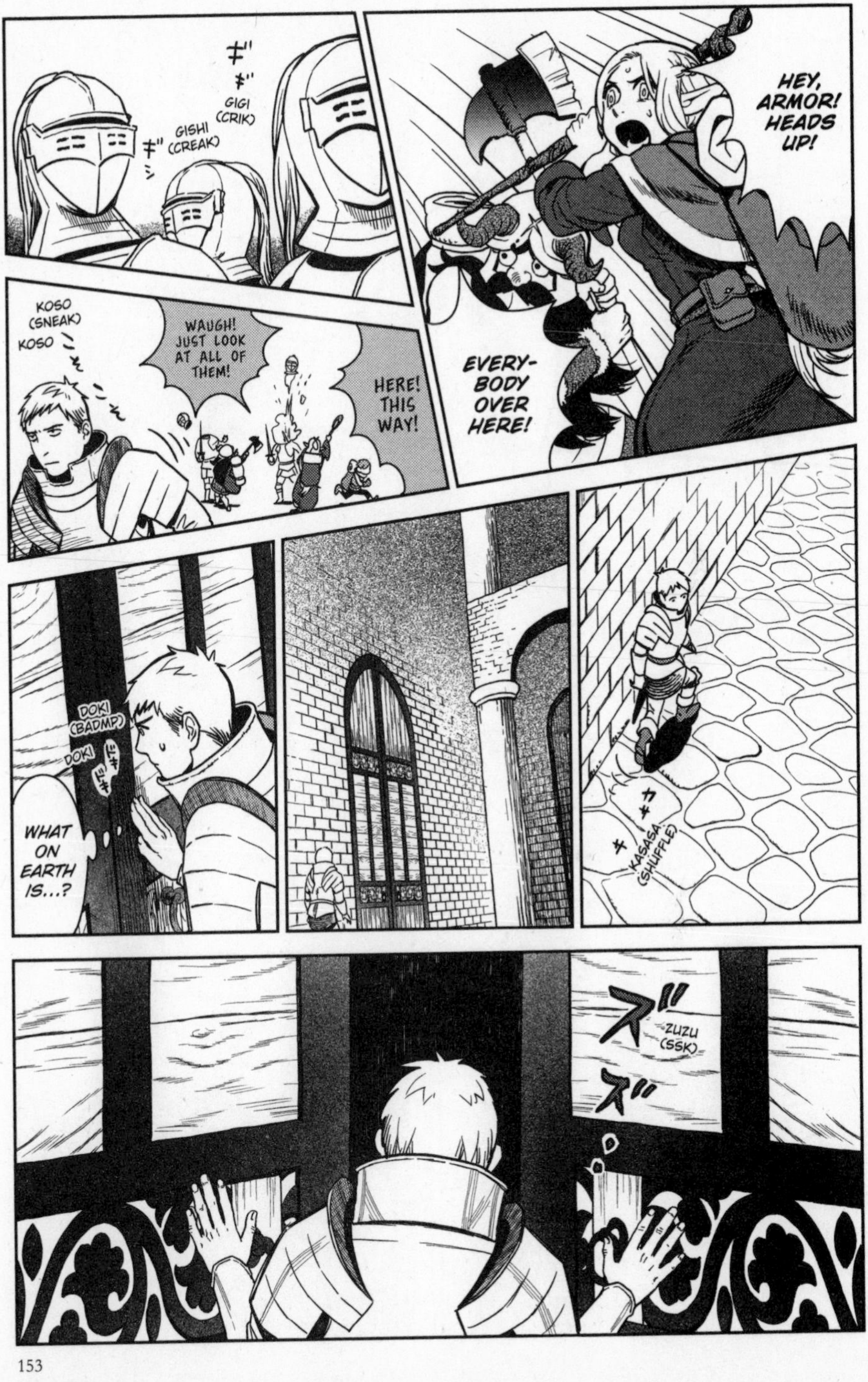
HEY, ARMOR! HEADS UP!
EVERYBODY OVER HERE!
GIGI (CRIK)
GISHI (CREAK)
WAUGH! JUST LOOK AT ALL OF THEM!
HERE! THIS WAY!
KOSO (SNEAK) KOSO
KASASA (SHUFFLE)
DOKI (BADMP) DOKI
WHAT ON EARTH IS...?
ZUZU (SSK)

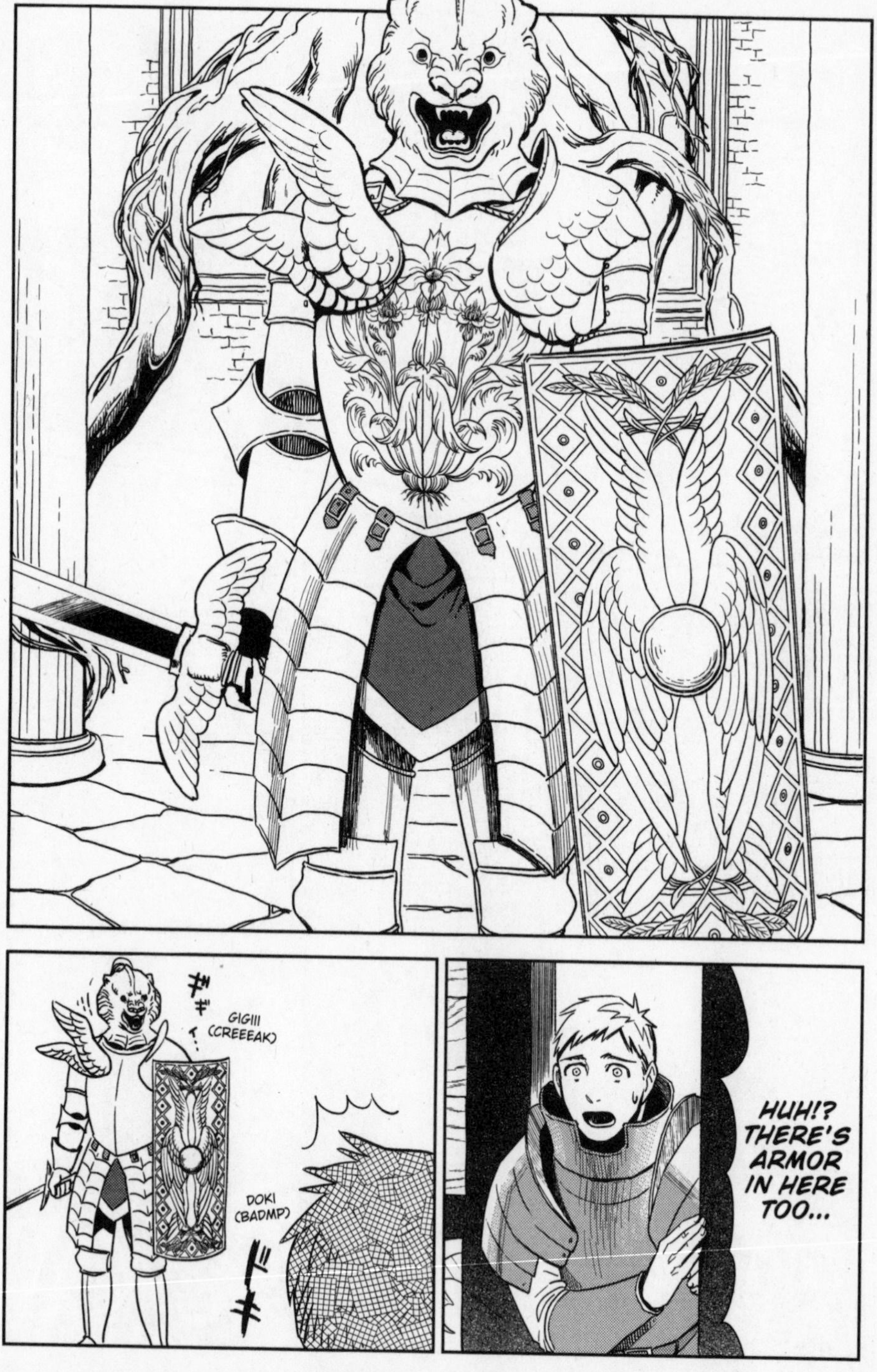
HUH!? THERE'S ARMOR IN HERE TOO...
ギギィ…
GIGIII (CREEEAK)
DOKI (BADMP)
ドキ

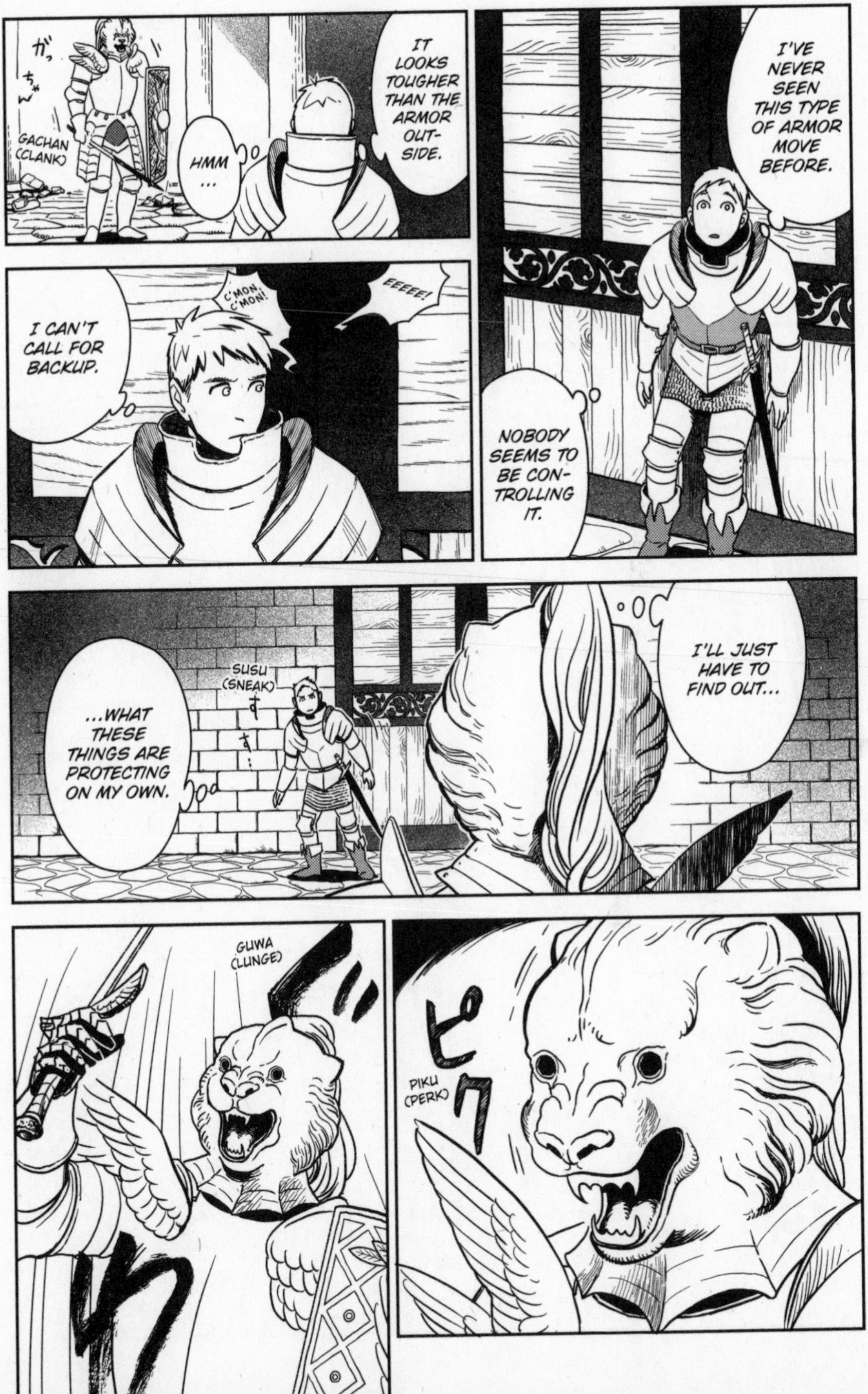
I'VE NEVER SEEN THIS TYPE OF ARMOR MOVE BEFORE.
NOBODY SEEMS TO BE CONTROLLING IT.
IT LOOKS TOUGHER THAN THE ARMOR OUTSIDE.
HMM...
ガっちゃん
GACHAN (CLANK)
EEEEE!
C'MON C'MON!
I CAN'T CALL FOR BACKUP.
I'LL JUST HAVE TO FIND OUT...
SUSU (SNEAK)
すす...
...WHAT THESE THINGS ARE PROTECTING ON MY OWN.
ピク
PIKU (PERK)
GUWA (LUNGE)

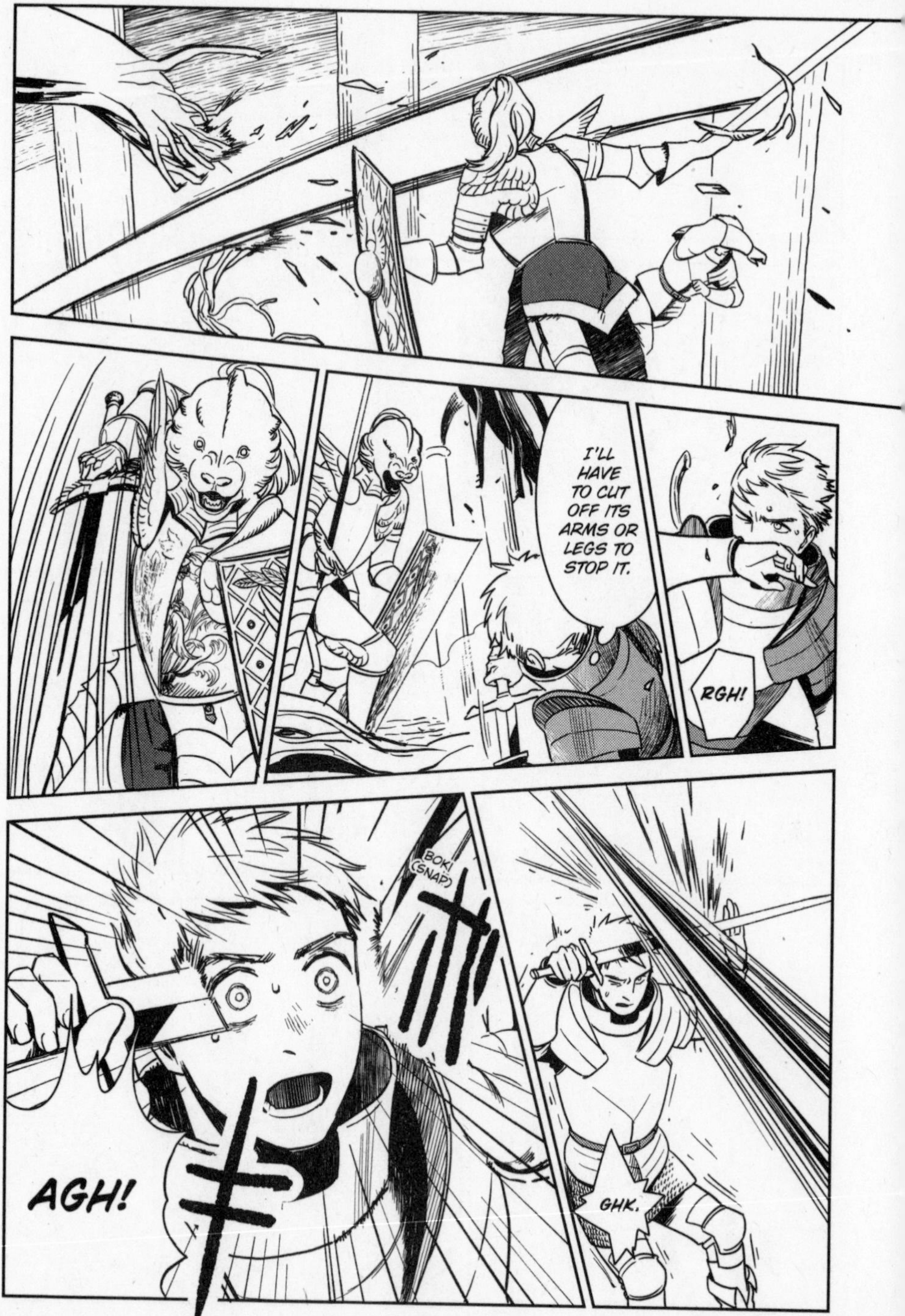
RGH!
I'LL HAVE TO CUT OFF ITS ARMS OR LEGS TO STOP IT.
GHK.
BOKI (SNAP)
AGH!

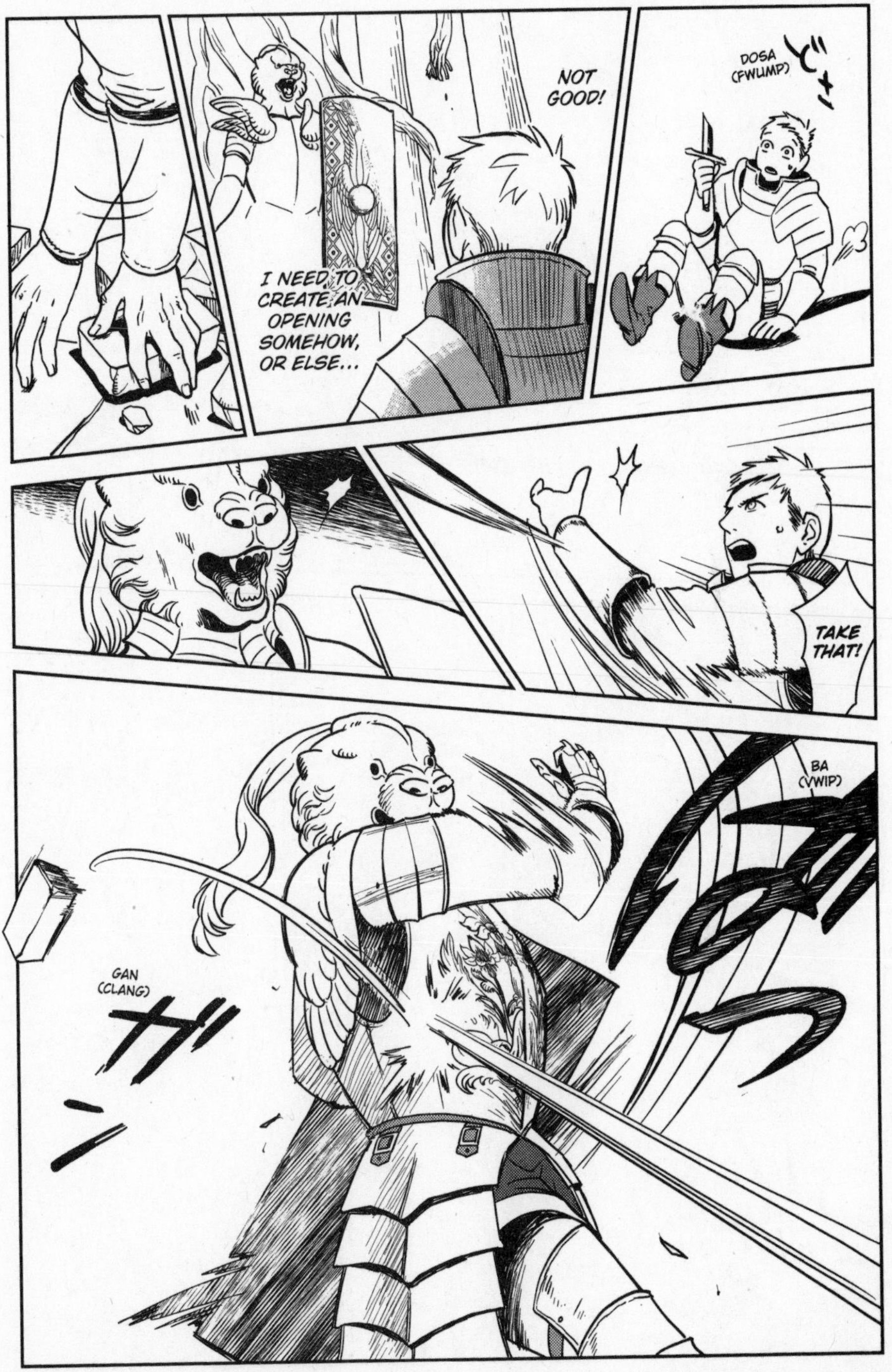
DOSA
(FWUMP)
NOT GOOD!
I NEED TO CREATE AN OPENING SOMEHOW, OR ELSE...
TAKE THAT!
BA
(VWIP)
GAN
(CLANG)

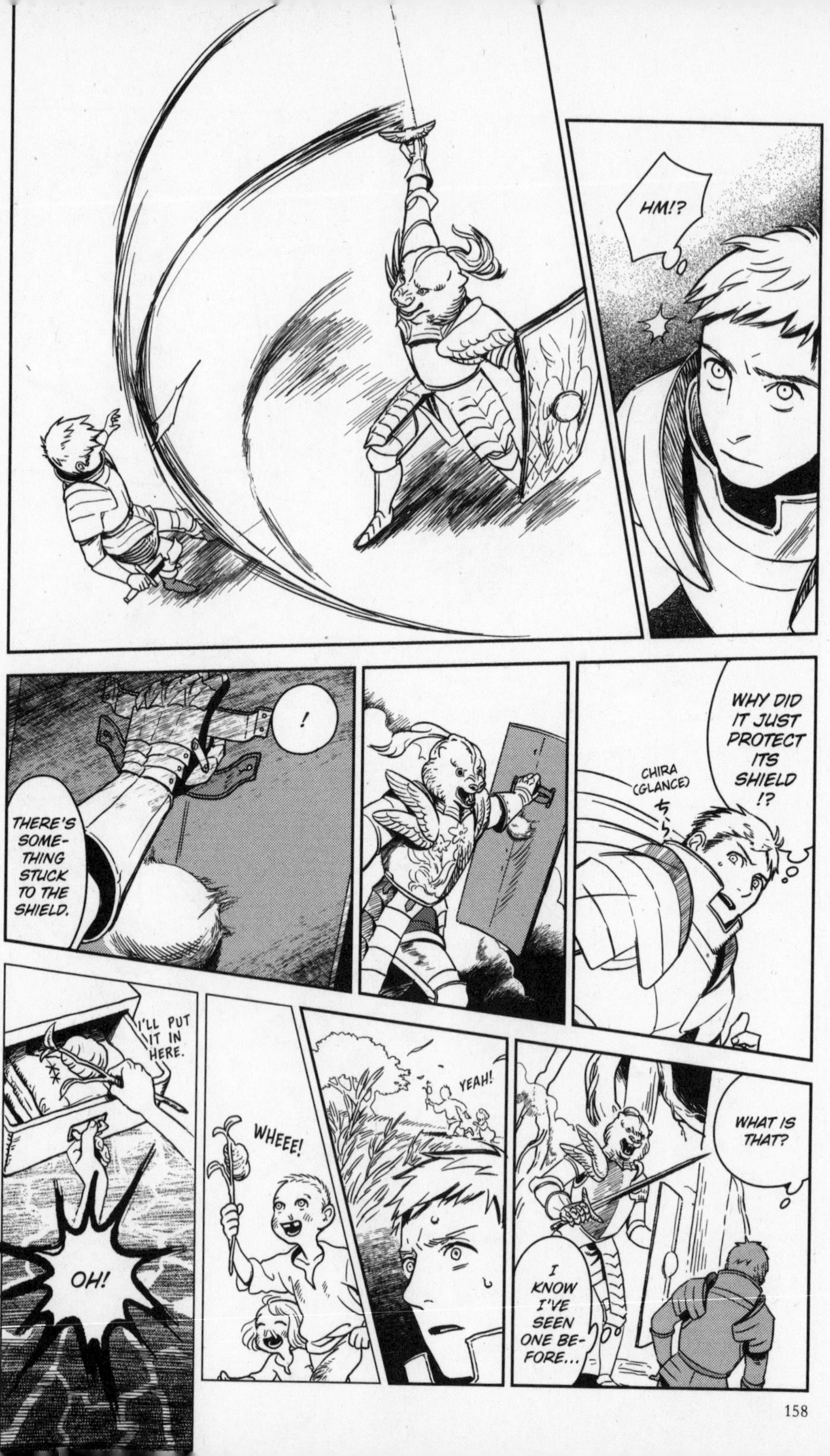
HM!?
WHY DID IT JUST PROTECT ITS SHIELD !?
CHIRA (GLANCE)
ちら
!
THERE'S SOME-THING STUCK TO THE SHIELD.
WHAT IS THAT?
I KNOW I'VE SEEN ONE BEFORE...
YEAH!
WHEEE!
I'LL PUT IT IN HERE.
OH!

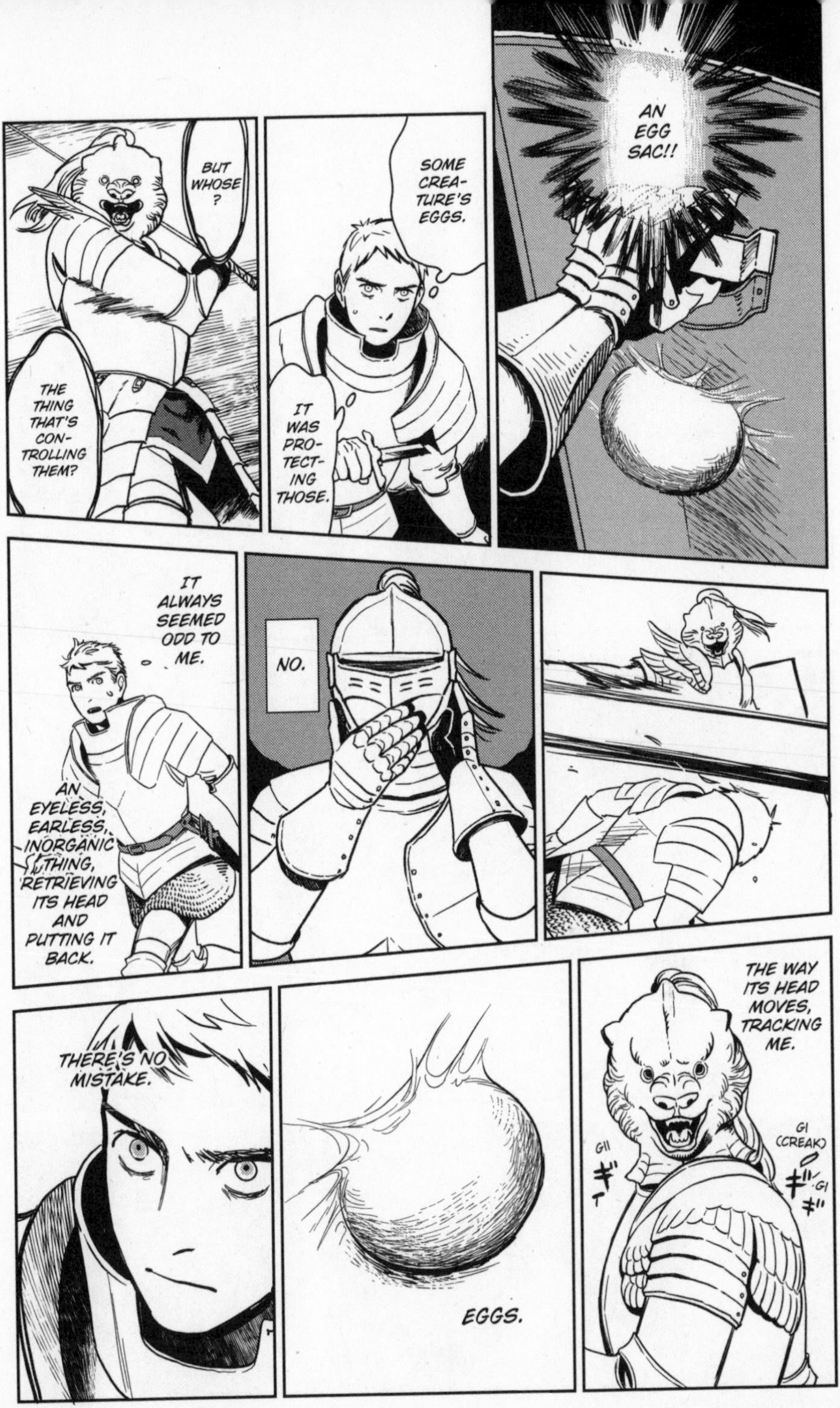
AN EGG SAC!!
SOME CREATURE'S EGGS.
IT WAS PROTECTING THOSE.
BUT WHOSE?
THE THING THAT'S CONTROLLING THEM?
NO.
IT ALWAYS SEEMED ODD TO ME.
AN EYELESS, EARLESS, INORGANIC THING, RETRIEVING ITS HEAD AND PUTTING IT BACK.
THE WAY ITS HEAD MOVES, TRACKING ME.
GI (CREAK)
GI
GII
EGGS.
THERE'S NO MISTAKE.

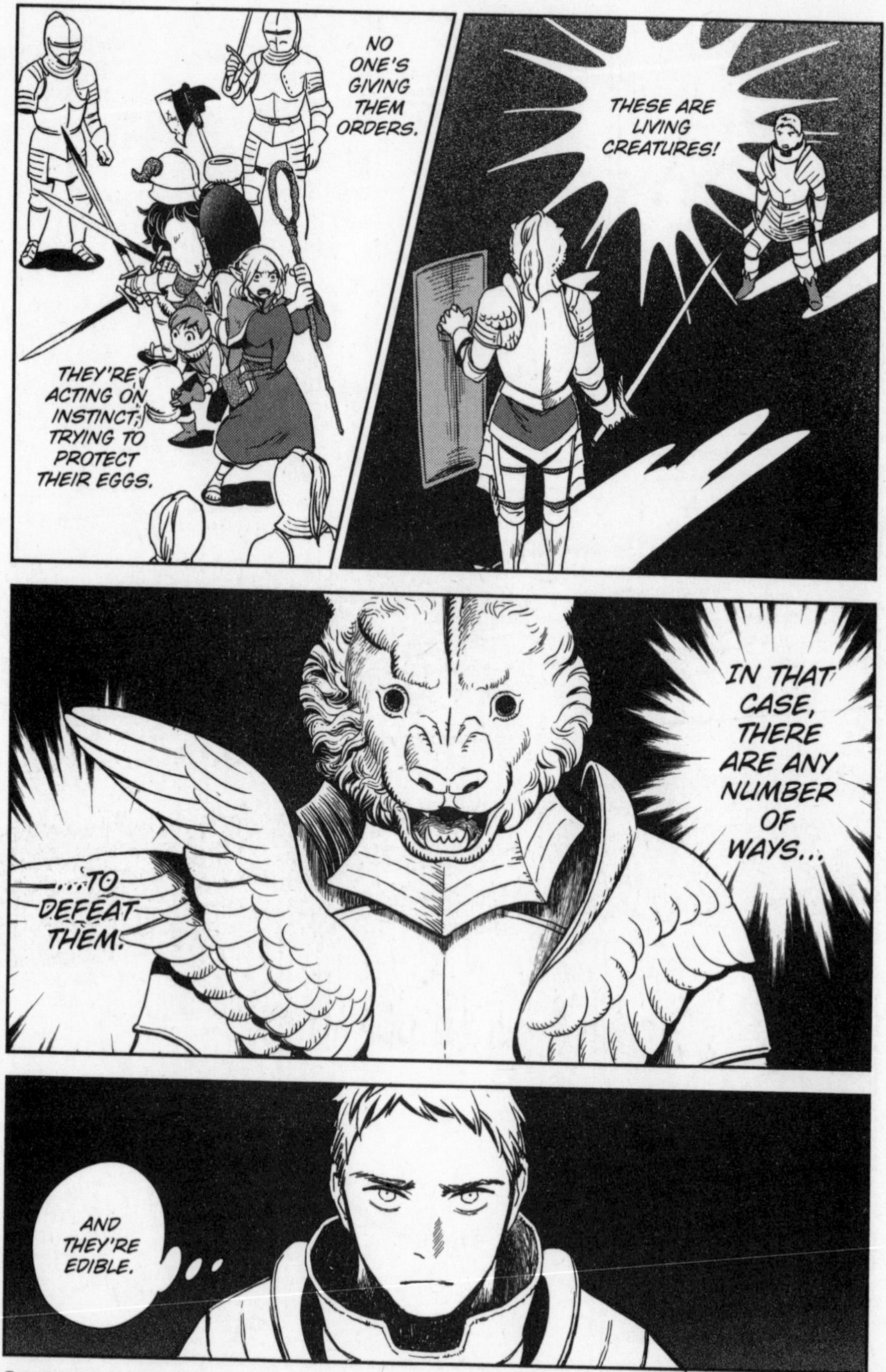
THESE ARE LIVING CREATURES!
NO ONE'S GIVING THEM ORDERS.
THEY'RE ACTING ON INSTINCT, TRYING TO PROTECT THEIR EGGS.
IN THAT CASE, THERE ARE ANY NUMBER OF WAYS...
...TO DEFEAT THEM.
AND THEY'RE EDIBLE.

Chapter 6: The End

7. Living Armor -2-

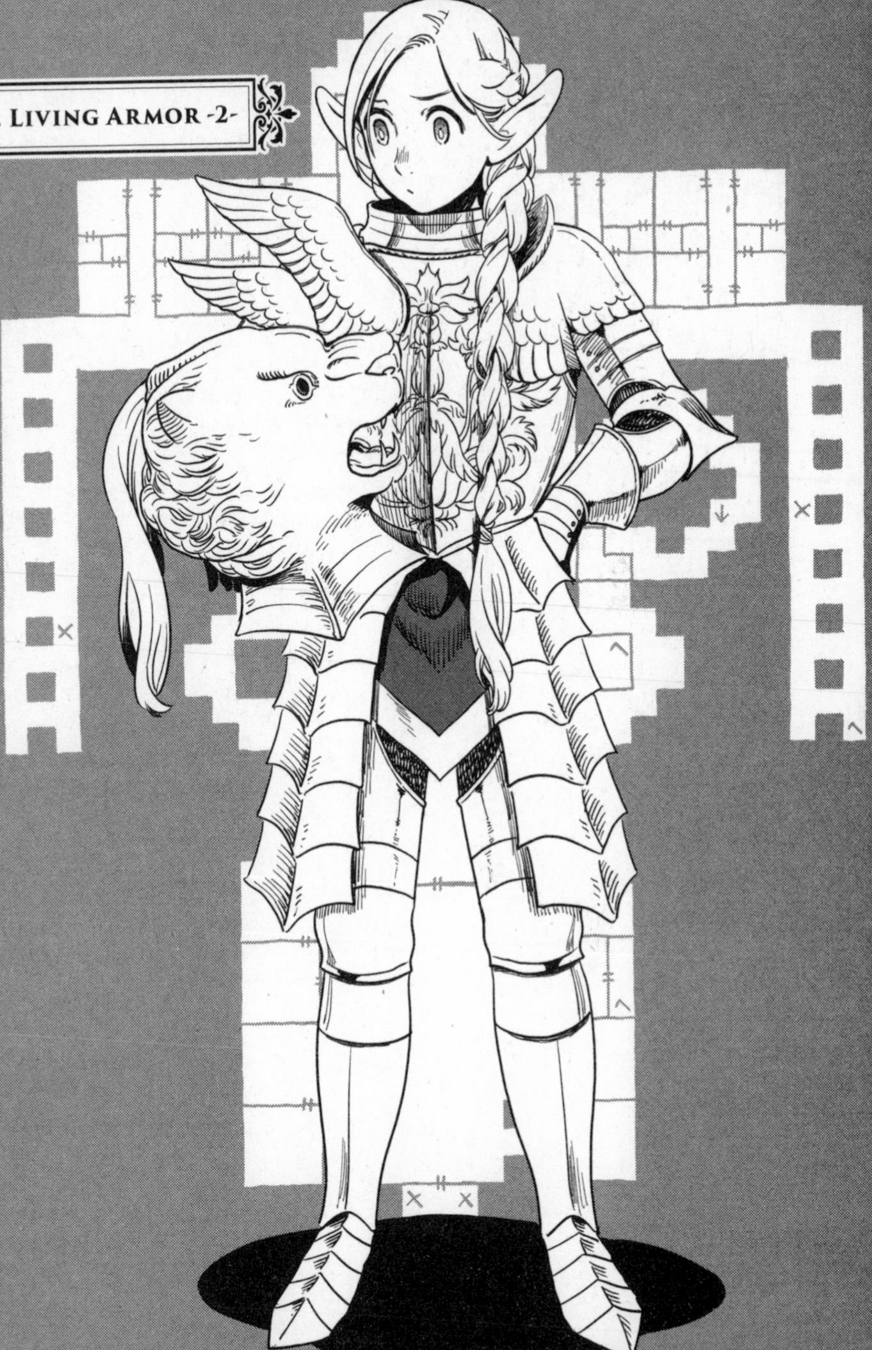

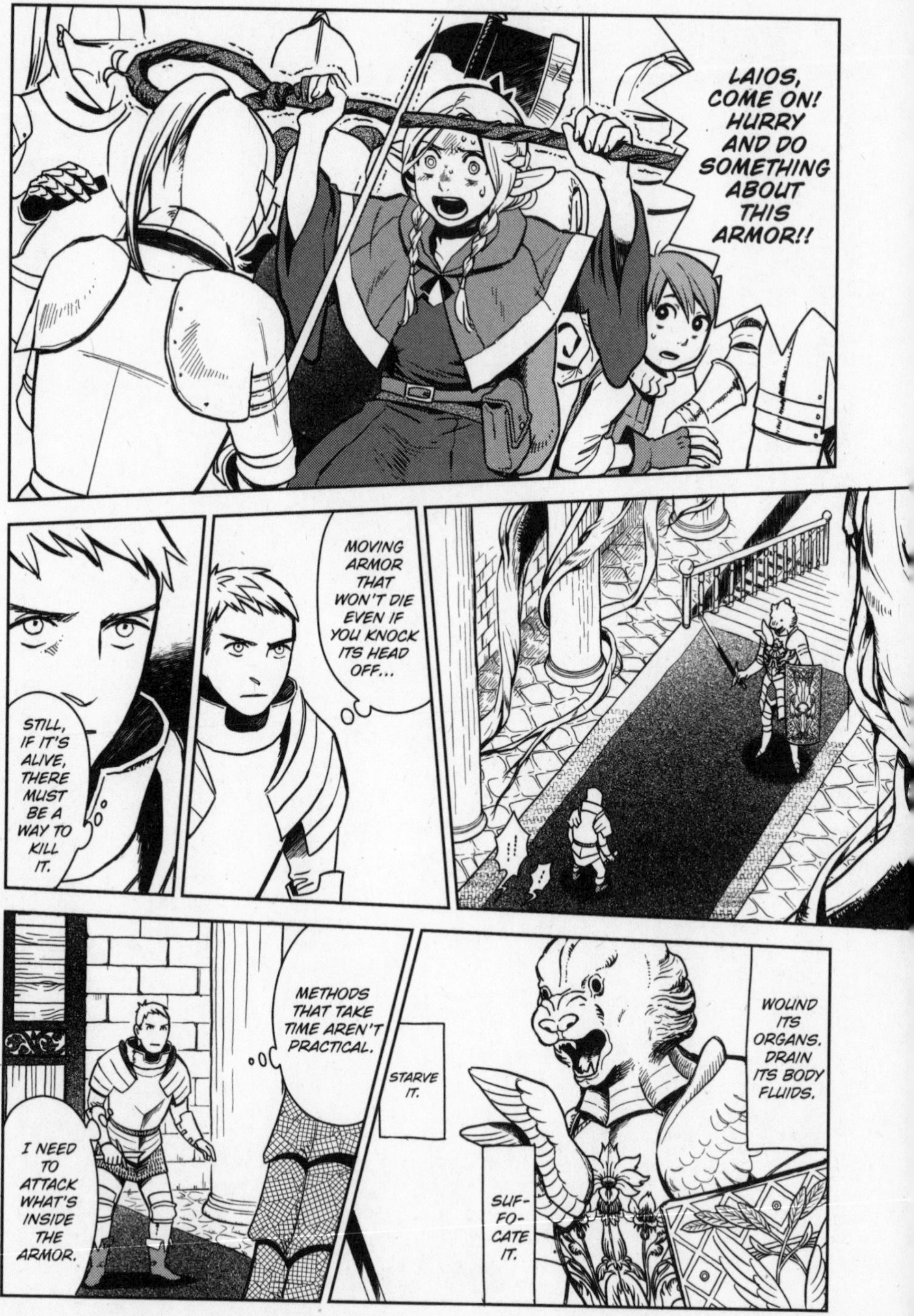

LAIOS, COME ON! HURRY AND DO SOMETHING ABOUT THIS ARMOR!!
MOVING ARMOR THAT WON'T DIE EVEN IF YOU KNOCK ITS HEAD OFF...
STILL, IF IT'S ALIVE, THERE MUST BE A WAY TO KILL IT.
WOUND ITS ORGANS. DRAIN ITS BODY FLUIDS.
STARVE IT.
SUF-FO-CATE IT.
METHODS THAT TAKE TIME AREN'T PRACTICAL.
I NEED TO ATTACK WHAT'S INSIDE THE ARMOR.

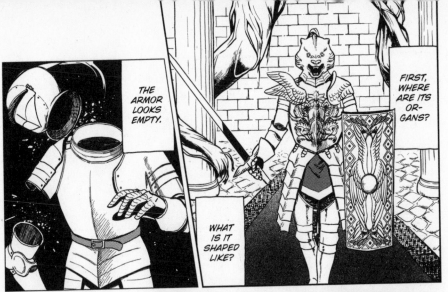

FIRST, WHERE ARE ITS OR-GANS?
WHAT IS IT SHAPED LIKE?
THE ARMOR LOOKS EMPTY.
SOME-THING AMOR-PHOUS, LIKE A SLIME?
AN EGG-LAYING QUEEN THAT'S GUARDED BY OTHER INDIVIDU-ALS... THAT SOUNDS LIKE BEES OR ANTS.
COLONY
IS IT HIDING DEEP INSIDE AND MOVING THE ARMOR BY STRETCH-ING ITS LIMBS OUT?
AROUND HERE?
HERE?
HERE?
HERE?
LIKE THIS?
FOR A FORM-LESS THING, ITS MO-TIONS ARE TOO REGU-LAR.
I DON'T HEAR ANY NOISE, SO INSECTS DON'T SEEM LIKELY.
IS IT LURKING IN A BLIND SPOT AFTER ALL?

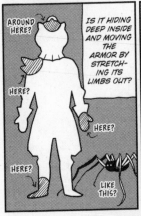

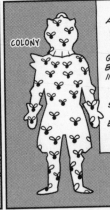

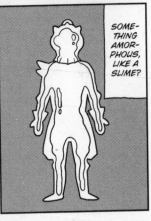

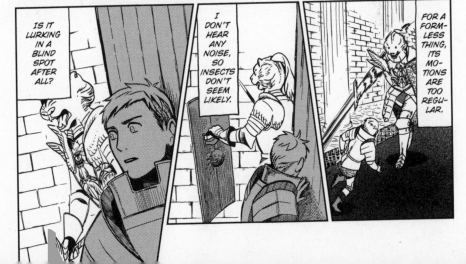

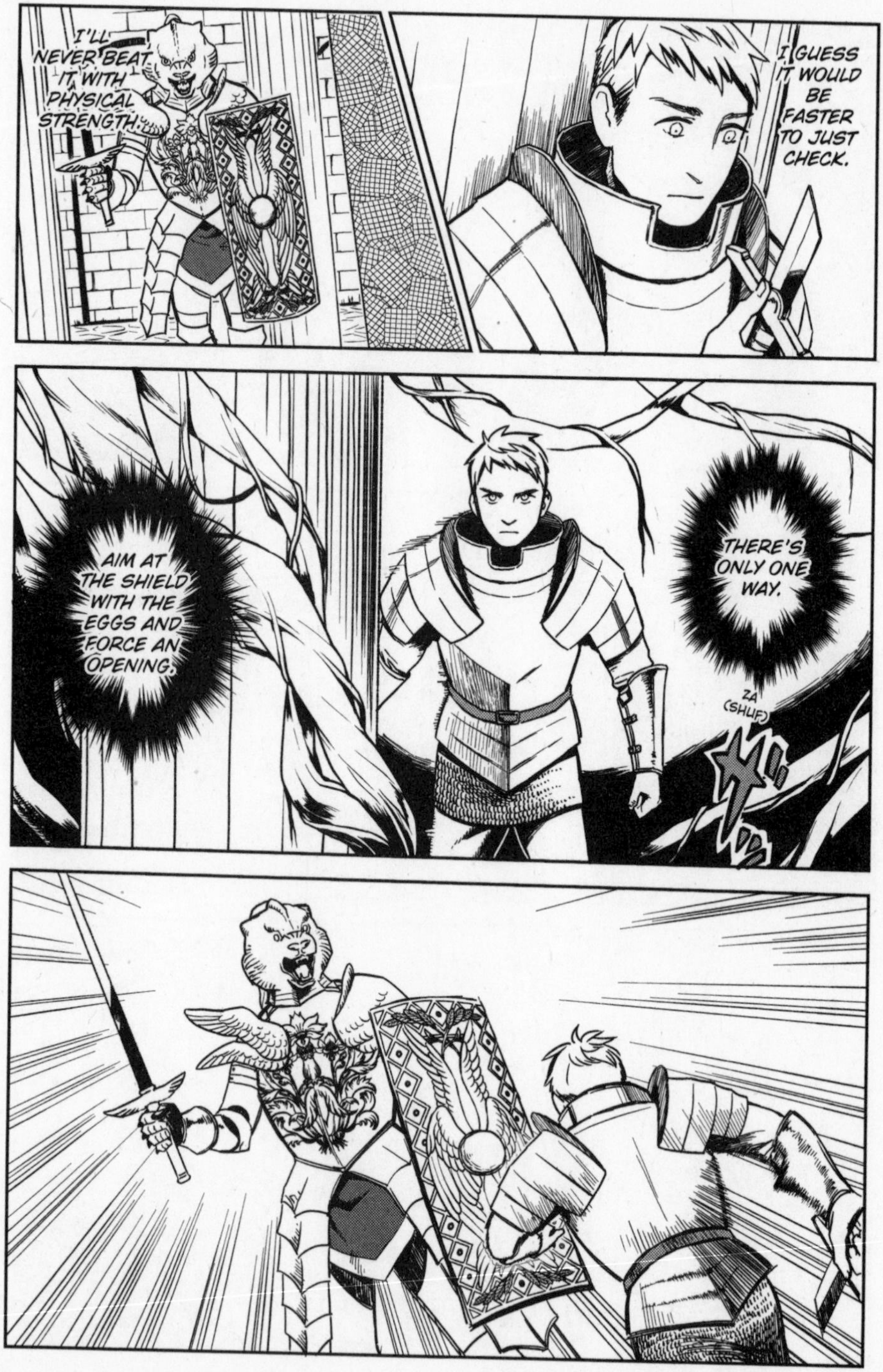
I GUESS IT WOULD BE FASTER TO JUST CHECK.
I'LL NEVER BEAT IT WITH PHYSICAL STRENGTH.
THERE'S ONLY ONE WAY.
ZA (SHUF)
AIM AT THE SHIELD WITH THE EGGS AND FORCE AN OPENING.

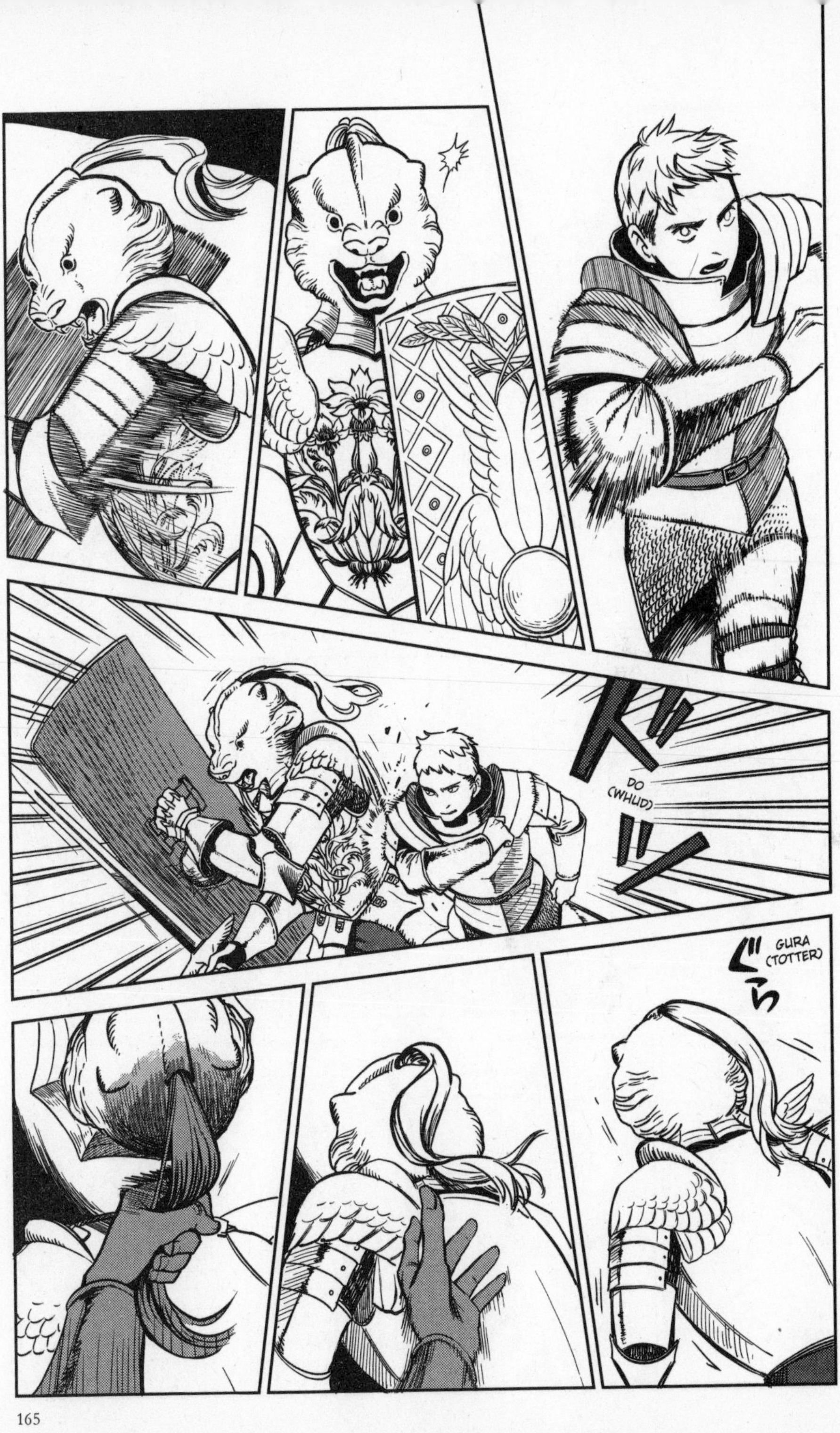
DO
(WHUD)
GURA
(TOTTER)

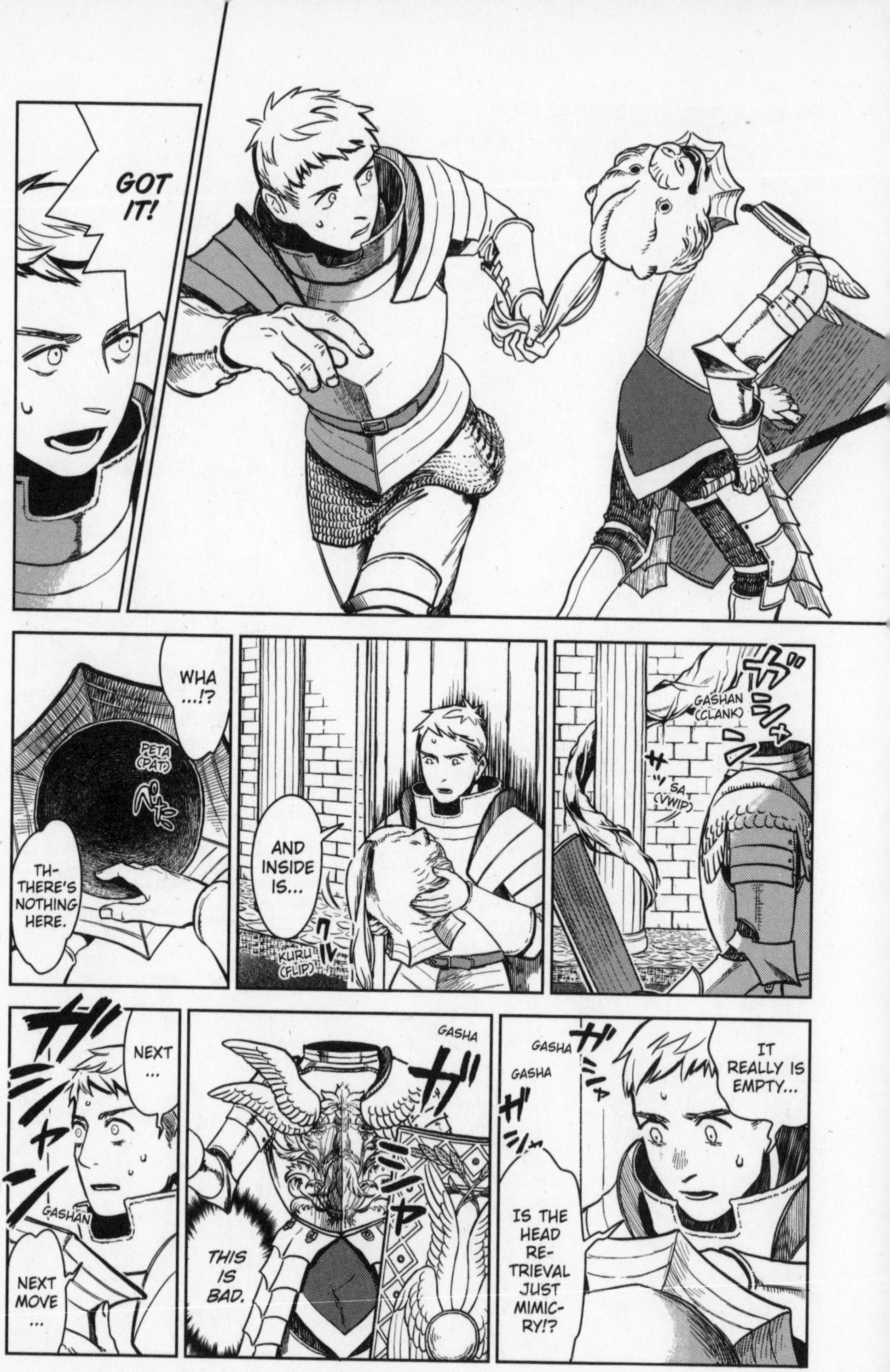
GOT IT!
GASHAN (CLANK)
SA (VWIP)
AND INSIDE IS...
KURU (FLIP)
WHA ...!?
PETA (PAT)
TH-THERE'S NOTHING HERE.
IT REALLY IS EMPTY...
GASHA
GASHA
IS THE HEAD RE-TRIEVAL JUST MIMIC-RY!?
GASHA
THIS IS BAD.
NEXT ...
GASHAN
NEXT MOVE ...

BIKU (FLINCH)

KAKIN (CLANG)

COULDN'T IT SEE WHICH PILLAR I HID BEHIND?

HUH?

GACHAN (CLANG)

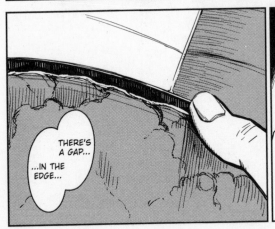

THERE'S A GAP...

...IN THE EDGE...

BA (WHP)

IS THERE SOMETHING IN THE HEAD AFTER ALL?

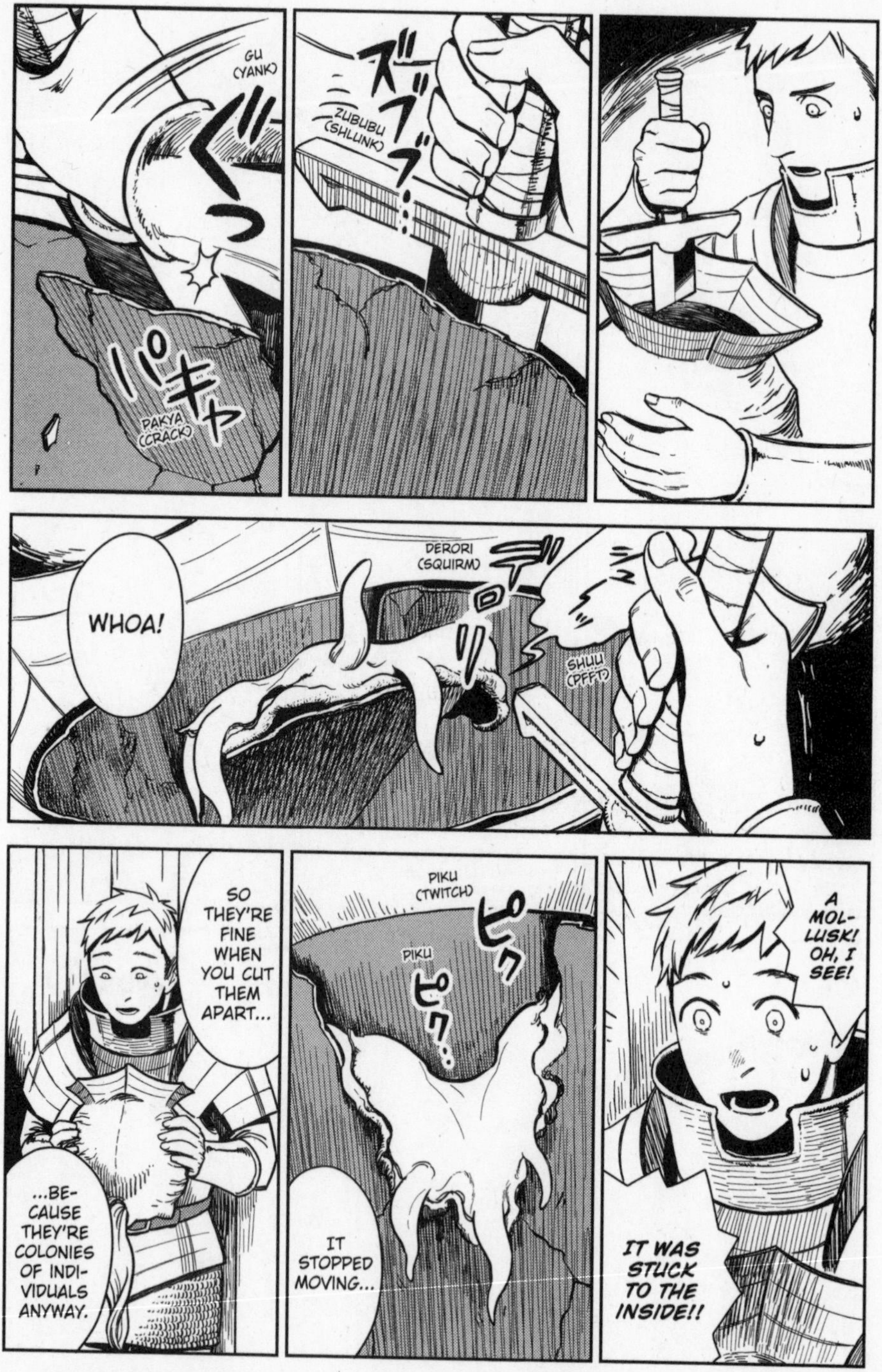
ズブブ…
ZUBUBU (SHLUNK)
ぐっ
GU (YANK)
パキャ
PAKYA (CRACK)
SHUU (PFFT)
デロリ
DERORI (SQUIRM)
WHOA!
A MOL-LUSK! OH, I SEE!
IT WAS STUCK TO THE INSIDE!!
ピク
PIKU (TWITCH)
ピク…
PIKU
IT STOPPED MOVING...
SO THEY'RE FINE WHEN YOU CUT THEM APART...
...BE-CAUSE THEY'RE COLONIES OF INDI-VIDUALS ANYWAY.

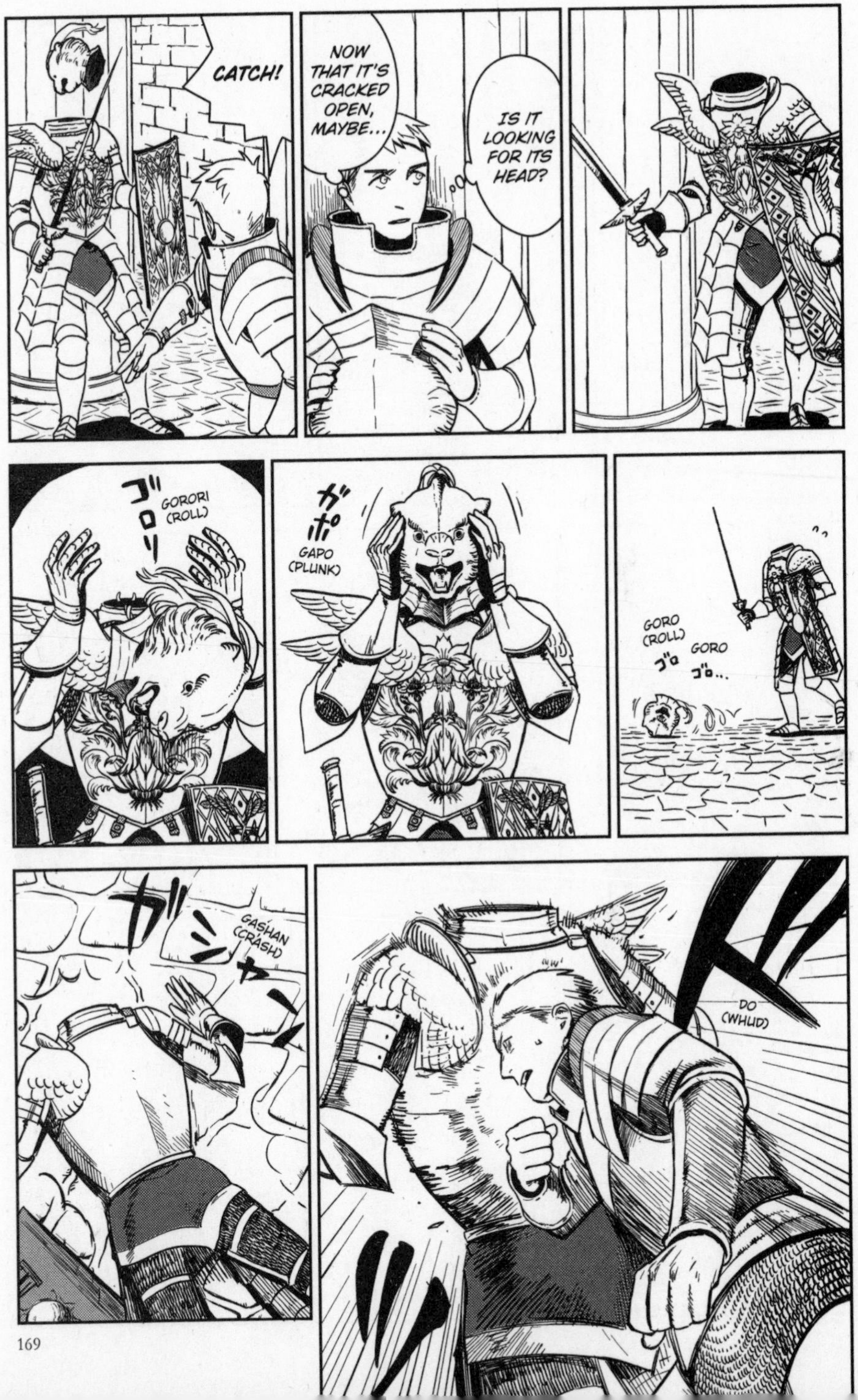
IS IT LOOKING FOR ITS HEAD?
NOW THAT IT'S CRACKED OPEN, MAYBE...
CATCH!
GORO (ROLL)
GORO
ゴロ
ゴロ...
ガポ
GAPO (PLUNK)
ゴロリ
GORORI (ROLL)
DO (WHUD)
ガシャン
GASHAN (CRASH)

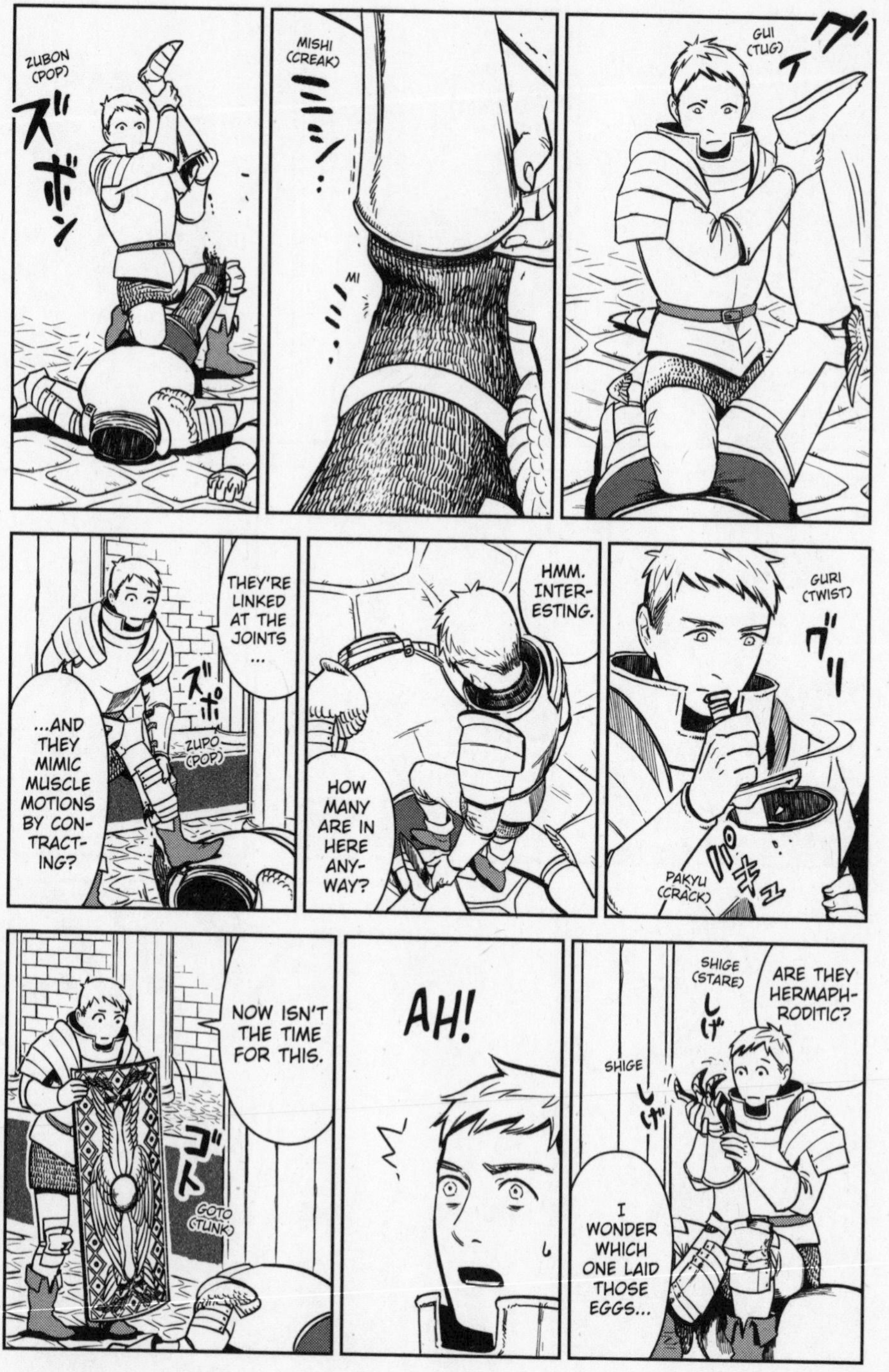
GUI (TUG)
グイ
MISHI (CREAK)
ミシッ
MI
ZUBON (POP)
ズボン
GURI (TWIST)
グリ
パキュ
PAKYU (CRACK)
HMM. INTERESTING.
HOW MANY ARE IN HERE ANYWAY?
THEY'RE LINKED AT THE JOINTS...
ズポ
ZUPO (POP)
...AND THEY MIMIC MUSCLE MOTIONS BY CONTRACTING?
SHIGE (STARE)
しげ
ARE THEY HERMAPHRODITIC?
SHIGE
しげ
I WONDER WHICH ONE LAID THOSE EGGS...
AH!
NOW ISN'T THE TIME FOR THIS.
ゴト
GOTO (TUNK)

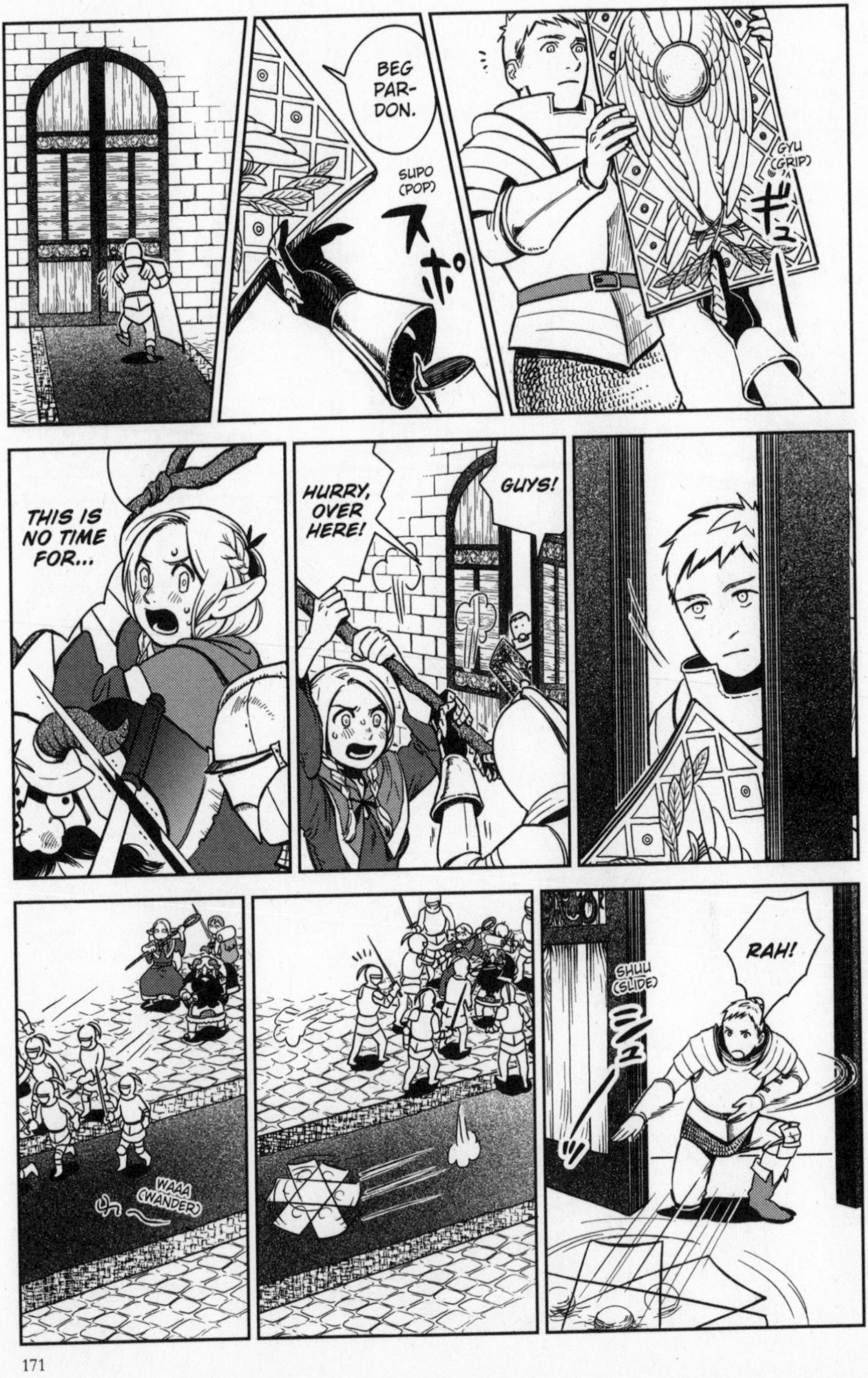

GYU (GRIP)
ギュ
BEG PAR-DON.
SUPO (POP)
スポ
GUYS!
HURRY, OVER HERE!
THIS IS NO TIME FOR...
RAH!
SHUU (SLIDE)
WAAA (WANDER)

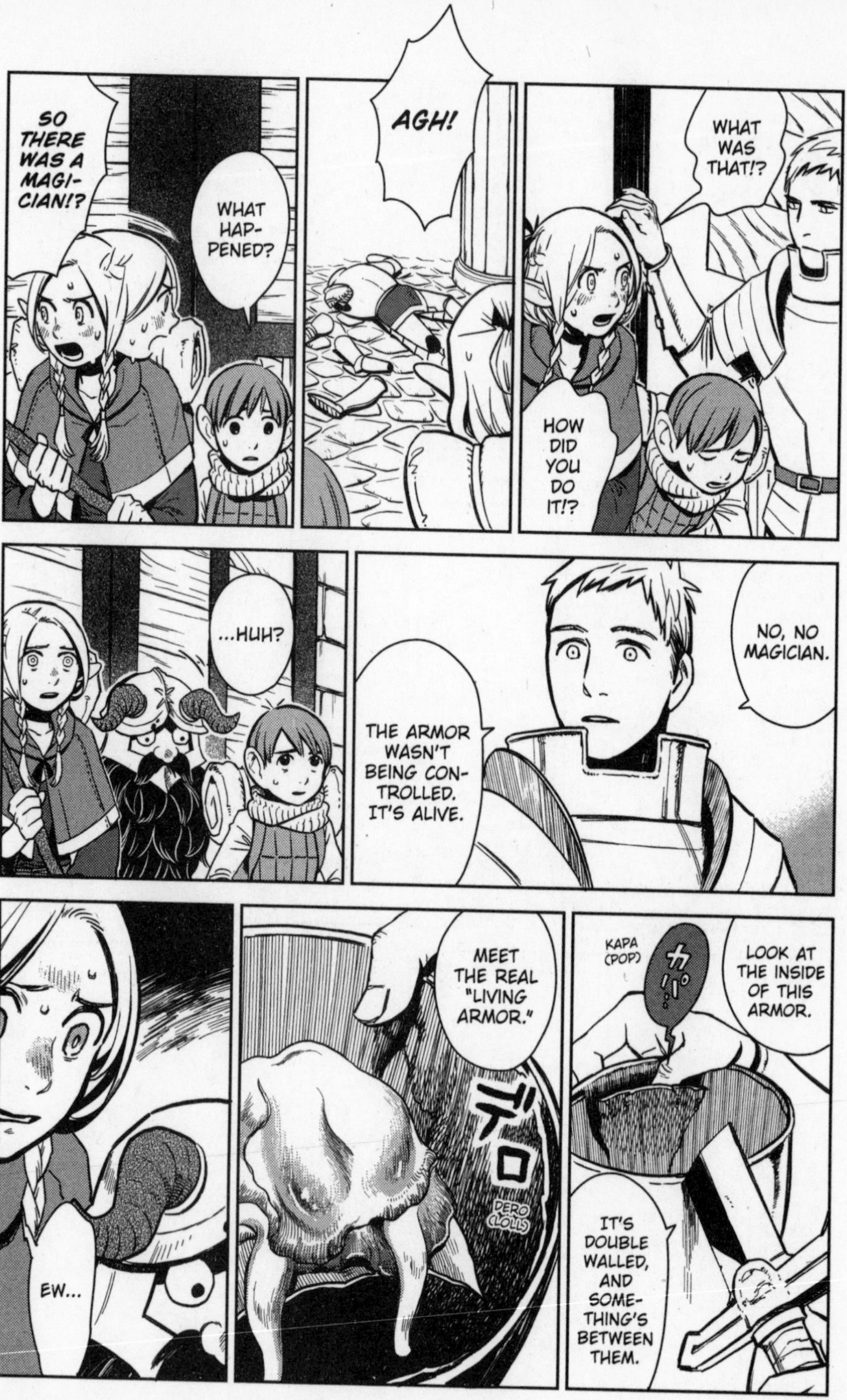
WHAT WAS THAT!?
HOW DID YOU DO IT!?
AGH!
WHAT HAPPENED?
SO THERE WAS A MAGICIAN!?
NO, NO MAGICIAN.
THE ARMOR WASN'T BEING CONTROLLED. IT'S ALIVE.
...HUH?
LOOK AT THE INSIDE OF THIS ARMOR.
カパ
KAPA (POP)
IT'S DOUBLE WALLED, AND SOMETHING'S BETWEEN THEM.
MEET THE REAL "LIVING ARMOR."
デロ
DERO (LOLLS)
EW...

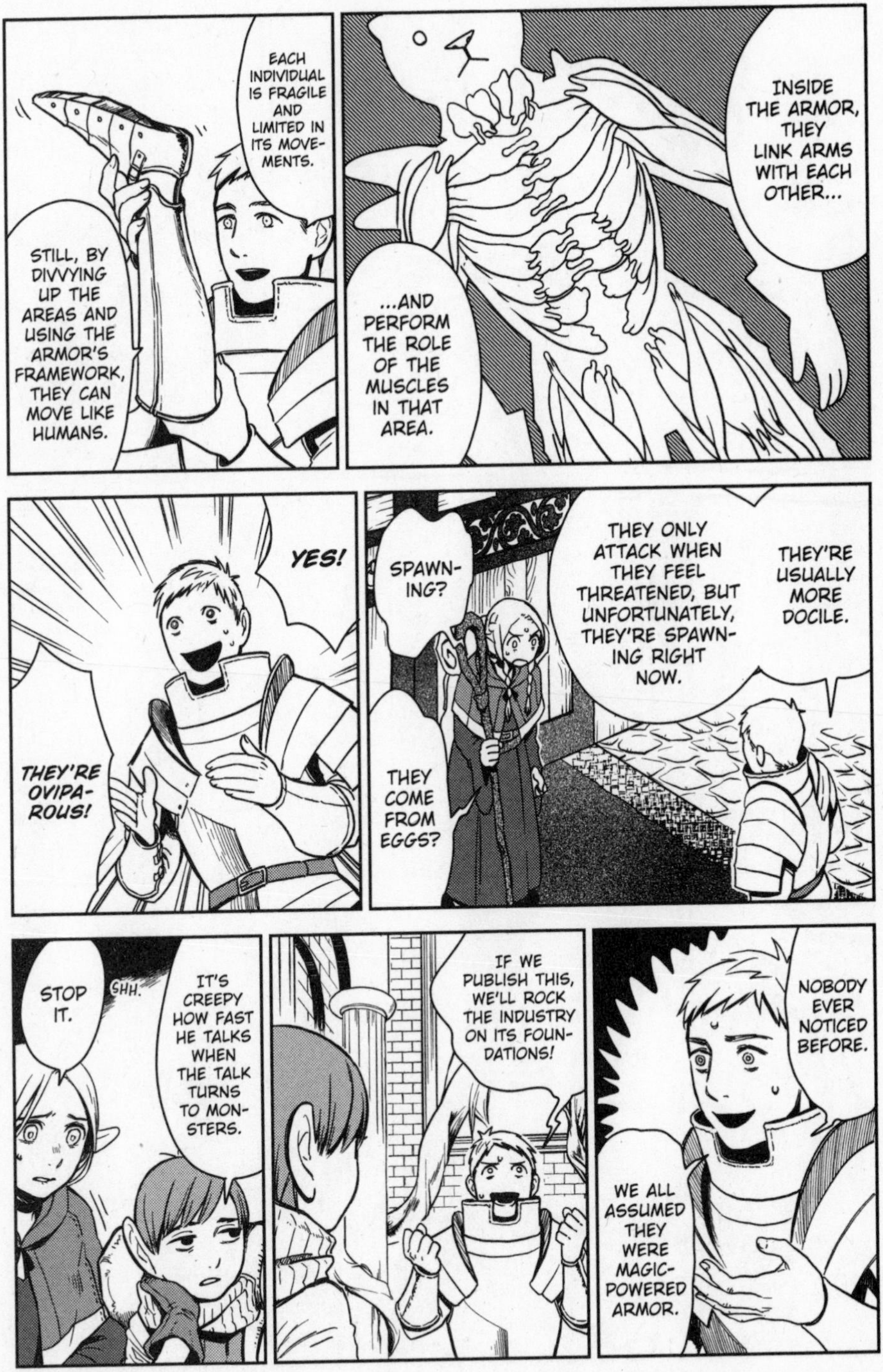
INSIDE THE ARMOR, THEY LINK ARMS WITH EACH OTHER...
...AND PERFORM THE ROLE OF THE MUSCLES IN THAT AREA.
EACH INDIVIDUAL IS FRAGILE AND LIMITED IN ITS MOVEMENTS.
STILL, BY DIVVYING UP THE AREAS AND USING THE ARMOR'S FRAMEWORK, THEY CAN MOVE LIKE HUMANS.
THEY'RE USUALLY MORE DOCILE.
THEY ONLY ATTACK WHEN THEY FEEL THREATENED, BUT UNFORTUNATELY, THEY'RE SPAWNING RIGHT NOW.
SPAWNING?
THEY COME FROM EGGS?
YES!
THEY'RE OVIPAROUS!
NOBODY EVER NOTICED BEFORE.
WE ALL ASSUMED THEY WERE MAGIC-POWERED ARMOR.
IF WE PUBLISH THIS, WE'LL ROCK THE INDUSTRY ON ITS FOUNDATIONS!
IT'S CREEPY HOW FAST HE TALKS WHEN THE TALK TURNS TO MONSTERS.
SHH.
STOP IT.

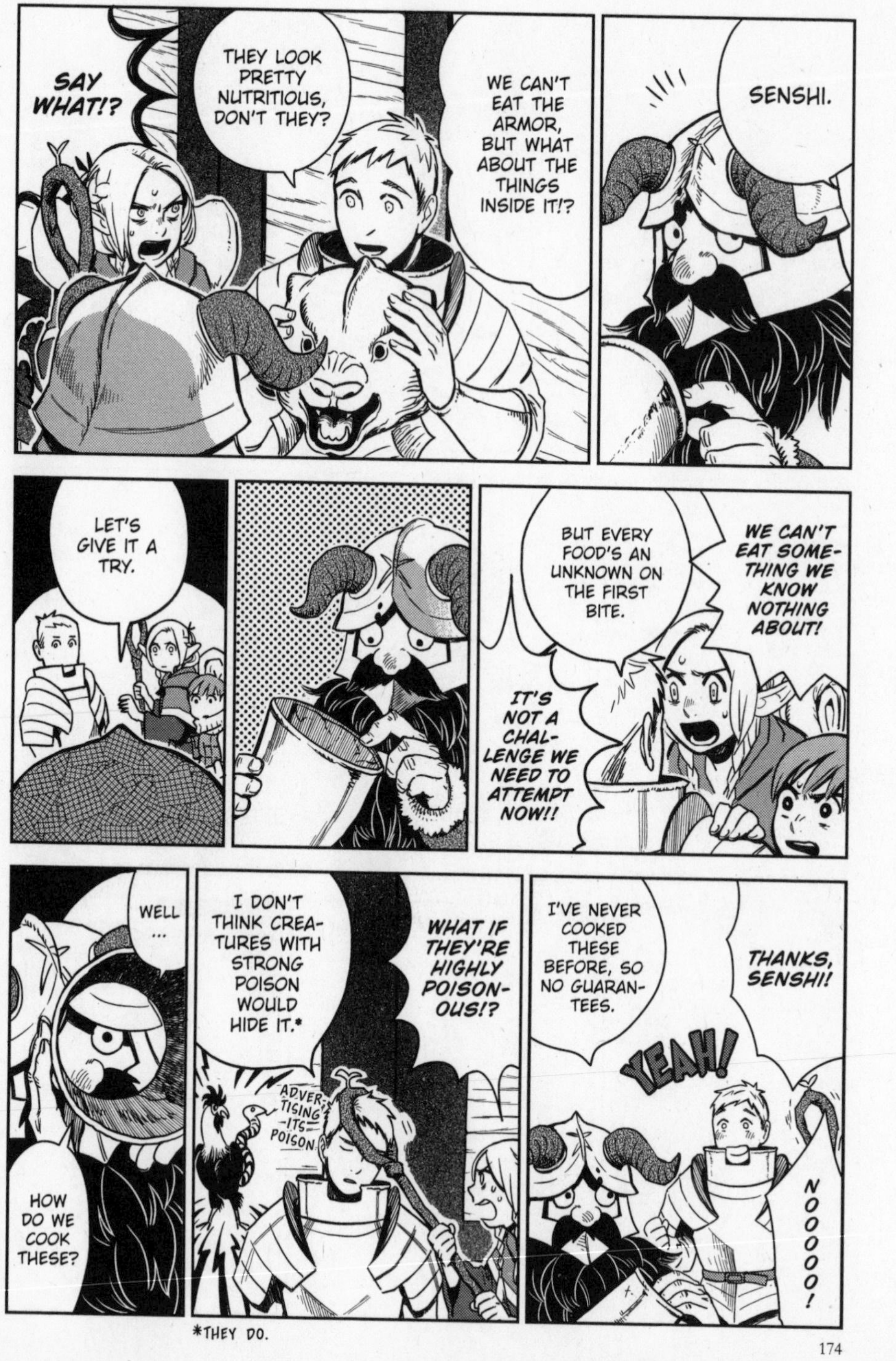
SENSHI.
WE CAN'T EAT THE ARMOR, BUT WHAT ABOUT THE THINGS INSIDE IT!?
THEY LOOK PRETTY NUTRITIOUS, DON'T THEY?
SAY WHAT!?
WE CAN'T EAT SOMETHING WE KNOW NOTHING ABOUT!
BUT EVERY FOOD'S AN UNKNOWN ON THE FIRST BITE.
IT'S NOT A CHALLENGE WE NEED TO ATTEMPT NOW!!
LET'S GIVE IT A TRY.
THANKS, SENSHI!
I'VE NEVER COOKED THESE BEFORE, SO NO GUARANTEES.
YEAH!
NOOOOOO!
WHAT IF THEY'RE HIGHLY POISONOUS!?
I DON'T THINK CREATURES WITH STRONG POISON WOULD HIDE IT.*
ADVERTISING ITS POISON
WELL...
HOW DO WE COOK THESE?

*THEY DO.

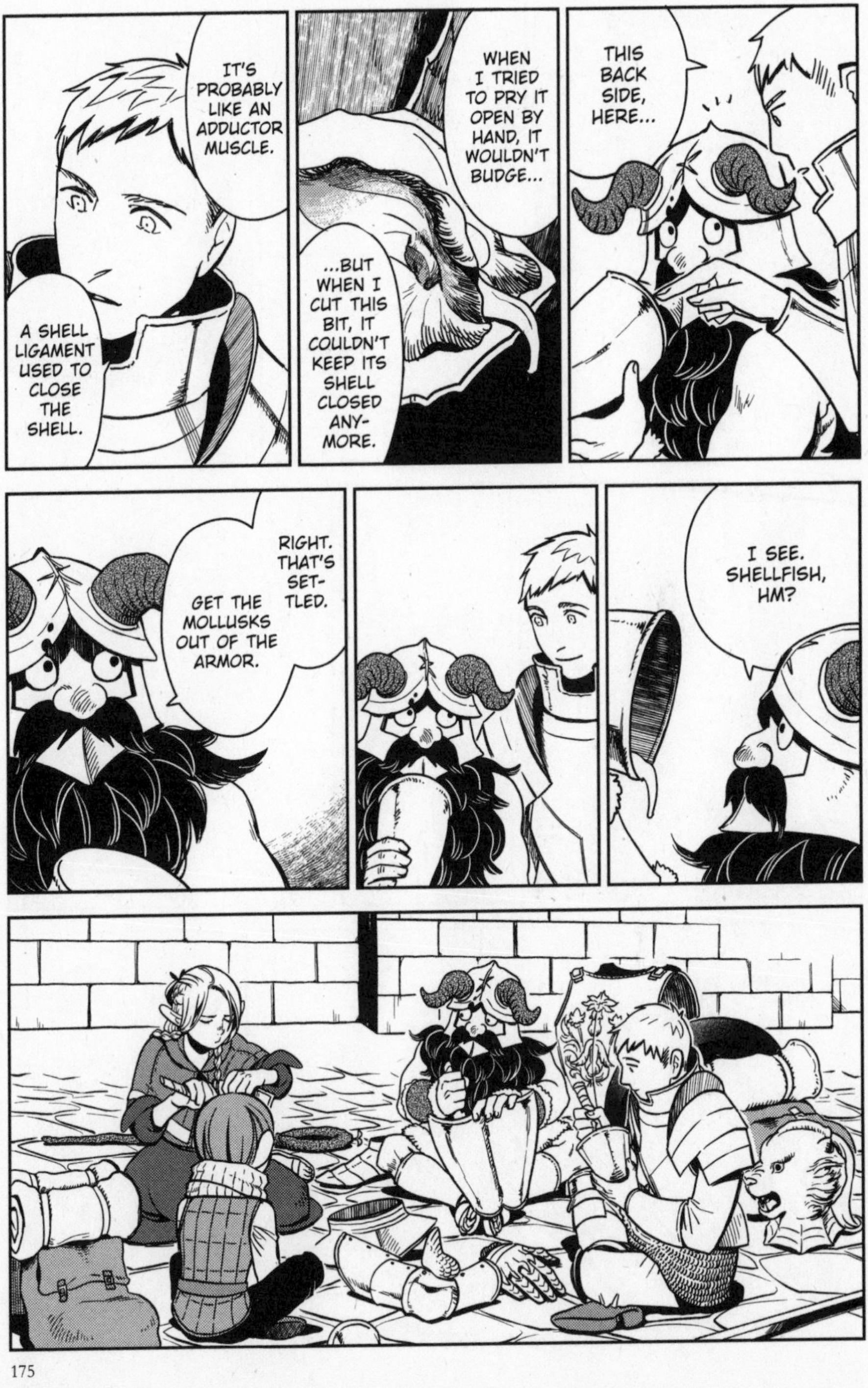

THIS BACK SIDE, HERE...
WHEN I TRIED TO PRY IT OPEN BY HAND, IT WOULDN'T BUDGE...
...BUT WHEN I CUT THIS BIT, IT COULDN'T KEEP ITS SHELL CLOSED ANY-MORE.
IT'S PROBABLY LIKE AN ADDUCTOR MUSCLE.
A SHELL LIGAMENT USED TO CLOSE THE SHELL.
I SEE. SHELLFISH, HM?
RIGHT. THAT'S SET-TLED.
GET THE MOLLUSKS OUT OF THE ARMOR.

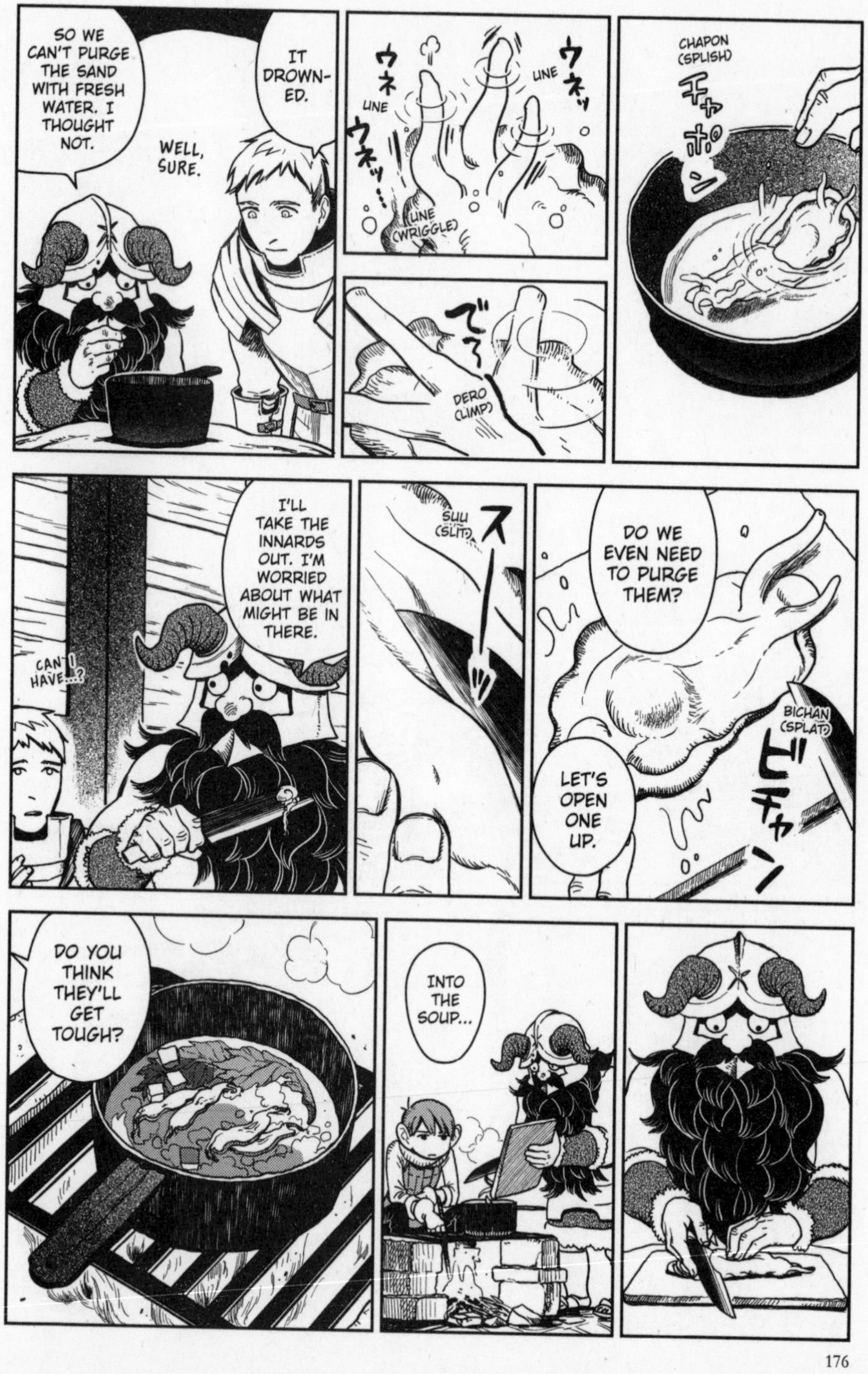
CHAPON (SPLISH)
チャポン
ウネッ
UNE
ウネ
UNE
ウネッ…
UNE (WRIGGLE)
でろ
DERO (LIMP)
IT DROWN-ED.
SO WE CAN'T PURGE THE SAND WITH FRESH WATER. I THOUGHT NOT.
WELL, SURE.
DO WE EVEN NEED TO PURGE THEM?
BICHAN (SPLAT)
ビチャン
LET'S OPEN ONE UP.
SUU (SLIT)
スー
I'LL TAKE THE INNARDS OUT. I'M WORRIED ABOUT WHAT MIGHT BE IN THERE.
CAN I HAVE...?
INTO THE SOUP...
DO YOU THINK THEY'LL GET TOUGH?

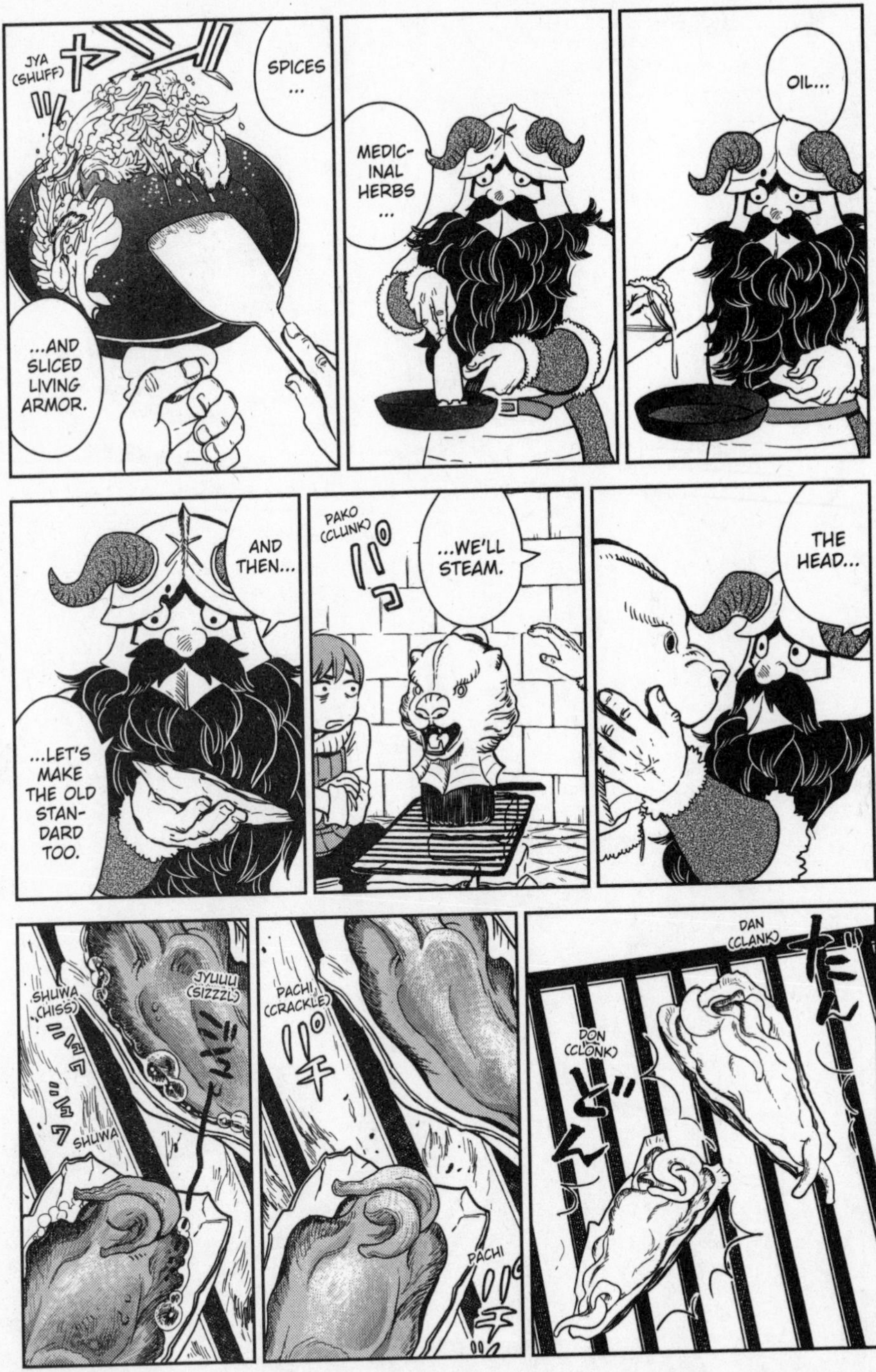
OIL...
MEDICINAL HERBS ...
SPICES ...
JYA (SHUFF)
...AND SLICED LIVING ARMOR.
THE HEAD...
...WE'LL STEAM.
PAKO (CLUNK)
AND THEN...
...LET'S MAKE THE OLD STANDARD TOO.
DAN (CLANK)
DON (CLONK)
PACHI (CRACKLE)
PACHI
JYUUU (SIZZZL)
SHUWA (HISS)
SHUWA

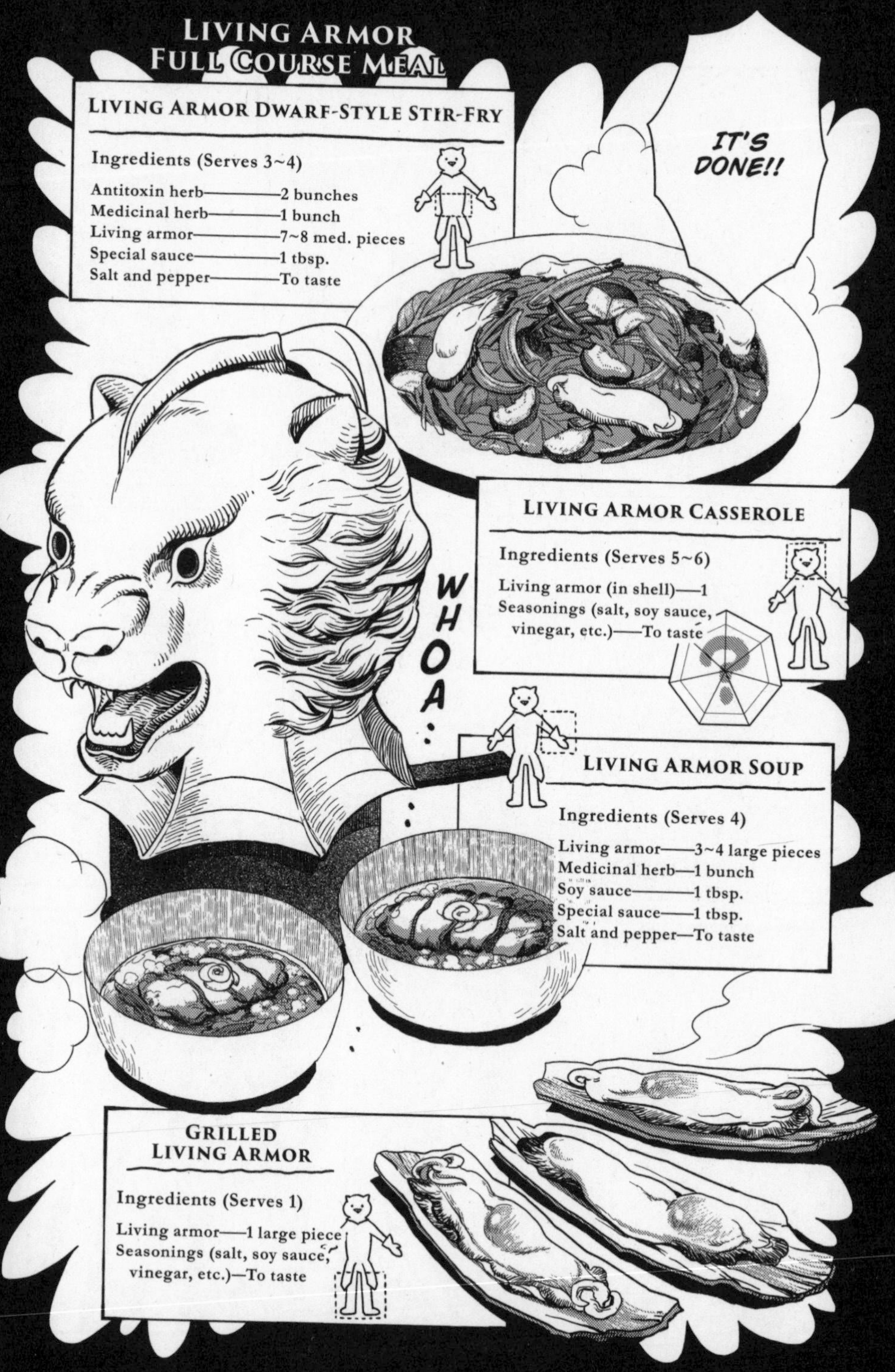

IT'S DONE!!
LIVING ARMOR FULL COURSE MEAL
LIVING ARMOR DWARF-STYLE STIR-FRY
Ingredients (Serves 3~4)
Antitoxin herb—2 bunches
Medicinal herb—1 bunch
Living armor—7~8 med. pieces
Special sauce—1 tbsp.
Salt and pepper—To taste
LIVING ARMOR CASSEROLE
Ingredients (Serves 5~6)
Living armor (in shell)—1
Seasonings (salt, soy sauce, vinegar, etc.)—To taste
WHOA...
LIVING ARMOR SOUP
Ingredients (Serves 4)
Living armor—3~4 large pieces
Medicinal herb—1 bunch
Soy sauce—1 tbsp.
Special sauce—1 tbsp.
Salt and pepper—To taste
GRILLED LIVING ARMOR
Ingredients (Serves 1)
Living armor—1 large piece
Seasonings (salt, soy sauce, vinegar, etc.)—To taste

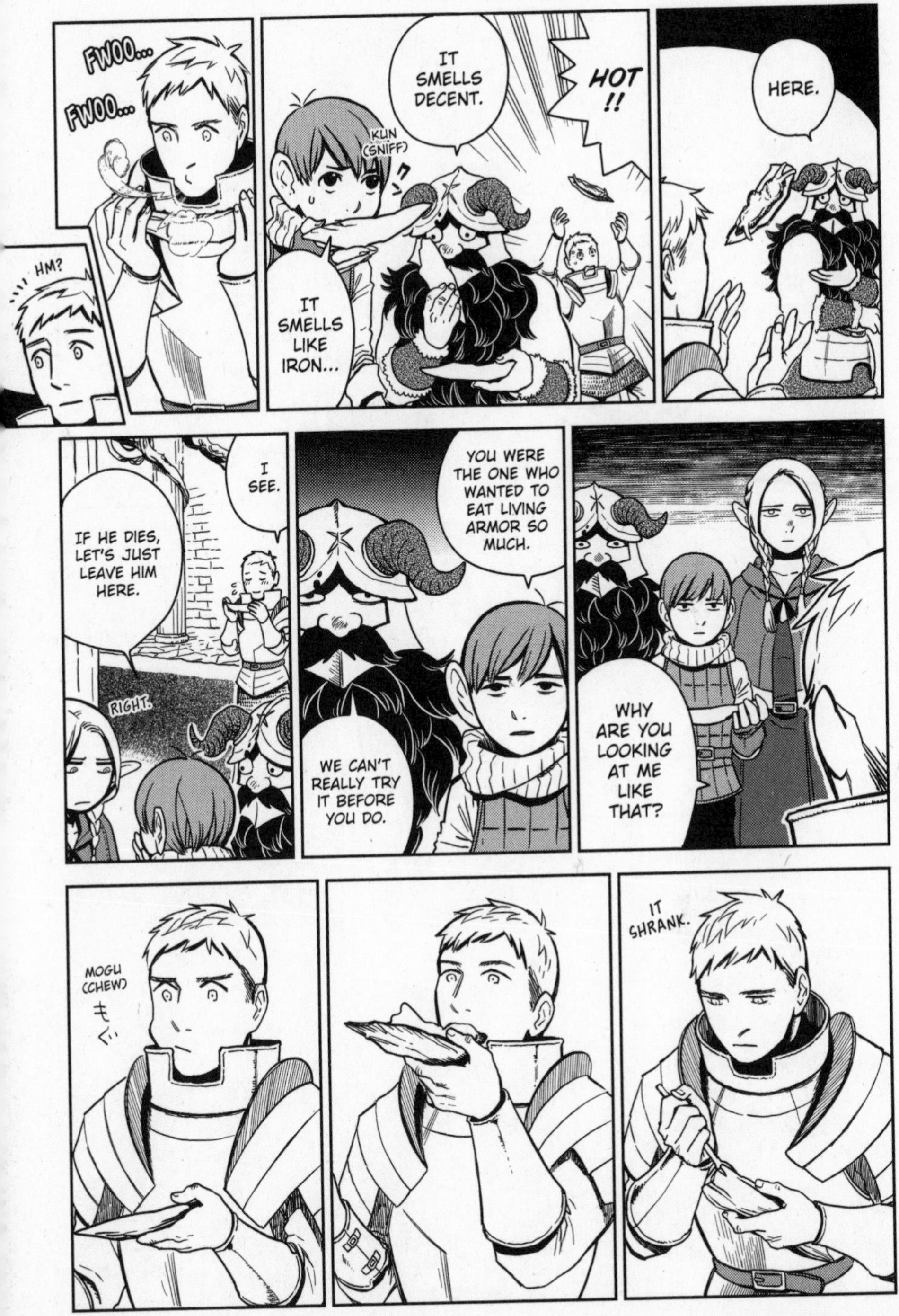
HERE.
HOT!!
IT SMELLS DECENT.
KUN (SNIFF)
IT SMELLS LIKE IRON...
FWOO...
FWOO...
HM?
WHY ARE YOU LOOKING AT ME LIKE THAT?
YOU WERE THE ONE WHO WANTED TO EAT LIVING ARMOR SO MUCH.
WE CAN'T REALLY TRY IT BEFORE YOU DO.
I SEE.
IF HE DIES, LET'S JUST LEAVE HIM HERE.
RIGHT.
IT SHRANK.
MOGU (CHEW)
もぐ

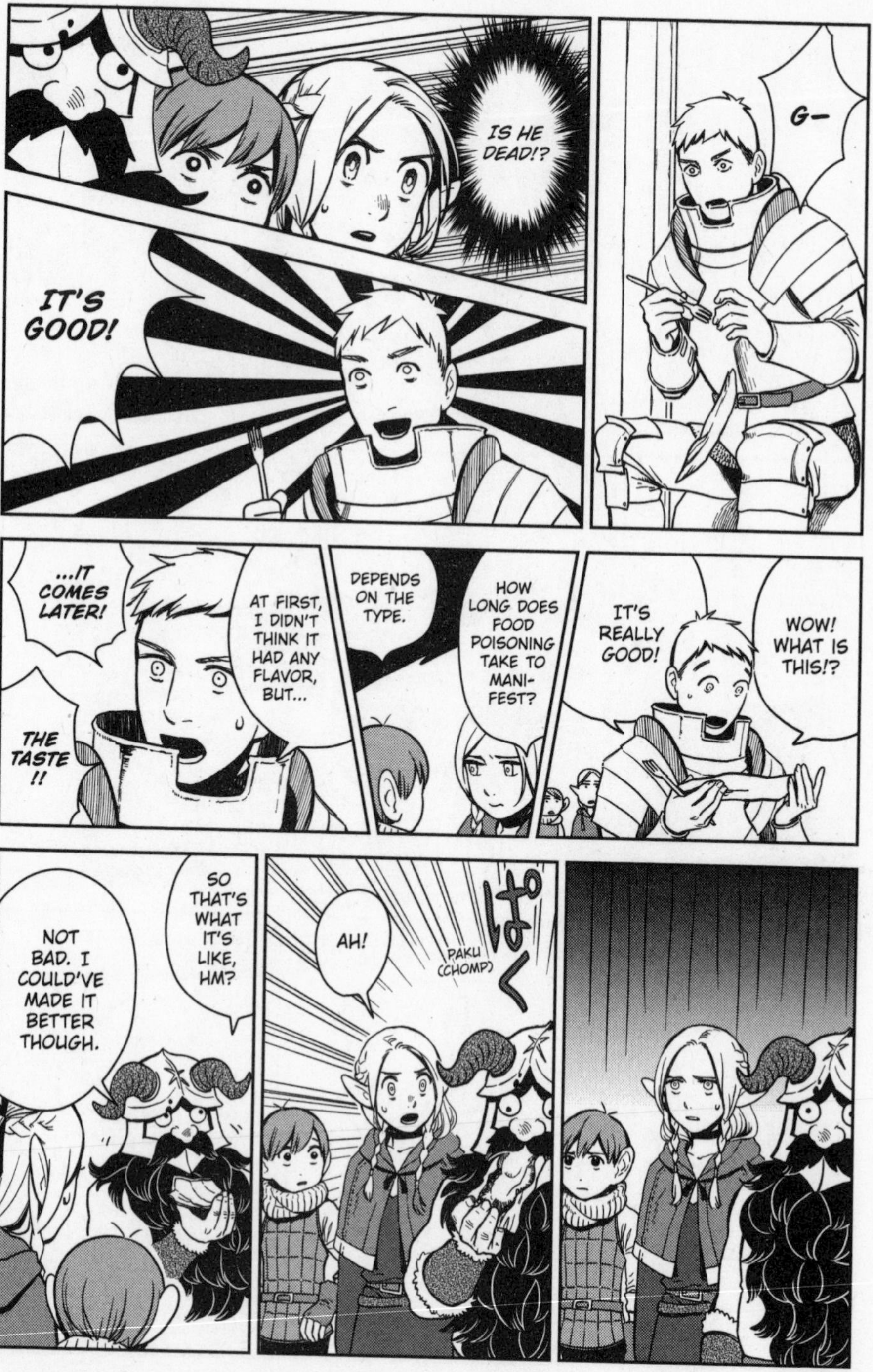
G–
IS HE DEAD!?
IT'S GOOD!
WOW! WHAT IS THIS!?
IT'S REALLY GOOD!
HOW LONG DOES FOOD POISONING TAKE TO MANI-FEST?
DEPENDS ON THE TYPE.
AT FIRST, I DIDN'T THINK IT HAD ANY FLAVOR, BUT...
...IT COMES LATER!
THE TASTE !!
ぱく
PAKU (CHOMP)
AH!
SO THAT'S WHAT IT'S LIKE, HM?
NOT BAD. I COULD'VE MADE IT BETTER THOUGH.

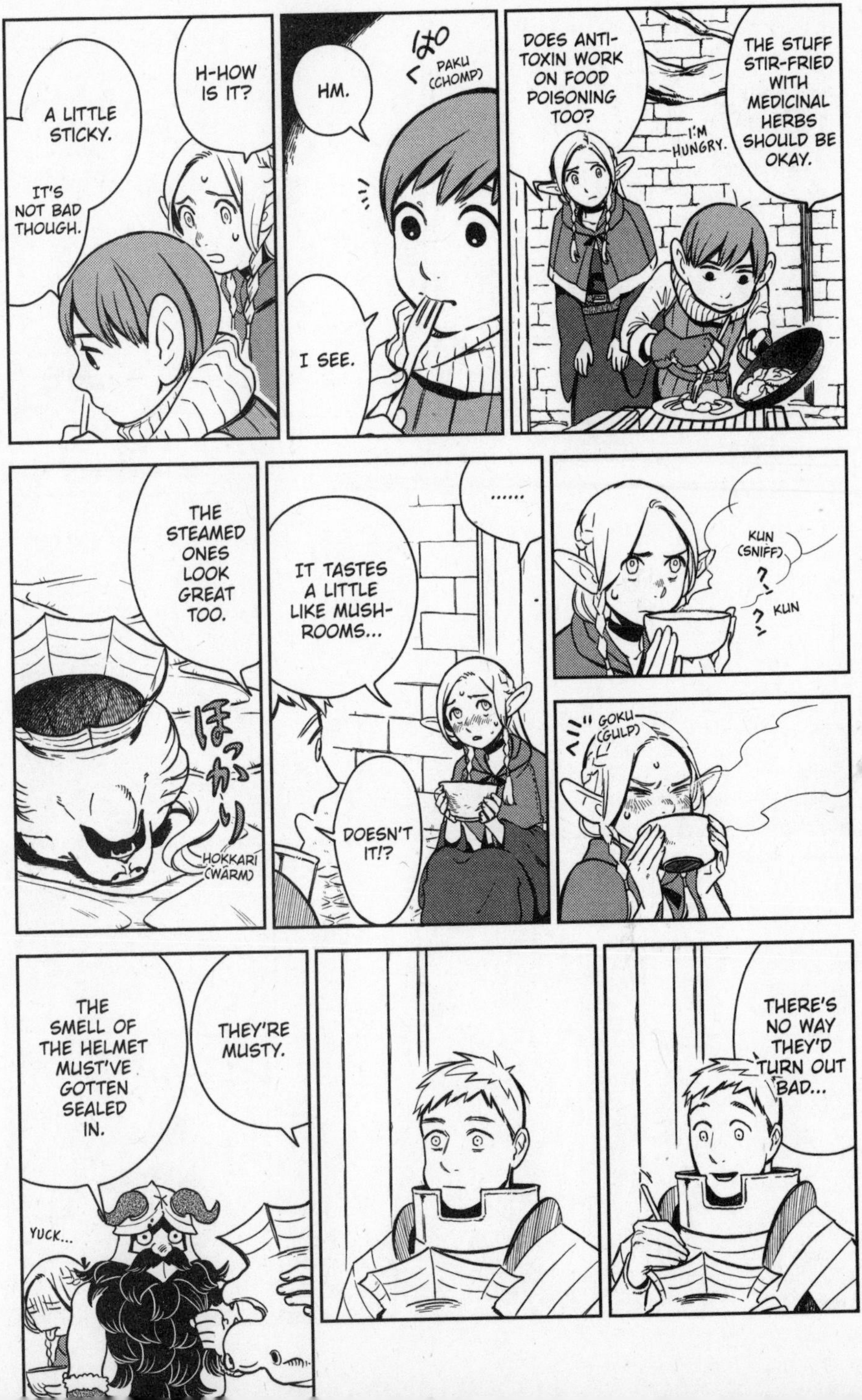
THE STUFF STIR-FRIED WITH MEDICINAL HERBS SHOULD BE OKAY.
DOES ANTI-TOXIN WORK ON FOOD POISONING TOO?
I'M HUNGRY.
ぱく
PAKU (CHOMP)
HM.
I SEE.
H-HOW IS IT?
A LITTLE STICKY.
IT'S NOT BAD THOUGH.
KUN (SNIFF)
KUN
GOKU (GULP)
......
IT TASTES A LITTLE LIKE MUSH-ROOMS...
DOESN'T IT!?
THE STEAMED ONES LOOK GREAT TOO.
ほっかり
HOKKARI (WARM)
THERE'S NO WAY THEY'D TURN OUT BAD...
THEY'RE MUSTY.
THE SMELL OF THE HELMET MUST'VE GOTTEN SEALED IN.
YUCK...

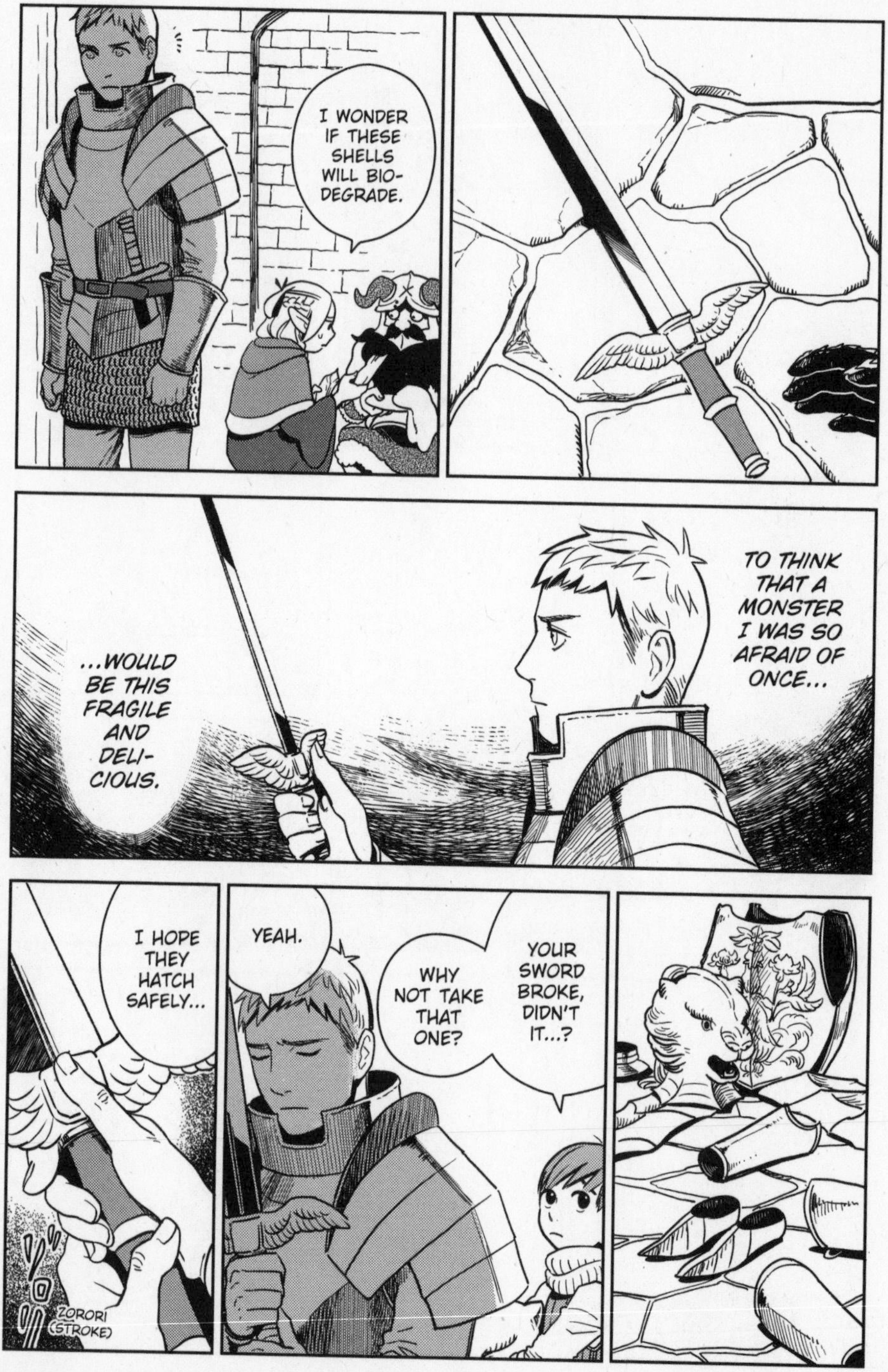
I WONDER IF THESE SHELLS WILL BIO-DEGRADE.
TO THINK THAT A MONSTER I WAS SO AFRAID OF ONCE...
...WOULD BE THIS FRAGILE AND DELI-CIOUS.
YOUR SWORD BROKE, DIDN'T IT...?
WHY NOT TAKE THAT ONE?
YEAH.
I HOPE THEY HATCH SAFELY...
ZORORI (STROKE)

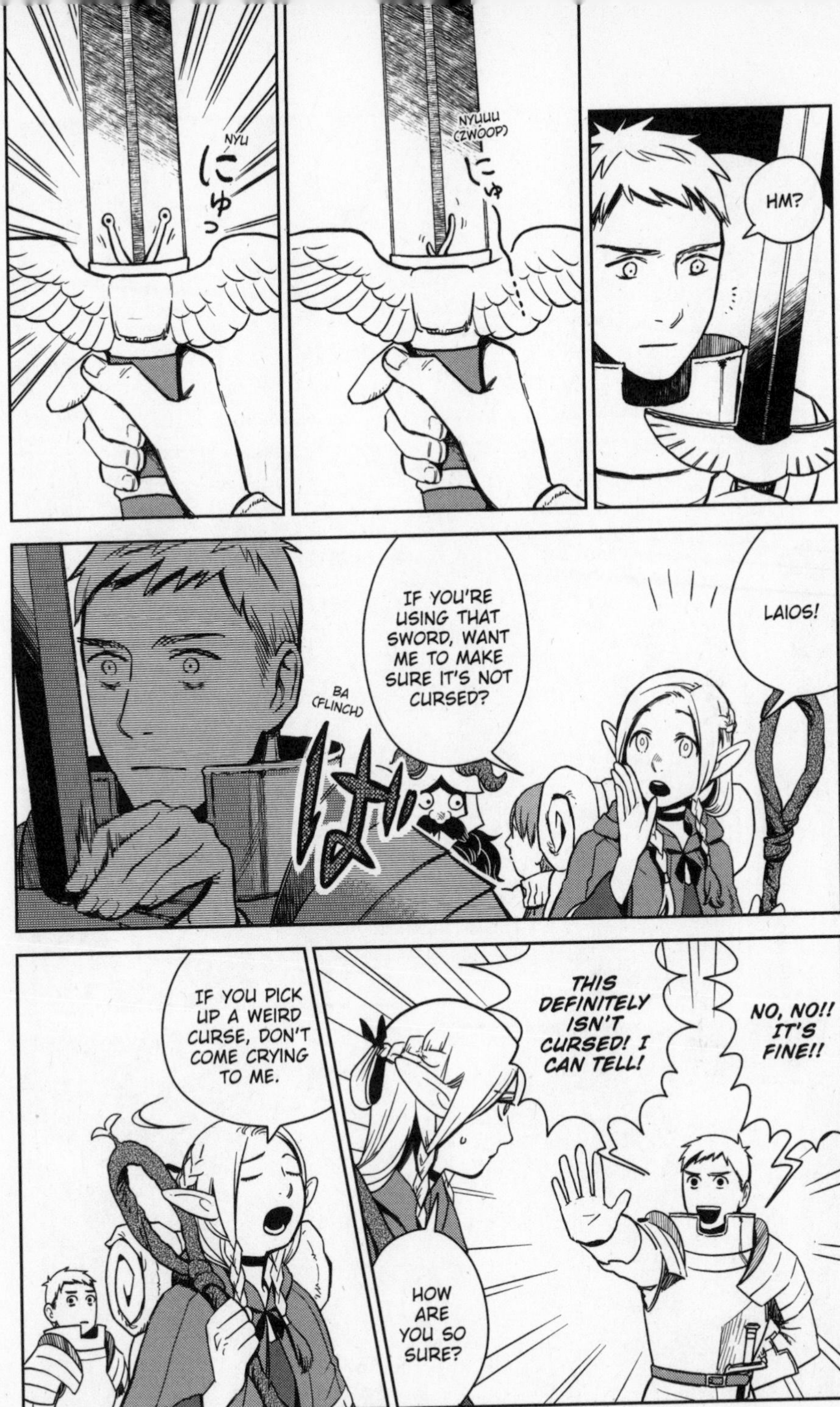
HM?
NYUUU (ZWOOP)
にゅ
NYU
にゅっ
LAIOS!
IF YOU'RE USING THAT SWORD, WANT ME TO MAKE SURE IT'S NOT CURSED?
BA (FLINCH)
ばっ
NO, NO!! IT'S FINE!!
THIS DEFINITELY ISN'T CURSED! I CAN TELL!
HOW ARE YOU SO SURE?
IF YOU PICK UP A WEIRD CURSE, DON'T COME CRYING TO ME.

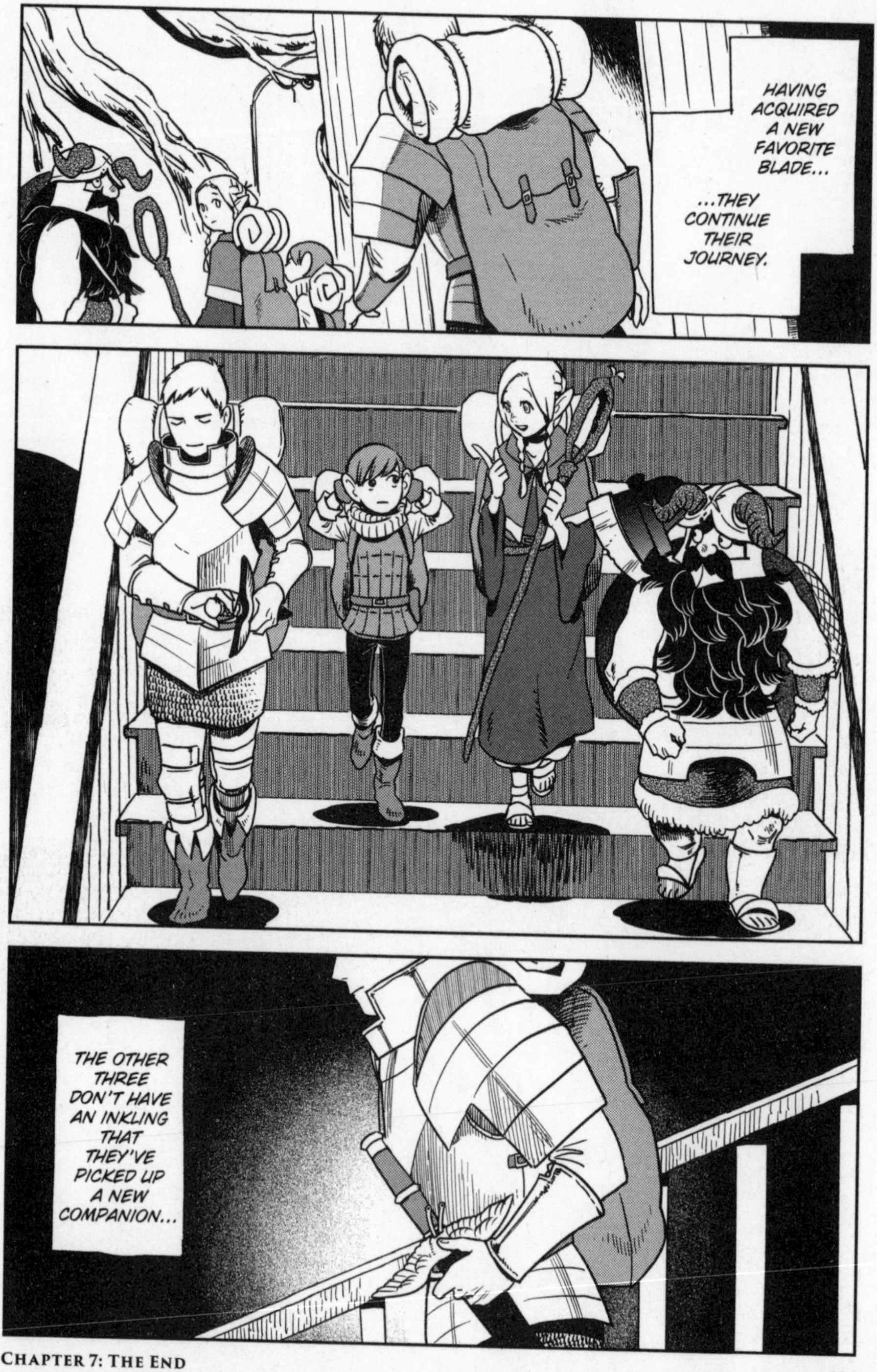
HAVING ACQUIRED A NEW FAVORITE BLADE...
...THEY CONTINUE THEIR JOURNEY.
THE OTHER THREE DON'T HAVE AN INKLING THAT THEY'VE PICKED UP A NEW COMPANION...

CHAPTER 7: THE END

TRANSLATION NOTES

Page 5
The specific hot pot being made here, *mizutaki*, is an unthickened stew of boiled, unseasoned meat and vegetables that is cooked at the table.

Page 39
Shabu-shabu is thinly sliced meat (usually beef) parboiled in hot broth, then dipped in sauce.

Oyako-don (mother-and-child rice bowls) usually consist of chicken, egg, and sautéed onions served over rice.

Page 47
The Matagi are people of Japan's Tohoku region who farm during the growing season and then form bands and hunt during the winter.

"Along comes a duck with a leek on its back" is a Japanese phrase used when something terribly convenient happens, as if a duck has arrived to dinner with its own seasoning in tow.

Page 49
According to Japanese urban legend, cherry trees are so beautiful because there are corpses buried under them. The legend stems from the folk belief that cherry blossoms were originally white but grew pink from the blood of the corpses buried under the trees.

Page 113
Kakiage are "cakes" made of assorted shredded vegetables and sometimes seafood that are then lightly battered and fried.

Page 120
Tempura refers to meat or vegetables that have been battered and deep-fried. Tempura is distinct from other deep-fry techniques in that breadcrumbs are omitted.

Page 186
Matango is a 1963 Japanese thriller about a group of castaways who are stranded on an island, eat the fungi that grow there, and find themselves slowly turning into mushrooms…which explains Marcille's reaction.

Page 125
Senshi is using degrees Celsius. Converted, 180°C is about 365°F. Ouch!

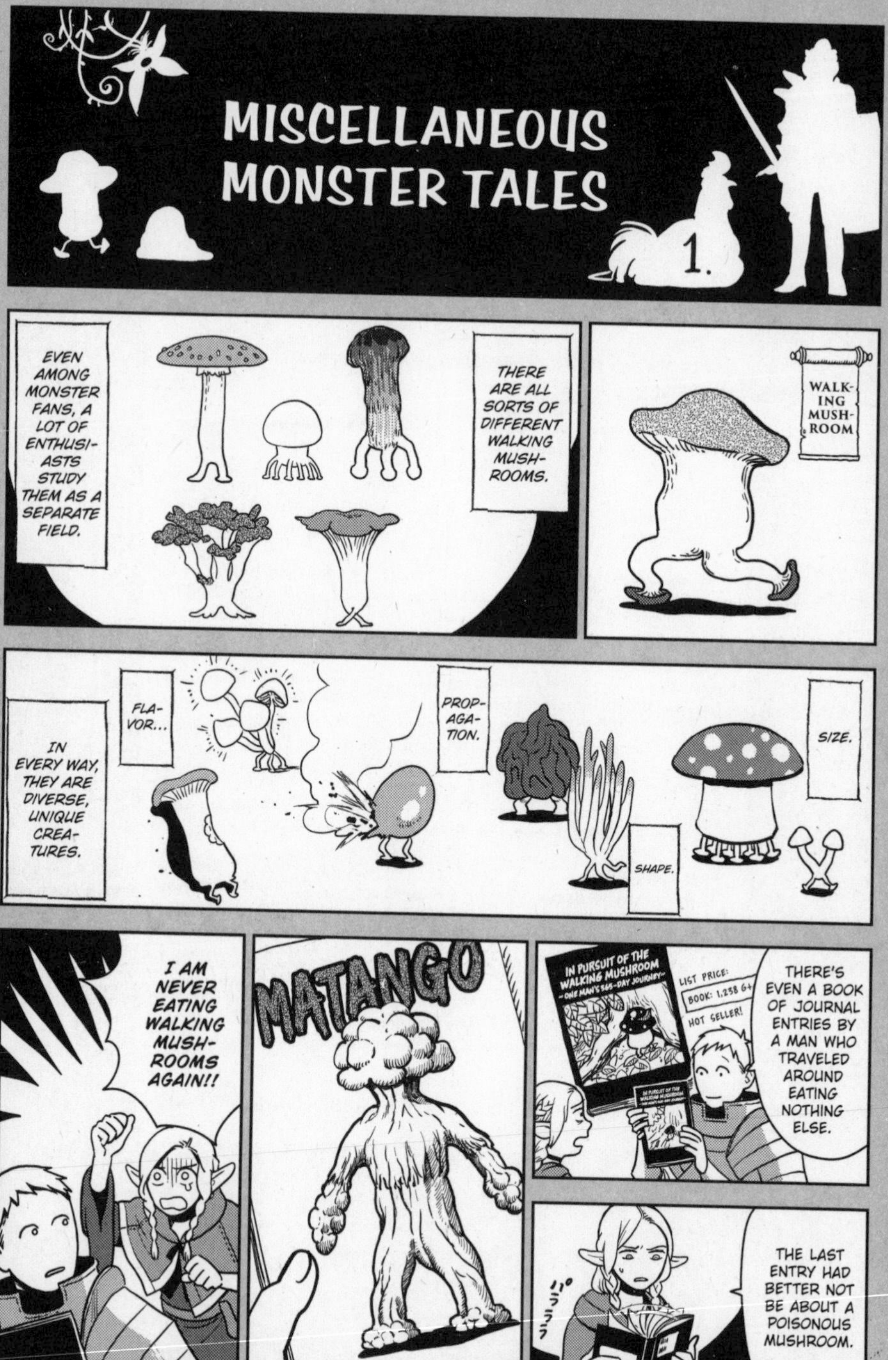
MISCELLANEOUS MONSTER TALES
1.
WALKING MUSHROOM
THERE ARE ALL SORTS OF DIFFERENT WALKING MUSHROOMS.
EVEN AMONG MONSTER FANS, A LOT OF ENTHUSIASTS STUDY THEM AS A SEPARATE FIELD.
SIZE.
SHAPE.
PROPAGATION.
FLAVOR...
IN EVERY WAY, THEY ARE DIVERSE, UNIQUE CREATURES.
THERE'S EVEN A BOOK OF JOURNAL ENTRIES BY A MAN WHO TRAVELED AROUND EATING NOTHING ELSE.
IN PURSUIT OF THE WALKING MUSHROOM ~ONE MAN'S 365-DAY JOURNEY~
LIST PRICE:
BOOK: 1,238 G+
HOT SELLER!
THE LAST ENTRY HAD BETTER NOT BE ABOUT A POISONOUS MUSHROOM.
MATANGO
I AM NEVER EATING WALKING MUSHROOMS AGAIN!!
SFX: PARARA (FLIPPP)

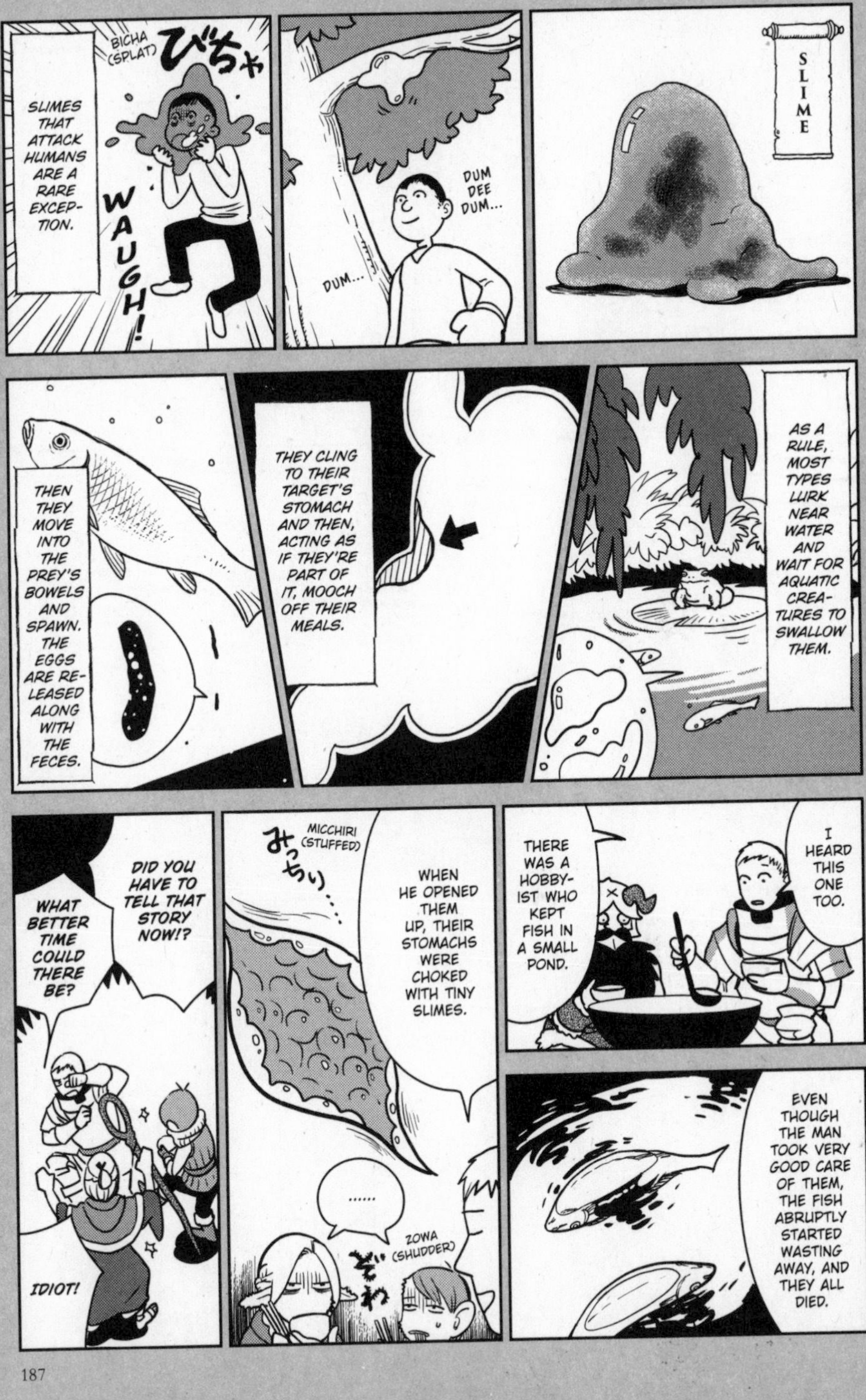
SLIME
DUM DEE DUM...
DUM...
BICHA (SPLAT)
びちゃ
SLIMES THAT ATTACK HUMANS ARE A RARE EXCEPTION.
WAUGH!
AS A RULE, MOST TYPES LURK NEAR WATER AND WAIT FOR AQUATIC CREATURES TO SWALLOW THEM.
THEY CLING TO THEIR TARGET'S STOMACH AND THEN, ACTING AS IF THEY'RE PART OF IT, MOOCH OFF THEIR MEALS.
THEN THEY MOVE INTO THE PREY'S BOWELS AND SPAWN. THE EGGS ARE RELEASED ALONG WITH THE FECES.
I HEARD THIS ONE TOO.
THERE WAS A HOBBYIST WHO KEPT FISH IN A SMALL POND.
EVEN THOUGH THE MAN TOOK VERY GOOD CARE OF THEM, THE FISH ABRUPTLY STARTED WASTING AWAY, AND THEY ALL DIED.
MICCHIRI (STUFFED)
みっちり
WHEN HE OPENED THEM UP, THEIR STOMACHS WERE CHOKED WITH TINY SLIMES.
......
ZOWA (SHUDDER)
ぞわ
DID YOU HAVE TO TELL THAT STORY NOW!?
WHAT BETTER TIME COULD THERE BE?
IDIOT!

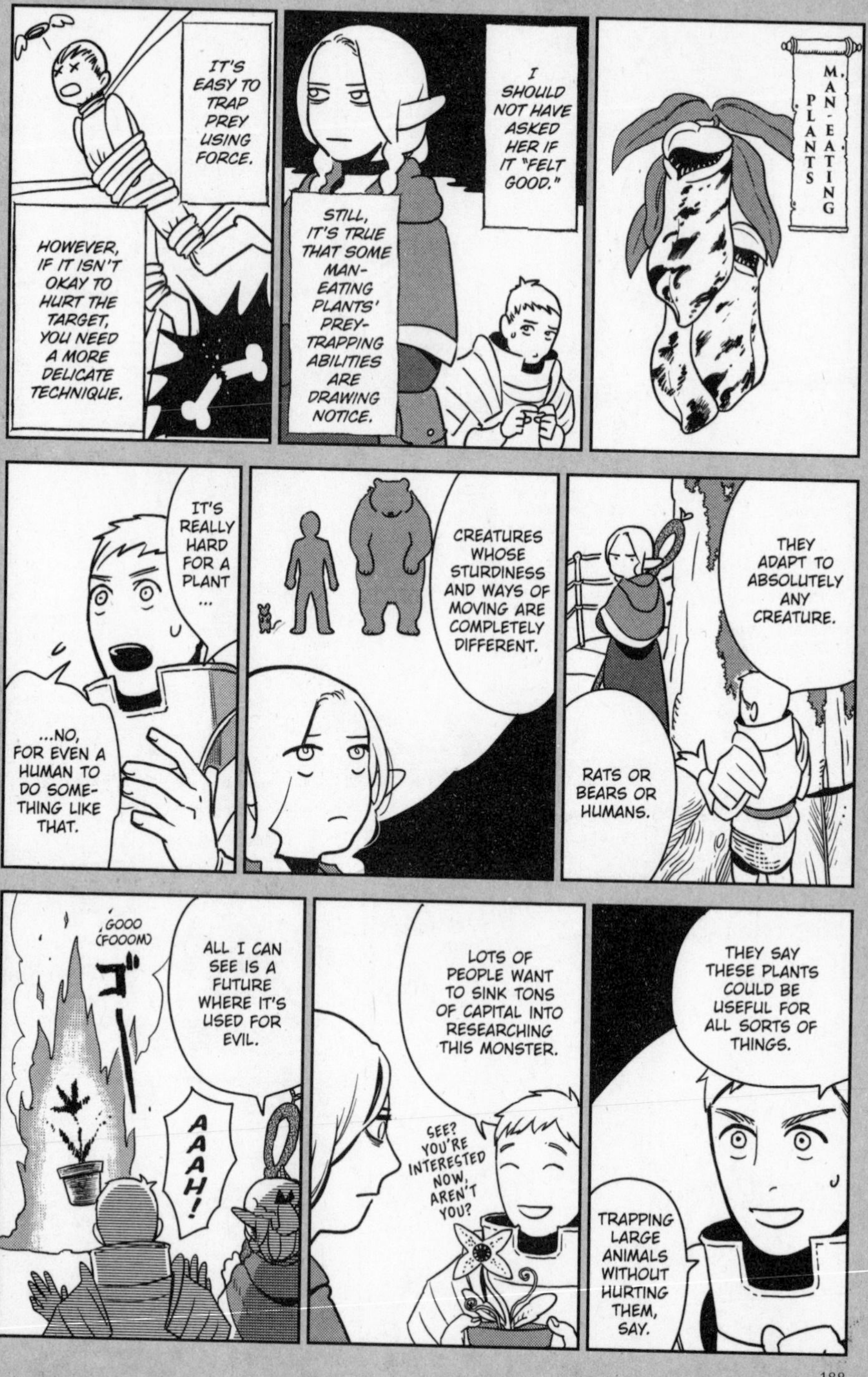
MAN-EATING PLANTS
I SHOULD NOT HAVE ASKED HER IF IT "FELT GOOD."
STILL, IT'S TRUE THAT SOME MAN-EATING PLANTS' PREY-TRAPPING ABILITIES ARE DRAWING NOTICE.
IT'S EASY TO TRAP PREY USING FORCE.
HOWEVER, IF IT ISN'T OKAY TO HURT THE TARGET, YOU NEED A MORE DELICATE TECHNIQUE.
THEY ADAPT TO ABSOLUTELY ANY CREATURE.
RATS OR BEARS OR HUMANS.
CREATURES WHOSE STURDINESS AND WAYS OF MOVING ARE COMPLETELY DIFFERENT.
IT'S REALLY HARD FOR A PLANT...
...NO, FOR EVEN A HUMAN TO DO SOMETHING LIKE THAT.
THEY SAY THESE PLANTS COULD BE USEFUL FOR ALL SORTS OF THINGS.
TRAPPING LARGE ANIMALS WITHOUT HURTING THEM, SAY.
LOTS OF PEOPLE WANT TO SINK TONS OF CAPITAL INTO RESEARCHING THIS MONSTER.
SEE? YOU'RE INTERESTED NOW, AREN'T YOU?
ALL I CAN SEE IS A FUTURE WHERE IT'S USED FOR EVIL.
AAAAH!
GOOO (FOOOM)
ゴー

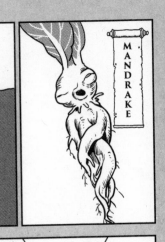

MANDRAKE
THEY DO LOOK SORT OF PERSON SHAPED, BUT...
...THERE ARE QUITE A FEW THAT DON'T.
LIKE HOW ANYTHING WITH THREE POINTS LOOKS LIKE A FACE.
EXACTLY!
WILD MANDRAKES DON'T FORM INTO HUMAN SHAPES EASILY.
AT THE ANNUAL MANDRAKE SHOW, WE COMPETE TO SEE WHO CAN GROW THE MOST BEAUTIFUL PERSON-SHAPED SPECIMEN.
LAST YEAR'S WINNING ENTRY
IN PARTICULAR, EYE LOCI SHOULD BE LEVEL.
ROOTS MUST BE AT PROPER LIMB SITES.
COLOR.
PROPORTIONS.
IF YOU BREAK UP THE ROOTS LIKE THAT, YOU WON'T HAVE AS MUCH TO EAT.
WE DON'T RAISE THEM TO EAT.
BY THE WAY, MANDRAKES (MANDRAGORA) ARE AN ACTUAL PLANT, BUT THEY'RE POISONOUS, SO YOU SHOULDN'T EAT THEM.

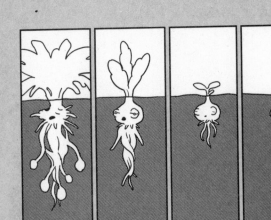

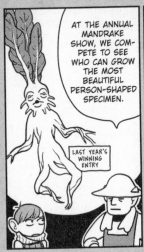

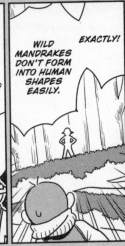

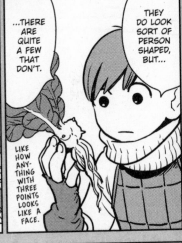

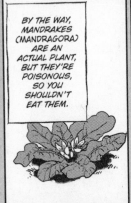

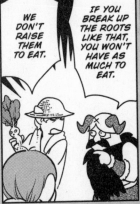

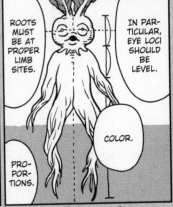

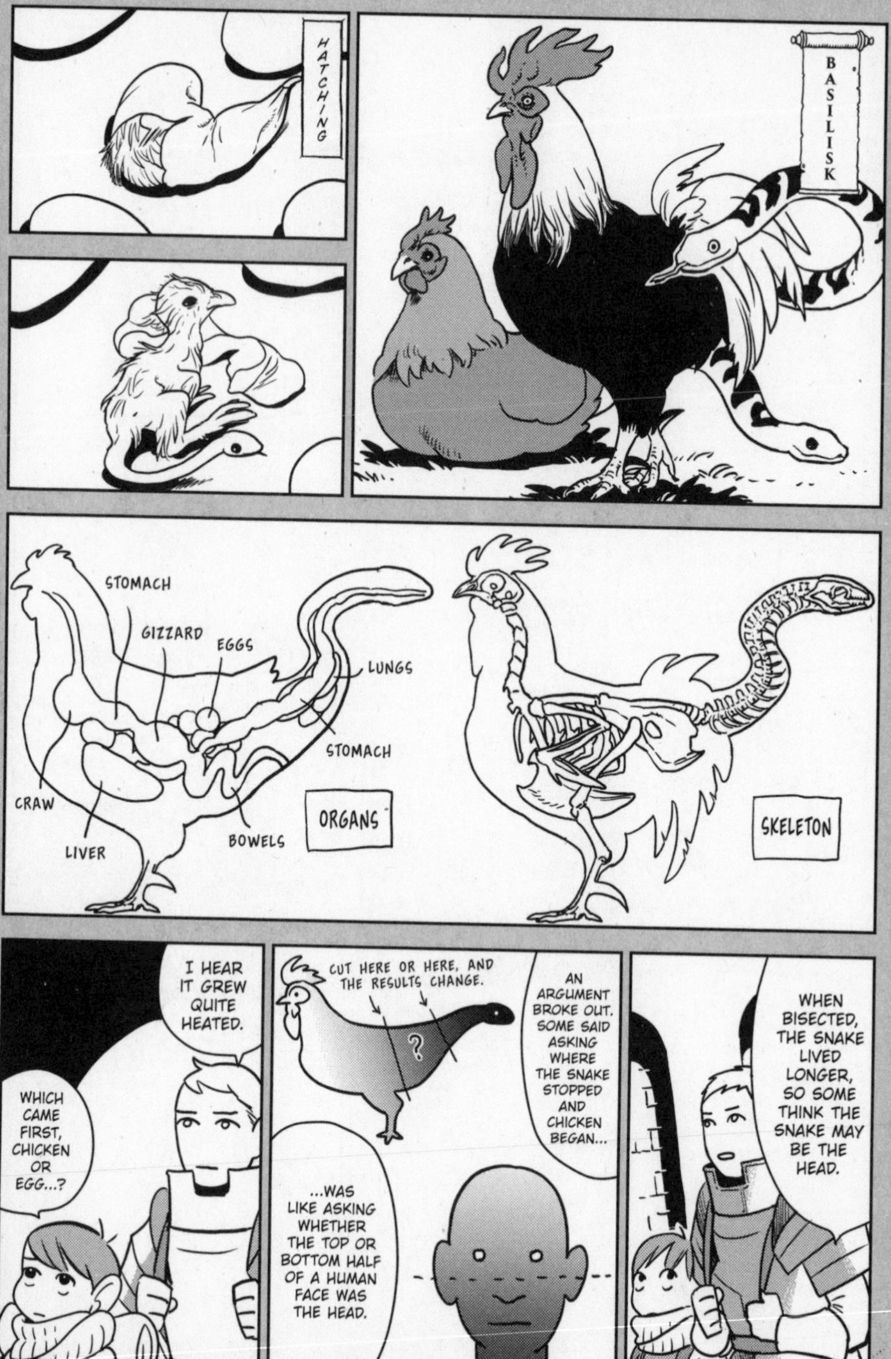
BASILISK
HATCHING
SKELETON
ORGANS
STOMACH
GIZZARD
EGGS
LUNGS
STOMACH
CRAW
LIVER
BOWELS
WHEN BISECTED, THE SNAKE LIVED LONGER, SO SOME THINK THE SNAKE MAY BE THE HEAD.
AN ARGUMENT BROKE OUT. SOME SAID ASKING WHERE THE SNAKE STOPPED AND CHICKEN BEGAN...
CUT HERE OR HERE, AND THE RESULTS CHANGE.
?
...WAS LIKE ASKING WHETHER THE TOP OR BOTTOM HALF OF A HUMAN FACE WAS THE HEAD.
I HEAR IT GREW QUITE HEATED.
WHICH CAME FIRST, CHICKEN OR EGG...?

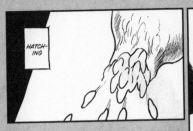

LIVING ARMOR
SPAWNING
THERE ARE LOTS OF EGGS IN AN EGG SAC.
HATCHING
TOTAL LENGTH, JUST 5MM
AS THEY GROW, THEIR SHELLS FORM.
ONCE THEY REACH A CERTAIN SIZE, THEY BEGIN TO SWARM.
GRADUALLY, THEY TAKE THE SHAPE OF ARMOR.
IT LOOKS LIKE A RUINED SUIT OF ARMOR.
ADULT
MUKURI (RISE)
ムクリ
ONCE IT CAN MOVE, IT GOES LOOKING FOR OTHER COLONIES.
THAT'S JUST A HYPOTHESIS, BUT...
...IF IT'S CORRECT, I THINK LINING UP LIKE THIS MAY BE A COURTSHIP RITUAL.
IT'S LIKELY THAT LIVING ARMOR IS HERMAPHRODITIC AND THAT THE BIGGEST COLONY LAYS THE EGGS...
WAIT! THEN...!?
AH!
THE ARMOR YOU SEE HOLDING HANDS SOMETIMES! MAYBE THAT WASN'T AN ADVENTURER PRANK! MAYBE THEY WERE MATING!
WHAT'S WITH THAT?
SUTA (STRIDE) SUTA
スタスタ

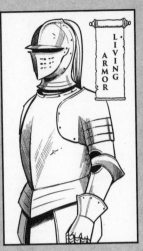

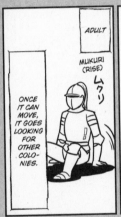

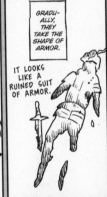

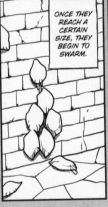

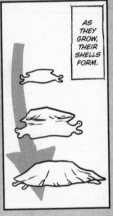

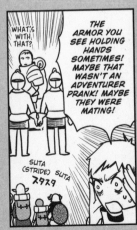

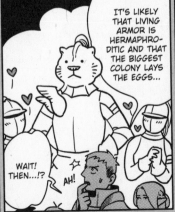

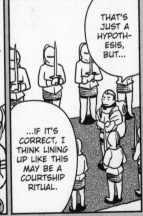

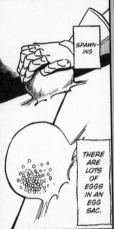

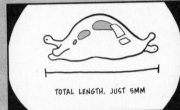

1

DELICIOUS IN DUN[ ]
RYOKO KUI

Translation: Taylor Engel Lettering: Abigail Blackman

DUNGEON MESHI Volume 1 © 2015 Ryoko Kui. All rights reserved. First published in Japan in 2015 by KADOKAWA CORPORATION ENTERBRAIN. English translation rights arranged with KADOKAWA CORPORATION ENTERBRAIN through Tuttle-Mori Agency, Inc., Tokyo.

English translation © 2017 by Yen Press, LLC

Yen Press
1290 Avenue of the Americas
New York, NY 10104

Visit us at yenpress.com
facebook.com/yenpress
twitter.com/yenpress
yenpress.tumblr.com
instagram.com/yenpress

First Yen Press Edition: May 2017

Yen Press is an imprint of Yen Press, LLC.
The Yen Press name and logo are trademarks of Yen Press, LLC.

Library of Congress Control Number: 2017932141

ISBNs: 978-0-316-47185-5 (paperback)
       978-0-316-47306-4 (ebook)

10 9 8 7 6

WOR

Printed in the United States of America